Created and Directed by Hans Höfer

INSIGHT GUIDES
THAILAND

Co-ordinated by Charles Levine

Updated by David Walls

Photography by Luca Invernizzi Tettoni

Editorial Director: Geoffrey Eu

APA PUBLICATIONS

THAILAND

Fourth Edition (Updated)
© 1995 APA PUBLICATIONS (HK) LTD
All Rights Reserved
Printed in Singapore by Höfer Press Pte Ltd

Distributed in the United States by:	Distributed in Canada by:	Distributed in the UK & Ireland by:	Worldwide distribution enquiries:
Houghton Mifflin Company	**Thomas Allen & Son**	**GeoCenter International UK Ltd**	**Höfer Communications Pte Ltd**
222 Berkeley Street	390 Steelcase Road East	The Viables Center, Harrow Way	38 Joo Koon Road
Boston, Massachusetts 02116-3764	Markham, Ontario L3R 1G2	Basingstoke, Hampshire RG22 4BJ	Singapore 2262
ISBN: 0-395-66181-1	ISBN: 0-395-66181-1	ISBN: 9-62421-054-3	ISBN: 9-62421-054-3

ABOUT THIS BOOK

Within the span of a few years, Thailand has changed from being the target for a small coterie of sophisticated travelers to one of the most popular tourist targets in Asia. No wonder. The beautiful country and warm, hospitable people have woven a spell that captivates those who visit for the first time and those who return time and again to learn more. From the dazzling temples and exciting street scenes of Bangkok, to the calm mountains of up-country and inviting beaches of the south and its islands, Thailand is a traveler's delight.

But there is a deep dimension to Thailand that is captured in *Insight Guide: Thailand*. Written for the international traveler, *Insight Guides* combine into a single well-written volume the history and development of this ancient land along with accurate reporting of the modern scene, good, bad and indifferent. Setting off this text is a collection of outstanding color photos. This concept of travel journalism was initiated by **Hans Höfer**, German-born founder of Apa Publications. In 1970, he published his first, model, prize-winning book *Insight Guide: Bali* that has been followed by a long series of Apa Publications that make up a complete travel library.

The Apa concept calls for assembling the best available writing and picture-taking talent from each subject country and giving a single project editor responsibility for the book. For *Insight Guide: Thailand*, the original team consisted of Apa founder and publisher Hans Höfer, Star Black and William Warren, a long-time American resident in Bangkok. While Warren honed his acute observations on the "City of Angels" and the complexities of Thai culture and lifestyle, Höfer and Black made four long sorties into the country's hinterland, south, northwest, east and northeast, covering more than 30,000km on highways, roads and back-of-beyond tracks.

Notes piled on notes. But even this was not enough. More writers with first-hand knowledge of Thailand were brought in – **Marcus Brooke**, **Robert Burrows**, **Jerry Dillon**, **Nancy Grace**, **Frank Green**, **John Stirling** and **Tony Wheeler**. Priya Rangsit, great-granddaughter of the Thai King Chulalongkorn, was commisioned to write a thorough history of the land while David DeVoss, Aporanee Buatong and Kultida Wongsawatdichart updated and revised the text and the Travel Tips section.

By 1990, rapid change had made a new country of Thailand. To keep up with the changes, we called upon **Steve Van Beek**, the editor and author of Apa's *Cityguide: Bangkok*, 1989 winner of PATA's Gold Award as the best travel book on Asia, to update and add some new features to *Insight Guide: Thailand*.

Van Beek, who is a long-time resident of Bangkok, is also the author of numerous books and films on Thai subjects, including *The Arts of Thailand*. He contributes regularly to the *International Herald Tribune* as well as Asian and European magazines. He was also enlisted to develop Apa's *Pocket Guides* series, later writing the Bangkok guide and writing and photographing the guides for Phuket and Chiang Mai.

Van Beek's exhaustive work on *Insight Guide: Thailand* was augmented by the talents of photographer **Luca Invernizzi Tettoni**, also a Bangkok resident with whom Van Beek had collaborated on several other

Van Beek   *Tettoni*   *Black*   *Rangsit*

books, and whose works appear extensively in this book.

California-born **Star Black** received degrees in art and English literature from Wellesley before going to live in Bangkok, traveling widely in Southeast Asia, and writing the first *Insight Guide*. She has since returned to the United States, where she works as a freelance photographer in New York. She took the photographs for a book, *Texas Boots*, published by Penguin-Viking.

William Warren, one of the most knowledgeable *farang* (foreigner) residents in Bangkok, is a freelance writer and journalist. A regular contributor to Asia-oriented publications, his books include *The Legendary American* and *The House on the Klong*, based on the life and art collections of Jim Thompson, the man who took Thai silk from the village looms to the international marketplace.

M.R. Priyanandana Rangsit attended the School of Oriental and African Studies, London University, where she read Sanskrit and History of India and Southeast Asia, with emphasis on the ancient period. Priya is a freelance writer whose works have appeared in *The Bangkok Post*, *The Nation*, *Vogue Magazine* (London), the *Monarchist*, and the *Taj Magazine* (Bombay). She belongs to one of Thailand's oldest literary families: her grandfather, Krom Muen Prince Bidyalongkorn, was regarded as the kingdom's "poet laureate", and her mother, V. na Pramuenmarg, was a renowned Thai novelist.

David DeVoss, *Time's* former Bangkok bureau chief, first came to Asia in 1972 when he joined *Time's* Saigon Bureau. He later covered Southeast Asia from Hong Kong. In early 1981 De Voss moved to Bangkok, a city that he had visited nearly 50 times over the previous three years. For the 1982 version, he was assisted by **Aporanee (Oi) Buatong** and **Wongsawatdichart** who updated and expanded the Travel Tips section.

Aporanee, an English literature graduate of Chulalongkorn University, was a Fulbright scholar in the United States. Wongsawatdichart, was a reporter and editorial assistant for *Time's* Southeast Asia bureau in Bangkok.

Charles Levine, who coordinated the efforts of *Thailand's* original contributors, worked with the Peace Corps in India for two years before settling in Bali. Subsequently, he worked in Singapore as a senior editor with McGraw-Hill and Apa.

Additional acknowledgement is given to the following books as sources of historical material: *A History of Siam* by W.A.R. Wood (Bangkok: Siam Barnakich Press, 1933); *1688: Revolution in Siam* by E.W. Hutchinson (Hong Kong: University Press, 1968); *Lords of Life* by Prince Chula Chakrabongse (London: Alvin Redman); *Louis and the King of Siam* by W.S. Bristave (London: Chatto and Windus, 1976).

Sincere thanks are also due to **John Gottberg Anderson** and **Yvan Van Outrive** for their invaluable help and advice in updating the guide; Tourism Authority of Thailand, the Montien Hotel, the Thai Consulate in Singapore, **General E. Black**, **Per Bang-Jensen**, **James Stanton**, **Henry Aronson**, **Leonard Lueras**, **Patrick (Shrimp) Gauvain**, **Sam Chan** and to the many unsung people who made this book possible.

—Apa Publications

De Voss   *Buatong*   *Van Outrive*   *Levine*

CONTENTS

History

People & Culture

PORTRAITS OF CONTEMPORARIES

Places

THE NORTHEAST

THE EASTERN GULF

THE SOUTH

Maps

TRAVEL TIPS

**For detailed Information
See Page 321**

Since the East discovered it a millenium ago and the West began trickling in during the 16th century, Thailand has been a powerful magnet for adventurers and entrepreneurs. An abundance of natural resources, ideal growing conditions, a wealth of natural beauty, a stunning cultural tradition revealed in dazzling architecture and art, and a warm, hospitable people have proved irresistible lures that continue to draw visitors in ever-increasing numbers year by year; over 5 million in 1993 alone.

Its traditional charms form only one side of the picture, however. Thailand is a country in transition, rapidly changing from a developing to a developed nation with a dynamism that is transforming its cities and countryside. Throughout its history it has shown a stubborn maverick streak and a sense of pragmatism that has created a solid economy based on fiscal responsibility and a determination to chart its own course. The result is a country that has never been colonized and which has unrepentantly retained its past while moving into the future.

These two aspects stand side by side in the Thailand of today. While it is hard to ignore the changes taking place, there is still much that sets it apart from nations on similar paths. The natural beauty is still there in superb beaches, seas of green rice and forested hills. And even in the most modern towns, the past continues to shine through in the form of temples, palaces and cultural presentations.

This uniqueness is not always apparent especially in a chaotic city like Bangkok which pounds on one's senses unceasingly. "This is not the exotic Orient I was promised," the visitor thinks. "This is madness; a city planner's worst nightmare". True. Yet even here, Thailand's beauty can be found. It often lies hidden and must be sought out but the reward is always worth the effort.

Most of all, Thais travel at their own pace, preferring to enjoy life rather than toil unendingly. Even with modern implements, farm families retain elements of traditional life. Undoubtedly, this too will change, but for the moment it is firmly intact. For the visitor, this means there is much to see and experience that will leave him or her with warm memories of a fabulous land.

Lying inland from the apex of the Gulf of Thailand, Bangkok is the country's international gateway, and seat of government, business and the monarchy. Bangkok is almost a city-state unto itself bearing little relation to the rest of the country. The rest of Thailand is a patchwork of rice fields, villages, plantations and forests whose largest town is 1/50th the size of Bangkok. Seven-eighths of the population live here and nearly 80 percent of it is engaged in agriculture.

Diversity and contrast characterize both its people and its geography. Within an area of 514,000sq km – roughly the size of France

Preceding pages: trumpeting the King's Birthday in front of the Giant Swing; early print depicting tourists stopping at a street stall for refreshments; contrasting images; verdant valley in Doi Inthanon. **Left**, Goverment officials on their way to present offerings at a monastery in Lampang.

– are tropical rain forests, broad rice plains and forest-clad hills that lie between 5° and 21° north of the equator, in the center of the geographical jigsaw puzzle of Southeast Asia.

There is an abundance of natural resources. Under the canopies of its rain forests, a wide variety of flora and fauna abound: iridescent kingfisher, parakeet, pheasant, blue-tailed broadbill, flying squirrel and lizard, gibbon, dozens of species of snake, hundreds of species of butterfly, and nearly a thousand varieties of orchid. A cornucopia of fruits grows as well, wild in the jungles, or tended carefully on small family holdings and in larger plantations: nearly thirty varieties of banana and plantain, coconut, durian, orange, lime, custard apple, mango, papaya, breadfruit, jackfruit, mangosteen, rambutan, *lychee* and *lamyai* can be found.

Elevations run from sea level along the 2,600-km long coastline to a peak of 2,596m in the North, a region of hills clad in teak forests and valleys carpeted in rice, fruit trees and vegetables, an area bordered by Myanmar and Laos.

The Northeast is dominated by the arid Korat Plateau where farmers struggle to cultivate rice, tapioca, jute and other cash crops. With strong cultural affinities with neighboring Laos, the region is rimmed and defined by the Mekong River.

In the Central Plains, monsoon rains transform the landscape into a vast hydroponic basin, which nourishes a sea of rice, the country's staple and an important export. Through this region flows the Chao Phya River, carrying produce and people south to Bangkok, washing rich sediment down from the northern hills, and during the monsoon season further flooding the rice fields.

The South runs down a long, narrow arm of land leading to Malaysia. Rubber and palm oil plantations alternate with rice and fruit trees, an area strongly influenced by Malay culture.

Across this landscape live Thailand's 55 million people, a rich cultural mix comprising ethnic Thais (who make up around 80 percent of the population), Chinese (about 10 percent), Malays (about 4 percent), and Lao, Mons, Khmers, Indians, Burmese and a scattering of hilltribes in the north about 6 percent.

FACTS AT A GLANCE

Area: 514,000sq km
Population: 55 million
Government: Constitutional Monarchy
Capital: Bangkok, officially 5.5 million people; unofficially, 8 million
Peoples: Thai 80%; Chinese 10%; Malay 4%, Lao, Burmese, Vietnamese, Indian, hilltribe, others 6%
Religions:Theravada Buddhism 92%; Islam 4%; Mahayana Buddhism 2½%; Christianity ½%
Highest Point: Doi Inthanon, 2,596m
Currency: Baht (25 baht = 1 US$)
Electricity: 220 volts AC

Looking pretty at the Loy Kratong parade in Chiang Mai.

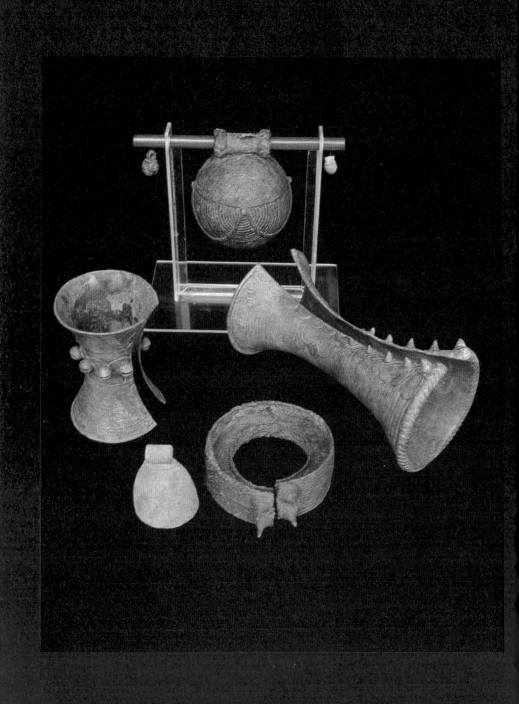

The Thai people have fiercely defended their country's independence for more than 800 years. They boast the distinction of being the only country in Southeast Asia never to have been a European colony. Nor has the country been divided by civil war, as tumultuous as Thai politics can be. Thai shrewdness in international diplomacy has won them the admiration of nations far more powerful. Moreover, they have proved themselves adept at absorbing outside influences without losing their national identity.

The name *Thai* means "free." Although the country was called "Siam" by foreigners from the 12th to the 20th centuries, to its citizens it always carried the name of its capital – Sukhothai, Ayutthaya, etc. In the l9th century, "Siam" was adopted as the official name of the Kingdom. This was changed to "Thailand" in 1939 after the advent of democratic government.

The original homeland of the Thais is a topic of much dispute and few facts. Linguistic studies indicate that they migrated from southeastern China to form communities in Yunnan, China's southernmost province. One theory suggests the Thais originated in Thailand, moved north and then migrated south again under pressure from Kublai Khan and his Mongol hordes.

Long before the Thai people migrated into what is today called Thailand, however, the Menam Chao Phya valley was inhabited by a high civilization.

The Ban Chiang culture: The first discovery of pre-historic relics was made during World War II by a Dutch prisoner of war forced to work on the Siam-Burma "Death Railway." He uncovered Stone Age implements at Ban Kao in the western province of Kanchanaburi, which led to the discovery of paleolithic and neolithic caves and cemeteries containing a wealth of pottery and tools.

The most important site, however, is the tiny village of Ban Chiang near Udon Thani in the northeast. Systematic excavation revealed painted pottery, jewelry, and bronze

and iron tools. If thermoluminescent dating is correct, the Bronze Age in Thailand corresponds to – and may even pre-date – that of the Tigris-Euphrates valley civilization, which preceded the Bronze Age in Europe.

The identity of the Ban Chiang people is a mystery. According to archaeological timetables, the existence of pottery normally suggests a culture already 2,000 years along the road to civilization; Ban Chiang's pottery dates from about 3600 BC. Settlement seems to have lasted until 250 BC after which the people mysteriously fade from history. While they thrived, they farmed rice, domesticated animals, and developed highly original pottery-decorating skills, with each design unique to that pot and not repeated in others. Their red-painted jars, decorated with finger-print whorl patterns, were buried in funerary mounds as offerings to the dead. Beads of glass and semi-precious stones were also included. Similar sites were excavated in nearby areas.

The Ban Chiang culture illustrates the high level of technology achieved by prehistoric man in Southeast Asia. It proves that China is not the sole birthplace of East Asian civilization as previously surmised.

Indian influence: Archaeological evidence has yet to be unearthed, but ancient texts discuss the presence of people of Indian origin around the 3rd century BC.

The Sinhalese Buddhist chronicle, the *Mahavamsa*, relates that India's great Emperor Ashoka (who ruled from 268 to 232 BC), the first royal patron of Buddhism, sent two missionaries to Suvannabhumi, the "land of gold" now identified as Southeast Asia. By the beginning of the Christian era, maritime trading between India and the south of Thailand had begun. Hindu statues found at settlements on river mouths in Southern Thailand suggest habitation from about the 4th century.

In later centuries, Buddhism and Hinduism, along with Indian ceremonial rites, iconography, law codes, and cosmological and architectural treatises, were adopted *en bloc* by the Southeast Asian ruling elite and modified to suit local requirements and tastes. Sanskrit became the court language, while

Pali was the language of the Buddhist canons. Native chiefs who wanted to consolidate their power and increase their prestige may have been responsible for this diffusion of culture by calling in *brahmins* (Indians of the priestly caste) to validate and consecrate their rule.

This transmission at court level had a vital and permanent impact, especially in Cambodia. The Mons and Khmers were the first Indianized peoples to form settlements in present-day Thailand. Mon influence is evident in the Buddhist art of the Dvaravati period (6th to 11th centuries); and the Khmers, famed as the builders of Cambodia's Angkor Wat, left many temples in Thailand's northeastern provinces. There is also archaeological evidence of Mon religious settlements at Lopburi and Nakhon Pathom from the 7th century onwards indicating the well-established presence of an indigenous population from an early date.

Arrival of the Thais: There are several theories to explain the early habitation of Thailand. The most persuasive one says that from perhaps as early as the 10th century, a people living in China's Yunnan province migrated down rivers and streams into the upper valleys of the Southeast Asian river system. There, they branched off. The Shans, also known as *Thai Yai* ("Great Thais"), went to Upper Burma, the Ahom Thais established themselves in Assam; another group settled in Laos and yet another occupied the island of Hainan off the Vietnamese coast.

The greatest number of Thai Noi ("Little Thais") first settled in the north of modern Thailand, around Chiang Saen and valleys to the south. They formed themselves into principalities, some of which later became independent kingdoms. The first was in 1238 at Sukhothai, at the southernmost edge of Thai penetration. Then came Chiang Rai in 1281 and Chiang Mai in 1296. Long after the main group of Thais moved farther down the peninsula to establish more powerful states, Chiang Mai continued to rule more or less autonomously over the northern region, maintaining a distinctive culture of its own.

By the 13th century, the Thais had begun to emerge as the dominant rulers of the region, slowly absorbing the weakened empires of the Mons and Khmers. Their rise to power culminated around 1238, when (according to inscriptions) the Khmers were expelled from Sukhothai.

The history of Peninsular Thailand is lesser known than that of the culturally richer north. The Isthmian region was once under the control of the mighty commercial and military empire of Srivijaya (7th to 13th centuries). Ancient chronicles state that in the Srivijayan capital, "a man at noon cast no shadow". This suggests an equatorial location but there is serious disagreement where that might be. Palembang in Sumatra, Chaiya in southern Thailand and a site in Kalimantan (Borneo) have been postulated.

The proof of claim forwarded for Chaiya is the discovery of an AD 775 inscription of a Srivijayan king at Chaiya, near the Kra Isthmus. The art of Srivijaya is heterogeneous in character showing influences from India, Champa and Java. The empire disintegrated during the 13th century and her dependencies were absorbed by Sukhothai.

Phra Ruang and the "Dawn" of Sukhothai: The name "Sukhothai" translates into "the dawn of happiness" and if early inscriptions are to be believed, its people enjoyed considerable freedom to pursue their livelihoods. This first independent Thai kingdom is considered the golden era of Thai history, and is often looked back upon with nostalgia as the ideal Thai state. It was a land of plenty, governed by just and paternal kings who ruled over peaceful, contented citizens. Sukhothai represented early Thai tribal society in its purest form.

Siamese tradition attributes the founding of the kingdom to Phra Ruang, a mythological hero comparable to King Arthur. Prior to his time, according to historical legend, the Thai people were forced to pay tribute to the Khmer rulers of Angkor. This tribute was exacted in the form of sacred water from a lake outside Lopburi: the Khmer god-king needed holy water from all corners of the empire for his ceremonial rites, a practice later adopted by Thai kings.

Every three years, the water tribute was sent by bullock carts in large earthenware jars. The jars inevitably cracked en route, compelling the tribute payers to make second and third journeys to fill the required quota. When Phra Ruang came of age, he devised a new system of transporting water in sealed woven bamboo containers which arrived in Angkor intact.

This success aroused the suspicion of the Khmer king. His chief astrologer said the ingenious Thai inventor was a person with supernatural powers, who constituted a threat to the empire. The king at once dispatched a gifted general who had the magic ability to travel swiftly underground, to eliminate the Thai menace. Phra Ruang perceived danger and went to Sukhothai, where he concealed himself at Wat Mahathat as a Buddhist monk. The Khmer general, who coincidentally surfaced in the middle of the *wat*, was turned into stone by Phra Ruang.

From then on, Phra Ruang's fame spread far and wide. He left the monkhood, married the ruler of Sukhothai's daughter, and upon

ruler to leave detailed epigraphical accounts of the Thai state, beginning with his own early life. He earned his title at age 19 on a campaign with his father against a neighboring state, in which he defeated the enemy leader in a Thai form of medieval jousts: hand-to-hand on elephant-back. As a result, he was granted the name Phra Ramkamhaeng (Rama the Brave) by his father.

The Sukhothai Kingdom at the time of Ramkamhaeng's accession was quite small, consisting only of the city and surrounding areas. By the end of his reign, he had increased its size tenfold: from Luang Prabang in the east through the Central Plains to the southern peninsula. The Mon state in Lower

Bird's eye view of fabled Sukhothai.

that monarch's death was invited to the throne by popular mandate. He assumed the title Sri Indraditya, sovereign of the newly-independent Kingdom of Sukhothai.

Fact and fiction are inseparable in this popular account. But there is no doubt that, since Sukhothai, Buddhism has been deeply rooted in the Thai way of life. Together with the monarchy, it provides a continuity lasting to the present day.

The rule of Ramkamhaeng: The most famous king of Sukhothai was the founder's second son, Ramkamhaeng. He was the first Thai

Burma also accepted his overlordship.

Ramkamhaeng was noted as an administrator, legislator and statesman; and sometimes as an amorous king. He is credited with the invention of Thai script, which he achieved by systematizing the Khmer alphabet with Thai words. A stone inscription bearing the date 1292 and employing the new script has been attributed to Ramkamhaeng. He depicted the idyllic conditions of his kingdom – fertile land and plentiful food, free trade, prohibition of slavery and guaranteed inheritance. However, some experts now doubt its authenticity and believe the inscription to be a much later work.

The king was a devout and conscientious Buddhist of the Theravada school practiced in Sukhothai. Exchanges were initiated with Sri Lankan monks which resulted in a purification of texts and an adoption of Sinhalese influences in *chedi* design.

There remained, however, a trace of animism in Thai Buddhism. Ramkamhaeng wrote about a mountain-dwelling ghost named Phra Khapung Phi, a spirit "above all others in the land." If correctly propitiated, he would bring prosperity to the country. The idea of a superior spirit looking after the nation survives today in the image of Phra Siam Devadhiraj, Siam's guardian angel.

One of the keys to Ramkamhaeng's success lay in his diplomatic relations with China. The Mongol Court pursued a "divide-and-rule" policy and supported the Thais' rise at the expense of the Khmers. Ramkamhaeng was said to have gone to China himself in 1299, and the *History of the Yuan* records seven missions from "Sien" (Sukhothai) between 1282 and 1323. Chinese craftsmen came to teach the Thais their secrets of glazing pottery, resulting in the production of the famous ceramic ware of Sawankhalok, whose kilns still remain and whose products were shipped to China aboard Siamese junks, remains of which have been found in the seabed near Pattaya.

The year Pagan fell to the armies of Kublai Khan in 1287, Ramkamhaeng formed a pact with two northern Thai princes, Mengrai of Chiang Rai and Ngam Muang of Phayao. The three agreed not to transgress but to protect each others' borders against common enemies. The alliance was maintained throughout their lifetimes.

The founding of Chiang Mai: Mengrai completed Thai political ascendancy in the north by annexing the last Mon kingdom of Haripunjaya about 1292. He first sent an agent provocateur to sow discord, and when the time was right, his army "plucked the town like a ripe fruit."

Wishing to found a new capital, Mengrai invited his two allies to help him select a site. The location they agreed upon as truly auspicious was one where two white sambars, two white barking deer, and a family of five white mice were seen together. On that spot by the river Ping, Mengrai laid the foundation of Chiang Mai ("New Town") in 1296, supplanting his former capital at Chiang Rai

and giving him a more centralized location from which to administer the southern portion of his newly-expanded kingdom. Chiang Mai, thus, became the capital of the Kingdom of Lanna, which translates as "Land of the Million Rice Fields."

Tradition says Ramkamhaeng drowned in the rapids of the Yom River at Sawankhalok. His son Lo Thai (ruled 1318 to 1347), preferring religion to war, lost the feudatory states as fast as he had gained them. He was called Dharmaraja, "the Pious King," an epithet his successors also bore. The relationship between Sukhothai and Sri Lanka, the center of orthodox Buddhism, intensified during his rule; Lo Thai recorded that he built many monuments to house sacred relics of the Buddha newly obtained from Sri Lanka.

Lo Thai's son, Li Thai, was as pious as his father. As heir to the throne, he composed a famous treatise on Buddhist cosmology, the *Traibhumikatha* or "Tales of the Three Worlds." When he became king in 1347, he declared a rule according to the 10 Royal Precepts of the Buddha. He pardoned criminals because he desired to become a Buddha, "to lead all creatures beyond the oceans of sorrow and transmigration."

The prioritizing of religion over military might permitted the meteoric rise of one of Sukhothai's former vassal states, Ayutthaya. The southern kingdom expanded rapidly extending control over the Chao Phya River valley until King Li Thai was forced to acknowledge its hegemony. Deprived of his independence, the pious king took deeper refuge in religion, eventually assuming the yellow robe. His family ruled for three more generations as hereditary governors but in 1378, the seat of power shifted to Phitsanulok and Sukhothai's population followed. By 1438, Sukhothai was a deserted city.

The Sukhothai period saw the Thais, for the first time, develop a distinctive civilization with their own administrative institutions, art and architecture. Sukhothai Buddha images, characterized by refined facial features, linear fluidity, and harmony of form are considered by many to be the most beautiful and the most original of Thai artistic expressions.

The majestic ruins of Wat Chetupon, Sukhothai.

History is ignorant of the ancestry of Ayutthaya's founder. But Thai folklore fills the lacuna.

The King of Traitrung unhappily discovered that his unmarried daughter had given birth to a child after eating an aubergine, which a vegetable gardener had fertilized with his own urine. The culprit – Nai Saen Pom, "Man With a Hundred Thousand Warts" – was summoned and promptly banished from the city, along with the princess and her son.

Ayodhya (Ayutthaya), an ancient Indianized settlement named after Rama's legendary kingdom in India.

The location of Phya U-Thong's new capital was blessed with several advantages. Situated on an island at the confluence of the Chao Phya, Lop Buri and Pasak rivers, not far from the sea and surrounded by fertile rice plains, it was an ideal center of administration and communications. Phya U-Thong officially established the city in 1350 after three years of preparation, when

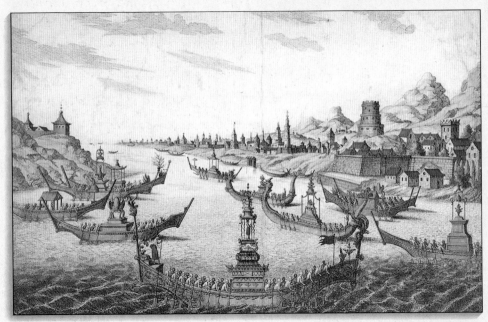

The god Indra, with his divine eye, saw the misery of the trio and decided to grant the gardener three magic wishes. Saen Pom first asked for his warts to disappear; next, he prayed for a kingdom to rule over; and lastly, he wanted a cradle of gold for his son. All his desires came true! The child was henceforth known as Chao U-Thong, "Prince of the Golden Crib."

Historically, U-Thong was an independent principality in today's Suphan Buri. Its rulers were members of the prestigious line of Chiang Saen kings. During the reign of Phya U-Thong, a cholera outbreak forced the ruler to evacuate his people to the site of

he assumed the title Ramathibodi I, King of Dvaravati Sri Ayodhya. Within a few years, the king united the whole of central Siam, including Sukhothai, under his rule, and extended control to the Malay Peninsula and Lower Burma. He and his successors pursued expansionist campaigns against Chiang Mai and Cambodia.

Ironically, although the Thais were responsible for the decline and eventual collapse of Angkor, the Ayutthaya kings adopted Khmer cultural influences from the very beginning. No longer the paternal and accessible rulers that the kings of Sukhothai had been, Ayutthaya's sovereigns were absolute monarchs, "Lords of Life", whose position was enhanced by trappings of royalty reflective of a Khmer *devaraja* (god-king). The *devaraja* concept was, however, tempered by the tenets of Theravada Buddhism, wherein the king was not actually divine, but was the protector and supreme head of the religion. Nevertheless, Khmer court rituals and language were emulated at the Ayutthaya court. Brahmins officiated side by side with Buddhist monks at state ceremonies, a legacy which remains in modern Bangkok.

Ramathibodi I divided his administration into four sections: ministries of Royal Household, Finance, Interior and Agriculture. This and his legislation provided a strong foundation for the kingdom, which survived with Ayutthaya as its capital for 417 years.

Ramathibodi died in 1369. His son, Ramesuen, captured Chiang Mai in 1390, reportedly with the use of cannon, the first recorded use of this weapon in Siam.

Left, a 17th-century impression of Ayutthaya. **Above**, a detail of a Thai manuscript showing a royal parade in the 17th century.

Ramesuen's army sacked Angkor three years later, and according to the *Pongsawadan*, the "Annals of Ayutthaya," 90,000 prisoners of war were taken. Given the economics of the time, manpower was more precious than gold.

The death blow to the Khmer capital was delivered in 1431 by King Boromaraja II, whose forces entered Angkor after a siege of seven months. The Khmer king abandoned his ancient capital in favor of Lovek and, later, Phnom Penh. The Siamese army returned from the campaign with much booty and many prisoners, including artists and brahmins.

The reign of King Trailok: Two centuries of wars between Chiang Mai and Ayutthaya reached a climax during the reign of King Boroma Trailokanath, more popularly known as Trailok (1448–1488). In his campaigns against Maharaja Sutham Tilok, guile and the occult complemented military might. A Burmese monk sent to spy for Trailok, for example, tricked Tilok into felling a sacred tree of Mengrai. As a result, a series of misfortunes befell him.

Envoys sent to Tilok from Ayutthaya were discovered to have buried seven jars containing ingredients which, it was feared, would magically bring doom upon Chiang Mai. The jars were cast into the river, followed by the ambassadors, whose feet were tied to rocks. The fighting between these rival kingdoms led to the transfer of Ayutthayan power from the capital to Phitsanulok during the last 25 years of Trailok's reign. The war, however, ended in a stalemate.

Trailok is important for having introduced reforms which shaped the administrative and social structures of Siam until the 19th century. He brought Ayutthaya's loosely controlled provinces under centralized rule, and regulated *sakdi na*, an ancient system of land ownership which stratified society, dictated responsibilities of both overlord and tenants, and determined salary levels of the official hierarchy.

Trailok also defined a system of corvee labor under which all able-bodied men were required to contribute their labor of part of each working year to the state. This system indirectly heightened the status of women, who were responsible for the welfare of their families in the absence of the menfolk.

Trailok's Palace Law of 1450 spelled out the relative ranks of members of the royal family, prescribed functions of officials, and regulated ceremonies. It also fixed punishments, which included death for "introducing amatory poems" into the palace or for whispering during a royal audience, and amputation of the foot of anyone kicking a palace door. While these sentences may not often have been carried out to the letter, they certainly exalted the aura of the king and dissuaded malefactors. Even royalty was not spared punishment, although the Palace Law

Burmese. Alfonso de Albuquerque of Portugal conquered Malacca in 1511, and soon thereafter his ships sailed to Siam. King Ramathibodi II (ruled 1491–1529) granted the Portuguese permission to reside and trade within the kingdom, in return for arms and ammunition. Portuguese mercenaries fought in campaigns against Chiang Mai and taught the Thais the arts of cannon foundry and musketry.

But this did nothing to stem the rising tide of Burmese aggression. King Tabinshweti of Pegu, upon unifying the Burmese Empire, had cast his eyes toward Ayutthaya, already weakened by wars with Chiang Mai.

In 1549, when Tabinshweti attacked, King

stipulated that no menial hands could touch royal flesh. It was therefore the executioner's task to beat the condemned royalty at the nape of the neck with a sandalwood club.

On the whole, the rules fixed by King Trailok helped to maintain the fluidity of Thai society. This persists today. Ranks of nobility were, and are, earned rather than inherited. Titles of royal descendants, what's more, are not retained in perpetuity; they degenerate, reaching a common status within five generations.

Enter the Portuguese and Burmese: The 16th century was marked by the first arrival of Europeans and by continual conflict with the

Mahachakrapat had just acceded to the throne. As the Burmese laid siege to his capital, Mahachakrapat led a sortie against them. Not only his sons, but his wife and daughter, accompanied him to the field of battle, mounted on elephants. Thai history proudly recalls how Queen Suriyothai, disguised as a warrior, galloped her mount between the king and his Burmese foe when she saw her husband in trouble. The queen saved the king's life, but lost her own in the process. A *chedi* enshrining her ashes can still be seen at Ayutthaya.

The Burmese invasion of 1549 was doomed to failure. Tabinshweti's armies withdrew, and Mahachakrapat refortified the kingdom's defenses with the help of the Portuguese. Three hundred wild elephants were captured and trained for further wars against Burma.

Seven of the new war elephants were white ones. The Buddhist kings of Southeast Asia have always treasured the possession of white elephants. They are considered to be auspicious, enhancing royal prestige and ensuring the country's prosperity. When Burma's King Bayinnaung, who had succeeded his father-in-law, heard about this, he launched another invasion.

In 1569, Ayutthaya fell to Bayinnaung's forces. The invading Burmese thoroughly

repatriated to Siam at the age of 15. Together with his younger brother, Ekatotsarot, Naresuen began immediately to gather armed followers.

Naresuen had gained an insight into Burmese armed strength and strategies during his formative gears. He trained his troops in the art of guerrilla warfare; their hit-and-run tactics earned them the nicknames "Wild Tigers" and "Peeping Cats."

Naresuen's opportunity to restore Siamese independence came following the death of Bayinnaung in 1581. Revolts in the Shan states and at Ava were tying young King Nandabayin down at home when Naresuen declared Ayutthaya's freedom in 1584. Dur-

ransacked and plundered the city, and forcibly removed much of Ayutthaya's population to Burma. King Mahachakrapat was among the captives; he died before arriving in Pegu.

Maha Thammaraja, the defeated king's leading deputy, was appointed by Bayinnaung to rule Siam as a vassal state. His eldest son, Naresuen, was taken to Burma by Bayinnaung as a guarantee for Maha Thammaraja's good conduct. The boy was

Left, **Ayutthayan royal jewelry found at Wat Ratburana.** **Above**, **Prince Naresuen engages the Burmese in a sea battle.**

ing the following nine years, the Burmese made several attempts to re-subjugate Siam, but Naresuen had taken thorough defensive measures and repulsed all invasions. On one of these occasions, he killed the Burmese crown prince in single combat mounted on elephants.

Naresuen assumed full kingship upon his father's death in 1590. He reconsolidated the Siamese kingdom, then turned the tables on Burma with repeated attacks which contributed to the disintegration of the Burmese Empire. The Khmers, who had been whittling away at Siam's eastern boundary during Ayutthaya's period of weakness, were also subdued. Under "Naresuen the Great," Ayutthaya prospered and became the thriving metropolis described by 17th-century European visitors.

Europe's "Door to the East": The reign of Naresuen's brother, Ekatotsarot, between 1605 and 1610, coincided with the arrival of the Dutch in Siam. Ekatotsarot was not interested in pursuing Naresuen's militaristic policies; instead, he sought to develop Ayutthaya's economy. To these ends, he decreed several measures to increase state revenue, among them the introduction of taxes on commerce. This gave him a reputation as a "covetous man" among Europeans.

The Dutch opened their first trading station at Ayutthaya in 1608. Keen to promote commercial relations, King Ekatotsarot in the same year sent emissaries to The Hague, the first recorded appearance of Thais in Europe. During the reign of King Songtham (1610-1628), the English arrived bearing a letter from James I. Like the Dutch, they were welcomed and allotted a plot of land on which to build a factory.

Europeans were primarily attracted to Siam as a door to the China trade. The nature of seasonal monsoons made direct sailing to China impossible, so Ayutthaya and her ports became entrepots for goods traveling between Europe, India and the East Indies, and China and Japan. The Siamese home market was also quite substantial. The peace initiated by Naresuen had given rise to a surplus of wealth, which created a demand in Thai society for luxury items like Oriental porcelain and silk. The Japanese, who already had established a sizable community of traders at Ayutthaya, paid silver bullion for local Siamese products such as hides, teak, tin and sugar.

Under the adventurer Yamada Nagamasa, who earned himself an official court rank, many Japanese gained employment as king's guards. These mercenaries played an important role in Thai history in 1628, when they helped King-to-be Prasat Thong to establish himself as regent to a boy-king, and subsequently to depose the rightful ruler. Unfortunately the shogun in Edo (Tokyo) refused to recognize him as Thai monarch, prompting Prasat Thong to take his revenge on the Japanese settlement in Ayutthaya. Several Japanese were killed; the rest hastily fled to Cambodia.

Prasat Thong ruled until 1655. He imposed a system of royal monopolies whereby all foreign trade was directly controlled by the king, represented by the Minister of Finance. (The minister's title, Phra Klang, was corrupted to "Barcalon" by European traders.) The importance of Ayutthaya as a trade center increased markedly during this period; because rare commodities were under state control, they could be procured only from royal warehouses in the capital.

The Dutch established maritime dominance in the Far East when they drove the Portuguese out of Malacca in 1641. Seven years later, in 1648, they made a show of naval force in the Gulf of Siam, thereby

persuading Prasat Thong to agree to certain trade concessions and giving them virtual economic control in Siam. Prasat Thong's son, King Narai (ruled 1656 to 1688), despised the Dutch and welcomed the English as a European ally to counter Holland's influence. But another Dutch blockade in 1664, this time at the mouth of the Chao Phya river, won them a monopoly on the hide trade and, for the first time in Thai history, extraterritorial privileges.

The "Greek Favorite": It was the French who gained greatest favor in King Narai's court. Their story is interwoven with that of one of the most fascinating characters in Thai history, a Greek adventurer named Constantine Phaulkon.

French Jesuit missionaries first arrived at the court of Ayutthaya in 1665, and were permitted to open a center of worship. The king's friendliness and religious tolerance were taken by the bishops as a sign of his imminent conversion. Their exaggerated accounts excited the imagination of Louis XIV, who hoped that the salvation of Siamese heathens could be combined with French territorial acquisition. King Narai was delighted to receive a personal letter from the Sun King in 1673.

Enter Phaulkon. The son of a Greek innkeeper, he began his career with the East

India Company as a cabin boy. He worked his way east with the British, and arrived in Siam in 1678. A talented linguist, he learned the Thai language in just two years, and with the help of his English benefactors, he was hired as interpreter by the Barcalon. Within five years, Phaulkon had risen through the strata of Thai society to the rank of Phya Vijayendra. In this exacted position, he had continual access to the king, whose confidence he slowly and surely cultivated.

Left, King Narai (1656–1688). **Above**, Constantine Phaulkon, the "Greek Favorite's" manipulation of Narai won privileges for the French.

The previous year, Phaulkon had fallen out of favor with the East India Company. He had also converted to Roman Catholic in order to marry a Japanese woman of that faith. As Phaulkon moved firmly into the French camp, so did King Narai. He sent two ambassadors to Louis' court, and the French reciprocated with a visit to Ayutthaya in 1685. While they failed to convert King Narai to Christianity, they did succeed in gaining many trade privileges.

Phaulkon, of course, served as interpreter during the French embassy. He secretly outlined to visiting Jesuit priests his plans to convert the entire country of Siam to Catholicism. To effect this, he said, he would need civilians and troops from France. Following another exchange of embassies between the courts of Louis and Narai, a French squadron under the command of Marshal Desfarges, accompanied French and Thai delegations aboard warships to Siam. The small but disciplined and well-equipped French force of 500 soldiers was given landing rights by King Narai, under Phaulkon's advice. For his pains, Phaulkon was created a Count of France and a Knight of the Order of St Michael.

Then the tables began to turn against Phaulkon. A number of high-ranking Siamese officials had become increasingly alarmed by the influence of the "Greek Favorite" over the king. Phaulkon's extravagant lifestyle was considered proof of his blatant robbery of the country. Contemporary European writers testify that at Phaulkon's Lop Buri mansion, the dinner table was laid for 40 guests every night, and a huge quantity of wine was consumed. His unpopularity was fueled not only by the ominous French military presence, but also by a rumor that Phaulkon had converted King Narai's adopted son to Christianity, with the intention of securing his succession to the throne.

When Narai fell gravely ill in 1688, a nationalistic, anti-French faction took immediate action. Led by Phra Phetracha, a commander of the Royal Regiment of Elephants, the rebels confined the ailing king to his palace. Phaulkon was arrested for treason, and in June was executed outside Lop Buri. Narai died the following month, and Phra Phetracha mounted the throne, declaring as his top priority the immediate withdrawal of French troops. The French forces had been diffused to man different garrisons, but Desfarges eventually agreed to remove his soldiers.

"The Most Beautiful City": The presence of Europeans throughout Narai's reign gave the West most of its early knowledge of Siam. Voluminous literature was generated by Western visitors to Narai's court. Their attempts at cartography left a record of Ayutthaya's appearance, though few maps exist today. Royal palaces and hundreds of temples crowded the area within the walls around the island on which the capital stood. Some Western visitors compared Ayutthaya to Venice and called it "the most beautiful city in the east." The Abbe de Choisy, an envoy of Louis XIV, was more reserved in his praise. "I have never seen anything fairer, despite the fact that the temples mark the only departure from unsophisticated nature," he wrote.

The kings who succeeded Narai terminated the open-door policy. A modest amount of trade was maintained and missionaries were permitted to remain; but Ayutthaya embarked on a course of isolation that lasted about 150 years. This left the rulers free to concentrate mainly on religious and cultural affairs. Internal communications were strengthened with the linking of numerous waterways.

The reign of King Boromakot (1733-1758) began with a particularly violent struggle for power, but Boromakot's 25-year term was an unusually peaceful one and became known as Ayutthaya's Golden Age. Poets and artists abounded at his court, enabling literature and the arts to flourish as never before. During this period, Ceylon invited a delegation of Siamese monks to purify the Sinhalese Sangha (monkhood), reversing the religious roles of the previous two countries.

The tranquil days proved to be the calm before the storm. Boromakot's son Ekatat ascended to the throne in 1758 after a bitter succession struggle with his brother, and surrounded himself with female company to ensure his pleasure. Meanwhile, a village headman united the Third Burmese Empire and assumed the royal title Alaungpaya. His invading Burmese armies were repelled in 1760 after Alaungpaya was wounded by his own cannon. But in 1767, a second Burmese invasion, led by Alaungpaya's son Hsinby-

ushin, succeeded in capturing Ayutthaya after a siege of 14 months.

In their hurry to withdraw from the conquered capital, the Burmese killed, looted and set fire to the whole city, thereby expunging four centuries of Thai civilization. Showing complete disregard for their common religion, the Burmese Buddhists plundered Ayutthaya's rich temples, melting down all the available gold from Buddha images. Members of the royal family, along with 90,000 captives and the accumulated booty, were removed to Burma.

Taksin's revenge: Despite their overwhelming victory, the Burmese didn't retain control of Siam for long. Attacks on Burma's northern borders compelled the Burmese to withdraw most of their forces and Thai tenacity in rebounding from setback combined to shorten the period of Burmese domination. Giving meaning to an ancient proverb that "Ayutthaya never lacks good men," a young general named Phya Tak Sin gathered a small band of followers during the final Burmese siege of the Thai capital. He recognized the hopelessness of the Siamese situation under the effete king and his decadent entourage. So instead of waiting for the holocaust to envelop the city, he and his comrades broke through the Burmese encirclement and escaped to Chantaburi on the southeast coast of the Gulf of Siam. There, Phya Tak Sin assembled an army and navy. Seven months after the fall of Ayutthaya, the general and his forces sailed back to the capital and expelled the Burmese occupation garrison.

Taksin, as he is popularly known, had barely spent a night at Ayutthaya when he decided to transfer the capital. He revealed to his troops that the old kings had appeared to him in a dream and told him to move. In fact, strategic considerations were probably more important than supernatural ones in Taksin's decision. A site nearer to the sea would facilitate foreign trade, ensure the procurement of arms, and make defense and withdrawal easier.

During the 17th century, a small fishing village downstream had become an important trade and defense outpost for Ayutthaya. Known as Bangkok, "village of wild olive groves," it contained fortifications built by the French. The settlement straddled both sides of the Chao Phya River, at a place where a short-cut canal had widened into the main stream. On the west bank, at Thonburi, Taksin officially established his new capital and was proclaimed king.

Taksin's reign was not an easy one. The lack of central authority after the fall of Ayutthaya had led to the rapid disintegration of the kingdom, and it fell upon Taksin to reunite the provinces. At the same time as he consolidated his power base at Thonburi, he contended with a series of Burmese invasions which he resolutely repulsed.

Taksin ruled until 1782. In the last seven years of his reign, he relied heavily on two trusted generals, the brothers Chao Phya Chakri and Chao Phya Sarasih, who were

the most sacred of all Buddha images, and is believed to guarantee the independence and prosperity of the nation.

But while the Emerald Buddha was in good health, Taksin was not. At Thonburi, his personality underwent a slow metamorphosis from strong and just leader to cruel and unpredictable eccentric, due perhaps, to over-exhaustion and the continuous strain of war and decision-making. He came to consider himself a *bodhisattva* or future Buddha, and flogged monks who refused to pay obeisance to him. Totally paranoid, he tortured his officials, his children, and even his wife to make them confess to imaginary crimes.

A 17th-century adventurer in a Thai mural.

given absolute command in military campaigns. They liberated Chiang Mai and the rest of northern Thailand from Burmese rule, and brought Cambodia and most of present-day Laos under Thai suzerainty.

It was from the victorious Laotian campaign that Thailand obtained the famed Emerald Buddha. Chao Phya Chakri carried the Buddha from Vientiane to Thonburi in 1779. Carved of solid jadeite, the image was allegedly discovered at Chiang Rai in 1436 inside a pagoda struck asunder by lightning. The Emerald Buddha is regarded by Thais as

When a revolt broke out in March 1782, Taksin was forced to abdicate and enter a monastery. A minor official named Phya San, who engineered the revolt, offered the vacant throne to Chao Phya Chakri upon his return from a Cambodian campaign. General Chakri assumed the kingship on April 6 – a date still commemorated annually as Chakri Day – and established the reigning Chakri dynasty. Taksin, still regarded by an advisory council of generals as a threat to internal stability, was executed in the traditional royal manner. It is said that Chao Phya Chakri's eyes were filled with tears when he said farewell to his former king and patron.

On assuming the throne, General Chakri took the name of Ramathibodi, like that of the illustrious founder of a new kingdom and dynasty. Later known as Rama I, he ruled from 1782 to 1809. His first action as king was to transfer his administrative headquarters across the river from the marshy ground and constricted confines of Thonburi to the more spacious Bangkok.

Understanding the value of tradition and symbol, he set about restoring the confidence of his war-shattered people. Buddha images were transported to Bangkok from Sukhothai and Ayutthaya, architects were instructed to design buildings in the Ayutthayan mode, and even bricks from ruined Ayutthaya were floated by barge to Bangkok to construct the city wall.

He assembled all surviving master craftsmen from the old city and had them design the first permanent building in the new capital: Wat Phra Kaew, or the Emerald Buddha temple. Constructed to house the Emerald Buddha, it took nearly three years to complete. When ready, the image was taken from Thonburi and installed on a canopied throne in the Royal Chapel. In commemoration of the event, a new word was added to the lengthy official title of the capital city (the longest city name in the world), Krung Thep Phra Maha Nakorn Amorn Rattanakosin (etc.). The new word altered the title to mean "City of Angels, Abode of the Emerald Buddha." Thais shorten the name to Krung Thep but the world knows it as Bangkok.

One of Rama I's chief concerns was to secure the borders of his kingdom. Early in his reign, King Bodawpaya of Burma launched a series of military expeditions involving the largest number of troops in the history of Thai-Burmese wars. Siamese troops boldly attacked the invaders at strategic border points, routing the Burmese before they could do serious harm. After Bodawpaya, Burma became embroiled in British colonial conflicts and Siam was left more or less in peace.

Modern Thailand is indebted to Rama I for his assiduous cultural revival program. He appointed commissions of experts to review and assemble fragments of historical and religious treatises, few of which had survived the destruction of Ayutthaya in 1767.

Rama I perpetuated another Ayutthaya tradition by appointing his brother as *Maha Uparaja*, or deputy king, with powers almost equal to his own. His home, the Wang Na or "palace at the back," now houses the National Museum and once extended across the northern half of Sanam Luang. Because the royal regalia had been destroyed with everything else during the siege of Ayutthaya, Rama I had a new crown and robes commissioned for his coronation. Similarly, in his old age, he commissioned a golden urn to be prepared for his body, according to ancient court protocol prescribing that the bodies of high-ranking royalty be placed in urns between the times of death and cremation.

The king was so pleased with the golden urn created by his craftsmen that he placed it in his bedroom to admire it fully. Upon seeing this, one of his wives burst into tears: it was a bad omen, she said. "Nonsense," replied the king, laughing. "If I don't see it from the outside while I'm alive, how the hell do you think I can ever see it?"

Rama II and Rama III: Rama I's successors, Rama II and Rama III, completed the consolidation of the Siamese kingdom and the revival of the arts and culture of Ayutthaya. Best remembered as an artist, Rama II (1809–1824), the second ruler of the Chakri dynasty, was responsible for building and repairing numerous Bangkok monasteries. His most famous construction was Wat Arun, the Temple of Dawn which was later enlarged to its present height by Rama IV. He is said to have carved the great doors of Wat Suthat, throwing away the special chisels so his work could never be replicated.

During his father's reign, Rama II had gained renown as a great poet. His *magnum opus* was the *Inao*, an epic poem adopted from a Javanese legend. His classic version of the *Ramakien*, the Thai version of the Indian classical saga, the *Ramayana*, was completed during his reign, with large sections composed by the king himself as well as by other poets. At his court, Rama II employed theatrical and classical *khon* and *lakorn* dance-drama troupes to enact his compositions as similar artists had performed for royal pleasure in the courts of Ayutthaya.

Rama II re-established relations with the West suspended since the time of Narai, allowing the Portuguese to open the first Western embassy in Bangkok. Rama III, who ruled from 1824 to 1851, continued to reopen Siam's doors to foreigners, successfully promoting trade with China.

The ready availability of Chinese porcelain led him to decorate many of his temples, including Wat Arun, with ceramic fragments.

Anna and the King of Siam: With the help of Hollywood, Rama IV (ruled 1851–1868) became the most famous King of Siam. Best known as King Mongkut, he was portrayed in *The King and I* as a frivolous, bald-headed despot. But nothing could have been further from the truth. He was the first Thai – and in many instances, first Asian – king to understand Western culture and technology, and his reign has been described as "the bridge spanning the new and the old."

The younger brother of Rama III, Mong-

This vogue did not survive his lifetime so that when viewing any temple with porcelain-decorated gables, one can immediately ascribe it to the reign of Rama III.

An extremely pious Buddhist, Rama III was considered to be "austere and reactionary" by some Europeans. But he encouraged American missionaries to introduce Western medicine to his country, including smallpox vaccinations.

Preceding pages: procession of royal barges at King Prajadhipok's 1925 coronation; and young classical dancers at the royal court. Above, century-old view of a city klong.

kut spent 27 years as a Buddhist monk prior to his accession to the throne. This gave him a unique opportunity to roam as a commoner among the populace. He learned to read Buddhist scriptures in the Pali language. Missionaries taught him Latin and English, thus enabling him to read European texts. As a monk, Mongkut delved into many subjects: history, geography and the sciences, especially astronomy.

Even as an abbot, he established himself as a reformer, ridding the Buddhist scriptures of their superstitious elements and founding a sect, the Dhammakaiya, which stressed strict adherence to Buddhist tenets. Today, these monks can be recognized by their brown robes. Mongkut realized that traditional Thai values would not save his country from Western encroachment. On the contrary, he believed that modernization would bring Siam in line with the West and reduce hostilities with foreigners.

England was the first European country to benefit from this policy when a 1855 treaty – not gained entirely without coercion by the British – granted extraterritorial privileges, a duty of only 3 percent on imports, and permission to import Indian opium duty-free. Other Western nations, including France and the United States, followed suit with similar treaties. And when Mongkut lifted the state

mer Palace at Bang Pa-in and the Palace on the Hill at Petchburi, he successfully calculated and predicted a total eclipse of the sun on August 18, 1868. European and Asian skeptics joined him on the southeastern coast of the Gulf of Siam to await the event. As the moon blocked off the sun's light from the earth, they raised an exclamation of admiration both among the Europeans and the scoffers among the royal astrologers, raising his esteem among both parties. But his triumph was short-lived. The king contracted malaria during the trip down the coast, and died two weeks later.

The beloved King Chulalongkorn: Mongkut's son, Chulalongkorn, was only 15 when he

monopoly on rice, that crop rapidly became Siam's leading export.

Rama IV wanted his children to gain the same benefits from the English language as himself. For this purpose, he engaged Anna Leonowens as an English teacher. The self-elevated governess greatly exaggerated her role in the Thai court in her autobiographical writings, misrepresenting the king as a cruel autocrat permanently involved in harem intrigues. Her residence in Siam (1862–1867) is hardly mentioned in Thai chronicles.

Mongkut's beloved hobby, astronomy, was the indirect cause of his death. From observatories at his favorite palaces, the Sum-

ascended the throne. But he reigned over Siam as Rama V for 42 years – longer than any Thai king until the present King Bhumibol who surpassed that record in 1988 – and transformed his country from a backward Asian land to a modern nation.

The farsighted Chulalongkorn immediately revolutionized his court by ending the ancient custom of prostration and by allowing officials to sit on chairs during royal audiences. He abolished serfdom in stages, giving owners and serfs time to readjust to the new order, and replaced corvee labor with direct taxation.

His reign was truly a "revolution from the

throne." When Chulalongkorn assumed power, Siam had no schools, few roads, railways, hospitals, or well-equipped military forces. To achieve the enormous task of modernization, he brought in foreign advisors and sent his sons and other young men abroad for education. He also founded a palace school for children of the aristocracy and followed this with the establishment of other schools and vocational centers. The only previous seats of learning in Siam had been the monasteries.

A watershed year was 1892, when the four government ministries were expanded to 12; a post and telegraph office was established; and construction of the first railway was be-

The first hospital, Siriraj, was opened in 1886 after years of unrelenting opposition. Most of the Thai common folk preferred herbal remedies to *farang* medicine. Besides, there was a distinct shortage of qualified doctors. Eventually, the obstacles were overcome.

In foreign relations, Rama V had to compromise and give up parts of his kingdom to protect Siam from foreign colonization. When France conquered Annam in 1883 and Britain annexed Upper Burma in 1886, Siam found itself sandwiched uncomfortably between two rival expansionist powers. Border conflicts and gunboat diplomacy forced Siam to surrender to France its claims to Laos and west-

gun. Chulalongkorn's brothers were leading figures in his government, especially Prince Devawongse, the foreign minister, and Prince Damrong, the first interior minister and a historian who has come to be known as "the father of Thai history." Chulalongkorn's elder children returned home from their European schools in the 1890s and contributed to modernizing the army and navy; one of them became Siam's first minister of justice.

From left to right: Rama IV and his Queen; a son of King Chulalongkorn; King Chulalongkorn and entourage in Heidelberg; Prince Damrong, "Father of Thai History".

ern Cambodia. Similarly, certain Malay Peninsula territories were ceded to Britain in exchange for renunciation of British extraterritorial rights in Siam. By the end of Chulalongkorn's reign, Siam had given up 120,000 sq km of fringe territory. But that seemed a small price to pay for maintaining the peace and independence of the Thai heartland in the Menam Chao Phya basin.

King Chulalongkorn made two European tours during his reign, in 1897 and 1907. These led him to seek more spacious surroundings than those of the Grand Palace, so he built the Dusit Palace on the site of a fruit orchard. It was directly connected to the

Grand Palace by the wide Rajdamnern Avenue. At Dusit, he held intimate parties and even fancy-dress balls, often cooking the food himself.

Chulalongkorn's many reforms bore fruit within his lifetime. During his reign, the economy of the country flourished, and Thai peasantry – by comparison with their counterparts in French Indochina and British Burma – were very well off. It is no wonder that Chulalongkorn was posthumously named Piya Maharaj, "the Beloved Great King." As Rama V, Chulalongkorn was conscious of worldwide democratic trends, but judged his country as yet unprepared for such a change. It is said that he brought progress to Siam

The law generated much initial bewilderment, especially in rural areas, and Vajiravudh personally coined patronymics for hundreds of families. To simplify his forebears' lengthy titles for foreigners, he invented the Chakri dynastic name, Rama, to be followed by the proper reign number. To start with, he proclaimed himself Rama VI.

As Thai standards of beauty did not conform to Western ideals of femininity, women were encouraged to keep their hair long instead of having it close-cropped, and to replace their *dhotis* or plus-fours with the *panung*, a Thai-style sarong. Primary education was made compulsory throughout the kingdom; Chulalongkorn University, the first

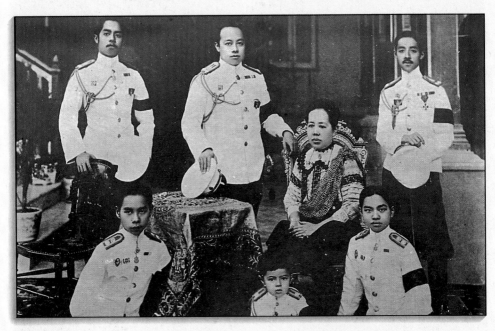

"through the judicious exercise of his absolute power."

Controversial brilliance: King Chulalongkorn's successor, Vajiravudh, began his reign (1910–1925) with a lavish coronation. Oxford-educated and thoroughly anglicized, his Western-inspired reforms to modernize Siam considerably affected the structure of modern Thai society.

One of the first changes was a 1913 edict commanding his subjects to adopt surnames. In the absence of a clan or caste system, genealogy was virtually unheard of in Thailand. Previously, Thais had used first names, a practice the king considered uncivilized.

in Siam, was founded and schools for both sexes flourished during his reign.

Rama VI's most significant political contribution was to promote the concept of nationalism. An accomplished author, he used literature and drama to foster nationalism by glorifying Thai legends and historical heroes in plays. Under a pseudonym, he also wrote essays extolling the virtues of the nation.

At the outbreak of World War I, Siam remained neutral but late in the War, Vajira-

Chulalongkorn's widow and family. Vajiravudh and Prajadhipok are at center top and lower right, respectively.

vudh joined the Allies by sending a small expeditionary force to fight in France in 1917, thereby securing Siam's admittance to the League of Nations. The Thai flag, a white elephant against a red background, was flown with others at Versailles but the pachyderm was unfortunately mistaken for a small domestic animal. The incident greatly discomfited the king who then changed the flag to red, white and blue stripes to represent the nation, the religion and the monarchy, elements now recognized as essential to the structure of modern Thailand.

King Vajiravudh preferred individual ministerial consultations to summoning his appointed cabinet. His regime was therefore criticized as autocratic and lacking in coordination. Members of his family were dissatisfied because he rarely saw them, enjoying more the company of his courtiers. To this clique, he was overly generous.

His extravagance soon emptied the reserve funds built up by Chulalongkorn; towards the end of his reign, the Treasury had to meet deficits caused by the ruler's personal expenses. Vajiravudh married late. His only daughter was born one day before he died in 1925. He was succeeded by his youngest brother, Prajadhipok, who reaped the consequences of his predecessor's brilliant but controversial reign.

Prajadhipok's short reign: The early death of his elder brother propelled Prajadhipok to royal succession although he, being an old Etonian, would have preferred a soldier's career to a ruler's. Once king, however, he stressed economy and efficiency within the government. Unlike his brother, he tried to cut public expenditure by reducing the Civil List and Royal Household expenses drastically. Prajadhipok's economic policies, combined with increased revenue from foreign trade, amply paid off.

In the early years of his reign, communications were improved by a wireless service and the Don Muang Airport began to operate as an international air center. It was also during his reign that Siam saw the establishment of the Fine Arts Department, the National Library and the National Museum.

Hard-working and conscientious, Prajadhipok was personally concerned with improving the welfare of his subjects. He was aware of the rising demand for greater participation in government by a small foreign-educated faction, but felt that the Siamese were, on the whole, not ready for democracy. In 1927, he publicly commented that the people must first be taught political consciousness before democracy could effectively be introduced.

The worldwide economic crisis of 1931 affected Siam's rice export. By the time Prajadhipok dropped the gold standard linking the Thai baht to the pound sterling, it was too late to stem the financial crisis. The government was forced to implement further economies by cutting the salary of junior personnel and by resorting to a retrenchment of the armed services. Thus, discontent brewed among army officials and bureaucrats, who felt that their promotions were hindered.

Rumors and speculation were rampant during the 150th anniversary celebrations of the Chakri dynasty in April 1932. Prajadhipok was the last regal representative of traditional Thai kingship to preside over grand pageantry which featured a royal barge procession. Two months later on June 24, a coup d'etat ended the paternal but absolute rule by Thai monarchs.

The coup was staged by the People's Party, a military and civilian group masterminded by foreign-educated Thais. The chief ideologist was Pridi Panomyong, a young lawyer trained in France. On the military side, Captain Luang Pibulsongram was responsible for gaining the support of important army colonels. With a few tanks, the 70 conspirators sparked off their "revolution" by occupying strategic areas and holding the senior princes hostage. Other army officers stood by and the public took no part in it, save as spectators. The king was in Hua Hin at the time; he quickly returned to the capital and to avoid bloodshed, accepted the provisional constitution by which he "ceased to rule but continued to reign."

From monarchy to democracy: Absolute monarchy was quickly replaced by a Party dictatorship. Once in power, the new regime declared that Thais were insufficiently educated to rule themselves; the new government's first 10 years was to be a trial period for democracy. In December 1932, the king signed the Constitution which promised universal suffrage and general elections every four years.

In 1933, the government was divided by

Pridi's economic policy advocating the nationalization of all agricultural land. The plan was considered communistic and Pridi was maneuvered into temporary exile. A counter-coup in the same year reshuffled members of the Executive Council, with Pibul (Pibulsongram) gaining ascendancy. Thai politics for the next two decades was alternately dominated by Pibul, who had the military backing, and Pridi, whose supporters were from the intelligentsia. The latter was allowed to return in 1934 when he was cleared of all charges.

Meanwhile, King Prajadhipok was finding his new role increasingly painful. Constitutional differences with the government

litical aimlessness and instability. The "permanent" constitution was revised several times; experiments with both uni-cameral and bi-cameral legislative systems were attempted. Unsuccessful democratic interludes usually paved the way for military intervention and dominance.

A series of governmental crises occurred between 1935 and 1938, enabling Pibul to assume control. Nationalism was intensified, economically as well as culturally, by his authoritarian regime. To demonstrate the new chauvinism, the name of the country was officially changed from Siam to Thailand. Pibul began a "civilizing campaign" which forced Western dress styles and social

culminated in his decision to abdicate in 1935. In his farewell speech to the nation, he said that he had given up his absolute power to the whole of the Thai people and not to any particular group. At the time of the abdication, Prajadhipok was in England; he remained there with the title "Prince Sukhothai" until his death in 1941. Ananda Mahidol, his 10-year-old nephew studying in Switzerland, was proclaimed King. A Regency Council of three members was appointed to act during his minority.

Aimlessness and instability: The abrupt transplanting of Western democracy to a traditionally deep-rooted society resulted in po-

mores upon the masses. The chewing of betelnut, favored by Thais from time immemorial, was outlawed and people were told to wear shoes and hats in public. Even expectant mothers and serious casualties, if shoeless or hatless, were refused admittance into hospitals.

The outbreak of World War II placed Thailand's traditional pro-Western stance on the line. The Japanese army invaded Bangkok and, Pibul, sensing that resistance would cost many Thai lives, capitulated.

His Ambassador in Washington, Seni Pramoj, could not accept the new overlords and refused to convey to the United States the Japanese-inspired Thai declaration of war. Instead, he placed the document in his desk drawer where it remained for the duration of the war. When hostilities ceased, Siam was relieved of war indemnifications on the grounds that as war had never officially been declared, it could not be condemned as an enemy.

In large part, it was the activities of overseas and pro-Ally Thais inside Thailand that influenced the Allies' decision. Anti-Japanese (and anti-Pibul), these Thais formed a pro-Ally underground resistance movement, the Seri Thai or Free Thai Movement. It received the active support of Pridi, who was acting as Regent, and was led by Seni Pramoj

improved by his war stance. King Ananda Mahidol, now aged 20, returned home to a tumultuous welcome in 1945. Only one year later, the young king was found shot dead in his bedroom. His tragic and unsolved death caused Pridi's political exit. Political opportunists insinuated that Pridi was implicated in the plot and hounded him out of the country and to exile in Paris and Peking.

Ananda Mahidol was succeeded by his younger brother King Bhumibol Adulyadej, the present monarch. Shortly after being appointed, the new king resumed his studies in Switzerland in 1946 and Prince Rangsit of Chainat, who had been released after six years of imprisonment, was appointed Re-

in the United States. The group participated in behind-the-lines sabotage to frustrate the Japanese war effort. Japanese became increasingly disliked and when the tide turned against them, Pibul's collaborative government collapsed. To bring about reconciliation with the West, Seni Pramoj was appointed Prime Minister in 1945.

The Seni government was soon replaced by that of Pridi, whose image had been

Left, pages from a period book, showing officers involved in the coup d'etat and the constitution of Thailand. <u>Above</u>, all dressed up for a Ploughing Day ceremony in 1930.

gent until his death in 1951.

The military consolidated its power with a bloodless coup in 1947. One of the main figures was Colonel Sarit Thanarat, army commander of the First Division controlling the Bangkok area. This coup saw the emergence of a younger generation of army officers, Thai-educated and less westernized than the coup leaders of 1932. Communist uprisings in neighboring countries were considered threatening by upper and middle-class Thais, and this helped to justify two decades of rule by military junta.

Field Marshal Pibul returned to politics in 1948. His premiership was to last 10 years, a rule characterized by an anti-communist foreign policy which led to closer cooperation with the United States against the People's Republic of China. Thailand joined SEATO (South East Asia Treaty Organization) to combat communist aggression and American economic aid began in 1950, most of it for military purposes. The total sum was to reach stupendous proportion, especially during the Vietnam War.

Subsequent to his world tour in 1955 Pibul decided to experiment with democracy by lifting the ban on political parties and permitting "Hyde Park" style free speeches. The program misfired and two years later, he declared a state of emergency. His govern-

controlling major financial, industrial, commercial and foreign enterprises. Sarit's government declared economic development its national priority and implemented a five-year plan. A Board of Investment was established to attract foreign capital. Recognizing the foreign exchange earning power of tourism, the Tourist Organization of Thailand, (later upgraded to the Tourism Authority of Thailand), was established. Sarit set in motion the machinery necessary for national development.

Upon his death in 1963, Sarit's aide General Thanom became Prime Minister and head of junta, with Prapass as the army commander-in-chief. The communist threat

ment, newly-elected in a corruption-ridden campaign that led to widespread public protest, was overthrown by Sarit.

Strongman politics: The 1957 coup saw the alignment of Sarit, General Thanom Kittikachorn and General Prapass Charusathien, a trio which controlled Thai politics from the later '50s to the early '70s. Sarit epitomized the strongman concept previously adopted by several kings. Although all but the trappings of democracy were abolished, his decisiveness and stress on discipline won popular support.

The military leaders, however, became involved in business activities, gradually

accounted for Thailand's complicity in the Vietnam war. By allowing the United States to build six air bases in 1965, American monetary aid was obtained for the construction of highways, much of which was allegedly siphoned by administrators into their private accounts.

The king proclaimed a new constitution in 1968 and the next year's general election saw Thanom democratically reassuming his premiership. But the internal situation soon deteriorated due to public dissatisfaction and what the rulers declared was terrorist insurgency, leading them to organize a coup against themselves, abrogate the constitution and declare martial law. Student leaders' demand for an end to military dictatorship, promulgation of a proper Constitution, and a return of parliamentary democracy culminated in the student uprising of October 1973. Most of the agitators were from the left-wing Thammasat University. A clash between students and the army produced 69 dead and 800 wounded and Thanom's clique was forced to resign and go into exile.

This heralded an era of open politics from 1973 to 1976. It was, according to the Institute of Southeast Asian Studies, "a nightmare for the bureaucratic and military elite." Hundreds of pressure groups were formed and strikes and demonstrations were common; elections led to brief coalition governments. Foreign policy-wise, the most successful government was that of M.R. Kukrit Pramoj. Kukrit started diplomatic relations with the People's Republic of China and strengthened Thailand's role in ASEAN (the Association of South East Asian Nations).

He also recognized that communist insurgency was fueled by dashed hopes among the rural poor. To alleviate their grievances, he established the Tambon Council Fund which provided money to construct irrigation canals, bridges and other rural development projects to remedy needs identified by the villagers themselves.

Despite its success, it was not enough to satisfy the students who felt the ruling and commercial elite was still entrenched and was resisting change. As a result, they increased the stridency of their protests. In 1976, Thanom Kittikachorn returned to Thailand ostensibly to visit his ailing father, and despite being banned, was allowed entry by certain military officials. The students once again protested which led on October 6 to another violent confrontation between the police and students. Using a trumped up pretext, the police and right-wing goons

A 1870 circa photo of the Royal barge by Thomson.

stormed Thammasat University, brutally murdering dozens of students and effectively ending the three-year experiment with democracy.

The army seized control from the elected government and instituted their own rule. Generals or ex-generals would continue to rule for the next decade and a half.

Ruling with Dharma: "We will reign with *dharma* (righteousness) for the benefit and happiness of the Siamese people," was the coronation pledge of King Bhumibol Adulyadej in 1950. The King alone provides stability and continuity lacking in the turbulent cycle of Thai politics.

Tirelessly touring the land with Queen Sirikit to inspect and improve the welfare of the people, the King has inspired universal reverence. As a constitutional monarch, he maintains neutrality at times of crises, and coupmakers have declared their loyalty to the Crown.

The King's moral authority was demonstrated in April 1981 when a group of army officers calling themselves the Young Turks staged a coup to overthrow the government of General Prem Tisulanonda. Although commanding formidable forces, their attempt quickly ended in failure when it was apparent that the group did not possess the king's tacit consent. Bangkok celebrated her 200th birthday as Thailand's capital with the Rattanakosin bicentennial celebrations in April 1982.

The 1980s saw Thailand's rapid emergence as an economic powerhouse and a reassessment of its role in the region. In a departure away from its former economic policy of promoting agro-based industries to capitalize on its competitive advantage of abundant harvests, Thailand has embarked on a policy of full-scale industrialization. The fuel for the growth is being provided by Taiwanese financiers as that country's increased prosperity threatens to price itself out of the market, by Hong Kong money which is flowing out of the colony as the 1997 reversion to Peking's rule approaches, and by Japanese financing which now accounts for 50 percent of all investment in Thailand.

Initially, cheap land and labor costs were the twin lures that helped transform the country. Bangkok's skyline continues to mushroom from horizontal to vertical and while the official population is set at 5.5 million, the unofficial tabulation is moving past 8 million, most of it day laborers no longer able to earn a decent income on the farm and drawn to live in Bangkok by the promise of higher wages.

While the cities are becoming more crowded, the biggest changes are occurring in the countryside. The long-dreamed of Eastern Seaboard development zone is now beginning to be realized with the completion of the Laem Chabang deepwater port. In the Central Plains, North and, to some extent, the Northeast, farm land is being turned into factories and forests into resorts and leisure homes.

Unfortunately, much of the new development is accelerating deforestation as farmers seek new land. It is also resulting in social dislocation and discontent which manifests itself in public protests. Income disparities, strains on existing infrastructure, an overheated economy, and what is viewed as tunnel-vision towards developing Thailand as a "Newly-Industrialized Country" is beginning to concern many who feel the changes are coming too rapidly and without sufficient consideration for social costs or the future.

Foreign policy in the 1990s has been governed by pragmatic and economic considerations. Anand Panyarachun, Prime Minister of an interim government formed after a February 1991 coup d'etat, continued the policies of his predecessor, Chatichai Choonhaven, in seeking to make Thailand a regional leader. Notably, he sought to expand trade relations with Thailand's former enemies in Indochina and to trade with Burma, despite foreign criticism support for a repressive regime.

In May 1992, there was a popular uprising against the ruling military junta and its appointment of a new Prime Minister to succeed the highly respected Anand Panyarachun. After the personal intervention of His Majesty King Bhumibol Adulyadej, again demonstrating his enormous moral authority, a brief interim government under the leadership of Anand Panyarachun preceeded new elections. The new, democratically elected government returned Thailand to political, economic and social stability.

In the 1990s, Thailand faces a series of important challenges in restructuring for the future. The government must take a more active, perhaps regulatory, role in stemming corruption, ensuring equitable distribution of wealth, preserving resources, and improving infrastructure.

Most observers feel Thailand will rise to the challenges. With its staunch reliance on religion, nation and monarchy, it has defeated colonialism and communism. This resiliency will serve to propel it into the 21st century as one of the most important nations in Asia.

On Chulalongkorn Day, students pay respect to the former King's statue.

PORTRAITS OF CONTEMPORARIES

Even a cursory glance at Thai history repudiates a simplified view of the country and its people. In the following pages we try to capture the more ineffable qualities that characterize the Thai nation by presenting a series of portraits of contemporary Thais.

Whether it is a young monk padding softly in the gentle light of a Bangkok dawn carrying an alms bowl; a chic Thai businesswoman closing a deal with her more traditional compatriot dressed in a silk *pasin* (full-length wraparound); or King Bhumibol flying by helicopter to an upcountry summer palace after a royal visit to a nearby village school – Thailand sparkles with remarkable individuals.

The king, a symbol from the distant past; a man vital to the present

His Majesty the King is to preside over a royal ceremony at Wat Phra Kaew, the Temple of the Emerald Buddha. The crowd that has begun to gather hours before the king's arrival, represents every walk of Thai life: elderly country women with cropped hair and betel stained lips, farmers in blue homespun cotton shorts, students in neatly pressed uniforms, society ladies in Thai silk dresses, office workers from nearby government buildings, and children brought by their parents to see their ruler. An air of excited anticipation animates the crowd.

It is not the first time they have seen the king, for within his kingdom he is one of the most visible rulers in the world. With age, he has reduced his schedule but he still opens fairs, presides over ceremonies, hands out university diplomas, and walks through the countryside overseeing rural development projects he has initiated. Yet the same sense of reverence and excitement grips his subjects every time he appears.

Swords clank, the honor guard snaps to attention, the crowd draws its breath and

Preceding pages, the Royal family at Wat Phra Kaew. **Left**, King Bhumibol at the investiture of the Crown Prince.

through the ornately carved doors that separate Wat Phra Kaew from the compound of the Grand Palace steps a slim man in an immaculate white uniform, followed by a beautiful woman in a shimmering traditional Thai-style dress. Their Majesties, King Bhumibol and Queen Sirikit, have arrived.

The king of Thailand is both a symbol and a man. Born in the distant past in fabled Sukhothai, the symbol has endured through wars, revolutions, the fall of dynasties, the smashing of traditions and governments, both dictatorial and democratic, and through times of tribulation and prosperity. While kings in many countries are little more than figureheads, in Thailand the monarch remains the

ing. His father, a son of King Rama V and later regarded as the father of modern medicine in Thailand, was a minor member of royalty. At his birth, there seemed little chance of Prince Bhumibol's becoming king. Between him and the throne, according to the laws of succession laid down by Rama V, stood any sons the ruling Rama VII might have, Bhumibol's own father, and his elder brother Prince Ananda.

But Rama VII had no sons, and Prince Mahidol died in 1929. On King Rama VII's abdication, Ananda, still a young student in Switzerland, became king, although he did not return to his kingdom until after the war. In 1946, he was killed under mysterious

most powerful unifying force in the country, respected by all groups. Pictures of the king and queen hang in almost every house in the nation. As the lights dim before the start of a movie, every Thai in the audience stands at attention as a portrait of the king is flashed on the screen and the royal anthem is played. The one thing the tolerant Thais will not forgive is a remark disrespectful of the monarchy.

The man himself is as extraordinary as the symbol. He was born in Cambridge, Massachusetts in 1927, where his father Prince Mahidol of Songkhla was studying medicine at Harvard University and his mother, nurs-

circumstances in the Grand Palace and his younger brother, Prince Bhumibol, ascended the throne as the ninth ruler of the Chakri dynasty.

In the 40 years since his coronation in 1950, King Bhumibol has proved himself a worthy successor to his celebrated ancestors. With Queen Sirikit, he has traveled to every part of the country; in 1955 he became the first monarch to tour the Northeast. He makes these visits not to make himself visible to his subjects but to talk with them and learn their problems firsthand. The most common portrait of him shows him in the countryside dressed in fatigues, one hand clutching a walkie-talkie, the other, a map.

His involvement with rural people began with a concerted effort to find new crops for hilltribesmen in order to wean them away from opium cultivation. He impressed on government officials the need to provide technical assistance, seeds and, most importantly, markets. This support extended to construction of roads and irrigation canals.

He incorporated this experience into programs to aid farmers in each of the country's four regions. From summer palaces – often little more than ordinary houses – in key areas, he traveled by road and helicopter to villages to learn what they needed to im-

where millions of *tilapia* fish have been bred. *Tilapia* fingerlings are given to farmers who release them in their rice fields at the beginning of the planting season and harvest the fattened fish along with the rice three months later.

Other members of the Royal Family operate similar programs to aid rural families. The Princess Mother, the King's octogenarian mother, founded the Flying Doctors program to provide medical and dental services in remote areas. Her Majesty, Queen Sirikit, established the SUPPORT foundation which serves a double purpose, preserving ancient arts and crafts, and providing skills and income for rural people who produce

prove their lives. He counts on their active participation in these projects, calling on the government to serve in a support role to their own efforts. He has also turned over his palace grounds to agricultural purposes.

It comes as a surprise to the visitor to drive past the moated fences of Chitralada Palace (the Grand Palace is used only for ceremonial occasions and state receptions) and see cows contentedly grazing. In the grounds are an experimental dairy and ponds

Left and above, King Bhumibol of Thailand – revered and respected, he's both man and symbol to the people of Thailand.

products which SUPPORT then markets locally and overseas.

In addition to all this, he and the queen take part in the numerous royal ceremonies that punctuate the year – the seasonal robing of the Emerald Buddha, the various Buddhist holy days, the opening of Parliament, the Trooping of the Colors parade, to name only a few. Only recently have they cut back considerably on handing out diplomas at the universities and sponsoring countless weddings and cremations.

If the Thais revere their king as a symbol, they also respect him as a man, a fact which makes the Thai monarchy stronger now than at any period since King Bhumibol's grandfather, Chulalongkorn (Rama V).

Buddhism: A total way of being

A young saffron-robed Buddhist monk walks with grave dignity along a city street in the pale light of early morning, a cloth bag over one arm, a metal alms bowl cradled in the other. Silently, he opens his alms bowl to receive the offerings of rice and curries placed in it by ordinary Thais who have stood for long moments before their homes, awaiting his arrival. He says not a word of thanks because, according to Buddhist tenets, he is doing them a favor, providing them a means to make merit so they can be reborn in the next life as higher beings. Turning, he continues to walk on bare feet to the next set of alms givers, following the steps of monks before him for 2,000 years.

The total number of monks at Thailand's 28,000 *wats* varies from season to season, swelling during the rainy season, the normal time for a young man to enter the priesthood. Tradition requires that every Buddhist male enter the monkhood for a period ranging from seven days to six months to a lifetime. Regulations require that government offices and the military give a man time off to enter the monkhood; companies customarily grant leave time with pay for this purpose.

Because there is no provision for the ordaining of women, the monk also makes merit for his mother and female relatives. There are nuns who wear white robes but they do not share the same rights as the monks. They live in side areas of the *wat*, chant in a group separate from the men, and receive whatever food has not been consumed by the monks.

Prior to being ordained, the would-be monk is shorn of all his hair. He then answers a series of questions put to him by the abbot which assures he is in good mental and physical health. He then takes up residence in a monks' dormitory or in a small *kuti* or meditation house.

While in the temple, he listens to sermons based on the Buddha's teachings, studies the Tripitaka or Three Baskets (the teaching of Buddha in Pali), practices meditation, and learns the virtues of an ascetic life free of material possessions. He also shares in the work of the monastery, washing dishes, sweeping and keeping his quarters clean. Like the regular priests, he goes out at dawn to receive his daily meals.

A Buddhist monk must not only abstain from stealing, lying and idle talk, taking life, indulgence in sex, intoxicants, luxuries and frivolous amusements, he must also obey no fewer than 227 rules that govern the minutiae of daily conduct and manners. In practice, however, except among the Dhammakaiya sect, monks observe ten basic rules. He can have no possessions except the yellow robe, the alms bowl and a few personal necessities. He eats two meals a day, the first early in the morning and the second before noon.

For all its spartan life, however, a Buddhist *wat* (or "temple") in Thailand is by no means isolated from the "real" world. Most *wats* have schools of some sort attached to them; for centuries, the only schools were those run by monks. *Wats* have traditionally been the centers of social and communal life in the villages with monks serving as herbal doctors, psychological counselors, and arbitrators of disputes. Monks also play an important part in many of the rituals of daily life, such as the blessing of a new building, a birthday or a funeral.

Except during the period of Buddhist Lent from July to October, monks are free to travel from one temple to another at will. Moreover, the *wats* are open to anyone who wishes to retire to them. On *wan phra* a day each week determined by the lunar calendar, Thais go to the *wat* to listen to monks chant scriptures and deliver sermons. In addition to providing monks with food, the laity earns merit by making repairs on the temple or, even better, replacing an old and derelict building with a new one. At the end of the Lenten season, groups of Thais board boats or buses to travel to distant villages to make donations, an occasion filled with as much riotous celebration as solemn ceremony.

The basic form of Buddhism practiced in Thailand is Hinayana (Buddhism of the Lesser Vehicle) also called Theravada. Originating in India, Hinayana is also practiced in neighboring Burma, but even a casual visitor to temples in both countries will quickly perceive differences between them. As they have done with most outside influences – Khmer temple decorations and Chinese food, for instance – the Thais over the centuries have evolved a Buddhism of their own, one suited to the Thai temperament.

In addition to Theravada Buddhism, there is the Mahayana (Greater Vehicle) Buddhism practiced by those of Chinese descent. Their shrines can be found throughout Bangkok and most towns of Thailand. To the visitor stepping into a *sanjao* or shrine, it is immediately evident that Mahayana is observed with more vigor. Incense smoke clouds the air, sticks are shaken out of canisters to tell fortunes, paper money is burned for use by deceased ancestors, bells are rung and the din of piety permeates every corner.

As a philosophy, as distinct from a religion, Buddhism has played a profound role in

Nearly 92 percent of the Thai people are Buddhist, but religious tolerance is (and always has been) extended to other religions. In Bangkok and the South, there are hundreds of mosques attesting to the presence of Muslims, Islam being the second largest religion in Thailand. Religious Affairs Department funds are provided for the repair or construction of mosques.

Christian missionaries have struggled for more than a century to win converts but without great success. King Mongkut, who welcomed them and learned English from them, suggested that missionaries had succeeded in countries where the indigenous religion was weak. It was a testament to the

shaping the Thai character, particularly their reactions to events. The Buddhist concept of the impermanence of life and possessions, and the necessity to avoid extremes of emotion or behavior, has done much to create the relaxed, carefree charm that is one of the most appealing characteristics of the people. Tension, ulcers, nervous breakdowns and the like are not unknown in Thailand, at least not in places like Bangkok; but that they are remarkably uncommon is in no small way due to the influence of Buddhism.

A monk ordination at Wat Suthat, Bangkok, is a solemn ceremony.

strength of Buddhism and to the cohesiveness of the society that few Thais needed to turn elsewhere for salvation. As a result, there are pockets of Christians and churches – most notably in Chiang Mai – but the few steeples are lost in a forest of *chedi* spires.

Hinduism and Sikhism are practiced by the descendants of Indian immigrants, most of whom reside in Bangkok.

Spirits: A commonplace belief

An old woman, kneeling reverently before a small spirit house, clasps her hands in the prayerlike gesture called the "wai". Before the house she places burning incense sticks and a garland of sweetly scented jasmine. These, she hopes, will persuade the spirit to look fondly on her and grant her a wish – to win a lottery, perhaps, or get a grandson, or good health. Though most Thais are Buddhist, other, older beliefs–in spirits, in astrology, in good and bad omens–also figure prominently in their lives.

Nearly every Thai male, and a large number of women as well, carry some sort of amulet, usually on a chain around their necks. Some wear as many as half a dozen charms, to protect them from automobile accidents, gunfire, snakebite and almost any other dis-

are Brahman in origin, and even today Brahman priests officiate at major ceremonies. The Thai wedding ceremony is almost entirely Brahman as are many funeral rites.

The rites of statecraft pertaining to the Royal Family are presided over by Brahman priests. One of the most popular and impressive of these, the Plowing Ceremony, takes place each May on the Phramane Ground north of Bangkok's Temple of the Emerald Buddha. To signal the beginning of the rice planting season, a team of sacred oxen is offered a selection of grains. Astrologers watch carefully as the grains the oxen choose determine the amount of rainfall and the degree of success or failure of

aster one can think of. In the provinces, tattoos are considered effective in warding off evil. According to official Thai chronicles, the first Thai embassy to the court of France's Louis XIV, astonished the king by telling him they possessed a magic charm that rendered them immune to bullets. A demonstration was arranged, and when the French squad fired, the chronicles relate, their bullets fell harmlessly to the ground.

Astrologers are consulted regularly to learn auspicious times for weddings, important journeys, moving into a new house, and even the promulgation of a constitution.

Many of the Thais' non-Buddhist beliefs

the year's crops. Afterwards, the oxen draw a gilded plow around the field and seeds are symbolically sown (and afterwards eagerly collected by farmers to bring them luck), and the head priest, after complex calculations, makes predictions on the forthcoming rainfall and the bounty of the next harvest.

The variety of *phis* (spirits) is legion, outnumbering the human population many times over. A seductive female *phi*, believed to reside in a banana plant, torments young men who come near. Another bothersome one takes possession of her victims and forces them to remove their clothes in public. (For some reason, the most destructive spirits seem to be female.)

A very common sight in any town in Thailand, including sophisticated Bangkok, is a miniature house, generally set on a post in a site selected after complex astrological consideration. In ordinary residences the small doll-like house may resemble a Thai dwelling; in grander establishments, hotels and offices, it may be an elaborate mini-temple, made of cement and painted and gilded.

In either case, they serve as the abodes of the resident spirits of the compounds. It is within their power to favor or plague the human inhabitants so the house is regularly

adorned with placative offerings of food, fresh flowers and incense sticks. If calamity or ill luck befalls the compound, it may be necessary to call in an expert (frequently a Buddhist priest) to consult the spirit to determine what is wrong.

One of the most famous spirit houses in Bangkok is in the compound of the Erawan Hotel, at the intersection of Rajdamri and Ploenchit roads. This shrine, honoring the

Left, a devotee makes an offering at a spirit house. **Above**, a Brahman blessing a newly installed spirit house in front of a plush residential estate in Bangkok.

Hindu god Brahma, was erected by the owners during the construction of the original hotel in the 1950s after several workers had been injured in mysterious accidents. The shrine soon acquired a widespread reputation for bringing good fortune to outsiders as well. Believers crowd the shrine, leaving huge mounds of garlands or wooden elephants, or paying a resident *lakhon* to perform a dance of thanksgiving.

A less well-known shrine sits in the compound of the Hilton Hotel. Its offerings consist entirely of phalluses, ranging from small to gargantuan, sculpted from wood, wax, stone or cement with scrupulous fidelity to life. They are left by women hoping to conceive a child.

To the average Thai, there is nothing inconsistent about the intermingling of such practices and beliefs with Buddhism. Their broad, easygoing tolerance allows them to accept, or at least to absorb, all such beliefs.

Public Service: An honorable career

She sits behind a desk, usually in a uniform of light brown that signifies her as a civil servant. If business is not occupying her attention, she turns to chat with friends. Her colleagues work at a leisurely pace, secure in the knowledge that long after politicians have faded from the scene, they will still be here, eternally. Her choice of career follows an old tradition in Asia. Although the pay is low, there is honor in holding a government position. Others may scurry after money, working as merchants but she has chosen the honorable way to earn her living. Her uniform gives her status and the knowledge that she will have a job until the mandatory retirement age of 60.

In Thailand, the term "civil servant" covers a segment of the population far beyond those who sit in government offices. It includes university and public school teachers, nurses in government hospitals, and employees of the various government monopolies and business enterprises as diverse as the State Railways of Thailand, the Lottery Bureau, the Thailand Tobacco Monopoly, and the Telephone Organization of Thailand. Altogether they number in the hundreds of thousands, after farmers, are perhaps the largest single workforce in the country.

Civil service pay scales are much lower than those of business and industry (a university lecturer with a Ph.D from abroad, for example, earns less than US$ 500 a month), but there is rarely a shortage of applicants for even the lowest positions.

Government service offers security; civil servants are almost never fired, except in cases of blatant dishonesty or corruption. It also carries a high degree of social prestige. For young women in particular the civil service has always been one of the few socially acceptable ways of earning a living, since business was regarded as unsuitable for a young woman from a good family.

But times are changing. The traditional *approval of his wife), is a strict vegetarian, sleeps on a thin mattress, wears a blue peasant's shirt, and is considered to be incorruptible.*

Major-General Chamlong Srimuang is one of the world's most unusual politicians. After 30 years in the Thai army, he found new direction in Buddhism, resigned his commission and set out to better the lot of the common people. In his 1985 campaign he gave new definition to "low-key, low-budget" and was swept up by an electorate long inured to corrupt city politics, to a four-year term as governor primarily on his reputation for sincerity and honesty.

Alert, smiling, energetic and eminently

view that business is best left to outsiders, such as the Chinese and Indian newcomers, is fast dying out. Expanded job opportunities and higher income are luring many who once would have become civil servants. Young people now go into advertising and airline offices, trading companies, or, in the case of teachers, into one of the private schools that offer better salaries than the government.

The politician: Chamlong the Great

He rises at 4 am to meditate before an 18-hour working day. He neither smokes nor drinks, has taken a vow of celibacy (with the

approachable, he worked to improve the corrupt city administration, and to instill a sense of pride in city workers, earning him the title "Maha Chamlong": Chamlong the Great. His reward came in 1989 when he was elected governor by a landslide, securing a large number of city seats for members of his Palang Dharma Party.

Many carved a future role for him by predicting that his refreshing style of leadership could transform the military-dominated nature of Thai politics. In 1992, the forecasts came true as Chamlong, dubbed the "conscience of the Thai nation," became the leading figure in the pro-democracy movement.

Thailand's dramatic economic growth had brought with it the desire for democratic government. Although the political scene was moving gradually towards this, a complex chain of events resulted in the military-backed – and unelected – General Suchinda Kraprayoon adopting the role of prime minister, bringing into his government civilians who had been accused of corruption. The Thais were shocked and a popular pro-democracy movement was born.

With Chamlong as their champion, the movement, made up from a broad spectrum of Thais, took to the streets to demand Suchinda's replacement by a democratically-elected leader. Chamlong went on a six-day stopped, and within hours the military withdrew and Bangkok seemed back to normal.

Chamlong, who had rejected a high-profile political role, stood by in the following general elections when voters gave a small majority to opposition parties, and Chuan Leekpai became prime minister. Chamlong's political role, however, was redefined in October 1994, when he became a deputy prime minister in the Chuan government.

Some commentators are puzzled by his political ambitions, but Chamlong's devotion to Buddhism has never been challenged. He has opened a restaurant at Chatuchak Park, which offers cheap vegetarian dishes, and the Tueng (Amazing) Shop providing

hunger strike and was arrested. In a week of unparalleled violence in Bangkok, the army, under Suchinda, killed or wounded hundreds of unarmed pro-democracy demonstrators. Tension increased with a deadlock between the army, focused around Suchinda, and Chamlong's pro-democracy movement.

Eventually the situation was defused by the intervention of the revered King Bhumipol Adulyadej. In a national broadcast, Suchinda prostrated himself before the king and later offered his resignation. The street protests

Left, government officers looking smart in their uniforms. **Above**, the people of Bangkok.

essentials at low prices. Profits go to charity.

"Chamlong the Great" has surprised both his supporters and enemies. Many are waiting to see what his next challenge will be.

The Military

The traditional avenue for advancement in all sectors of society is the military. The Thai soldier, like the civil servant, belongs to a sprawling, complex organization whose activities go beyond the bounds of defending the country. Thai conscripts serving their obligatory two-year terms fill most of the lower ranks and perform the traditional duties of military life in defending borders against invaders. The upper ranks, however, perform a wider function, being intimately involved in the business and government of the country.

It is a role vastly different from that performed in Western Europe or North America but one which has its roots in Thai history when rulers rose out of the ranks of the military. In Thailand, the ruler's role as "Commander in Chief" is more than an empty title; it defines his origins and what he sees as his chief role in the society.

High-ranking military officers sit on the boards of banks, own hotels, and take part in business even as they actively pursue mili-

old Thai proverb, "A woman is the hind legs of the elephant," and Thai tradition requires that she honor and obey her husband. That image has changed considerably in recent decades so that today, the hind legs are pushing and even outpacing the front legs.

During the drafting of the 1974 constitution a proposal that for the first time equality between men and women be clearly spelled out (made by the sole woman member of the drafting committee) was soundly defeated. From all this it would appear that the women of Thailand are sorely oppressed, and that a fertile field exists for feminists. In truth, this is yet another example of how Thai appear-

tary careers. This reflects the attitude that the military is a career not unlike that of the civil service, and is one of the few occupations in which a bright but poor young man can achieve advancement on merit. The military establishment is now such an integral part of Thai society that it is difficult to imagine life without it.

The Thai Woman: Gracefully balancing tradition and modernity

A Thai businesswoman, small, soft-spoken, gentle-mannered is the antithesis of the Western "career woman." According to an

ances can be misleading. Among the upper classes at least, women wield considerable power and would be amazed at the suggestion that they are downtrodden.

If you rent a house in Thailand, you will probably pay your monthly check to a woman, no matter whose name might be on the title deed to the property. If you move in business circles, especially in Bangkok, you will sooner or later have dealings with one of the famous "lady tycoons" who have been written about with wonder by several American magazines.

Women helm major companies and own several of the largest hotels in the capital.

There are women who head villages or occupy top positions in the civil service and women doctors, and the university population is divided almost equally between male and female students.

In Thailand, lower class women have less power but often control the family purse strings and moral upbringing of the children. Women can generally be found on construction sites, cleaning offices, running small businesses, and even driving buses. Although in democratic Thailand, all may be equal under law, there are lapses in its enforcement and interpretation which have contributed to the exploitation of lower class women in Thailand's sex industry.

her fellows because she is bright, pretty, funny, very articulate, and by her own admission, *jai ron* (hot headed) and not afraid to state an opinion. When she's in her dress clothes, she could pass for an office worker or a student.

"I like pedaling a *samlor*," she says with a bright smile. "I could have worked in a restaurant or a hotel but then I would not have any freedom. Here, I can work the hours I want. I can even take the day off when I need to."

A few moments later, another *samlor* rolls up. Off steps her husband, Mun, 25, who cheerily joins the conversation. Their happy-go-lucky attitude is infectious. It is only after

Noi, *samlor* driver

She's so petite that at first you think she is merely resting on the back seat of the *samlor* (trishaw) parked next to the market on Hua Hin's main street. As you approach, however, she climbs onto the driver's seat, and asks you your destination.

Noi, 22, is one of a handful of women *samlor* drivers in town. She stands out from

Left, soldiers taking part in a religious ceremony. **Above left**, prominent Thai ladies, elegantly attired; and **right**, Noi, one of the few *samlor* drivers in Hua Hin.

talking with them for a few moments that you realize that it masks very difficult lives. But they do not complain.

"I was born in a poor family in Surin and spent several years in Bangkok working around a relative's house," says Noi. "When I was 18, I went with a girlfriend to visit her home in Petchburi."

"One evening, I looked out the window, and there he was," she says with a shy smile and glowing eyes. "He was a construction worker, relaxing after work, bathed and powdered, and smoking a cigarette. We started talking..." she trails off, leaving one to guess the rest.

They decided to live in Mun's hometown of Hua Hin, in a filmsy shed of matting and a tin roof next to the railway tracks where most of the trains roar by between midnight and 6am. Their lives are simple; they cannot afford anything better.

They rent their *samlors* for 15 baht a day but often do not make enough money even to cover the rental costs.

"Last year, on some days, we used to make 600 baht between the two of us. Then somebody brought the motorcycle taxis to Hua Hin (the passenger rides on the pillion seat) and suddenly business dropped off. Sometimes we can make 100 baht a day but sometimes we don't have enought to eat," she says

matter-of-factly.

The couple has one daughter but they cannot afford to keep her. "She stays with my mother in Surin. She is three. We see her once every year for about two or three days when we can afford the train fare. We would like her to stay with us but who would take care of her while we are working?"

There is no bitterness as they talk. They are young and they hope for better times. They would like to buy their own *samlors* but a new one costs 20,000 baht and even a good used one costs 5,000 baht. Mun says that if they had the money, he would buy a second-hand motorcycle and build a small sidecar

that could carry three passengers and baggage. Noi quietly listens to his optimistic plans, a hint of resignation written on her unlined face.

The Chinese: Thailand's largest minority group excels in trade and commerce

An old Chinese storekeeper sits in shorts and singlet behind the counter of his goods shop in one of the long, narrow, two or three-storey rows of shop houses that can be found in every town in Thailand. On his desk is an abacus, on his wall, a calendar with Chinese characters. Across the street, his nephew runs a consultancy firm, his desk topped by a computer, a fax machine spewing out orders.

The uncle lives with his large family on the floor over the shop. Every day of the year (many now close on Sundays) he opens for business except for a short break at Chinese New Year, when the iron grates are drawn across the doors for two or three days and the family enjoys feasting, visiting ancestral graves, and the rare luxury of doing nothing. His nephew has opted for one of the housing estates on the outskirts of the city, living in a house indistinguishable from those in America, commuting to work down the Expressway in his BMW.

Like every country in Southeast Asia, Thailand has had Chinese merchants since the earliest days of commerce. When King Rama I selected Bangkok as his new capital, the site on which he wanted to build the Grand Palace was occupied by Chinese shops. He asked the owners to move a kilometer or so down the riverbank to Sampeng where they settled and formed what is today the Chinese center of the capital.

Throughout the 19th century and through the first half of the 20th, immigrants from China poured into the country. Only with the coming of the communist regime to mainland China did the flow slow to a trickle and finally stop altogether. As in other Asian countries these immigrants were denied ownership of land and participation in government so drifted naturally towards trade. They opened banks, pawnshops, export-import firms, and the innumerable little variety shops and restaurants found in even the smallest hamlet.

One thing, however, has long distinguished the Thai Chinese from their counterparts in most other countries in the region: they have been assimilated to a remarkable degree into the life of their adopted land. In part this has been due to deliberate government policy: all children, Chinese or otherwise, are required to learn the Thai language in primary school (Chinese language was not even taught at the university level until a few years ago). Moreover, the Chinese were encouraged, sometimes pressured, into taking Thai names when they wanted a passport, a government scholarship, or an official document.

Similarity of religions has eliminated some

The most outstanding result of this has been that the Thai Chinese have never really lived in an exclusive separate world as they do elsewhere. Even areas like Yaowaraj, where the atmosphere is as Chinese as Hong Kong, have never been ghettos, and the various Chinese associations are charitable rather than cultural in purpose.

There is no deep-rooted anti-Chinese bias in Thailand, nor have there been any of the serious racial conflicts that have marred the recent histories of neighboring countries. Only among the older generation will you find many people who think and speak of themselves specifically as "Chinese." The younger generation thinks of itself as Thai,

of the problems of integration faced by the Chinese in Malaysia and Indonesia.

As a result, Chinese and Thais have intermarried freely, so that today, especially in the cities, it is difficult to point to anyone and say with assurance that he or she is "pure" Thai. King Taksin who avenged Ayutthaya and established his capital at Thonburi, had a Chinese mother; and most of the prominent Thai families have a Chinese branch somewhere on their genealogical tree.

Left, a Chinese temple in Nakorn Pathom. **Above**, the Chinese in Thailand have been assimilated into the mainstream of Thai society.

speaks the language, voices loyalty to Thailand, and have only cursory interests in affairs in China.

Rural life: The backbone of the country

A "phu yai ban," or Thai village headman, middle-aged usually, or older (experience and stability are important qualities in a leader), must have a sharp perception of the nuances of village life. Far more important to the villagers than the government-appointed district officers, the headman is the backbone of Thai rural society. Selected by his fellow villagers in an open election, the "phu yai ban" plays a major role in village affairs, speaking for the village in negotiations with the outside world, settling disputes, organizing cooperative village undertakings, listening to complaints and responding to village needs.

Most Thai villages, even those lying a relatively short distance from large towns and cities, are remarkably insular; some have no electricity, and for many in the dry Northeast, the nearest fresh water may be an hour's walk away. Their concerns, like those of most insular people, are mainly inward and personal.

When university students from Bangkok village and told people about the doors, no one believed them.

The land and the crops it produces, the vagaries of weather; the local temple and the opportunities it offers for earning merit as well as the special pleasures of its fairs and ceremonies; the strange spirits that lie everywhere in wait for the unwary; the love affairs and small scandals that provide occasional diversion from everyday cares; illness and death, these are the immediate concerns of rural life, as they have been from time immemorial.

Given their choice, villagers would prefer to stay at home; the city holds no allure for them. But poverty and insufficient land drive

embarked on an ambitious "political education" plan in the countryside before the 1975 elections, some of them were surprised to discover that many villagers were totally uninterested in what was going on in Bangkok, and a number had no news of events in the capital or the country at large.

An elderly couple from a village in the South, taken on their first visit to the capital by their city-dwelling son, found only one thing that really impressed them in the noisy, confusing place: the electrically operated automatic doors of a department store. But even this turned out to be a somewhat droll discovery, for when they returned to their

them to seek their fortunes in the metropolis. When a young man leaves the village to try his luck in the city, his family views his departure with a mixture of hope and sadness. While they hope he will find a good job and send money home each month they are sad because they know that a young man who leaves his village rarely ever comes back except to visit, and when he does he has changed beyond all recognition. Yet, within every transplanted person's veins, the village flows, a theme that runs through hundreds of folk songs that express longing for home. Even if he is resident in Bangkok for 10 years, his heart is still in the village.

Hilltribes: Semi-nomadic peoples living in the misty hills of the North

Wearing an enormous turban, a costume of heavy, shiny black cotton, and a large quantity of silver jewelry that gleams dully in the sun, a Hmong (popularly called the "Meo") tribeswoman down from the hills for a look at Chiang Mai, is an exotic, even a bizarre, sight to the foreigner. But Thais pay her little attention; in the last decade hilltribesmen have become a common sight in the cities of the North and even on the streets of Bangkok where they sell their crafts.

Approximately 20 distinct tribes of cause their relative isolation has enabled them to retain, almost unchanged, customs and traditions that go back centuries. To the Thai government, they are a matter of concern because of their slash-and-burn form of agriculture, which tends to deplete the land and their reliance on illegal opium as their chief cash crop.

For a long time, the main contact between the hilltribes and the outside world was the missionaries, mostly American. These foreigners elected to work among them, learning their languages and often living as far as five days' walk from the nearest town. As the government became more aware of the problems, actual and potential, presented

semi-nomadic peoples live in the mountains along the Burmese and Laotian borders of the North. They range from large, relatively sophisticated groups like the Hmong to tiny groups like the elusive Phi Thong Luang ("Spirits of the Yellow Leaves"), whose very existence was in doubt until an expedition tracked them down some years ago.

Culturally, the tribes are of interest be-

Left, Yao tribeswomen and child, resplendent in their traditional finery. **Above**, Hmong tribeswomen, distinguished by their costume of heavy, shiny black cotton.

by the tribes, it began to take more definite steps to aid them, initiating a now sizable tribal development program. The king takes a personal interest in developing new crops like coffee, tea and fruit trees for the tribespeople to grow. The Border Patrol Police are establishing schools and the Princess Mother's Flying Doctors are bringing medical care. Moreover, the distinctive tribal handicrafts, first revealed by the missionaries and now sponsored by Queen Sirikit's SUPPORT Foundation, have found popularity not only in Bangkok but also abroad, providing the hilltribes with another source of income.

Literature: A long tradition, a short history

A popular novelist, a thin, rather intense woman in her early forties, the author of a half dozen successful romances, most of which have been adapted to the movies or television. All of her novels first appeared serially in a woman's magazine and all appealed primarily to a female audience. A typical plot concerns a well-born young girl who falls in love with a poor boy and is forbidden by her family to marry him. True love finally triumphs after many chapters and many obstacles, as the boy at last convinces her parents of his sterling character.

young Thais which deal with social themes, the general reading public prefers escapist, sentimental stories generally written by and for women.

Many of the works of the action genre are, surprisingly, written by policemen experienced in the shadier side of life and with time on their hands. Like Dickens, writers are compelled by paltry payments to produce the books in installments for popular magazines; only on completion are the chapters bound into books. In recent years, readers of serious literature have turned to Thai versions of modern Western novels which local translators turn out by the bushel basket.

What is known as classical Thai literature, which consists mainly of the *Ramakien* (the Thai version of the Sanskrit epic *Ramayana*), folk tales in verse, and court poetry, are ancient stories in modern rendition. Most of Thailand's classical literature was burned to ashes in Ayutthaya's destruction in 1767. Early kings of the Chakri dynasty gathered scholars and story tellers and patiently reconstructed what had been lost. Today, they and Thai translations of Western classics (*The Merchant of Venice* was translated by King Rama VI), are studied by university students.

While there are books popular among

The Movies: A kaleidoscope of Thai myth and legend

A Thai movie star, like movie stars every where, represents an ideal, a dream, of beauty. She has pale, flawless skin and an artfully made-up face; she speaks in a soft, almost childlike voice, often hardly more than a whisper. Her clothes are the latest fashion, and her jewels look expensive yet she manages, somehow, to suggest purity and the promise of sex at the same time. She can usually be seen smiling demurely from calendars and gigantic advertising billboards. At any given time she is making several movies simultaneously, playing more or less the same role in all of them.

Few foreign visitors go to see a Thai movie during their stay. This is understandable in view of the language barrier, but it is also unfortunate, for popular arts like the movies reveal much about the contemporary culture and tastes of a country. There are several major movie studios in Thailand, all of them in Bangkok, and they produce several hundred films a year. Although they have a large audience in the capital their greatest popularity is in the provinces, where the average price of a ticket is ten baht and movies together with village fairs are still the major

and Thais, indifferent to orientation, sat on the ground on either side of the screen to view them.

Today, most Thai movies are made in 35mm with sound tracks. Producers have adopted sophisticated moviemaking techniques of the West and a few directors have even experimented with departures from the tried-and-true story formulas of the past. But only a few, for the Thai-film audience knows what it wants.

To begin with, it wants familiar faces, the same stars over and over again, playing predictable roles. Leading superstars make twenty to thirty movies a year, usually featuring the same pairings. Audiences also

entertainment despite the advent of television and videos.

Until the 1970s, most Thai movies were silent 16mm films and the sound was provided by narrators–often a *single* narrator–who sat near the projector, a sound system amplifying his voice and the snatches of records he played as musical interludes. Movies were often presented by patented medicine salesmen who used them to lure prospective customers. Huge, translucent screens were erected in temple courtyards

want the same classic romance stories, with only slight variations. The Cinderella theme is highly popular; poor girl (or boy) meets bright boy (or girl), encounters many difficulties along the way, finally gets him (or her) at the end when all the misunderstandings are cleared away.

Another popular story is the poor boy from the country who comes to the wicked city, is subjected to all sorts of temptations (usually sexual), and finally settles for the virtuous girl who has loved and stood by him all along. A city variation of this involves students who pull pranks and fall in love and generally act silly.

<u>Left</u>, young performers of Likay, a popular dance form. <u>Above</u>, a 1960s Thai movie poster.

Ghost stories, the gorier the better, are also favorites. No matter how sad the theme, Thai audiences also insist on comic relief, and there are several slapstick comedians who are as much in demand as the superstars; a good deal of singing and dancing is also considered a powerful asset. Finally, they want their money's worth in length; two and a half hours is common for a Thai film, and many go for three or more.

Whether they go to Thai or Western films, Thais have similar tastes in foreign movies; one that is too "talky" or slow moving will have a short run, while comedies, musicals and action films attract large crowds. The two most popular western movies ever shown

in Thailand have been *The Sound of Music* and *McKenna's Gold*.

Traditional Dance:
The classical epitome

A group of Thai classical dance students solemnly practice the complicated movements essential to this ancient form of theater. Most of them are girls, for traditionally the masked "khon" dances were performed only by women in the inner court of the Royal Palace where no men were allowed. Today, young men also take part, especially in such athletic roles as Ha-

numan, the white monkey god. The students in the school are quite young, for after a certain age it is difficult to train the body to contort into some of the positions by which a dancer is judged; the fingers, for example, must be able to bend gracefully backward almost to the wrist.

In a *khon* performance, masks are worn for all roles except the three leads where heavy make-up and elaborate jeweled costumes and head-dress subordinate the personality of the dancer. To purists, it is a cardinal sin to smile or otherwise indicate the human being behind the role. Every gesture is highly stylized and immediately recognizable to a connoisseur. A normal performance can last for as long as eight hours; a full presentation of the *Ramakien* requires 720 hours.

The *khon* has never been an art form for the masses. Born in the royal palaces, and for many centuries only performed there, the *khon* was created for the pleasure of the king and his retinue. It lives today largely through the efforts of the Fine Arts Department which maintains a school to train dancers and sponsors occasional performances at Bangkok's National Theater. The excerpts presented at certain tourist restaurants are, like the Thai food served, pale imitations of the originals, but worth seeing for the costumes alone.

Two dance forms popular with the general Thai public are *lakhon*, which uses no masks and in which the movements are somewhat less stylized; and the *likay*, which might be described as a burlesque form of the classical dance, relying heavily on pitfalls and bawdy lyrics. A prominent feature of almost every provincial Thai fair, *likay* occupies a place roughly analogous to popular folk singing in the West.

In the early hours of the evening, low comedy fills the stage, but once the children have been put safely to bed, sex comes to the fore in a flurry of puns and double entendres which can keep the show going and the audiences wide awake and laughing until the wee hours of the morning.

Left, backstage in the TV studios. Right, the personality of the masked Khon dancer is subordinated by his elaborate jeweled costume and head-dress.

Eating is a favorite pastime of many Thais. Not surprising when you consider the variety, colors and flavors of Thai cuisine. Good food is found in fascinating places, from seafood markets to floating restaurants to hawker stalls. Wherever you travel in Thailand, you are bound to be tempted by overpowering aromas and attractive food presentations. Each region offers its own distinct taste treats and traditional dishes.

Northern cuisine is somewhat heavier and oilier than that of the Central Plains, but no

pork curry, cucumbers in brine and broth with chunks of gourd. Such dinners are normally part of a package that includes a performance of northern dancing and hilltribe singing and can be found at a number of restaurants in Chiang Mai.

These are other important dishes of northern cuisine worth sampling:

Sai Oua. A chewy, oily, spicy pork sausage also called *naam* and associated with the North. It is roasted over a fire fueled by coconut husks which impart an aroma to the

less delicious. It tends to make extensive use of pork and has been spiced by the dishes of neighboring Burma and Laos. Like Northeastern meals, it is eaten with *khao niew* or glutinous (sticky) rice. One kneads a bit of rice into a ball and dips it in the various sauces and curries.

The best way to experience the variety of Northern food is to have a Kantoke Dinner. A half dozen small dishes are served in a single setting, allowing one to sample the range of northern cuisine. Included in a typical dinner is sticky rice, crispy pork rind, chicken curry, boiled cabbage, plain thin egg noodles, minced pork in a tomato-based curry,

meat. While it is generally prepared hygienically, it is best to buy it only at better restaurants. Beware the fiery *prik khii nuu* (rat dropping) chilies buried inside, lurking to present an unpleasant surprise to the unwary.

Khao Soy. Originally from Burma, this tasty egg noodle dish is filled with chunks of beef or chicken and is lightly curried in a gravy of coconut cream and sprinkled with crispy noodles and crispy garlic, and accented with half a boiled egg.

Nam Prik Ong. Minced pork, chilies,

Thai food is a feast for the palate and for the eyes.

tomatoes, garlic and shrimp paste are blended and cooled. It is served with crisp cucumber slices, parboiled cabbage leaves and pork rind.

Larb. A minced pork, chicken, beef and even fish dish normally associated with Northeastern cuisine and usually eaten raw; *larb* in the North is thoroughly cooked. It is served with long beans, mint leaves and other condiments.

Gaeng Hang Lay. Another Burmese dish, this is one of the spiciest of northern dishes and should be approached with caution by those with tender palates. Pork and tamarind flesh give this curry a sweet and sour flavor. The sauce is especially suited to dipping with a ball of sticky rice.

Mieng. This is not so much a dish as a snack; fermented tea leaves. Place a wad in your cheeks and chew away.

Northeast cuisine: The Northeast has never been a land of plenty and its diet reflects it. Grubs, insects, frogs, land crabs and other delicacies is not the cuisine of gourmets but of necessity. It is flavored by the food of its close cousin to the east, Laos, and offers some of the fieriest dishes known to humankind. Yet, even in toned down form, it is still delicious.

Like Northern food, it is eaten with steamed sticky rice, an excellent soporific. Residents of I-sarn (the Northeast) claim that if you eat sticky rice for lunch you will spend the afternoon napping, so heavy will it weigh on your stomach. If so, it is a pleasantly tasty weight. Knead the rice into small balls with your fingertips and dip it in one of the delicious sauces, the honeyed sauce with the flecks of chili being the tastiest.

These are the mainstays of I-sarn cuisine:

Kai Yang. Roast chicken, basted with herbs and turned over an open fire to release its juices. In Bangkok, the tastiest Gai Yang (and I-sarn food in general) is found at a string of shops behind the Thai Boxing Stadium on Rajdamnern Nok Road beside the Tourism Authority of Thailand office.

Nua Yang. Strips of beef are sun-dried much like jerky. Better restaurants serve *Nua Nam Tok Salika* referring to an area where tasty beef is found.

Larb. Like that found in the North, *larb* can be made from beef, chicken, pork or fish. In its village form, it is eaten raw but that found in restaurants is minced and lightly fried with bits of mint leaf added.

Som-dtam. One's success at becoming an adopted child of I-sarn will depend on how much of this fiery salad one can down. The base is raw papaya sliced into noodle-sized strips. To it is added lime juice, chilies, dried shrimps, and, if available, tiny salted land crabs. The whole is pounded in a pestle and served as is. It leaves even the Thais with their hardened palates, fanning their mouths, wheezing and panting.

Southern cuisine: This is strongly influenced by Muslim dietary proscriptions and flavored by Malay cooking. It is generally eaten with plain rice and can be very spicy. Whatever flavor a dish has, it will be uncompromisingly distinctive; no bland food here.

Khao Yam. A rice dish heavily flavored with *kapi*, a paste made of fermented shrimp that sounds a lot worse than it tastes. Various condiments are offered to let you alter the flavor as you wish.

Phat Phet Sataw. Sataw *looks* like a lima bean but bite into it and discover a bitter difference. Cooking removes much of the bitterness but it still imparts a very strong flavor to the dish it inhabits. An acquired taste, converts soon become addicts.

Khao Mok Gai. A Muslim dish, it features roasted chicken on a bed of saffron rice, mixed with ginger which has been fried lightly to make it crisp.

Khanom Chin. This is a breakfast dish, generally sold out by 9am. Look for it in markets. Found throughout Thailand, the South claims to be its birthplace. Tiny bits of minced beef are stewed in a red sauce and served atop rice noodles.

Nam Prik Kung Siap. Dried prawn on a stick. The concoction is grilled and served with chilies, *kapi* and lime. It is one of the most memorable dishes in southern cuisine.

Gaeng Dtai Plaa. This is a bachelor's dish, created by fishermen who wanted a meal that would last them a long time. Fish kidneys, chilies and vegetables are blended in a curry sauce and stewed for up to seven days. Fans claim that curries that have run the full week are the most delicious. It is eaten over rice noodles.

Gaeng Luang. A curry in a broth similar to the lemony *Gaeng Som* served in other parts of Thailand. Fish bits are stirred into the broth.

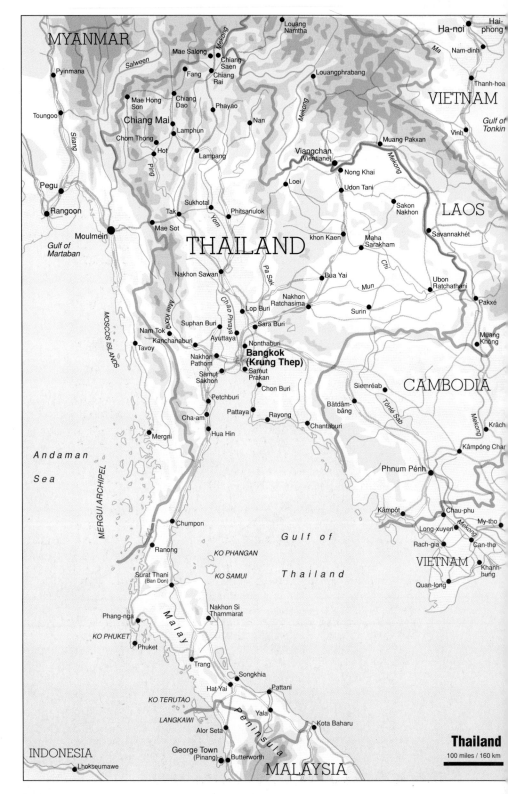

MYANMAR

Pyinmana

Toungoo

Salween

Mae Salong

Chiang Saen

Fang Chiang Rai

Louang Namtha

Louangphrabang

Ha-noi

Hai-phong

Nam-dinh

Thanh-hoa

VIETNAM

Gulf of Tonkin

Vinh

Mae Hong Son

Chiang Dao

Phayao

Nan

Chiang Mai

Lamphun

Chom Thong

Hot

Lampang

Pegu

Rangoon

Moulmein

Gulf of Martaban

Sukhotai

Tak

Mae Sot

Nakhon Sawan

THAILAND

Phitsanulok

khon Kaen

Maha Sarakham

Sakon Nakhon

Savannakhét

LAOS

Viangchan (Vientiane)

Nong Khai

Loei

Udon Tani

Muang Pakxan

Mekong

Mekong

Salween

Ping

Yom

Chi

Mun

Chao Phraya

Pa Sak

Nakhon Ratchasima

Bua Yai

Ubon Ratchathani

Pakxé

Muang Khong

Lop Buri

Suphan Buri

Sara Buri

Surin

Nam Tok

Kanchanaburi

Ayuttaya

Nonthaburi

Bangkok (Krung Thep)

Samut Prakan

Chon Buri

Siemréab

CAMBODIA

Tavoy

Nakhon Pathom

Samut Sakhon

Petchburi

Bàtdàm-bâng

Mae Klong

Cha-am

Pattaya

Rayong

Chantaburi

Tonlé Sàp

Kràch

Kâmpóng Char

Mergni

Hua Hin

Andaman Sea

MOSCOS ISLANDS

MERGUI ARCHIPEL

Phnum Pénh

Chumpon

Gulf of Thailand

Kâmpôt

Chau-phu

My-tho

Ranong

KO PHANGAN

KO SAMUI

Long-xuyen

Rach-gia

Can-tho

Surat Thani (Ban Don)

Phang-nga

Nakhon Si Thammarat

Malay

VIETNAM

Quan-long

Khanh-hung

KO PHUKET

Phuket

Trang

Songkhia

Hat Yai

Pattani

KO TERUTAO

LANGKAWI

Yala

Kota Baharu

Alor Seta

Peninsula

INDONESIA

George Town (Pinang)

Butterworth

MALAYSIA

Lhokseumawe

Mekong

Thailand

100 miles / 160 km

THE LAND OF SMILES

Imagine a land of infinite variety with high, tree-carpeted mountains, jungles rich with wildlife, orchids and exotic plants: shining rivers tumbling to the plains on their way to a warm-water gulf rimmed by miles of golden sands. This is what the gods have given Thailand.

Picture orange temple roofs, golden spires glowing softly in the dusk light, silver canals crisscrossing the lowlands through a patchwork of fertile rice paddies;fragile arts of breathtaking beauty. This is what Thais have created from their exquisite land. Together god-made and man-made Thailand has for eons served as a magnet of endless appeal for travelers, many of whom journeyed for a look and stayed a lifetime.

Land of the Free. Land of Smiles. The former is a literal translation of the name "Thailand": the latter describes the cheerful demeanor of its people. Thais are proud of their ancestors rejection of foreign domination making their country the only one in Southeast Asia to escape the yoke of colonialism. This independent spirit is evident in everything they do. Beneath their graciousness is a strong sense of self, a humanity without subservience. It is this pride in themselves which underlies their sense of nationalism and their ability to smile at the vicissitudes of life.

But then Thais have much to smile about: A sunny culture filled with color and brilliance, sparkling waterways that offer cooling comfort from the heat of the sun, food that is a match for any other cuisine in Asia, handsome men and beautiful women, a healthy economy, and a tolerance of religions, politicians, and especially foreigners. All these contribute to the Thais natural warmth, hospitality and genuine concern for the traveler.

Boasting a population of 55 million and a land area of 198,460sq miles (514,000sq km). Thailand is very nearly the size and shape of Central America. Its climate is tropical with three seasons: hot (March–June), monsoon (July–November) and cool (December–February). Its capital, Bangkok (population, 8 million) lies on the same latitude as Madras, Khartoum, Guatemala City, Guam and Manila.

The country is commonly divided into four regions; the Central Plains which includes Bangkok, the North, the Northeast and the South. Each region has its own culture and appeal and must be explored thoroughly to gain a proper appreciation of Thailand's vast richness. Bangkok is but one small patch in the cultural quilt. When a Thai says "I'm heading up-country tomorrow," he could mean anywhere outside Bangkok's city limits; north, east, south or west. This is where the real Thailand begins. Up-country.

Preceding pages, a bird's eye view of Bangkok.

A CITY OF MANY FACES

To each person who encounters it, Bangkok is a different city. Some are repelled by its din and flee to the countryside, others ignore the main street and plunge into the warren of sidestreets where the mystique of the Orient still thrives. Some see only the grandeur of its monuments while others bathe in the balm of its cool canals and lose themselves amid its tropical beauty. Some prefer luxury hotels far removed from the streets, others opt for budget guesthouses in the old part of town, accommodation that allows them to mix freely with ordinary Thais.

Some cities are easy to learn. After only a few days you have a clear sense of their design, their personality, and you do not hesitate to set out boldly on explorations. Others are less accessible: they sprawl, they are confusing, without logic, and seem to have not one but a dozen, often contradictory, personalities. Nearly every visitor without hesitation would put Bangkok in the second category.

At first glance, this metropolis of between six and eight million people (nobody can agree on the exact number) appears to be a bewildering conglomeration of new and old, East and West, serenity and chaos, the exotic and the commonplace, all thrown together haphazardly into a gigantic urban stew.

You can stand at one moment in a hushed temple courtyard, lulled by the rhythmic chanting of priests and the silvery tinkle of bells, and at the next, risk life and limb crossing a street down which hurtles some of the most lethal traffic in Asia. You can start out with the most up-to-date city map and find yourself on streets that do not exist (at least on the map), searching for bus routes which have been altered or abolished, discovering that a two-way street is now a one-way street. If you are searching for a graphic example of this complexity, look no farther than some of the modern office buildings and condominiums which combine half a dozen seemingly disparate architectural styles into a single whole.

If Bangkok is not an orderly city it is because it never has been; city planning has been haphazard at best. It began as a city of canals and elephant paths and, instead of redesigning it for 20th-century vehicular traffic, administrators simply paved the former in concrete and carried on doing business. The first macadamized road was not built until 1863 and other roads followed slowly. It was as if the Thais had a portent of the Pandora's Box they were opening and opted for the more leisurely pace canal travel afforded.

Sections of the city developed almost by whim and a desire to escape from the hubbub of the city center. Chinatown was a fairly cohesive unit next to the thatched and floating Thai houses of the district to the north. King Chulalongkorn built a country estate at the end of Rajdamnern Road and other royals built their country homes nearby. Foreigners built their legations and commercial businesses

Preceding pages, bumper to bumper traffic is a common sight in Bangkok. **Left**, larger than life size movie poster in Bangkok.

along the new New Road in the vicinity of the Post Office but sited their homes at the end of New Road in an area called Bangkolem. Here, at the end of New Road, at Thanon Tok (literally, "the road falls" into the Chao Phya River), the fresh river breezes blew and the only disturbance was ships moving up and down the river.

The biggest, most disorderly building boom started in the late 1950s, and a large part of what strikes the eye most forcibly today has appeared since then: the lofty office buildings, the airconditioned supermarkets and shopping centers, nearly all the broad streets, movie theaters and international hotels, the endless blocks of row shops following what one critic called the "egg-crate principle of design." Before the boom the now fashionable residential streets on either side of Sukhumvit Road and Phaholyothin Road, were primiarily rice paddies.

Until 1955, you could go by boat along Rama IV Road from where the Dusit Thani Hotel now stands to the river. Sathorn, Silom (Windmill Road), Siphya, Wittayu, Rajdamri and others now in the city center were built alongside and, as traffic increased, atop canals. Thais moved north and east in search of land on which to build homes. The Erawan Hotel was regarded as rather inconveniently located on the city's outskirts; today, it is *west* of the geographical center of the capital.

After the boom, it seemed to some, a whole new Bangkok had emerged; and yet there were large areas around the old Grand Palace, in the Chinese district, and across the river in Thonburi (now included in the Greater Bangkok Metropolitan Area) that were hardly touched by the building fever, and still looked almost exactly as they did 50 years ago. Yet change is coming even to these areas. New construction in Chinatown is replacing the squat, squashed buildings with skyscrapers as the area becomes yet another layer of many stratas future archaeologists will one day study.

Today, about one out of every eight Thais live in Bangkok; the second largest city (Chiang Mai or Khon Kaen, depending on who you are talking to) is 1/40th its size. About 80 percent of all the automobiles in the country are registered there. At least 55 percent of Bangkok's population is of Chinese descent. The population has grown eight-fold since World War II, augmented by the migration of day laborers who do the actual work of building and maintaining the city. About 70 percent of the country's university students study there, and the monarchy has reigned there for over two centuries.

To many lovers of Bangkok, it is precisely its vital, changing, clashing, unpredictable nature that gives the city its special flavor. Quite apart from its celebrated tourist attractions, you are constantly being confronted, and sometimes amused, by unexpected sights: a narrow *klong* meandering tranquilly in the shadow of a modern 400-room hotel; a leafy tropical garden with full-sized trees and an elegant little Chinese pagoda on the roof of an otherwise commonplace row shop.

Elsewhere, a slightly derelict but still noble Victorian palace,

A wooden soldier keeps steadfast guard at the doors of Wat Rajabophit in Bangkok.

with turrets and gingerbread hides behind a cinema; a massage parlor whimsically called the Darling is down the street from a restaurant called Cabbages and Condoms; an old woman calmly strings ropes of jasmine blossoms on a busy sidewalk; a mammoth standing Buddha, three storeys high, is inadvertently glimpsed between two glass-and-cement office blocks; a ring-shaped apartment house is engulfed by glass-box office buildings.

A little Greek temple sits in the grounds of a hospital once the palace of a crown prince; a short-time hotel is called the Bungalow Home Fun; a group of street urchins move like ballet dancers as they kick a rattan ball from one to another with the side of their feet; in a vast movie poster a smiling woman's entrails spill down the side of a building; thousands of migratory swallows roost unperturbed over one of the noisiest streets in the city; sunlit Thai classical dancers entertain on a velvet green lawn at a tea party. All in Bangkok.

As a clue to getting your bearings in the sprawl of present-day Bangkok, think of it as being roughly (very roughly) divided as follows:

1. *Early Royal Bangkok* (1782–present): The area between the river and Klong Lawd and including the Grand Palace, Wat Phra Kaew, Wat Po, Sanam Luang, Wat Rajabophit. The second stage of development extended the boundaries to the city wall at Klong Ong Ang and included Wat Suthat and the Giant Swing.

2. *Later Royal Bangkok* (1900 onwards): Chitralada Palace (the residence of the present king), the Marble Temple, Parliament, Dusit Zoo.

3. *Military Bangkok*: Actually a part of No. 2, the military having taken over many of the palaces and government offices built during the latter part of Rama V's reign in the Dusit area.

4. *Chinese Bangkok*: Yaowaraj Road and surrounding districts.

5. *Old Tourist Bangkok*: New Road, the Oriental Hotel, lower Suriwong and Silom roads.

6. *New Tourist Bangkok*: Upper Silom and Suriwong roads; the river between Siphya and Sathorn roads; the Rajprasong area around the Erawan Shrine; lower Sukhumvit Road.

7. *Old Residential Bangkok*: The streets leading off both sides of Phaholyothin Road and Sukhumvit Road east to Prakanong and beyond.

8. *New Residential Bangkok*: Vast middle- and upper-income housing estates beyond New Petchburi Road, on the superhighway leading north from the city and west of Thonburi.

9. *Principal Thai Markets*: Pratunam, Bangrak, Thevet, Klong Toey, to mention some of the largest.

The Chao Phya glides its sinuous way through the city.

Hotels ①–㉖

1 Century	40 Manohra
2 Continental	41 Narai
3 Federal	42 Royal River
4 Florida	43 Silom Plaza
5 Fortuna	44 Windsor
6 Honey	45 Asia
7 Malaysia	46 Dusit Thani
8 Miami	47 Hilton International
9 Miramar	48 Central Plaza
10 Morakot	49 Imperial
11 New Fuji	50 Indra
12 Park	51 The Menam
13 Prince	52 Meridien President
14 Rajsubhamit	53 Montien
15 Reno	54 Rama Gardens
16 Rex	55 Regal Landmark
17 Rose	56 Royal Orchid Sheraton
18 Royal	57 Siam Inter-Continental
19 Suriwongse	58 Tawana Ramada
20 Swan	59 Oriental
21 Thai	60 Regent
22 Viengtai	61 Shangri-la
23 Bangkok Center	
24 First	
25 Grace	
26 Majestic	
27 Manhattan	
28 New Nana	
29 Peninsula	
30 Rajan	
31 Siam	
32 Trocadero	
33 Victory	
34 Airport	
35 Ambassador	
36 Bangkok Palace	
37 Erawan	
38 Impala	
39 Mandarin	

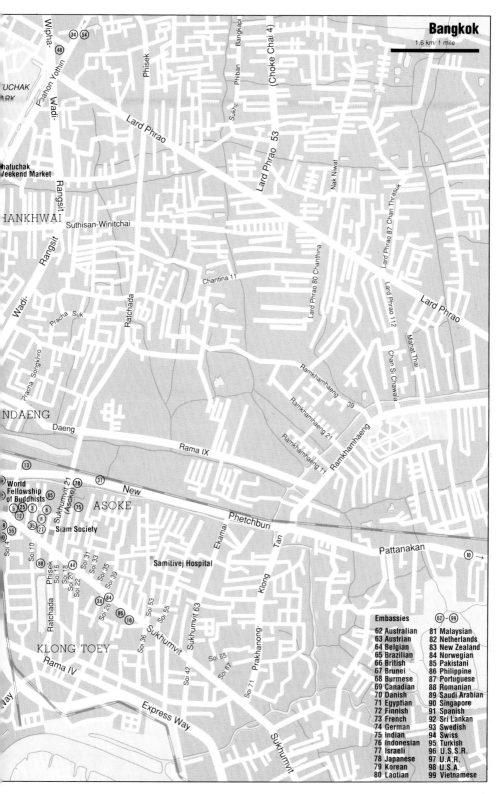

Bangkok

1.6 km/ 1 mile

Wipha-
Phahon Yothin
Wadi-
Phisek
Bangkapi
Phiban
Sukhe
(Choke Chai 4)
Lard Phrao
Lard Phrao 53
Nak Niwat
Lard Phrao 87 Chan Thrasuk
Lard Phrao 80 Chanthina
Lard Phrao 112
Lard Phrao
Chan Si Chawala
Mahat Thai
Chantina 11
Ratchada
Pracha Suk
Pracha Songkhro
Ramkhamhaeng
Ramkhamhaeng 39
Ramkhamhaeng 21
Ramkhamhaeng
Ramkhamhaeng 11
Daeng
Rama IX
New
Phetchburi
Pattanakan
Sukhumvit 21 (Asoke)
ASOKE
Siam Society
Ekamai
Tan
Klong
Samitivej Hospital
Soi 31
Soi 33
Soi 35
Soi 39
Soi 53
Soi 55
Sukhumvit 63
Soi 65
Soi 67
Prakhanong-
Phisek
Soi 16
Soi 18
Soi 22
Soi 20
Soi 10
Soi 26
Sukhumvit
Soi 36
Soi 42
Soi 71
Sukhumvit
KLONG TOEY
Ratchada
Rama IV
Express Way
Way

UCHAK
ARK
hatuchak
Weekend Market
Rangsit
HANKHWAI
Suthisan-Winitchai
Rangsit
Wadi-
NDAENG
World
Fellowship
of Buddhists

34 54
48
13

Embassies

	62 – 99
62 Australian	81 Malaysian
63 Austrian	82 Netherlands
64 Belgian	83 New Zealand
65 Brazilian	84 Norwegian
66 British	85 Pakistani
67 Brunei	86 Philippine
68 Burmese	87 Portuguese
69 Canadian	88 Romanian
70 Danish	89 Saudi Arabian
71 Egyptian	90 Singapore
72 Finnish	91 Spanish
73 French	92 Sri Lankan
74 German	93 Swedish
75 Indian	94 Swiss
76 Indonesian	95 Turkish
77 Israeli	96 U.S.S.R.
78 Japanese	97 U.A.R.
79 Korean	98 U.S.A.
80 Laotian	99 Vietnamese

93

THE INNER CITY

Search for the Chao Phya River on the left-hand side of any map of Bangkok. To its right is Klong (Canal) Lawd, leaving the river on the north and re-entering it on the south. Together, river and canal define a mango or a conch shell, a man-made island called Rattanakosin on which Bangkok was born.

At its heart is the Grand Palace, Wat Phra Kaew (Temple of the Emerald Buddha), the broad expanse of grass called Sanam Luang (Phramane Ground) and most of the principal royal and religious buildings of the city. It is here that an exploration of Bangkok should begin. Approach this island from the Democracy Monument on Rajdamnern Avenue (King Rama V's version of the Champs Elysees). The tree-rimmed lawn of Sanam Luang will appear ahead; if it is the hot season, it will be covered with kite fliers speckling the sky overhead with dots of bright color. At its far end, flashing in the sunlight is Wat Phra Kaew, a sight so majestic that it will stir even the most jaded traveler.

A good place to start your tour of the inner city is at the official center of Bangkok, for contrary to what many people think of the sprawling metropolis, it does have one: a shrine next door to the Ministry of Defense which bristles with cannons. In this shrine stands **Lak Muang**, a gilded pillar placed there by Rama I at the beginning of his reign and a second pillar placed there at a later date. Similar to the Shiva lingams which represent potency, the Lak Muang is regarded as the foundation stone of the capital, the point from which the power of the city emanates. Distances within Bangkok are measured from this stone.

Sheltered by a graceful, recently-renovated building, Lak Muang and its attendant spirits are believed to have the power to grant wishes, revealing a winning lottery ticket number, granting fertility to a childless couple or a passing examination score to a student. Floral offerings pile high around the pillar, and the air is laden with the fragrance of incense. Devotees bow reverently before the pillar before pressing gold leaf to the millions of other squares of gold that layer the monument.

In an adjoining *sala*, a performance of Thai *lakhon* classical dance and music is usually underway. The troupe is hired by supplicants whose wishes have been granted; for spectators, the performance is free. The best times to visit the shrine are in the late afternoons, on holidays, and especially on the day before the drawing of the lottery.

The grounds of the **Grand Palace**, open to visitors from 9am to 6pm daily (dress properly – no shorts, no sleeveless dresses – or be turned away), occupy part of a larger compound which also includes the royal chapel, the Temple of the Emerald Buddha. Here too is the Royal Collection of Weapons, the Coin Pavilion and a small museum containing artifacts from the Grand Palace. A 100-baht ticket grants admission to the Grand Palace, the Temple of the Emerald Buddha and the Vimarn Mek Palace near the Dusit Zoo.

The palace compound embodies Thailand's characteristic blend of temporal and spiritual elements. Surrounded by high, crenellated walls and entered by the huge Phiman Jayasri double gate, the Grand Palace was begun by King Rama I in 1782. Almost every king since then has added to it, so that today the complex is a melange of architectural styles ranging from Thai to Italian.

After the palace murder of King Ananda in 1946, his brother, the present King Bhumibol, moved to the more modern and comfortable Chitralada Palace. Today, the Grand Palace is used only for state banquets, presentation of ambassadorial credentials, and other royal ceremonies.

The grandest of the buildings was the last to be built. The triple-spired royal residence that commands the courtyard is called the **Chakri Maha Prasad**. This two-story hall set on an elevated base, of which visitors are allowed to see only the reception rooms, was con-

Preceding pages, the Phramane Ground royal cremation ground durin the funeral o Queen Rambhai Bharni in 1985. **Below** the majestic Chakri Throne Hall.

96

structed during King Rama V's reign (1868–1910) to commemorate the hundredth anniversary of the Chakri dynasty in 1882. It is an impressive mixture of Thai and Western architecture. The lower part of the building was designed by a British architect; the very Thai spires were added at the last moment after protests by purists that it was improper that a hallowed Thai site be dominated by a European building.

The top floor, under the tall central spire, contains golden urns with ashes of the Chakri kings. The large reception rooms are decorated with pictures of past kings, busts of foreign royalty (most of whom Rama V met on his trips abroad), and a quantity of objets d'art, most of them European. The central hall is the magnificent Chakri Throne Room, where the king receives foreign ambassadors on a niello throne under a nine-tiered white umbrella made originally for King Chulalongkorn.

The building to the west of the Chakri Maha Prasad is the **Dusit Maha Prasad**, built by Rama I in 1789 to replace an earlier wooden structure. A splendid example of classical Thai architecture, its four-tiered roof supports an elegant nine-tiered spire. The balcony on the north wing contains a throne once used by the king for outdoor receptions; the last occasion was when Rama VI received the oath of loyalty from his court after his coronation in 1911. Today, deceased kings and queens lie in state here before their bodies are cremated on Sanam Luang.

Just in front of the Dusit Maha Prasad is Thailand's most exquisite pavilion, the **Arporn Phimok Prasad**, or "Disrobing Pavilion". It was built to the height of the king's palanquin so he could alight from his elephant and don his ceremonial hat and gown before proceeding to the audience hall. It was reproduced by Rama V at Bang Pa-in, his summer palace just south of Ayutthaya; a replica was exhibited at the 1958 World Fair in Brussels.

To the left of the Chakri Maha Prasad, a door leads to the **Forbidden Quarters**, an area where the king's many wives used to live. The king himself was the only male above the age of 12 allowed to enter the door which led to the harem's lovely garden of cool fountains, pavilions and carefully pruned trees; it was guarded by armed women. Even today this inner section is closed to visitors, except when the king throws a garden birthday party for diplomats and government officials. North of the women's quarters lies **Borompiman Hall**, built in a Western style by King Chulalongkorn as a residence for the then crown prince who later became Rama VI. It was in this building that the young King Ananda was killed.

The **Amarin Vinichai Hall**, just east of the doorway leading to the former harem, is another of the palace's few remaining original buildings. Built by Rama I, the three-room building originally served as a royal residence, the bedroom lying just beyond the main audience hall. Today, the audience hall is used for coronations and special ceremonies such as that held when the king presents medals to government officials. During these ceremonies, the boat-

e throne at e Amarin rone Hall which are splayed urns ntaining hes of akri kings.

shaped throne is at first concealed by two curtains, called *Phra Visud* in Thai. The king takes his seat unseen by those in the hall. A fanfare is then sounded on conchshell trumpets, the curtains part dramatically, and the king appears resplendent in royal regalia.

Wat Phra Kaew, **Temple of the Emerald Buddha**, adjoins the Grand Palace and serves as the Royal Chapel where the king performs his various religious duties. Unlike the rest of the kingdom's 28,000 *wats*, no monks live here. Wat Phra Kaew ranks among the world's great sights: a dazzling, dizzying collection of gilded spires and sparkling pavilions and towering mythological gods both awesome and delightful. It is what most foreigners expect to see when they visit Thailand, and it is the single most powerful image they take away when they leave.

For a full appreciation, Wat Phra Kaew deserves at least two visits. The first should be on a weekday when the compound is relatively uncrowded and you can wander about at leisure inspecting its treasures. The second visit should be on a public holiday for only then can you witness the vital role of the temple and its celebrated image. Then, ardent worshippers fill the sanctuary, prostrating themselves on the marble floor before the golden altar. The air is alive with the supplicants' murmured prayers, yet heavy with the scent of floral offerings and joss sticks. Bathed in an eerie green light, high on its pedestal, the small image looks serenely down on the congregation. Only then can you sense the power the Emerald Buddha has exercised over the Thai people for centuries.

Wat Phra Kaew was the first permanent structure to be built in Bangkok. Begun by King Rama I in 1782 in imitation of the Royal Temple of the Grand Palace in Ayutthaya it was created to house the most celebrated image in the kingdom. No one knows the precise origin of the 75-cm-high jadeite image, the most sacred in the country.

Today, the Emerald Buddha sits atop an 11-m-tall gilded altar, protected by a

An illuminated view of Wat Phra Kaew, the temple of the Emerald Buddha.

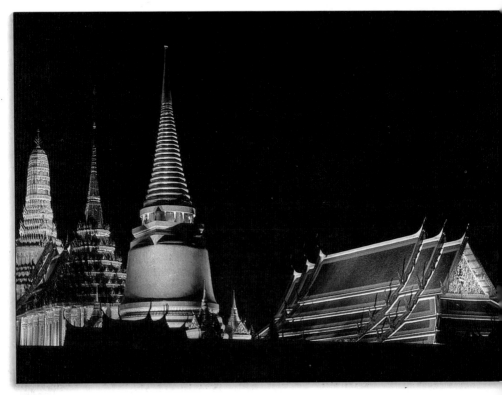

nine-tiered umbrella. Crystal balls on either side represent the sun and the moon. Three times a year, at the beginning of each new season, the king changes the Emerald Buddha's robes, cladding it in a golden, diamond-studded tunic for the hot season; a gilded robe flecked with blue for the rainy season; and a robe of enamel-coated solid gold for the cool season.

A spectacular collection of structures crowds the compound of Wat Phra Kaew: buildings, pavilions, *chedis* (spires), *prangs* (rounded spires), and mythological gods and goddesses, most of which are gilded or encrusted with porcelain or glass.

The walls of the cloister that surround the temple courtyard are painted with murals telling the *Ramakien* story, the Thai version of the Indian *Ramayana* epic. The murals were originally painted during the reign of Rama III (1824–1850), but have been restored several times. The story begins on the left as you walk around the cloister.

Epic battles, processions, consulta-
tions and other elements from the *Ramakien* story crowd the murals. Just beyond each principal scene are depictions of everyday life, including gambling, love and opium smoking. Marble slabs set in pillars in front of the paintings are inscribed with poems relating each episode of the story.

On a broad, raised marble terrace, higher than the rest of the compound are (from east to west) the **Royal Pantheon**, the library (Mondop), and a golden stupa erected by Rama IV. The Royal Pantheon contains life-sized statues of the Chakri kings and is open to the public only on Chakri Day, April 6. In front of it stand marvelous gilded statues of mythological creatures, including the charming half-bird, half-male (or female) *kinaree* and *kinnara*.

Behind the Pantheon is the library, surrounded by statues of sacred white elephants, symbols of royal power, that were found roaming in the kingdom during the reigns of the first five Chakri kings. Nearby is a large, detailed model of the famous Khmer temple of Angkor

left, ornate, glitterring entrance of Wat Phra Kaew; right, painstakingly crafted interior frames the Emerald Buddha.

Wat. The model was built by Rama IV to show his people what the temple looked like during the 16th century when Thailand ruled it.

Wat Po is the popular name for Wat Phra Jetupon, the oldest and, at eight hectares, the largest temple in Bangkok. Located just south of the Grand Palace, it is divided into two sections, one containing the living quarters of the monks and the other, a variety of religious buildings. The two sections are separated by the narrow Jetupon Road, down which King Rama I marched on his way back from Cambodia to Thonburi on April 6, 1782, the day he officially founded the Chakri dynasty.

There are 16 gates in the huge, massive walls of Wat Po, but only two of them, both on Jetupon Road, are open to the public. While the temple compound is large, it is crammed with buildings, pavilions, statues and gardens.

The first temple building on this site was built in the 16th century, but the *wat* did not achieve real importance until the establishment of Bangkok as the capi-tal. Wat Po was a particular favorite of the first four Bangkok kings, all of whom added to its treasures. The four large *chedis* to the west of the main chapel are memorials to them, the earliest being the green-mosaic *chedi* built by Rama I, and the last being the blue one built by Rama IV in the mid-19th century. Around the cloisters leading to the chapel are 91 other *chedis*, 71 small ones and 20 large ones.

The vast quantity and variety of things to be seen at Wat Po are more meaningful if you bear in mind that the early kings regarded the temple as a primary source of public education; it is sometimes called "Thailand's first university." Objects were placed in the compound as a way of letting people acquire knowledge, not necessarily connected with Buddhism. Murals illustrated treatises on such diverse subjects as military defense, astrology, morality, literature and archaeology. Twenty small hills around the compound serve as a useful geology lesson, displaying stone specimens from

An early view of Wat Po, taken by Robert Lenz (circa 1890).

different parts of Thailand.

Wat Po is still regarded as a center for traditional medicine. The dozen stone statues of hermits that sit under trees or on rocks, were used as diagnostic tools by herbal physicians. The patient pointed to the statue depicting the pain he was feeling and the physician prescribed a remedy. On the walls of a small pavilion, which you pass on your way to the Reclining Buddha, are plaques that prescribe treatments for different ailments. The building to the left is the headquarters for Bangkok's traditional medicine practitioners. Each day, in the late afternoon, people flock here for herbal treatments.

For most tourists, Wat Po's big attraction is its gigantic **Reclining Buddha**. The largest in Thailand, the 46-m long and 15-m high image is entirely covered with gold leaf. The soles of the feet, 5½m high, are inlaid with mother-of-pearl designs depicting the 108 auspicious signs by which a Buddha may be recognized.

The *bot* or main chapel of the complex is similarly interesting for its mother-of-pearl work. They decorate the east and west doors, illustrating in brilliant detail, scenes from the *Ramakien*. Along the base of the *bot* are a series of superb sandstone panels with bas-relief carvings of similar scenes from the *Ramakien*. Elsewhere in the courtyard, vendors sell rubbings taken from the panels. Along the eastern wall of the complex, masseurs offer traditional Thai massages for a nominal fee.

The huge, top-hatted stone figures (which supposedly represent Europeans) that guard the gates of Wat Po and the delightful little stone animals and pagodas scattered around the compound came to Thailand as ballast on the rice boats returning from trade with China. Similar statues are found at Wat Suthat and other temples in Bangkok.

One of the most beautiful buildings in the courtyard is the library. Located near the four big *chedis*, it is covered with bits of broken pale-colored porcelain. Near it is a walled Chinese garden that once contained crocodiles.

monk preparing medicine, the traditional way.

PHRAMANE GROUND

North of Wat Phra Kaew is a large oval lawn known as **Sanam Luang** (Royal Field) or **Phramane Ground** (Royal Cremation Ground). Originally, the palace of the second king (now the National Museum) occupied the northern half. It is written that when the Vietnamese threatened an invasion, King Rama III ordered that the area be planted in rice. Vietnamese generals, told that the Thais could hold off indefinitely with such supplies of food, called off the invasion.

The ground has served as the cremation site for high royalty, the most recent being the funeral in 1985 of Queen Rambhai Bharni, widow of King Prajadipok. In a significant departure from tradition, the bodies of those killed in the 1973 revolution were given a royally sponsored cremation in the field. The annual Plowing Ceremony is held here each May to mark the official beginning of the rice planting season.

It is also a place for recreation. Thais come here to *pai tio* (take a leisurely stroll) or picnic in the late afternoon. Impromptu soccer games are played and children chase each other around the trees. From around mid-February through April, vendors set up racks decorated with dozens of styles and sizes of kites including the "snake" kite with its four-meter-long tail. Children of all ages launch these colorful kites into the air.

About 4pm each day, teams set up winches in preparation for a kite contest. Teams are divided according to the type of kite they fly. One flies the 2-m-tall star-shaped *chula* kite and another flies the tiny *pakpao* kite representing male and female respectively. The object is to snare the opponent's kite and drag it across a dividing line. It is often the female kite that drags down a lumbering *chula*.

During the kite contests, *takraw* competitions are held in the northwest corner of the ground. Two teams of three

A sanctuary of peace inside Buddhaisawa Chapel.

men stand on either side of a net and, using their feet, knees, shoulders, elbows and heads, propel a rattan ball over a head-high net. It is a demanding sport, one of the most exciting in Asia.

Until it was moved to Chatuchak Park north of the city, Sanam Luang played host to the Weekend Market. Its removal in 1982, was intended to give the area the dignity the city fathers felt it deserved but its demise, and that of the book stalls across the street and the flower market on Klong Lawd, has taken away much of the liveliness that formerly animated the old city.

Between Sanam Luang and the river is another group of buildings that form the core of the old city. Closest to the entry gate to the Grand Palace on Na Prathat Road, is the Fine Arts Department. Up the street towards the river is **Silpakorn University**, the University of Fine Arts, where students are trained in painting, sculpture, archaeology and architecture. The oldest building of the university was once a palace. Despite many modern additions to the complex there are still attractive, shady courtyards where students can relax between classes. Frequent art exhibitions are held here, and there is a small but interesting archaeological museum.

Behind the umber-colored building that faces Sanam Luang and which formerly housed the National Library is **Wat Mahathat** Temple of the Great Relic. Built during the reign of Rama I, it is an important Buddhist teaching institution, specializing in meditation. During his 27 years in the priesthood before becoming king, Rama IV was abbot of this temple.

Behind it is the **Mahachulalongkorn University** which provides higher education for monks. An interesting warren of lanes meander between the monks' dormitories. Also in its grounds is a market selling religious items including the small amulets Thais wear around their necks. An even bigger amulet market runs along the river directly west of Mahachulalongkorn.

North of Prachan Road which extends from the middle of Sanam Luang

to the river is **Thammasart University**. Founded just before World War II, it is now one of Thailand's leading educational institutions, especially for students of law and economics. The students of Thammasart tend to be less conservative than those of the older Chulalongkorn University. Many leaders of the 1973 revolution came from Thammasart.

To the north is the **National Museum**. It consists of a number of buildings housing art and ethnology exhibits. It is open every day, except Monday and Friday, from 9am until noon, and from 1 until 4pm; admission is free on Saturday and Sunday, and 20 baht on other days. On Tuesdays, Wednesdays and Thursdays at 9.30am there are special English, German and French-language tours that start from the entry pavilion at the main gate and last about two hours.

Besides housing a vast collection of antiquities, the museum has an interesting history of its own. The oldest buildings in the compound date from 1782 and were built as the palace of the second king, a sort of deputy ruler, a feature of the Thai monarchy until 1870. Originally, the palace included a large park that went all the way to Wat Mahathat and covered the northern half of the present Phramane Grounds.

The first building to the left of the entrance is the **Sivamokha Biman Hall**, which was originally an open-sided audience hall. It now houses the pre-historic art collection, in particular the bronzes and handsome painted earthenware jars found in Ban Chieng in Northeast Thailand which are arousing much interest among archaeologists around the world.

Directly behind the entrance is the **Buddhaisawan Chapel**, built by the second king as his private place of worship. It contains some of Thailand's most beautiful and best-preserved murals, depicting the life of the Buddha. It also holds the famous *Phra Buddha Sihing*, a bronze Sukhothai-style image, the second most important in the kingdom. The image is paraded through the

NATIONAL MUSEUM

For the museum visitor in a hurry, the following are the main periods of Thai art, with a brief description of the principal characteristics of their statues or images, and the rooms where they are displayed.

Dvaravati (6th–11th centuries): Mon in appearance, with broad, usually smiling faces and tight curls, often showing Indian influence especially in the robes and the slightly curved bodies of standing figures. In rooms 32 and 33 you will find Dvaravati figures in terra-cotta, Buddha images and lively groups of dancers and musicians.

Srivichaya (8th–13th centuries): Contemporaneous with Dvaravati but from areas farther south and strongly influenced by Javanese art. Bronzes are in room 35.

Lopburi or *Khmer* (11th–14th centuries): Similar, sometimes identical in style to the art of Cambodia, with many stone and bronze figures of Hindu deities as well as Buddha images. Figures look strong and masculine. Rooms 29 and 31.

Chiang Saen (12th–20th centuries): From North Thailand. Rather plump, somewhat Chinese-looking faces and curled hair. Room 41.

Sukhothai (13th–15th centuries): The first purely Thai style and still regarded as the most original; images displaying long, flowing, idealized bodies and faces with enigmatic smiling expressions. Many of the features are based on descriptions in Sanskrit poetry of gods and heroes. Be sure to see the famous black bronze of the walking Buddha. Rooms 42 and 43.

Ayutthaya (15th–18th centuries): A mixture of styles with graceful but stylized figures, the lavish decoration reflecting the wealth and power of the kingdom. Rooms 44 and 45.

Bangkok or *Rattanakosin* (late 18th century to present): Round, rather sweet faces and elaborate Thai costumes more decorative than figures of earlier periods; unfortunately not well represented.

streets of Bangkok each year on the day before Songkran.

Also in the museum compound is the **Tamnak Daeng**, or Red House. It was the residence of an elder sister of King Rama I and was formerly located in the grounds of the Grand Palace. It has a fascinating collection of furniture used by early royalty.

The finely-proportioned old palace of the second king, which formerly held the museum's entire collection, is now reserved for ethnological exhibits of elephant howdahs, ceramics, palanquins, royal furnishings, weapons and other old objects. The Buddhist art collection, in the new wings on either side, includes sculptures from other Asian countries, but its main exhibits are its Thai images ranging from Hindu statues of the 5th century, up through Rattanakosin (Bangkok) art. Brochures and pamphlets available at the museum entrance explain the evolution of the various artistic styles.

Directly north of the National Museum is the **National Theater**, a huge building that is not an entirely happy mixture of Thai and Western architecture. This is where performances of Thai classical dance are presented on special occasions. Check newspapers for dates, for they are worth seeing.

Behind it is **Nattasin**, a dance school run by the Department of Fine Arts. Here, in old buildings of the second king's palace, young students learn the complex gestures and steps of the *khon*, and *lakhon* dance dramas once performed only for the king and his court.

One last temple remains on the royal island: Wat Rajpradit. It sits in a quiet area on Saranrom Road, one street south of the Defense Ministry. Built by King Rama IV, it is a study in the contrasting architectural styles of Asia. Behind the gray marble *bot* is a stupa of the Sinhalese style of Sri Lanka. On the left is an Ayutthayan-style *prang* and on the right is a Bayong-style prang from 12th-century Angkor Thom in Cambodia. Within the *bot* are a series of 12 lovely murals depicting the royal ceremonies for each month of the year.

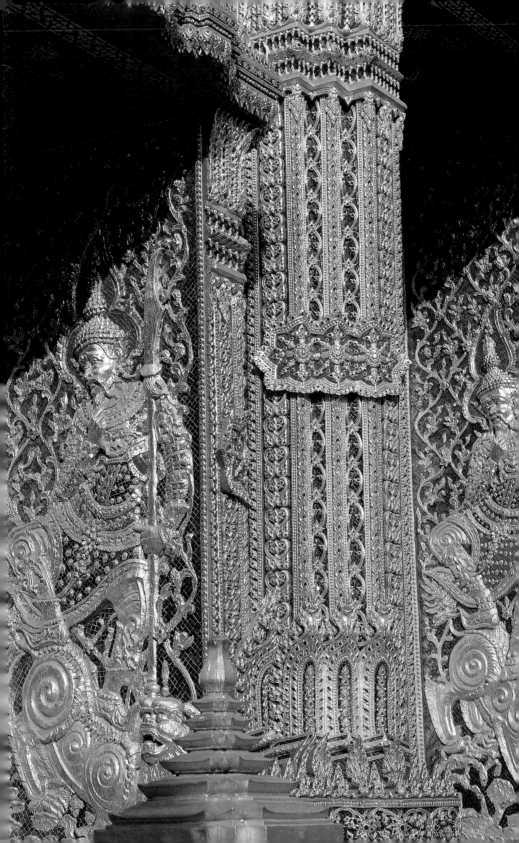

OTHER BANGKOK TEMPLES AND SITES

Many of the principal administrative and religious buildings of the original city of Bangkok lie between the first and second canals, Klong Lawd on the west and a canal with two names – Banglampoo on its northern half and Ong Ang on its southern half – on the east. The latter canal served as a moat for a crenellated wall that ran from one riverbank to the other. Along it were 14 watchtowers. Unfortunately only two have survived, one at the canal's northern mouth on Phrasumane Road and the other at the intersection of Rajdamnern and Mahachai roads in the shadow of the Golden Mount.

This section of the old city holds temples whose beauty rivals those on Rattanakosin Island. One of the most attractive, an architectural curiosity visited by relatively few tourists, is **Wat Rajabophit**, located near the Ministry of Interior east of Klong Lawd. You can easily recognize it by its distinctive doors, carved in relief with jaunty-looking soldiers wearing European-type uniforms. Built by King Chulalongkorn in 1870, the temple reflects the king's interest in blending Western art with traditional Thai forms.

The design of the principal structures is a departure from the norm, a form that makes it unique among Thailand's religious buildings. At the center of the courtyard stands a tall, gilded *chedi* enclosed by a circular cloister like that encircling the Phra Pathom Chedi in Nakhon Pathom. Built into the northern side of the yellow tile-clad cloister is the *bot*, itself covered in brightly-patterned tiles in a variety of hues.

The windows and entrance doors of the *bot* are works of art. Tiny pieces of mother-of-pearl have been inlaid in lacquer in an intricate rendition of the insignias of the five royal ranks. In a recess beside one of the doors is a bas-relief of a god named Khio Kang (Chew Hard) "the one with long teeth," who guards this sanctuary. Four chapels,

connected to the central gallery by small porticoes, further enlarge this colorful temple.

The doors open into one of the most surprising temple interiors in Thailand. Instead of the murals and the dark interior normal in Thai temples, this one has been rendered like a gothic European chapel with all the light and delicacy of a medieval cathedral combined with a Versailles salon. Wat Rajabophit was built before King Chulalongkorn made his first trip to Europe, so its design is even more remarkable. The king mixed the indigenous and the foreign even further when, 30 years later, he built Wat Benjamabophit.

Bamrungmuang Road, beside the Ministry of the Defense heads east and, three name changes and several kilometers later, becomes Sukhumvit Road. As you are passing the second canal, you can see directly ahead of you the tall, gate-like structure known as *Sao Ching Cha* or the **Giant Swing**. Bamrungmuang, on either side of the swing, is filled with shops selling religious objects for temples and homes. They are worth peeking into to see what they have to offer.

The Swing itself consists of two tall red poles in the center of a wide square, bounded on the north by the city hall and on the south by Wat Suthat. The Swinging Ceremony, now no longer held, was a popular Brahminist ritual held in honor of the god, Phra Isuan, who was believed to visit the earth for ten days every January. Teams of men pumped back and forth to set the swing in motion, struggling to ascend high enough to snatch a bag of gold that was hung from a tall pole. The Brahman temple, the only one in Bangkok, is a plain building on Dinsor Road just northwest of the Swing.

Wat Suthat, which faces the Giant Swing, was begun by Rama I and finished during the reign of Rama III (1824–1851). It is noted for its enormous *bot* (chapel), said to be the tallest in Bangkok, and for its equally large *viharn*, both of them surrounded by a gallery of gilded Buddha images. The Buddha image dominating the *bot* is called the

aborately
lded stucco
corations
ace the
alls of Wat
ajabophit,
angkok.

Phra Buddha Chakyamuni. Cast in 14th-century Sukhothai, its size and beauty so impressed Rama I that he brought it down to Bangkok by river. The murals that decorate the walls date from the reign of Rama III and are in a variety of styles; most intriguing are the depictions of fabulous sea monsters and foreign ships on the columns.

The *bot* doors are among the wonders of Thai art. Carved to a depth of 5cm, they follow the Ayutthayan tradition of floral motifs, tangled jungle vegetation hiding small animals. Accounts vary as to whether Rama II only designed the doors or actually carved them himself but it is known that when they were finished, he ordered the chisels to be thrown into the river so that no one could duplicate the fine carving. Bronze horses and stone pagodas and gods dotting the courtyard are gifts from China.

Almost due north of Wat Suthat, past the Democracy Monument, and on to Phrasumane Road is **Wat Bovornivet**. It was built by Rama III for Rama IV when he was still a monk and it was here that he reformed many of the Buddhist texts, ridding them of their superstitious elements. Since then, it has served as the temple where kings are ordained as monks; King Bhumibol donned the saffron robes here not long after his coronation.

Nothing of note marks the buildings but the *bot* contains some of the most unusual murals in the kingdom. They were painted by an innovative painter named Krua In-khong, a man who had never traveled outside Thailand but who understood the concept of Western perspective and must have seen pictures of American buildings. Unlike the flat, two-dimensional paintings of classical Thai art, these recede into the distance and are characterized by muted, moody colors. What is most interesting is their subjects: ante-bellum southern United States mansions, race tracks, people dressed in the fashions of 19th-century America, all being used to relate Buddhist teachings and fables.

Across Mahachai Road from the watchtower below the Golden Mount,

Dawn breaks gently over Wat Suthat, casting a warm glow of the Giant Swing.

is **Wat Rajnadda** and its **Amulet Market**. Thais are firm believers in the protective powers of amulets. They wear them on gold or silver chains around their necks and take great care in selecting precisely the right one.

The majority are Buddha images, often pressed into terra-cotta but there are amulets imprinted with portraits of monks renowned for their wisdom. There are also other gods and goddesses who are supposed to protect the wearer. A ten-eyed deity, for example, protects not only from the front, but from the back and both sides as well. There are amulets that attract women to men and vice versa, and amulets that ward off bullets, or protect one from harm while riding in a car or airplane. Among these are phalluses which men wear on strings around their waists to enhance their virility.

Now visible behind Wat Rajnadda since the city removed the old Chalerm Thai theater is **Lohaprasad**, the "iron palace" so named because of the metal spikes that rise from its many spires. It

is said that the model for this unusual building was the thousand-room Brazen Palace in Polonaruwa in Sri Lanka. Unfortunately, visitors are not allowed inside.

The most prominent monument in the area is the **Golden Mount**, (Phu Khao Thong) for many years the highest point in the city. Ayutthaya had had a great artificial hill, and King Rama III decided to reproduce it in Bangkok. Because of Bangkok's soft earth, however, he was never able to raise it to the desired height, and it was not until the reign of King Rama IV that the hill and the *chedi* topping it were completed.

Standing 78m high, the top level is reached by a stairway of 318 steps that ascends around the base of the hill. The gilded *chedi* contains relics of the Buddha given to Rama V in 1877 by Lord Curzon, then Viceroy of India. The climb is fairly exhausting, especially on a hot day, but the view of Bangkok is simply superb.

At the bottom of the Mount, Wat Saket was built during the Ayutthaya

period, and was originally called Wat Sakae. On his return from Laos in 1782 General Chakri stopped here and ceremonially bathed on his way back to Thonburi to be crowned King Rama I. The name of the temple was later changed to Saket, which means "the washing of hair."

The temple is associated with a more grisly history. Commoners were cremated here. During a series of cholera epidemics in the 19th century, their numbers became so great that undertakers resorted to laying out the bodies and allowing great flocks of vultures to consume them.

Every November, Wat Saket and the Golden Mount are the scene of one of Bangkok's noisiest fairs. Food stalls and dozens of stage shows are set up in the grounds. The mount is bathed in colored lights and the devout make their way in candlelight processions to the top of the wat.

Crossing the *klong* at Pan Fah next to the watchtower, Rajdamnern Avenue turns left into a pleasant, tree-lined boulevard, that leads to the square in front of the old **National Assembly**. The square is dominated by an equestrian statue of King Chulalongkorn who was responsible for so much of the construction of this part of Bangkok. On the anniversary of his death each October 23, the square is crowded with students and government officials who honor him by laying wreaths at the base of his statue. The square resounds to the thud of booted heels at the annual Trooping of the Colors ceremony held each year on December 3 as royal regiments resplendent in bright uniforms march in review before the King and Queen.

To the left of the square is **Amporn Gardens**, a spacious park with fountains and trees. It is the setting for many royal social functions and fairs, among them the annual Red Cross Fair in January. At the back of the square stands the former National Assembly building, an Italian-looking hall of gray marble crowned by a huge dome. It was built in 1907 by King Chulalongkorn as his Throne Hall and only later became the

Parliament Building, gloriously decked out with strings of lights, in honor of the King's birthday.

Parliament building. Special permission is required to go inside the building, which is decorated with huge murals depicting famous events in Thai history. In 1974, Parliament moved to new premises a short distance north.

Behind the old National Assembly is **Vimarn Mek**, billed as the world's largest golden teak building. As much a work of art as the treasures it holds, Vimarn Mek (Cloud Mansion), was built by King Chulalongkorn as a rural residence for his family in what was in 1900, the suburbs of Bangkok. The airy, 100-room home is filled with crystal, Faberge jewelry and other objects brought from Europe. Open daily; 50 baht admission or free as part of the 100-baht entrance fee for the Grand Palace.

East of the National Assembly building is **Dusit Zoo** also known as Khao Din (Mountain of Earth) for the small hill it holds. There is an entrance here and on Rajawiti Road. Dusit Zoo is the city's main animal park and one of the most popular places in Bangkok for family outings.

A lake with boats for rent, is surrounded by cages containing the exotic wildlife of Asia. Gibbons, orang-utangs from the jungles of Sumatra, an aviary, snakes and a host of other animals are found here. Among the most interesting are the king's white elephants. By tradition, every white elephant found in Thailand belongs to the king. To the newcomer, the elephants look nearly as gray as the normal variety. It is only by a complicated process involving an examination of skin color, hair and eyes by special court officials that the elephant's albino traits are discovered.

Historically throughout Southeast Asia, the white elephant has denoted regal power. Buddha's mother is said to have dreamed of a white elephant touching her side with his trunk, causing her to conceive. Buddha, in one of his previous incarnations as Prince Vessanthorn, was expelled from his palace after giving a white elephant to a rival kingdom.

The number of white elephants a king owned signified his power; the more he

had, the more powerful he was. Wars were fought over ownership of white elephants. One could not own a white elephant without providing all the care their exalted status demanded. Special quarters were provided for them and rare foods were found for them. If the king suspected that a minor prince was becoming too powerful, he would give him a white elephant. The prince would generally go bankrupt trying to feed and house it, hence the term "white elephant" that has come into the English language to denote a gift which costs the recipient dearly to maintain.

East of the zoo is **Chitralada Palace** where the king and queen reside. To the southeast is **Wat Benchamabophit**, the **Marble Wat**, the last major temple built in Bangkok. Started by King Chulalongkorn in 1900, it was finished ten years later, the year he died. It was designed by Prince Naris, a half-brother of the king. A talented architect, Naris made a number of departures from the traditional style. The most obvious of these must be the Carrara marble used to

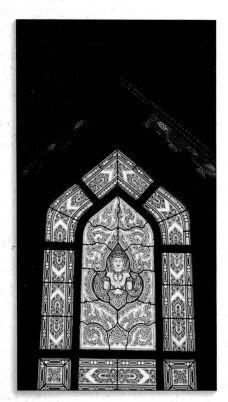

cover the main buildings; the enclosed courtyard; and the curved, yellow Chinese tiles of the roof. Another innovation is the use of stained glass windows in the *bot*.

The *bot's* principal Buddha image is a replica of the famous *Phra Buddha Jinnirat* of Phitsanulok. Behind the *bot* is a gallery holding 51 Buddha images from various countries of Asia. The gallery serves as instruction in the various ways in which the Buddha has been depicted throughout Asia.

Through the rear entrance of the courtyard is a huge Bodhi tree, 80-odd years old. It was brought as a seedling from a tree in South Thailand that came from Bodhgaya in India, the Buddha's birthplace. A canal filled with large turtles released by people wishing to earn merit, separates the religious buildings from the monks' quarters. Visit Wat Benchamabophit early in the morning when monks gather before the front gates to receive alms from Thais who stop there with food on their way to work. The scene affords some excellent photo opportunities.

On the northern edge of the city is the Thai equivalent of an Oriental supermarket. **Chatuchak Weekend Market** operates only on Saturdays and Sundays so it is thronged by Thais eager to find as many bargains as they can. It is a sprawling market covering 31 acres and containing 5,000 stallholders who set up displays under canvas awnings. An enormous variety of goods are sold including fresh produce, meats, antiques, clothes, tropical fish, pets and others which make for a fascinating morning. Stroll through displays of blue-and-white porcelain or used books. Half the fun is in the bargaining.

On the southern end of the market is a vegetarian restaurant operated by Chamlong Srimuang, a former Governor of Bangkok. Open at 1am, it offers a surprising range of excellent dishes for unbelievably low prices. Even if you are not a vegetarian, you will enjoy a meal here. Plan a morning visit as the sun can heat up the market to intolerable temperatures by noon.

Left, stained glass at the Marble Wat, an example of fine craftsmanship. Right, devotees with lighted candles and lotus buds converge in the temple grounds of Marble Wat

CHINATOWN AREA

Bangkok's **Chinatown** is a sprawling area concentrated between Chakrawat Road and Klong Krung Kasem on the west and east, and from a bit north of Charoen Krung (New Road) to Song-wat Road near the river. It began its life along Sampeng Lane, the area to which the Chinese merchants moved in the 1780s after vacating the land where the Grand Palace now stands. In 1863, King Mongkut built New Road, the first paved street in Bangkok and Chinatown began to expand northwards towards it. Shortly thereafter, a third road, Yaowaraj, was built between Charoen Krung and Sampeng and this became the principal road of Chinatown and the other name by which the area is known.

Sampeng has had a somewhat rowdy history. What began with mercantile pursuits soon degenerated into an entertainment area. By 1900, side alleys led to opium dens and houses whose entrances were marked by green lanterns (khom khiew). Green light meant red light and while the lanterns have disappeared, the term "khom khiew" still signifies a brothel. Sampeng was tamed and eventually metamorphosed into a sleepy lane of small shops selling sundry goods imported from China.

The lane begins on Mahachai Road and is bound at either end by Indian and Muslim shops. The western end, Pahurat has a warren of tiny lanes filled with Indians and Sikhs selling cloth. Along the canal are Indian, Nepalese and Burmese restaurants. Across the canal is Sampeng proper.

Here are shops selling inexpensive jewelry, tools, cloth, clothes, toys, shoes and novelties. The prices are low because this is where ordinary Thais go to shop. On crossing Chakrawat Road, turn right a short distance to the entrance to **Wat Chakrawat** (it is no longer possible to enter from Sampeng Lane itself).

The *wat* is an odd amalgam of buildings. Dating from the Ayutthaya period and thus pre-dating Chinatown, it has a small grotto with a statue of a laughing monk. Myth says that it is the likeness of a monk who was once slim and handsome, so handsome he was constantly pestered by women. His devotion to Buddhism led him to the unusual remedy of eating until he grew so gross, the women lost interest.

Wats in Thailand normally serve as humane societies. Thais with a litter of puppies or kittens they cannot feed, leave them at the *wat* to be fed the leftovers from the monks' daily meals. This *wat* is a departure from the norm as the animals it houses are crocodiles.

Back on Sampeng, continue east. Halfway down on the left is a handsome building that once served as the gold exchange. In the side alleys are quiet Chinese temples; farther down on the right are sweet-scented shops selling slabs of cinnamon and other spices. Here and there are small, dark wet markets that throb with life at dawn and are dead by 9am.

Near the end of Sampeng, notice that the shops bear Muslim names. The merchants here trade gems. Marking the eastern end of Sampeng is **Wat Pathooma Kongka**, another temple from the Ayutthaya period. It was here that criminals of royal birth were executed for crimes against the state.

At places, Yaowaraj Road looks like a Hong Kong street with its forest of signs. It is best known for its gold shops, all of which seem to have been designed by a cookie cutter, so alike do they look. Daily prices are scrawled on the windows of shops painted red for good luck. Mirrors and neon lights complete the decor. Prices are quoted in *baht*, an ancient unit of weight.

Yaowaraj is also an old entertainment area. Halfway down on the north side of the street is the famous "Seven Storey Mansion" that flourished well into the middle part of this century. It was designed so that those interested only in dining could do so on the ground floor. As the evening progressed and as one relaxed, one would ascend the stairs, floor by floor, to more sybaritic delights; unrepentant hedonists heading straight for the top floor.

Between Yaowaraj and New roads

near the west end of Chinatown is **Nakorn Kasem** or **Thieves Market**. A few decades ago, it was the area a householder searched after he had been robbed. It was likely he would recover his stolen goods for a very reasonable price after a short tour of the market. It later became an antique dealer's area. The antiques have been nudged aside by more prosaic items like cement mixers but it is still possible to find a few shops selling pottery and images.

Near the eastern end of New Road is Chinatown's biggest Mahayana Buddhist temple, **Wat Monkhonkamalawat**, normally shortened to Wat Mongkhon. From early in the morning it is aswirl with activity and incense smoke reminiscent of ancient China.

The most interesting lane is Issaranuphap which runs south from Plaplachai Road. It begins near a busy Mahayana Buddhist temple called Wat Hong Kong, and passes a Thai temple called Wat Kanikaphon, better known as Wat Mae Lao Fang for the brothel madam who built it to atone for her sins.

Around the entrance to Issaranuphap are shops selling miniature houses, Mercedes-Benz, household furniture and other items made of paper. These are for the Chinese "kong tek" ceremony. The items are taken to the temple and burnt in a special furnace to send them to deceased relatives. Other shops sell the bright red and gold trimmed shrines the Chinese install in their homes to propitiate the spirits.

Down Issaranuphap are shops selling candles, incense and other religious items. There are temples off to the sides and stalls selling exotic Chinese foods. A walk down here is a walk through an area quite unlike any other in Bangkok.

Just east of the point where Yaowaraj Road meets Charoen Krung Road (not far from Hualampong Railway Station) is **Wat Traimitr**. It holds the famous **Golden Buddha,** found by accident in the 1950s at a riverside temple when a construction company was extending its dock. The huge stucco figure was too heavy for the sling. It snapped and, to the horror of all, smashed to the ground,

Believers appease hungry ghosts with offerings in a Bangkok wholesale market, a Chinese stronghold.

116

breaking one corner. A close examination showed a glint of yellow through the crack. Further investigation revealed that stucco was only a thin coat and that inside was an image of solid gold weighing 5½ tons. Like many similar statues, it was probably made elsewhere in Thailand during the Ayutthayan period. To preserve it from Burmese invaders, it was covered in stucco to conceal its true composition and rested undetected for centuries. The image now stands at Wat Traimitr.

New Road (Charoen Krung) runs over 6km from the royal palace to a point where it drops straight into the river just south of the Krung Thep Bridge. Along it, the principal minorities settled and set up shop during the 1800s. The Chinese section was succeeded at Krung Kasem Canal by a Muslim district which, in turn was followed by a *farang* area.

Mementos of the *farang* era are found in the many old buildings that line the river. They begin with the Portuguese Embassy and continue downriver with the old Customs House, the French Embassy, the Oriental Hotel and the East Asiatic Company. The General Post Office sits atop the former site of the British Embassy. Until the 1950s, this area is where the hotels and shops patronized by the foreign community were found. At the far end of New Road was Bangkolem, an exclusive area among the trees where the wealthier foreigners built their houses. They commuted by tram which until 1965 ran the length of New Road.

While the land along the river between Sathorn and Siphya roads is still covered by luxury hotels and shops, much of the commercial activity is now concentrated around Rajprasong. On New Road between Silom and Sathorn is Bangrak market with a wealth of simple but excellent sidewalk restaurants. Bangrak is also a flower market where you can buy the fragrant *puang malai* floral garlands.

Here, also, you can find two fruits prized by Thais: mangoes and durians, both of which appear on the market only in the hot season. If the only mangoes you have ever eaten are the Caribbean or Mexican varieties, you are in for a treat, for the pale Thai mangoes have an infinitely more delicate flavor. The Thais eat them green in a salad or dipped in sugar; or ripe as a dessert with glutinous (sticky) rice and coconut milk.

Durian is a large, spiky, pungent prehistoric-looking fruit that you either like or loathe; nobody seems neutral about it. If you have a taste for it, be prepared to pay anywhere from 50 baht for one of the ordinary specimens to several hundred for a superior *kanyao* ("long stem"), the most prized of all. If you are having your first durian, it might be helpful to remember that a very ripe fruit at room temperature tastes much stronger than a chilled one just ripening.

Located a few blocks south of Sathorn along New Road is **Wat Yannawa**. Rama IV built it in the shape of a Chinese junk as he feared that one day these useful boats would disappear from the seas and no one would remember what they looked like.

GARDENS AND PARKS

For plant lovers, especially from temperate lands, visiting a tropical country can be a dream come true. **Tropical gardens** virtually know no season, and countries like Thailand are perennially abloom.

For those who like to look at other people's gardens, however, Bangkok tends to be a city of high walls, many of them studded with intimidating bits of broken glass, so a drive through a residential area is not very rewarding. To the delight of plant lovers, Bangkok has recently acquired a botanical park. Located deep down Soi 101 off Sukhumvit Road just east of Bangkok is the **Rama IX Park**. It was opened in 1987 as a birthday gift for King Bhumibol on the occasion of his 60th birthday, the completion of his fifth 12-year cycle, an auspicious achievement in Asia. Found here are tropical plants as well as specimens donated by other countries.

One can also visit private gardens. One of the prettiest is the **Suan Pakkad Palace** at 352 Sri Ayutthaya Road (just east of the intersection with Phya Thai Road). The splendid residence belonged to the late Princess Chumbhot of Nagara Svarga, one of Thailand's leading gardeners and art collectors. The beautifully landscaped grounds (*suan* means "garden," *pakkad* means "cabbage") contain numerous plants the princess brought from all over the world as well as varieties found in the Thai jungle.

The gardens are only one reason for visiting Suan Pakkad; another is its superb art collection. Five old, traditional Thai houses overlook gardens, ponds and lawns around which pelicans strut imperiously. In the open-walled houses are antique lacquer book cabinets, Buddha images, Khmer statues, old paintings, porcelain, musical instruments, the regalia of the late Prince Chumbhot, and other art objects.

At the back of the garden stands an exquisite little lacquer pavilion which Prince Chumbhot discovered in a temple near Ayutthaya, brought in pieces to Bangkok, and had carefully restored. The pavilion's black and gold panels are considered masterpieces of Thai decorative art.

Other buildings at Suan Pakkad contain collections of seashells, mineral crystals, and painted pottery and bronze objects from the pre-historic burial ground at Ban Chiang in Northeast Thailand. The palace is open every day except Sundays from 9am to 4pm; admission is 50 baht.

The **Flower Market in Thevet** (or Thewes) is a gardening supply market which affords an excellent opportunity to see tropical plants (tell the taxi driver you want to go to *talat dokmai Taywait*). It runs along a pretty street that parallels Klong Krung Kasem, from Samsen Road to the river. Shaded by flame trees (a showy relative of the poinciana) are about 50 shops selling all the ornamental plants found in Bangkok gardens.

Across Klong Krung Kasem is Bangkok's main coconut market, where the barges from plantations unload their produce. Note the large, handsome, cone-shaped baskets which are used only for loading and measuring coconuts.

There is a flower market at **Phak Klong Talat,** Bangkok's largest wet market, next to the Memorial Bridge. From the early hours of the morning, the docks receive produce and flowers grown in market gardens along the canals in Thonburi. On Chakraphet Road which runs along the northern edge of the market, vendors sell freshly-cut flowers.

Chatuchak Flower Market south of Yan Paholyothin Road across from the Chatuchak weekend market offers a similar variety of plants and shrubs. Bangkok's gardeners come here to select everything from potted flowers to 3-m-high palm trees. It is worth strolling for an hour or two along the row of a dozen or so shops.

erdant
ardens with
ush plants
ourish in the
'opical Thai
limate.

The flower that comes closest to being Thailand's national flower, expressing through its multicolored petal, leaf, and stem much of the character of the land, is the **Orchid**. Nearly a thousand species grow native to the country, and the home cultivation of hybrid varieties has long been a popular hobby. Just about every Thai house, even in a slum, has at least one pot of orchids. Trees in parks and along many Bangkok streets now wear orchids on their trunks. In the past two decades, orchid growing has turned into a booming commercial enterprise.

Orchid lovers can visit one of the numerous nurseries where orchids are grown commercially for export. The majority of these are in Thonburi (you will likely come across several during a canal tour) or along the superhighway leading to the airport, where the air and water are fresher and cleaner.

The **Siam Society** on Soi 21 (Soi Asoke), off Sukhumvit Road, is a royally sponsored foundation established in 1904 to promote the study of Thai history, botany, zoology, anthropology and linguistics. It publishes a scholarly journal containing articles by experts on those subjects, and also special books on specific subjects like the orchids of Thailand, Thai customs and gardening. Copies of these are on sale at the society's headquarters. There is also an excellent reference library for anyone doing research on Thailand.

Any visitor interested in the culture of North Thailand should visit the **Kamthieng House** in the Siam Society compound. This lovely old house, which is approximately 130 years old, was the ancestral home of a prominent family in Chiang Mai, one of whose members donated it to the society. With the help of a grant from the Asia Foundation, it was dismantled, brought to Bangkok and carefully reassembled in a garden composed mostly of traditional Thai plants. It has been converted to an ethnological museum devoted to folk art and implements of the North, an important addition to Bangkok since the National Museum has no such collection.

Bonsai and water lilies on display at the Chatucha Flower Market.

Among the items on display are everyday objects used by farmers and fishermen, fine wood carvings from Northern temples and houses, lacquerware and hilltribe costumes. Notice in particular the beautifully carved teak lintels from traditional domestic houses, which are fast vanishing in the North. These were placed over the doorway leading to the inner main room of the house and are called in northern dialect *ham yon*, meaning "sacred testicles", so named because the inner room was believed to contain not only the ancestral spirits of the family but also the virility of the present inhabitants. When an old northern house is dismantled, or when a new owner moves in, the *ham yon* are often symbolically castrated by beating them severely to destroy the powerful magic accumulated in them under the old owner. A guide to the Kamthieng House and the collection in it is available in the Society library.

In the same compound is the **Saengaroon House**, a superb example of Central Thai architecture, the "Thai-style" house everyone talks about but no one sees.

On Klong Maha Nag at the end of Soi Kasemsan II, across from the National Stadium on Rama I Road, stands **Jim Thompson's House**, open daily except Sundays from 9am to 4.30pm. This Thai-style house is, in truth, a collection of seven Thai-style houses joined together by the remarkable American who came to Thailand at the end of World War II and revived the Thai silk industry. In 1967, while on a visit to the Cameron Highlands in Malaysia, Thompson mysteriously disappeared; despite an extensive search, no trace has been found of him.

Besides his contribution to the silk business, Thompson is remembered for his fabulous collection of Asian art and the house in which he displayed it; his heirs have decided to keep it as he left it. "Not only have you beautiful things," Somerset Maugham once wrote Thompson after dining with him, "but what is more rare, you have displayed them beautifully."

Tropical blooms add brilliant splashes of color to the Pak Klong Talat Flower Market.

The garden around the house is a luxuriant tropical mini-jungle. Volunteer guides explain the collection to visitors. Admission is 80 baht, which goes to a favorite charity of Thompson, the local School for the Blind.

Wildlife parks: Thailand has 42 national parks and more are being created each year. Most have nature trails, bungalows and camping facilities; one normally has to carry one's own provisions. This is a brief listing of the most popular:

Khao Yai. This is probably Thailand's most visited park by virtue of its close proximity to Bangkok, and the large variety of wildlife it contains. Within its boundaries lie some of the richest remaining rain forest in mainland Asia. It was the first of Thailand's national parks to be established and in 1971, was listed among the world's top five parks. The best developed of Thailand's parks, it has over 50km of hiking trails ranging from easy to rugged. There are bungalows and camp sites.

Erawan. Located in the Kancha-

naburi area, it has what is regarded as the most beautiful waterfall in Thailand. Covered mainly in deciduous forest, some areas are dominated by bamboo, the result of denudation by Burmese armies in the 17th and 18th centuries as they made their way east to attack Ayutthaya.

Phu Kradung. Near Loei, it holds a 60sq km plateau covered in savanna and magnificent pines making it one of the most picturesque parks. A story says that its name (bell mountain) derives from a local belief that on each Buddhist holy day (*Wan Phra*) a mysterious bell can be heard ringing across the hills.

Khao Chamao-Khao Wong. In Rayong province, it has abundant wildlife including pileated gibbon, serow, sambar, barking deer, tiger, elephant, Asiatic black bear, gaur and monkeys. Chamao means "to get drunk". Villagers say that the carp in the river eat the fruit of a strange tree which has no effect on them but makes people who eat the carp tipsy.

Kang Krachan. Thailand's largest park lies southwest of Petchburi. It also holds a large variety of wildlife and has numerous trekking trails. The reservoir has boats and bungalows for rent.

Khao Sam Roi Yot. North of Prachuap Khiri Khan this rugged mountain has forest trails which lead to rarely-seen serow (goat-antelope). There are also numerous species of shore birds, as well as Irrawaddy dolphins. In Phraya Nakhon Cave, a 30-minute climb from Laem Sala Beach, is a pavilion built for King Rama V's visit on June 20, 1890.

Thale Noi. Near Songkhla's huge Thale Sap, this small lake covers 28sq km and is a birdwatchers paradise. More than 200 species of water birds nest here.

Tarutao. This collection of islands lying in the Andaman Sea near Satun is the northern portion of Malaysia's Langkawi group. The islands offer superb snorkeling opportunities as well as Koh Lipe with its sea gypsy villages. The islands are also home to dusky langurs, crab eating macaques, mousedeer and dolphins.

Left, doorway to Jim Thompson's Thai-style house. Right, the silk king house contains a fine collection of Asian art.

MODERN BANGKOK

Besides the many temples and traditional sights of the old city, the newer sections of Bangkok invite exploration and shopping. The areas along Rama I Road extending from Phya Thai to Rajprasong offer some of both.

Three of the four corners of Rama I and Phya Thai offer some of the city's best shopping opportunities. On the southwest corner next to the National Stadium is the air-conditioned **Mahboonkrong Shopping Center**, one of Bangkok's biggest complexes. Five floors of shops sell everything from computers to chinaware. Terrace restaurants invite one to relax and sip a soft drink or a coffee.

Across Phya Thai to the east is one of the oldest shopping malls in Bangkok, Siam Square. It holds the British Council with its excellent library, three movie theaters, book stores and a wealth of restaurants ranging from Thai and Chinese shark's fin to the famous fast-food establishments imported directly from the United States. Recently, the covered walkways have become a mini-mart of crafts and clothes where students and others sell small items; a good place to browse.

Across Rama I from Siam Square is Siam Center. This is an up-market emporium offering the latest pop fashions for Bangkok's teens and post-teens. Next to it is the Siam Inter-continental Hotel, with one of the more interesting architectural designs. Just beyond it stands **Wat Pathumawanaram**, whose name means "The Lotus Temple," because of the great number of lotuses and water lilies blooming in the large pond behind it.

The temple was built by Rama IV in a large park that also held a palace in which the king could escape the summer heat of the Grand Palace. A few years ago you could become so lost in it you could not hear or see the city. The palace is gone, the trees have been cut and the ponds filled in to build yet another shopping complex.

The temple's *bot* contains attractive murals painted during the reign of Rama V (1868–1910). Just before it is a lovely stone stele bearing a bas-relief of the Buddha's face. If the style looks un-Thai it is because the stele was carved by an Italian sculptor who resided at the *wat* a few years ago. Wat Pathumawanaram is the most popular temple in Bangkok among taxi drivers who drive here to have their vehicles blessed against accidents.

Along Henri Dunant Road (still called by Thais by its old name of Sanam Ma, "Race Course Road") are found two important old Bangkok institutions. On the left, walking south from Siam Square, is the **Royal Bangkok Sports Club**, a multi-national private club with sports facilities, golf course, swimming pool, tennis courts and horse racing on alternate Sundays during all but the rainiest months. The club is closed to non-members, but the race course is open to the public. The program commences at 12.15pm and consists of 10 races. On all other Sundays, races are held at the Royal Turf Club on Sukhothai Road opposite Chitralada Palace.

Across the road from the Sports Club stands the temple-like buildings of **Chulalongkorn University**, the country's oldest and most prestigious institution of higher learning. The campus extends from Henri Dunant to Phya Thai Road and holds 14 faculties. Built in a mixture of Thai and Western styles, with spacious yellow roofed pavilions, an open gallery and an assembly hall, the university was founded by King Rama VI (1911–1925) and named after his father, King Chulalongkorn.

South of Chulalongkorn University is the Pasteur Institute or, as it is better known, the **Snake Farm**. The entrance is on Rama IV Road directly opposite the Montien Hotel. Operated by the Thai Red Cross, its primary function is to produce anti-venom serum to be used on snakebite victims. One may also obtain internationally-certified cholera, smallpox, rabies and typhoid fever inoculations here. The Snake Farm, the second oldest of its kind in the world,

receding
age,
itrance to
impini
ark, in the
eart of
angkok.
eft, the
biquitous
r-
anditioned
apartment
ore.

produces serum from seven types of snake: the King Cobra, Siamese Cobra, Banded Krait, Russell's Viper, Malayan Pit Viper and the Green and Pope's Pit Viper.

The farm offers free educational shows at 11am and 2pm daily. A slide show in the back building is followed by a show at the arena during which the various snakes are handled and their characteristics discussed. Technicians show how they milk Siamese Cobras of their venom. Small doses of this venom will then be injected in horses at a farm near Si Racha. After a period, the horses' blood will be extracted in small amounts. The antigens separated from this blood will form the anti-venom serum which will be distributed to hospitals around the country.

Other, non-poisonous snakes like pythons are also shown. Of most interest to visitors is the deadly King Cobra which can grow up to 5m. While the workers are somewhat casual in handling the Siamese Cobras and Kraits, they concentrate intently when handling the King Cobra and for good reason. Several years ago, one bit a worker and even though he was injected immediately with anti-venom serum, he went into a coma that lasted for three days and left him with massive scarring on his forearm.

At the end of Rama I is **Rajprasong** intersection where the street changes its name to Ploenchit Road. The attraction here is the **Erawan Shrine**. To improve their fortunes or pass their exams, Thais make offerings at a statue of the Hindu god, Brahma. Originally erected by the Erawan Hotel to counter a spate of bad luck, the shrine is redolent with incense smoke and jasmine. To repay the god for wishes granted, supplicants place floral garlands or wooden elephants at the god's feet or hire a resident troupe to dance. Day or night, the shrine provides a fascinating spectacle, an enclave of peace amid the din of one of the city's busiest streets.

Nearby is another cluster of shopping malls. The showcase is the **Peninsula Plaza** on Rajdamri Road near the Re-

Lumpini Park, the city's only green lung, provides a welcome contrast to the busy cityscape.

gent Hotel. **Galeries Lafayette** and other prestige shops sell luxury items from around the world.

A short distance east of the Shrine on Ploenchit Road is Amarin Plaza with McDonalds for those who miss American food. Up the road, where Ploenchit and Chidlom meet is the largest of the Central department stores. **Central** has a large section on the fourth floor selling Thai products for those who forgot to buy souvenirs elsewhere. One block east before reaching the railway tracks is a duty free shop which offers Thai craft items in addition to the normal duty free liquors, perfumes, cigarettes and other products.

North of the Shrine, on Rajdamri Road is a street called Gaysorn which curves to run in front of Le Meridien President Hotel. It has a number of stalls selling inexpensive but stylish clothes. Beyond it, still on Rajdamri is the government's handicrafts store, **Narayana Phand**. It has an excellent selection of goods and is worth exploring if for no other reason than to learn of the wide variety of Thai crafts and the approximate prices.

Continue up Rajdamri to **Rajdamri Arcade** and **Bangkok Bazaar**. Both have the air of markets with numerous small shops crammed into a small space and vendors spilling off the sidewalks. One can often find some good handicraft bargains at small shops in Rajdamri Arcade.

The pair serve as a link between the chic shops of **Rajprasong** and the bazaar atmosphere of a vast, sprawling **Pratunam**, one block north, a favorite shopping place for many Thais. *Pratunam* means "Water Gate," referring to the lock at the bridge to prevent **Klong Saen Sap** on the right (east) from being flooded by the one on the left (west) which leads to the Chao Phya River. Under the bridge are shops selling wicker goods. The noodle shops of Pratunam Market are popular late-night eateries after the bars and movie theaters close.

On the other end of Rajdamri, at the intersection with Rama IV Road is **Lumpini Park**, central Bangkok's only park. In the morning, Bangkok jogs, does *tai chi chuan* exercises, lifts weights, even tangoes under its trees. Along the two lakes, kiosks rent rowboats or paddleboats which not only provide exercise but a ringside seat of the activities on the banks. On Sundays, Chinese gather on the island to play and sing old songs. In the afternoons, boys play *takraw* and soccer or, during the hot season, fly kites. The park is Bangkok's only island of green and is a superb respite from the heat and traffic that prevail in the rest of the city.

In the evenings, tranquil pastimes give way to one of Thailand's most popular indigenous sports, Thai boxing (*Muay Thai*).

Bouts are staged at two venues: Lumpini Stadium on Tuesdays and Fridays at 6.30pm and on Saturdays at 1pm and 6.30pm; Rajdamnern Stadium on Mondays, Wednesdays and Thursdays at 6pm and on Sundays at 4.30 and 8.30pm. There are also televised bouts on weekends.

vening
eace
mbraces the
ark.

NIGHTLIFE

When night falls, a different Bangkok emerges. **Bangkok at night** has many faces, offering just about any form of amusement you could want. Some areas are transformed into an unbroken neon jungle of bars and nightclubs, with touts hawking their attractions at each doorway. Restaurants (themselves an evening's entertainment), movie theaters and massage parlors are jammed, especially on weekends; and almost any taxi driver you encounter in the vicinity of a big hotel is prepared to offer, sometimes on a card printed in several languages, a mind-boggling menu of vices for every imaginable taste, and not couched in innuendoes either.

While no part of the city's night life could be described as strictly *farang*, meaning that Thai patrons rarely go there, certain areas do have a pre-dominantly European and North American clientele. Foremost among these is **Patpong**, a short, privately owned street that runs between Silom and Suriwong roads a short walk from the Dusit Thani Hotel. Twenty-five years ago Patpong boasted only one or two rather sedate nightclubs and a couple of good restaurants. Now, it is nearly all night spots from one end to the other, spilling over to Patpong 2, which runs parallel, and to the gay bars of Patpong 3.

Patpong clubs change name, ownership and decor with bewildering frequency, so that printed guides become obsolete almost before the ink dries, but at any given time they run the gamut from raunchy to reasonably refined. Most of them have some gimmick to attract customers: topless go-go dancing, old movies, dart throwing contests, and "special shows" that are occasionally raided by police (who do not, however, arrest the customers).

Several of Bangkok's better massage parlors are located on Patpong 2. If you happen to see lovely young ladies loitering around the sidewalks, especially between Patpong and the Dusit Thani on Silom Road, the chances are that they are not ladies at all but what the Thais call *kra-toeys*, or transvestites, some of whom could fool even a sober expert. Thaniya Road is a mini-Ginza with bars patronized by Japanese and are quite reluctant to welcome *farangs*.

In the years when Bangkok was the leading rest and recreation center for the American military in Vietnam, a similar stretch of night life sprang up along the New Petchburi Road, starting roughly around the intersection of Soi Asoke (Soi 21) and generally referred to as **The Strip**.

There were clubs with names like The San Francisco and Jack's American Star Bar, featuring soul food and country music, and massage palaces that looked like a cross between a bowling alley and a mansion.

While the New Petchburi bar scene of the 60s and 70s has disappeared, there is one survivor: the "short time" hotel which is almost as much a feature of Bangkok's evening world (and afternoon, too) as the massage parlors. They are discreet, motel-like establishments where you can drive your car straight into a garage adjoining the room, and a curtain is immediately drawn around it to conceal you. Thousands of such places are found all over Bangkok, catering to every pocketbook; many are full from mid-morning until late in the evening. These are not brothels but trysting places.

The ones in the Sukhumvit-New Petchburi Road areas are among the fanciest; one has mirrors on the ceilings as well as on the walls, and a control board over the bed with push buttons for lights, music, air-conditioning and *sanuk* (if you press *sanuk* the bed begins to undulate slowly). However, most of these places now offer blue videos instead of blue movies.

To see what Patpong or New Petchburi once were like, travel to Soi Cowboy. The atmosphere here is more informal than Patpong but there is less of its raunchiness. The area around the Washington Theater near Soi 22 of Sukhumvit Road houses a few bars and restaurants.

Nana Entertainment Plaza, with its

ight revel-
ers live it up
t one of the
any discos
Bangkok.

lively go-go bars and open air "bar beers" on Soi 4 Sukhumvit Road, is preferred by the expatriate community as unlike Patpong all the bars are well run and at the end of the evening there are no padded bills or hidden charges to pay. Soi 3 is dominated by the Grace Hotel whose coffee shop is a seedy supermarket for bargirls. The clientele here is primarily Arab. The area also boasts some excellent Middle-eastern restaurants.

Whether the **massage parlor** originated in Bangkok, as some local enthusiasts claim, or whether they have merely reached their apotheosis here is a question best left for scholarly debate. Certainly they have been a feature of the city for a quarter century. They now number in the hundreds, from rather suspicious-looking establishments in dark, narrow streets to glass-and-marble palaces that the sybaritic Romans might have envied.

And these places really do offer genuine massages, either pure and simple or with such local embellishments as the method called B-course, in which the masseuse does the job with her naked body as well as her hands. In the larger massage parlors, the girls are on display behind a one-way glass show window and customers select the one they want by her number. Having made your choice, you then proceed to a comfortable private room that contains a massage table and a bathtub with hot water; refreshments such as beer and soft drinks can be ordered.

The usual length of a massage is an hour and prices vary beginning at 300 baht, depending on the grandeur of the establishment. The girl receives part of the fee but a tip is expected. The amount varies. A small tip will suffice in the case of a simple massage, more is expected if it has been accompanied by what is euphemistically referred to as "special services."

To clear up one persistent misunderstanding: massage parlors are not brothels, and massage girls are not per se prostitutes. The price you pay for a massage in most places entitles you to precisely that and no more. Whatever

After sundown, Bangkok shows a different face.

arrangements you may make with your masseuse are strictly between you and her. On the other hand, the popularity of massage parlors with Thais as well as *farangs*, can scarcely be credited solely to a passion for bodily health or greater cleanliness. Some, like Cleopatra, fearful of the consequences of AIDS (Acquired Immune Deficiency Syndrome), have closed their doors to *farangs* in the belief they are protecting their girls and their Thai customers. With AIDS rampant in Thailand, it would be foolish to assume anyone is safe; take appropriate precautions.

For the pure of heart, there are massages without the naughty bits. Called **Traditional or Ancient Massages**, they employ centuries of knowledge to knead and relax a body.

A 1980s addition to the nightscene are the music bars along Sarasin Road and Ratchadapisek Road. Light music, often live bands, serves as background to conversation and casual drinking. These establishments attract primarily a young Thai crowd but *farangs* are welcome. Brown Sugar on Soi Sarasin is one of the most popular.

Bangkok has numerous **discos.** **Diana's** in the Oriental Plaza, **Capitol City** on Ratchadapisek Road, **Rome Club** (which until 11pm functions as a gay bar) on Patpong 3, **Peppermint Lounge** on Patpong (also comes to life at 11pm, **Bubbles** in the Dusit Thani Hotel and the enormous **NASA Spacedome** at the end of New Petchburi Road offer music and music videos.

Quieter music can be found in the Oriental Hotel's famous **Bamboo Bar** and in lounge bands found in most hotel lobbies in the city.

Stage shows are offered in the Dusit Thani Hotel's top-floor **Tiara Lounge** and at the **Galaxy** on Rama IV Road between Suriwong and Siphya. Next to the Galaxy is the **No-hands** restaurant in which the diner can enjoy the novel experience of being fed a delicious meal by a delectable lass. On Sunday nights, **Bobby's Arms** on the second floor of the Patpong Carpark on Patpong 2, offers rousing Dixieland jazz.

n all too bvious atpong night cene.

THAI BOXING

The Marquis of Queensbury would definitely not approve but no one in the audience is going to quibble because Thai boxing (*Muay Thai*) is far more exciting than anything he ever devised. It began its life on Ayutthayan battlefields as a lethal martial art. It has not really gone much beyond that except some of its nastier elements have been eliminated. It is a curious combination of balletic grace and murderous ferocity, accompanied and whipped up by the music, making it a thrilling sport to watch.

"Wrestling, judo, throwing, butting, biting, spitting and kicking your opponent while he is down" are forbidden by the rules; but a fighter can use his feet, elbows, legs, knees and shoulders, almost every part of his body to pummel an opponent into submission. The bare feet are the favored weapons. You do not have to watch a fight long before you realize that diminutive size is no measure of a Thai boxer's capacity to inflict injury. A well-delivered kick (often to the groin) can floor an opponent of any size. It is an open secret in martial arts' circles that a good Thai boxer is virtually unstoppable.

Until about 40 years ago, Thai boxers did not wear gloves but bound their hands with hemp, in which ground glass was sometimes embedded for added effect. Fights went on for as long as both fighters could stand up. Now there are five rounds of three minute duration, no ground glass, and if one fighter appears to be injured the referee stops the bout.

Several other elements distinguish Thai boxing from its overseas relative. Boxers wear the familiar gloves and baggy boxing trunks, but also a colored cord around their biceps (usually containing a lucky amulet). Women are not allowed in the ring as they would contaminate it but bouts between women are often staged in separate arenas.

Traditional Thai boxing originated as a lethal martial art in the battlefields of ancient Ayutthaya.

A bout is preceded by an elaborate stylized dance as the boxer honors his teacher and invokes the spirits of the ring to intimidate his opponent. To an outsider, the dances look pretty much the same, but in fact each boxing camp has its own distinctive version and connoisseurs can tell immediately from which camp a fighter originates.

A somewhat mournful-sounding four-piece orchestra composed of a Java pipe, cymbals and a pair of drums accompanies the dance and also the fight itself, spurring the combatants to action. It generally stirs the audience to action also, as gamblers lay down heavy money on their favorites. Indeed, the action outside the ring can be as interesting as that inside the colored ropes.

Thai boxing has so caught the popular imagination that bouts are regularly staged in France and foreign boxers travel to Bangkok to square off against Thai opponents. They usually do not fare very well but there are several promising newcomers. Thai television presents bouts on Saturdays and Sundays and several weekday nights. But if you want to catch all the color and action, not only in the ring but among the gamblers in the stadium audience, you should watch it live in the stadium.

Thai boxing can be seen in Bangkok at Rajadamnern Stadium (Rajadamnern Avenue) and at Lumpini Stadium (Rama 1V Road). Two Thai fighters have held the World Flyweight Championship, and as a result, western-style boxing now rivals the older Thai style. Programs in Bangkok's boxing stadiums now usually include both styles.

Although programs at the Bangkok stadiums start around 5pm, the main fight of Thai boxing takes place around 7pm. Spectators in the cheaper seats are often separated by wire mesh from the more expensive ringside seats, to protect the better-paying (and presumably more sedate) customers from the unruly masses who are known to hurl bottles when angered by a referee's decision.

he feet have
– a well-
imed kick
an floor the
pponent.

ACROSS THE RIVER

Wat Arun, the Temple of Dawn, sitting majestically on the Thonburi bank of the Chao Phya River is, perhaps more than any monument, the one associated with Bangkok. It is reached by taking a ferry from the Tha Tien landing just behind the Grand Palace.

It began its life as a short *prang* next to an old temple called Wat Cheng. In the few moments when he was free from repelling incessant invasions by neighbors on east, north and west, King Taksin established his capital here. He sited his palace nearby and used Wat Cheng as his royal temple. His successor, Rama I, moved the capital across the river in 1782.

In the early years of the 19th century, King Rama II decided to enlarge the temple and raise the height of the central tower from 15 to its present 104m (a base of 37m, a prang of 67m) to make it one of the tallest religious structures in the country. The soft earth defeated his engineers and it was not until the reign of Rama III that a solution was found. Hundreds of *klong* jars were turned upside down and the *prang* was erected on this floating support. It worked and Wat Arun has stood to this day with only minor repairs in 1971 after lightning split a portion of the upper spire.

The great *prang* (rounded spire) represents Mount Meru with its 33 heavens. Its decoration is a mosaic of multicolored Chinese porcelain embedded in cement. The builders ran out of porcelain for this large edifice, compelling Rama III to call upon his subjects to contribute broken crockery to complete the decoration. He was rewarded with thousands of pieces which artisans fashioned into flower petals or used to decorate the costumes of the small gods and mythical figures which ring each tier, guarding it from evil.

You can climb about half-way up the central tower by one of four steep staircases and get a fine view of the temple compound and the river; though anyone suffering from vertigo would be well advised to think twice before doing so. The niches at the foot of each stairway contains images of the Buddha in the four key events in his life: birth, meditation while sheltered by a seven-headed *naga* serpent, preaching to his first five disciples, and at death. The four outer *prangs* hold statues of Phra Phai, god of the wind.

The complex is guarded by mythical giants called *yaksas,* similar to those that protect Wat Phra Kaew. More of the stone statues brought from China are scattered around the courtyard. Some good murals cover the inside of the *bot.*

A short distance upriver, in an open space opposite the Grand Palace, is **Wat Rakang** (the bell *wat*). It has a lovely collection of bells which are rung each morning. Behind it are three wooden houses that once belonged to King Rama I. The *wat's* treasure is its library which sits directly behind the *bot.* Superb murals dating from 1788 depict scenes from the *Ramakien* and the *Traiphum* (Three Worlds), the Buddhist cosmology.

A visit to Wat Arun can be combined with one to the **Royal Barges**, on the north bank of Klong Bangkok Noi, which opens into the river at the Bangkok Noi Railway Station. These splendidly carved boats are used during the rare Royal Barge Procession when the king makes a royal *kathin* at the end of the rainy season, taking robes and gifts to the monks of Wat Arun.

His Majesty rides in the largest of the 51 barges, the magnificent *Sri Supannahong.* Some 44m long, it requires a crew of 54 oarsmen, two steersmen, two officers, one flagman, one rhythm keeper and one singer who chants to the cadence of the oars. Two seven-tiered umbrellas are placed in front of and behind the golden pavilion that shelters the king. The gilded bird's head that forms the prow of the barge represents a *hong*, or sacred swan.

This spectacle is so costly that it is only rarely held, the last occasions being for the Chakri dynasty's Bicentennial celebration in 1982, and the King's 60th birthday in 1987.

The purity of Wat Rakang, framed in the window of the library.

WATERWAYS

For centuries, the river and *klongs* served as the highways of Thailand. In delta land subject to annual flooding when the monsoon rain-swollen river overflowed its banks, it made little sense to build roads which would be washed away. Rivers also provided natural defenses, serving as moats against the attacks of invaders.

Ayutthaya and the Central Valley showed the Thais to be master engineers. They diverted a river to turn Ayutthaya into an island and protect it from its enemies. In Thonburi, engineers dug a canal across a neck of land between the present site of Thammasart University and Wat Arun, thereby eliminating a long roundabout route to the mouth of the Chao Phya. Erosion widened the canal which has now become the main course of the river. The abandoned river loop became Bangkok Noi and Bangkok Yai, the principal canals that run through Thonburi.

When Rama I established Bangkok, he repeated the pattern, digging three concentric canals to turn the capital into an island. Other canals were dug to connect them. Residents lived on houses built atop bamboo rafts that rose with the floodwaters. Travel was by boat; in the 19th century, it was estimated that more than 100,000 boats plied the canals. Little wonder that Bangkok, like Ayutthaya before it, was dubbed the "Venice of the East".

The most extensive rural canal expansion came during the reign of King Chulalongkorn. His engineers mapped the central valley and the monarch gave farm land to whoever would dig the section of canal passing his property. Within a few years, thousands of kilometers cris-crossed the Central Plains. The magnitude of this enormous project can only be appreciated from an airplane. Silver lines run arrow-straight through green fields, the farm houses clustered along their banks.

As Bangkok progressed towards the mid-point of the 20th century it made a hard choice, abandoning boats for cars. Canals were filled in to create roads. Houses were built on solid ground. The result is evident at first glance: congested noisy streets in the hot season, flooded streets in the monsoon season. Some would say it was a bad trade.

Exploring the canals is one of the highlights of a Thailand trip. Zipping along at water level in a *rua hang yao* (long-tailed boat) is also one of the coolest ways to tour. A typical route through Thonburi takes you past houses where mothers bathe babies on the landings, children flip and dive and splash on a hot afternoon, coconut plantations shade you, monks in their orange robes sweep old temple courtyards, orchid nurseries fill the air with color, tiny shops, barbershops and even gasoline stations stand on spindly stilts, waiting for customers.

The *rua hang yao* is a particularly Thai invention. Like the *rot e-tan* the small trucks powered by rototiller or "iron buffalo" engines that move along country roads, the long-tailed boat was born of necessity. In engineering terms, it is simplicity itself. A car or truck engine is mounted on a pivot at the stern of a long, low, narrow boat. A long shaft, or "tail", extends from the back of the boat, the small propeller spinning furiously, churning the water, spitting a rooster tail and propelling the boat at quite rapid speeds. In the narrow canals, the pivot allows the boatman to turn the craft in a very tight radius.

Long-tailed boats run regular routes through the Thonburi canals, leaving hourly from the foot of the Memorial Bridge and the Tha Tien landing for a 10 baht trip into various canals. You can also arrange your own tour. Boats can be hired by the hour at the northern end of the Oriental Hotel terrace, at Tha Chang Wang Luang next to the Grand Palace and at Tha Maharaj, just up the river. Prices vary but should be no more than 300 baht per hour.

A lovely 90-minute route takes you upriver to Klong Bangkok Noi. A short way beyond the Bangkok Noi Railway Station is the Royal Barge Museum. If

Preceding pages, barges pass one of the many beautiful Ayutthayan temples. Below, spick and span tourist launches await passengers a the Shangri-La Hotel.

you ask, the driver will stop for a few minutes so you can tour the museum and take photos. Continue up the canal, turning left into Klong Chak Phra which soon changes its name to Bang Kounsri and eventually to Bangkok Yai which re-enters the river near Wat Arun and returns to your departure point. Stop along the way at a canalside restaurant for a soft drink or an iced coffee.

An alternative route is to travel up the river to a point opposite the Grand Palace. Turn left into Klong Mon, continue to the intersection with Bang Kounsri where you turn left. Shortly after entering Bangkok Yai, you arrive at another intersection on the right whose entrance is marked on the left by an open shop selling coffins and on the right by the enormous Wat Pratunam. Turn right into Klong Ban Don which becomes Klong Wat Sai, site of the original Floating Market. Continue into Dao Khanong and the area known as Suan Phak (vegetable garden). The canal eventually re-enters the river below the Krung Thep Bridge for a journey home up a quiet section of the river.

A more comfortable (and quieter) journey can be made aboard a goods boat with cushioned seats and a roof. Boats can be rented at the same piers as for the long-tailed boats. At certain times of the day or year, the boats may have problems navigating the canals, either being too tall to pass under the bridges at high tide (the river is tidal affected which is why half the time, it flows in reverse) or too low to avoid scraping the canal bed.

One of the most scenic *klongs* on the eastern section of Bangkok is **Klong Saen Sap**, dug to carry troops to Chachoengsao to fight invaders from the east and to join the Bangpakong River for a journey into the sea. The canal begins at Pratunam but the water is so filthy and fetid, you will be holding your nose the entire journey. It is better to start at the Ekamai Bridge on Soi 63 off Sukhumvit Road or at Phrakanong Klong Tan Bridge on Soi 71, also off Sukhumvit Road. The canal is straight and unshaded so is less attractive than the

twisting Thonburi canals but it takes you through some lovely rice country. Take the boat as far as Nong Chok or Min Buri; the journey to Chachoengsao is too far for most people.

Perhaps Bangkok's most famous water attraction is the **Floating Market**. Agencies may try to talk you into going to the Wat Sai market but it is moribund; insist on the **Damnern Saduak Floating Market**. A day-tour normally begins early in the morning with an hour's bus ride to the canal west of the city. There, you board a boat for a ride into the market itself.

Its popularity has grown so much over the years that tourists outnumber the vendors and souvenir stalls outnumber the *sampans* the blue-shirted ladies paddle. Nonetheless, it is an interesting experience with plenty of photo opportunities. The normal tour includes a visit to **Phra Pathom Chedi**, the world's tallest, in Nakhon Pathom and on to lunch and a cultural show at the **Rose Garden**. The show introduces you to Thai boxing, a wedding ceremony, folk dances and other village entertainments. It ends with a demonstration of elephant prowess at moving heavy teak logs and a chance to ride on the back of these pachyderms.

Purists or perseverers can reach the canal on their own by driving across the Memorial Bridge, following Route 4 to Nakhon Pathom. About 25km farther, turn left onto Route 325, the road to Samut Songkram, and arrive at Damnern Saduak.

The Chao Phya River also offers possibilities for exploration. The cheapest and most common form of transport are the *rua duan* or express buses which run between the Krung Thep Bridge south of Bangkok and Nonthaburi, an hour north of the city. The boats make frequent stops along the river and as they run every 20 minutes or so, you can hop off, explore a temple, and board another boat later. The most popular boarding points are at the Oriental Hotel, Tha Chang Wang Luang next to the Grand Palace, and Thewes at the flower market. The fare is based on distance traveled

Paddling down a *klon*

and begins at 5 baht.

Not only does the boat pass the principal monuments and buildings of the city – Wat Arun, Wat Po, Wat Phra Kaew – but the hotels and houses that hug the riverbanks. Once out of the city, the scenery changes to houses on stilts and coconut plantations. The river has an endless array of boats: elephantine rice and sand barges, so heavily laden their gunwales are level with the water; crowded passenger ferries; *sampans*; fishermen; double-decked boats; produce boats and more.

Nonthaburi is a provincial town with a lively market and some superb restaurants. It is famed for its durians, plaster replicas of which hang from lamp standards along the promenade. The last boat leaves for Bangkok at 6.30pm. If you miss it, catch Bus 32 which takes you to Sanam Luang.

Converted rice barges serve as floating restaurants. Evening cruises offer set Thai meals. The *Tassaneya Nava* is the best known of these dinner cruise boats.

The *Oriental Queen* is a relaxing way to see both the river and the old capital at Ayutthaya. The boat leaves the Oriental Hotel pier at 8am, cruising upriver past the principal landmarks of the city. An excellent buffet lunch is served on board after which the boat pulls into Bang Pa-in, the former Summer Palace. A bus transports you further north to tour Ayutthaya, returning you to Bangkok at 5pm. The journey may also be done in reverse, returning to Bangkok by boat. Contact World Travel Service for reservations.

A recent addition to river travel is the *Mekhala* another converted rice barge which leaves from a pier opposite the Oriental Hotel for a cruise upriver. It moors at Wat Kai Tia for the night and the passengers sleep below decks in air-conditioned cabins. The next morning, the boat continues upriver, stopping at Bang Pa-in, and a bus conveys you to the tour of Ayutthaya. As with the *Oriental Queen*, it is possible to do the tour in reverse. Contact Asian Voyages for reservations.

e lush,
rtile
nterland
elds a rich
rvest in
pical fruit
r these
ter-borne
ndors.

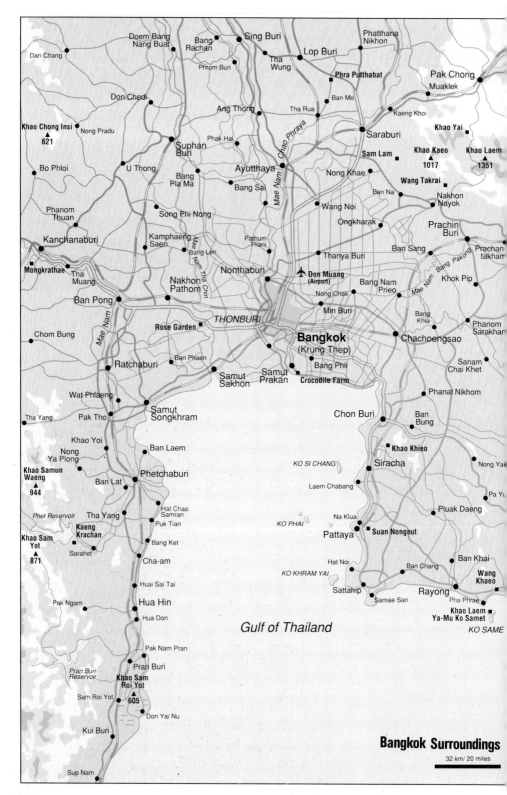

Dan Chang

Doem Bang
Nang Buat

Bang
Rachan

Sing Buri

Phatthana
Nikhon

Lop Buri

Phrom Buri

Tha
Wung

Phra Putthabat

Pak Chong

Muaklek

Ban Mo

Ang Thong

Tha Rua

Kaeng Khoi

Khao Yai

Phak Hai

Saraburi

Khao Chong Insi
▲
621

Nong Pradu

Suphan
Buri

Sam Lam

Khao Kaeo
▲
1017

Khao Laem
▲
1351

Bo Phloi

U Thong

Ayutthaya

Nong Khae

Wang Takrai

Bang
Pla Ma

Bang Sai

Ban Na

Nakhon
Nayok

Phanom
Thuan

Song Phi Nong

Wang Noi

Kanchanaburi

Kamphaeng
Saen

Bang Len

Pathum
Thani

Ongkharak

Prachin
Buri

Prachin
takhan

Ban Sang

Khok Pip

Mongkrathae

Tha
Muang

Nakhon
Pathom

Nonthaburi

Don Muang
(Airport)

Bang Nam
Prieo

Ban Pong

Nong Chok

Bang
Khla

Phanom
Sarakhan

Chom Bung

Rose Garden

THONBURI

Min Buri

Chachoengsao

Ratchaburi

Ban Phaen

Bangkok
(Krung Thep)

Bang Phli

Sanam
Chai Khet

Wat Phlaeng

Samut
Sakhon

Samut
Prakan

Crocodile Farm

Phanat Nikhom

Tha Yang

Pak Tho

Samut
Songkhram

Chon Buri

Ban
Bung

Khao Yoi

Ban Laem

Khao Khieo

Nong
Ya Plong

KO SI CHANG

Siracha

Nong Yai

Khao Samun
Waeng
▲
944

Ban Lat

Phetchaburi

Laem Chabang

Pa Yu

Phet Reservoir

Tha Yang

Hat Chao
Samran

Puk Tian

KO PHAI

Na Klua

Pattaya

Suan Nongnut

Pluak Daeng

Khao Sam
Yot
▲
871

Sarahet

Kaeng
Krachan

Bang Ket

Ban Khai

Cha-am

Hat Noi

Ban Chang

Wang
Khaeo

Pak Ngam

Huai Sai Tai

KO KHRAM YAI

Sattahip

Samae San

Rayong

Pha Phrae

Hua Hin

Hua Don

Gulf of Thailand

Khao Laem
Ya-Mu Ko Samet

KO SAME

Pak Nam Pran

Pran Buri
Reservoir

Pran Buri

Khao Sam
Roi Yot
▲
605

Sam Roi Yot

Don Yai Nu

Kui Buri

Bangkok Surroundings

32 km/ 20 miles

Sup Nam

SOUTHEAST OF BANGKOK

Bangkok is the hub of Thailand, not merely for commerce and government but also for tourism. Though today more and more visitors venture upcountry into the far provinces, the great majority still do their sightseeing in or around the city. For this reason many of the newer attractions, like the Ancient City, the Rose Garden and the Crocodile Farm, have been located within easy driving distance of the capital. They join traditional sights such as Bang Pa-in and the ruins of Ayutthaya which lie on the southern rim of Thailand's Central Plains.

The most popular resorts on the East Coast of the Gulf of Thailand are also within convenient reach of Bangkok for a weekend outing. Excellent highways now lead out of Bangkok in all directions, and a trip that used to take three or four hours, to Ayutthaya, for example, can now be made in just over an hour, assuming the roads are not clogged with traffic. We profile here the main attractions near Bangkok, each of which can be visited in a day's round trip from the capital. The places of interest are covered in a counterclockwise spiral, starting southeast of the city.

The **Crocodile Farm** is located in Samut Prakarn Province, near the river-mouth town of Paknam, half an hour's drive (30km) southeast of Bangkok on the old Sukhumvit Highway (Route 3). A brochure describes it as "a happy marriage between wildlife conservation and commercial enterprise," and while the crocodiles that get turned into ladies' handbags might argue about the first part, no one can deny the second.

Started in the 1960s with about 10,000 baht (less than US$500), the owner now has three farms (two in the Northeast) worth 100 million baht (US$4.4 million). At present the Samut Prakarn farm has about 30,000 fresh- and salt-water Siamese Crocodiles, as well as some South American caimans and Nile River

crocodiles. They are hatched in incubation cells and raised in tanks. The young must be protected by netting from mosquitoes which can blind them by biting their eyes.

The highlight of a visit to the farm is a show in which handlers enter a pond teeming with crocodiles and toss them about rather roughly. While this sounds dangerous in print, the lethargic, leathery beasts are more likely to bite less because of innate viciousness than because their quiet snooze in the hot sun has been interrupted.

The odd fact is that the owners have succeeded in preserving the animal; all the wild specimens have been hunted to extinction. After the crocodiles are skinned, incidentally, their meat is sold to restaurants in Samut Prakarn and Bangkok, where diners claim it tastes like frog. The farm also has a zoo and amusement park with rides.

Also in Samut Prakarn, a few kilometers from the Crocodile Farm, is the **Ancient City** which bills itself as "the world's largest outdoor museum." The brainchild of a Bangkok millionaire with a passion for Thai art and history, it took around three years to construct. In what used to be 80 hectares of rice fields, designers sketched an area roughly the shape of a map of Thailand and placed the individual attractions as close to their real sites as possible.

There are replicas (some full size, others one-third the size of the originals) of famous monuments and temples from all parts of the kingdom. Some are reconstructions of buildings that no longer exist, like the Grand Palace and Royal Chapel of Ayutthaya, and some are copies of real places like the huge temple of Khao Phra Viharn on the Thai-Cambodian border, which was awarded to Cambodia by the World Court some years ago after a long dispute over its ownership. Experts from the National Museum worked as consultants to ensure historical accuracy of the reproductions. At present there are more than 60 monuments, covering 15 centuries of Thai history.

In addition to the monuments, the Ancient City also has a model Thai village, in which you can see artisans at work on various native handicrafts, such as lacquerware, ceramics and paper umbrellas. It has its own version of the floating market, picturesquely staged for photographers; assorted shops for buying souvenirs; and a Thai restaurant. Several times, the king of Thailand has taken royal visitors around the site. Among the first, in 1972, were Queen Elizabeth and Prince Philip.

For those with time, Paknam is a bustling fishing town with an interesting market along its docks. Cross the river by ferry to the famous **Wat Phra Chedi Klang Nam** which, contrary to its name (the *chedi* in the middle of the river) is now on solid land, the result of the river shifting its course. Thai kings used to stop at this temple on their way in and out of the country on state visits, praying for success in their journeys or thanks on their return.

You can also take a bus from the temple into **Phrapadaeng**. The town celebrates Songkran a week later and much more boisterously than Bangkok.

One of the many replicas on display in Ancient City

NORTHEAST OF BANGKOK

Located near enough to Bangkok for a comfortably paced day trip, the eastern province of **Nakhon Nayok** offers waterfalls and a pretty park. The most scenic route to this province is Road 305, which branches off Route 1 just north of Rangsit, 30km north of Bangkok. A wide road runs northeast along a lovely canal, passing rice fields and small rivers to reach Nakhon Nayok, about 140km from the capital.

From the town, Road 33 heads northwest and then, within a few kilometers, another second road leads off to the right towards two waterfalls and Wang Takrai Park. After 11km you reach an intersection: straight ahead is **Salika Waterfall**. Near the parking lot are pleasant outdoor restaurants and stalls selling fruits and drinks. The waterfall itself is impressive around the end of the rainy season (September to November).

Left of the intersection is **Wang Takrai Park**. On the way is the **Temple of Chao Pau Khun Dan**, named after one of King Naresuan's advisers whose spirit is believed to protect the area. Prince Chumbhot (of Suan Pakkad Palace in Bangkok) established the 80-hectare Wang Takrai Park in the 1950s; a statue of him stands on the opposite bank of the small river flowing through the park. His wife, Princess Chumbhot, planted many varieties of flowers and trees, including some imported species. Cultivated gardens sit among tall trees that line both banks of the main stream flowing through the 2-km-long park. Bungalows are available for rent.

Before returning to Bangkok, dine at the park restaurant. Just outside the park entrance, the road on the left crosses a river and continues 5km to **Nang Rong Waterfall**, an inviting three-tier cascade situated in a steep valley. Here are open-air restaurants and fruit stalls.

Khao Yai National Park, the nearest hill resort to Bangkok, lies 205km north of the capital, and covers 2,000sq km.

This cool retreat boasts bungalows, motels, restaurants, an 18-hole golf course, and many nature trails and roads. You can drive to Khao Yai ("Big Mountain") in about three to four hours from Bangkok via one of two routes.

The long route takes you up Route 1. Just before entering Saraburi, about 107km from the capital, turn right onto the Friendship Highway (Route 2) and go 58km. Turn right again on to Dhanarajata Road and, about 24km later, arrive at the foot of the park. The road climbs and twists among the hills for 16km until reaching **Nong Khing Village**. Dine at the Khao Yai Restaurant and check out the accommodations.

The second route requires driving to Nakhon Nayok via the roads described above. About 3km beyond Nakhon Nayok, a road leads to the left for about 50km along a twisting road to the park headquarters. Accommodations can be booked through the T.A.T. office in Bangkok. If you camp in the park, notify officials as to your campsite and take mosquito nets and repellent. If you want a quick view of the park, the State Railways of Thailand offers a day trip each Saturday at reasonable rates.

Khao Yai's highest peaks lie on the east along a land form known as the Korat Plateau. Khao Laem is 1,351m high and Khao Kaeo, 1,017m. Evergreen and deciduous trees, palms and bamboo provide ample greenery throughout the park. At night winter temperatures may drop to below 15°C. Monkeys, gibbons and langurs are commonly seen. Wild, but not considered dangerous, elephants, bears, gaurs, tigers, boars and deer also roam the huge, protected reserve. After dark, the park conducts "hunts" in large trucks, shining spotlights on night-feeding animals like deer.

Many trails snake through the park, taking one to waterfalls like Haew Sawat, and grassy areas where one may see elephants roaming. In several clearings, park officials have erected observation towers; sit there at sunset and watch the animals come out to browse. Everywhere in Khao Yai, orchids and other flowers bloom.

Monkey business in Khao Yai National park.

NORTH OF BANGKOK

Were one to know nothing of the importance and fabulous history of **Ayutthaya** one would nonetheless be impressed by the beauty and grandeur of this city built by 33 Ayutthayan kings over a period of 400 years. Founded around 1350, by the 1600s, Ayutthaya was one of the richest cities in Asia, boasting a population of one million, greater than that of contemporary London. Merchants came from Portugal, England, France, Holland and China to trade in its markets. Ayutthayan kings engaged Japanese soldiers and Persian men-at-arms to serve in their retinues. Europeans wrote awed accounts of the fabulous wealth of the courts and of 2,000 spires clad in gold. By any standards, Ayutthaya was one of the fabled cities of the Orient.

It seems odd, then, that it could have suffered a destruction so complete that it was never rebuilt. Burmese armies had been pounding on its doors for centuries, occupying it for a period in the 16th century before Siamese kings expelled them and re-asserted their independence. In 1767, however, the Burmese triumphed. In a rampage, they burned and looted, destroying most of the city's monuments, and enslaving, killing, or scattering the population. Within a year, Ayutthaya was a ghost town with fewer than 10,000 inhabitants. Even after Taksin defeated the Burmese garrison force, he was forced to concede that Ayutthaya was beyond repair; a fabled city was left to crumble to dust. Only 200 years later would the Fine Arts Department begin to restore it to its former grandeur. A town would continue to thrive on the man-made island but far from the ruins which had ruled it in its glory days.

From the ruins, it is possible to gain a clear idea of the genius of the kings who built this great city. Located 85km north of Bangkok, Ayutthaya was laid out at the junction of three rivers; engineers had only to cut a canal across the loop of

Wat Phra Ram – dreaming of fame and glory of long ago. Built in 1369, it is one of the oldest *wats* in Ayutthaya.

the Chao Phya to create an island. Canals were also etched across the city to serve as streets; palaces and temples were erected.

Today, the ruins stand by themselves on the western half of the island. Modern Ayutthaya is a bustling commercial town concentrated in the northeast corner of the island not far from the **Pridi Damrong Bridge** over which one crosses to enter the city. The majority of Ayutthaya's visitors see it on a day trip from Bangkok.

Should you feel Ayutthaya's long history requires more time to absorb, there is a modern hotel, the U-thong Inn, on the main highway as well as several clean, inexpensive Chinese hotels across from the Chandrakasem Palace. There are restaurants and open-air food stalls in the market area and some superb floating restaurants along the eastern edge of town, just below the Pridi Damrong Bridge.

To appreciate the city as 17th-century visitors did, travel up the Chao Phya River from Bangkok. The Oriental Queen and Mekhala (see "Bangkok Water Tours") make a pleasant voyage of the journey. Alternatively, there are convenient bus and train connections from Bangkok, both taking 1œ hours.

Once in Ayutthaya a river tour around the island in a long-tailed boat can be arranged on the landing stage close to Chandrakasem Palace provided the tide is not receding. This provides an excellent introduction to the ruined city; it is also the only way to reach some of the more isolated sites on the mainland side of the river. A boat hired for about an hour should cost no more than 100 to 150 baht.

Start your boat tour close to the junction of the Nam Pasak and Chao Phya rivers, passing the imposing **Wat Phanan Choeng**. Established 26 years prior to Ayutthaya's foundation in 1350, the temple houses a huge seated Buddha, so tightly crowded against the roof that he appears to be holding it up. Wat Phanan Choeng was a favorite with Chinese traders who prayed there before setting out on long voyages; it still has an

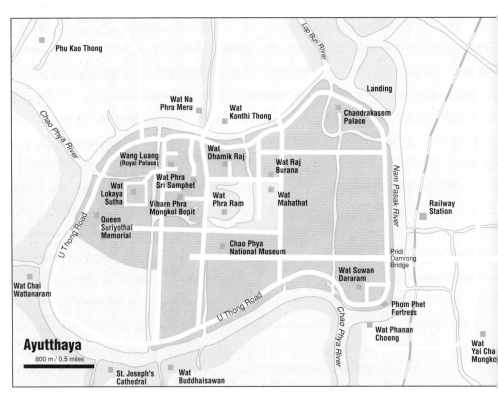

Ayutthaya
800 m / 0,5 miles

unmistakably Chinese atmosphere.

Ayutthaya was at one time surrounded by stout walls, only portions of which remain. One of the best-preserved sections is at **Phom Phet**, across the river from Wat Phanan Choeng. Vendors sell ceramics they claim were dropped overboard by 17th-century sailors and only recently brought to the surface. Given the volume of the wares and length of time they have been on sale, the sailors must have been extremely butterfingered.

Upstream from Wat Phanan Choeng, the recently-restored **Wat Buddhaisawan** stands serenely on the riverbank. It is seldom visited so is quiet; its landing is an excellent place to enjoy the tranquillity of the river in the evenings. Farther upstream, the Catholic **Cathedral of St Joseph** is a reminder of the large European population that lived in the city at its prime.

Where the river bends to the north, stands one of Ayutthaya's most eloquently romantic ruins, **Wat Chai Wattanaram**. Perched high on a pedestal in front of the ruins, a Buddha keeps solitary watch. The stately *prang* with its surrounding *chedis* and rows of headless Buddhas make a fine contrast to the restored **Queen Suriyothai Chedi** on the city side of the river. The valiant Ayutthaya queen, dressed as a man, rode into battle, her elephant beside that of her husband. When she saw him attacked by a Burmese prince, she moved between them with her elephant and received the lance blow intended for her husband.

Chandrakasem Palace, known as the Palace of the Front, was originally constructed outside the city walls close to the junction of the old rivers and the new canal. King Naresuen built it as a defensive bastion while he was engaged in wars against his northern rival, Chiang Mai. In 1767, the Burmese destroyed the palace but King Mongkut rebuilt it. Now housing a small museum, the palace looks out on the noisiest part of the modern town.

The old royal palace, **Wang Luang**, was razed by the Burmese. The bricks were later removed to Bangkok to build

its defensive walls so only remnants of the foundations survive to mark the site. Close by stands the three stately *chedis* of **Wat Phra Sri Sanphet**, which honor three 15th-century kings. The identical *chedis* have been restored and stand in regal contrast to the surrounding ruins.

For two centuries after Ayutthaya's fall, a huge bronze Buddha sat unsheltered near Wat Phra Sri Sanphet. Its flame of knowledge and one of his arms had been broken when the roof, set afire by the Burmese, collapsed. Thirty years ago, a new building, the **Viharn Phra Mongkol Bophit** was built around the restored statue. With a large car park and rows of souvenir stalls facing it, this is often used as a starting point for Ayutthaya tours.

Across the road to the east, **Wat Phra Ram** is one of Ayutthaya's oldest temples. Built in 1369 by the son of Ayutthaya's founder, it has been completely restored twice. Elephant gates punctuate the old walls, and the central terrace is dominated by a crumbling *prang* to which clings a gallery of stucco *nagas*, *garudas* and statues of the Buddha. The reflection of Wat Phra Ram's *prang* shimmers in the pool that surrounds the complex. Once a marshy swamp, the pool was dug to provide landfill for the temple's foundations.

Two of Ayutthaya's finest temples stand side by side across the lake from Wat Phra Ram. Built by the seventh king of Ayutthaya as a memorial to his brothers, **Wat Rajburana** dominates its surroundings. Excavations during its restoration in 1958 revealed a crypt containing gold jewelry, Buddha images and other art objects, among them a charming, intricately-decorated elephant. These treasures are now kept in the **Chao Sam Phya Museum** to the south. Other relics can be seen in Ayutthaya's fine **Chao Phya Museum.**

At the crossroads stand the ruins of two *chedis*. They contain the ashes of the royal brothers, Princes Ai and Yo who killed each other in an elephant-back duel to decide which one would rule the kingdom.

Across the road, **Wat Mahathat** is one of the most beautiful temple complexes in Ayutthaya. Its glory is its huge *prang* which originally stood 46m high. The *prang* later collapsed but was rebuilt 4m higher. Stone Buddha faces, each a meter-tall, stand silently around the ruins. These, together with the restored *chedis* that ring the *prang*, combine to make this one of the most impressive sites in Ayutthaya. Next door, the Fine Arts Department has built a model of how it thinks the royal city once looked.

Wat Suwan Dararam, constructed near the close of the Ayutthaya period, has been beautifully restored. The foundations of the *bot* dip in the center in emulation of the graceful deck line of a boat. This typical Ayutthayan decoration is meant to suggest a boat that carries pious Buddhists to salvation. Delicately carved columns support the roof, and the interior walls are decorated with brilliantly colored frescoes. Still used as a temple, the *wat* seems embraced in a magical aura in the early evening as the monks chant their prayers.

Across the river from the old palace stands another restored temple, **Wat Na Phra Meru**. Here, a large stone Buddha is seated in the "European fashion" on a throne, a sharp contrast to the yoga position of most seated Buddhas. Found in the ruins of Wat Mahathat, the statue is believed to be one of five that originally sat in a recently-unearthed Dvaravati-period complex in Nakhon Pathom. The *bot* contains an Ayutthaya-style seated Buddha on the altar. Across a bridge from Wat Na Phra Meru are the ruins of **Wat Konthi Thong.**

A winding road from Queen Suriyothai's *chedi* leads to **Wat Lokaya Sutha**. Little remains here, apart from a massive reclining Buddha. A scattering of food stalls stand close by, their owners gazing back with equal equanimity.

East of the roundabout on the road from Bangkok is **Wat Yai Chai Mongkol** with its huge *chedi*. In single-handed combat on elephant-back, King Naresuan slew the crown prince of Burma in 1592. The *chedi*, built to match the Phu Khao Thong Pagoda just north

Wat Rajburana, built by the seventh king of Ayutthaya, is one of the finest temple in the ancien city.

of Ayutthaya, was erected in celebration of the victory. Contemporary Buddha statues line the courtyard.

North of Ayutthaya the **Chedi Phu Khao Thong**, better known as the **Golden Mount Chedi**, stands alone amidst the rice fields, its upper terraces commanding a panoramic view of the countryside. Built by the Burmese after their earlier and less destructive conquest in 1569, it was later remodeled by the Siamese in their own style. To mark 2,500 years of Buddhism in 1957, a 2,500-gram gold ball was mounted on top of the *chedi* spire.

Heading the opposite direction from the Golden Mount, the road runs to the only **Elephant Kraal** left in Thailand. This kraal is a reminder of the days when elephants were not only caught and trained to work in the jungles, but were also an essential requisite for a strong army. Standing at the edge of the stockade with its huge teak columns, one can imagine the thunder of the mighty beasts that helped raise Ayutthaya to its peak. After years of decay, the kraal has recently been rebuilt.

Bang Pa-in, a charming collection of palaces and pavilions once used by the kings of Thailand as a summer retreat, lies a short distance downriver from the ruins of Ayutthaya. It can be reached by water on a tour boat like the Oriental Queen or by road in about an hour from Bangkok. The rulers of Ayutthaya used Bang Pa-in in the hot season as long ago as the 17th century, but the buildings one sees today date from the late 19th- and early 20th-century reigns of Rama V and Rama VI, who used to come up from Bangkok.

On the lake, the pretty palace, a mixture of Italian and Victorian styles built by Rama V, is closed to the public but visitors can tour an ornate Chinese-style palace in which the king stayed during visits. A Thai-style pavilion called the **Aisawan Tippaya Asna** in the middle of the lake as one enters the grounds, is regarded as one of the finest examples of Thai architecture.

The former summer capital of Siam, **Lopburi** lies 155km north of Bang-

scene from ne of the last eat ephant ints at the aal of yutthaya, notographed 1895.

kok. You can drive to Lopburi from Bangkok in less than four hours on a pleasant journey that takes you through the fertile rice bowl of Thailand. Just 10km north of Ayutthaya, the hills of the Korat Plateau appear on the horizon, the first break in the flatness of the Central Plains.

Artifacts of the Neolithic and Bronze ages have been found in quantity in Lop Buri, testifying to the great antiquity of the city. In the Dvaravati Period (6th to 11th centuries) it was a major religious center thought to have attracted savants from around the region. At the height of the Angkorian Empire (11th and 12th centuries), it was a provincial capital. Then came the Thais, who put their imprint on most of the old buildings which now survive.

Tentative contacts with Dutch and Portuguese explorers came in the 16th century, but it was not until the mid 1600s that Ayutthaya became a bustling international city with missionaries from Italy and Spain and traders from Britain, Indonesia and China. Some French architects even ventured to Lop Buri, where King Narai retreated each summer to escape Ayutthaya's heat and humidity.

Narai was one of the most luckless kings of the Ayutthaya period. The last scenes of his life were played out in Lopburi in the **Suttha Sawan Pavilion**. In May 1688, as he lay mortally ill in this pavilion, a regimental commander, Phra Phetracha, seized the throne. According to one tradition, the dying king was attended by only ten royal pages who remained loyal to him.

Realizing that the rebels might never allow them to leave the palace alive, the king called in a Buddhist abbot to ordain the pages as monks, so that the saffron robe of Buddhism would guarantee their safety. In return, he offered the Suttha Sawan Pavilion to the monkhood as a temple. The truth of this tradition is attested by the actions of a later king, Mongkut, who, when he came to reoccupy the Lopburi palace in the 19th century, had to offer other lands to the Buddhist authorities in exchange for the palace and its grounds.

The grounds of the **Lopburi Palace** (Narai Raja Niwes Palace) are enclosed by massive walls which still dominate the center of the modern town. The inner side of the walls flanking the gates are honeycombed with hundreds of leaf-shaped niches meant to contain small lamps fed by coconut oil. In the heyday of the palace, they were lighted on state and religious occasions.

Of King Narai's buildings, the only one which has substantially survived is the **Dusit Maha Prasat Hall**. This was built for the audience granted by the king in 1685 to Chevalier de Chaumont, ambassador of Louis XIV. It is recorded that the walls of the front structure were paneled with mirrors given by the French king. Holes for the mirrors can still be seen.

Another surviving building of the Narai period is the **Chantra Paisan Pavilion**, also in the palace grounds. Now part of the Fine Arts Museum, it was the first structure built by King Narai, and was later restored by King Mongkut. The wooden decorations of the roof are not in good proportions, somewhat spoiling the overall effect, but the classic Ayutthaya-period curve of the base is good. The sagging line of the multiple roofs is also classical and designed for elegance.

Adjoining the Chantra Paisan Pavilion is the **Phiman Mongkut Pavilion**, a three-storied mansion in the colonial style built in the mid-19th century by King Mongkut. The immensely thick walls and high ceilings show how the summer heat was averted most effectively before air-conditioning arrived. The mansion, small but full of character, and also part of the Fine Arts Museum, displays a mixture of bronze statues, Chinese and Sukhothai porcelain, coins, Buddhist fans and shadow play puppets. Some of the pieces, particularly the Ayutthaya bronze heads and Bencharong porcelain, are extremely fine. On the top floor are displayed some of King Mongkut's personal effects. They reveal the character of this remarkable man who, though one of Siam's "Lords of Life," led a surprisingly spartan existence.

Other buildings in the palace complex which should be visited are the eight bijou houses behind the museum. In King Mongkut's time they accommodated the court ladies, their children and servants. One of the buildings has now been converted into a **Farmer's Museum**, which displays the traditional implements of Thai agriculture.

King Narai had a Greek adviser, Constantine Phaulkon, whom the king ennobled with the title of *Chao Phya Vijayendra* ("The Noble Victorious Lord"). Though not officially the foreign minister, it was Phaulkon who managed Siam's relations with the European powers. However, his ambition also led him to meddle in domestic matters, making him most unpopular with the Buddhist clergy and also with officials of King Narai's government. When the king lay dying in his pavilion, Phra Phetracha seized power and had Phaulkon beheaded.

The remains of a grand palace in Lop Buri, said to have belonged to Phaulkon, rival those of the royal palace.

Located just north of Narai's residence, the buildings show traces of European influence, straight-sided walls and pedimental decorations over Western-style windows. The estate is kept locked to prevent vandalism.

Of particular interest in Lop Buri are two important relics of the Khmer (Cambodian) and pre-Khmer periods. One, located just west of the railroad and north of the town's main road, is a 13th-century laterite block shrine with three spires which give it its Thai name of **Phra Prang Sam Yod** ("Sacred Three Spires").

Restored in 1926 by the Fine Arts Department, the stone carvings on the towers and the door columns are particularly fine. It has been taken over by monkeys which scamper over it and the nearby bodhi tree shrine. The second *prang* is the Hindu Spire (**Prang Khaek**) in the center of the town, also of great antiquity. A group of three laterite spires, it was probably built during the 11th century and restored by King Narai in the 17th century.

Phaulkon's palace in Lop Buri – distinctively European in style.

WEST OF BANGKOK

Located on the Tachin River, less than an hour's drive from Bangkok, the **Rose Garden** is the brainchild of a former lord mayor of the capital. The garden, known as *Suan Sam Phran* in Thai, lies 32km west of the capital on Route 4, the road to famous Nakhon Pathom. It covers a large area of well landscaped gardens that contain roses and orchids and includes accommodations, restaurants and a golf course. Its premier attraction is the daily Thai Cultural Show it presents.

In a large arena, beautifully-costumed Thai actors demonstrate folk dances, Thai boxing, a wedding ceremony, cock fighting and other entertainments of rural villages. After the show, guests gather outside to watch elephants move huge teak logs as they would in the forests of the North. The elephants then trade cargoes, carrying tourists around the compound for a small fee.

One sport demonstrated is *takraw* which you may see being played in parks and temple courtyards throughout Thailand. There are two forms: basket and net. In the former, a basket is suspended about 5m off the ground. A team, normally of six men, stands in a circle below it. They kick a small rattan ball back and forth, using their feet, knees, elbows and heads – everything except their hands. After several of these passes, they propel the ball upwards, trying to place it in the basket. After a set time period during which the players try to score as many baskets as they can, it is the turn of the opposing team. *Takraw* is a graceful game requiring great agility; a match proceeds languidly but there are many special or showy moves which keep it interesting.

In the second form, two teams of three men stand either side of a net stretched head height as in badminton. A server starts each point attempt by lobbing the ball over the net. Back and forth it goes, the loser being the team that allows the ball to touch the ground.

Many consider this the more exciting type as there are a lot of flashy moves including doing a somersault kick to send the ball across the net at great speed. Semi-professional *takraw* teams put on performances at temple fairs and parties. If you are in Bangkok during the kite-fighting season, you can see the teams in action at the Rajdamnern Avenue every weekday afternoon.

Just 54km west of Bangkok beyond the Rose Garden on Route 4 is the town of **Nakhon Pathom**. As you drive towards town a colossal landmark rises from the flat countryside ahead of you. Standing 127m high, **Phra Pathom Chedi** is the tallest Buddhist monument in the world.

The original Phra Pathom Chedi was small and was built more than a thousand years ago by the Mon empire whose culture flourished in Burma and Thailand. They established Nakhon Pathom as a religious center. In 1057, King Anawrahta of Burma besieged the town, leaving it in ruins for the next hundred years.

It was not until King Mongkut visited the old *chedi* and was impressed by its significance as the oldest Buddhist monument in Thailand, that restoration of the temple began in 1853. The original structure was in such a state of collapse that repair proved impossible, and a new *chedi* was built to cover the old one. Unfortunately, this too collapsed in a rainstorm, and eventually the present structure was completed by King Chulalongkorn.

Set in a huge square park, the massive *chedi* rests upon a circular terrace accented with trees connected with the Buddha's life. In November each year, a huge fair in the temple grounds attracts crowds from far and near.

In former times, a royal visit to Nakhon Pathom was more than a day's journey, so it is not surprising that a number of palaces and residences were built there. **Sanam Chand Palace** has a fine *sala*, a meeting pavilion now used for government offices, and a building in a most unusual Thai interpretation of English Tudor architec-

ıra Pathom
ıedi – a
ılossal
ndmark in
akhon
athom.

ture, used appropriately as a setting for Shakespearean drama. In front of this building stands a statue of Yaleh, the pet dog of King Rama VI. The fierce dog, unpopular with the court, was poisoned by the king's attendants. Even as a statue, Yaleh looks insufferable.

A good way to approach the port of Samut Sakhon, for a view of Thailand's coastal life, is by the branch railway connecting it with Thonburi, Bangkok's sister city. The line, called the Mae Klong Railway, runs at a loss, but has been reprieved from extinction because of its usefulness to the population of the three provinces west of Bangkok.

For a few baht, you can take the "express" which leaves approximately every hour, from Wong Wien Yai station in Thonburi. The express train moves at a leisurely pace. The 40-minute journey passes first through the suburbs, then through thriving vegetable gardens, groves of coconut and areca palms and rice fields.

A busy fishing port, **Samut Sakhon** (also called Mahachai) lies at the meeting of the Tachin River, the Mahachai Canal and the Gulf of Thailand. The main landing stage on the riverbank has a clock tower and a restaurant which serves excellent seafood, including grilled crab with vegetables. Nearby at the main **Fish Market** fishermen unload hauls of fish, crabs, squids and prawns from their boats.

At the fish market pier, you can hire a boat for an 80-baht round trip to Samut Sakhon's principal temple, **Wat Chom Long**, at the mouth of the Tachin River. Most of the buildings are modern except for an old *viharn* immediately to the right of the temple's river landing. The *viharn* dates back about a century. The extensive grounds overlooking the water are charmingly laid out with shrubs and flowering trees. There is also a bronze statue of King Chulalongkorn commemorating his visit to the temple. His homburg hat does not in the least detract from his immense dignity.

From Samut Sakhon, cross the river to the railway station on the opposite

Fishing boats anchored at the harbor in Samut Songkhram.

ver Kwai
agedy re-
nacted at
e light and
und show.

side. Here, you can board a second train for another 45 minutes to **Samut Song-khram** on the banks of the Meklong River. The journey takes you through broad salt flats with their picturesque windmills revolving slowly in the sea breezes. Samut Songkhram is another pretty fishing town; wandering its wharf is an olfactory and a visual experience. Return to Bangkok along the same rail route or hire a long-tailed boat for a trip up the Meklong River to Rajburi.

An odd-looking railway bridge crosses the Meklong River a few kilometers from **Kanchanaburi**. The bridge leaves the bank over a series of elliptical spans; in the center of the river the spans become awkwardly rectangular, without apparent reason, and then revert to their elliptical form before disappearing into the vegetation on the other side.

Over the bridge flows a constant stream of pedestrians taking vegetables home from the market or just out for a walk. Occasionally a motorcycle buzzes across the bridge skirting between the railway tracks. When the river's other name is mentioned the mystery behind the strange pattern of spans becomes clear.

The Meklong River, also known as the Kwai Yai (Large Branch) is spanned by the infamous **Bridge on the River Kwai**. Towards the end of World War II, the central spans were knocked out by Allied bombers and which were later rebuilt with those incongruous angular replacements.

Kanchanaburi town, in the province of the same name, is about 122km northwest of Bangkok, past Nakhon Pathom, and not far from the Thai border with Burma. It was here that the Japanese forced Allied prisoners of war to construct 263km of rail leading to the Three Pagodas Pass at the Burmese border.

It is estimated that 100,000 impressed Asian laborers as well as 16,000 Allied prisoners of war lost their lives due to beatings, starvation, disease and exhaustion when constructing the railroad. In Kanchanaburi, endless rows of war

graves mark the resting places of 6,982 of those Allied soldiers.

There are two cemeteries in Kanchanaburi, the larger is on the main road nearly opposite the railway station; the second, Chungkai, is across the river on the banks of the Kwai Noi. Maintained by an Allied foundation, they hold the remains of Dutch, Australian, British, Danish, New Zealand and other Allied prisoners of war. American war dead were removed to the Arlington cemetery in Washington D.C.

An appreciation of the enormous obstacles the prisoners faced in their struggle to survive is provided by the **Jeath Museum** near the end of Lak Muang Road. Established in 1977 by the abbot of Wat Chaichumpol next door, the museum was constructed like the bamboo huts in which the war prisoners lived.

Utensils, paintings, writings and other objects donated by prisoners who survived convey some of the horror of their animal-like existence. A walk through is a sobering experience.

Although the Bridge on the River Kwai owes much of its fame to the novel by Pierre Boulle and to the film, it is worthwhile visiting from an historical point of view. It can be reached by boat or *samlor* from Kanchanaburi. Agencies can arrange tours or you can simply hire a car for the 5km journey; the train to Nam Tok stops briefly at the bridge for passengers to disembark.

With the eruption of an entire town of souvenir shops, the bridge has lost some of its mystery but standing on it one can appreciate the terrible sacrifices its construction entailed. Walk across it. The pedestrian walkway over the bridge is not as unsafe as it looks, niches between the spans provide an escape in case a train happens along.

A steam locomotive used shortly after the war is displayed beside the tiny Kwai Bridge station platform, along with an ingenious Japanese supply truck that could run on road or rails. Up and downstream from the bridge are floating restaurants and hotels on the banks of what, in spite of

Huts afloat on the River Kwai.

its grisly history, is an attractive river. Bamboo rafts can be rented in Kanchanaburi, towed here by tugboats with lunch served on board.

The entire railway was bought by the Thai government from the Allies for 50 million baht. It was a "pig in a poke" purchase, as the British had already dismantled several kilometers of track at the Burmese border, and the whole line was in need of considerable repair. The prisoners had done their utmost to make the worst possible job of constructing the railway. Quite apart from frequent bombings, the wooden supports were often rotting even before they were put in place.

Shortly before the end of the war, British bombers from Ceylon succeeded in destroying the fourth, fifth and sixth spans of the bridge. As war reparations, the Japanese replaced these three spans with two larger ones, the "Made in Japan" signs on the newer girders strike an ironic note.

Today, the quiet little railway runs peacefully from Kanchanaburi to the terminus at Nam Tok, a 50km-journey that takes about one-and-a-half hours. It carries you across one of the ricketiest bridges in the world; the wooden pillars and sleepers creak and groan as the train moves slowly across them. The construction of numerous "flotels" along the banks has robbed the river of some of its wilderness allure but the journey is still worthwhile.

The Asian Highway now runs from Kanchanaburi to the border at Three Pagodas Pass, a distance of 241km. Sporadic fighting between the Burmese Army and ethnic groups has made the site unsafe to visit but there are many other interesting stops along the way. The river and its many branches are dotted with beautiful waterfalls. **Erawan Falls**, or "Elephant Falls," about 67km north of Kanchanaburi is one such magnificent sight.

Near Nam Tok, at the end of the railway line, are the **Khao Phang Falls** where the water trips down a series of limestone steps. From here you can take a three-hour boat ride to the **Sai Yok Falls** where the water plunges directly into the river. On the way to Sai Yok, the river passes the **Cave of Tham Kung** which contains impressive stalactites and stalagmites.

Nearly the entire length of the river is now dappled with resorts, most of them perched on bamboo rafts. These resorts provide an unusual form of accommodation and a starting point to explore Mon and Karen villages, waterfalls, caves and bamboo forests that lie either side of the river. Stays can be booked at Bangkok reservation offices (see Travel Tips).

The State Railways of Thailand offers an all-day trip from Bangkok's Hualampong Station to the Nakhon Pathom chedi, the Bridge, the POW cemetery, Khao Phang waterfalls, and travels a short stretch of the Death Railway to its terminus at Nam Tok. Saturdays, Sundays, holidays; 60 baht.

One fortunate outcome of railway construction was the discovery by a Dutch prisoner of what he thought to be evidence of a Neolithic site. Not until 1961 did a Thai-Danish archaeological search party confirm the find and open a whole new page of Thai pre-history. A small museum close to the original excavations has many of the finds on exhibition, including a skeleton from one of the burial sites.

The bulk of the finds from this first Neolithic site found in this part of Southeast Asia is on display in the National Museum in Bangkok. Sugar cane has long overgrown the archaeological site, but university students still conduct diggings from time to time. The dusty little town of Ban Keo near the site, and a couple of kilometers walk from the small museum, lies 30km north of Kanchanaburi and can be reached by bus or train from the provincial town.

Long before it assumed its strategic role in the last war, Kanchanaburi had been a continual battlefield between the warring Siamese and Burmese; evidence of old battlements can still be seen. North of Ban Keo, before the station of Wang Po, are the ruins of the Khmer town of **Muang Sing**, City of the Lion.

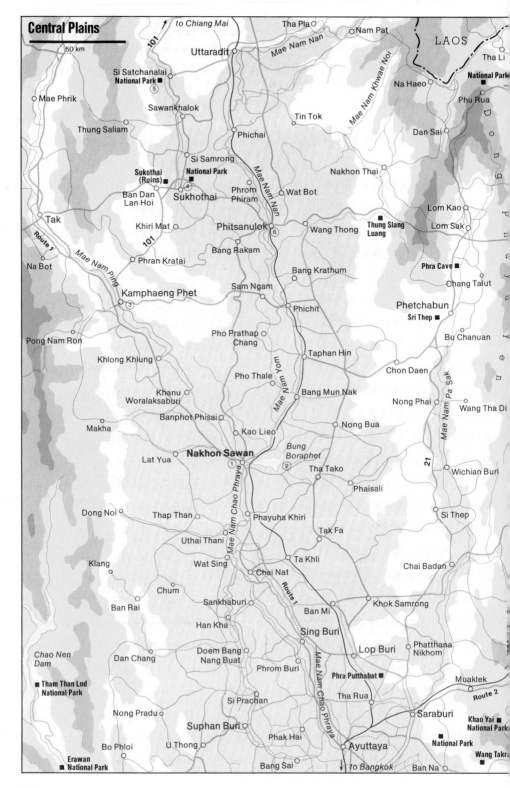

Central Plains

50 km

to Chiang Mai

LAOS

Tha Pla
Nam Pat
Tha Li
Uttaradit
Mae Nam Nan
National Park
Si Satchanalai
National Park (5)
Na Haeo
Phu Rua
Mae Phrik
Sawankhalok
Tin Tok
Dan Sai
Thung Saliam
Phichai
Nakhon Thai
Si Samrong
Lom Kao
Sukothai (Ruins)
National Park (4)
Phrom Phiram
Wat Bot
Lom Sak
Ban Dan Lan Hoi
Sukhothai
Thung Slang Luang
Tak
Khiri Mat
Phitsanulok (6)
Wang Thong
Na Bot
Bang Rakam
Bang Krathum
Phra Cave
Route 1
Phran Kratai
Chang Talut
Mae Nam Ping
Sam Ngam
Phetchabun
Kamphaeng Phet (3)
Phichit
Sri Thep
Pong Nam Ron
Pho Prathap Chang
Taphan Hin
Bu Chanuan
Khlong Khlung
Pho Thale
Chon Daen
Khanu Woralaksaburi
Bang Mun Nak
Nong Phai
Wang Tha Di
Makha
Banphot Phisai
Nong Bua
Kao Lieo
Lat Yua
Nakhon Sawan (1)
Bung Boraphet (2)
Tha Tako
Wichian Buri
Phaisali
Dong Noi
Thap Than
Phayuha Khiri
Tak Fa
Si Thep
Uthai Thani
Klang
Wat Sing
Ta Khli
Chai Badan
Chai Nat
Chum
Sankhaburi
Khok Samrong
Ban Rai
Ban Mi
Han Kha
Sing Buri
Chao Nen Dam
Dan Chang
Doem Bang Nang Buat
Lop Buri
Phatthana Nikhom
Tham Than Lod National Park
Phrom Buri
Phra Putthabat
Muaklek
Si Prachan
Tha Rua
Route 2
Nong Pradu
Saraburi
Khao Yai National Park
Suphan Buri
Phak Hai
Erawan National Park
U Thong
Bang Sai
National Park
Wang Takra
Bang Na
to Bangkok

Mae Nam Khwae Noi

Mae Nam Nan

Mae Nam Yom

Mae Nam Chao Phraya

Mae Nam Pa Sak

Route 1

Mae Nam Chao Phraya

170

CENTRAL PLAINS: THE HEARTLAND

A cluster of simple, thatched-roof farmhouses, almost hidden amid tall, graceful plumes of bamboo swaying lazily in the breeze. The village sits like a small island in the vast, chartreuse sea that stretches for seemingly endless kilometers in all directions, broken only by similar islands of darker green or, occasionally, by the swooping orange roof and glittering gilt of a Buddhist temple that flashes out of the sea like an improbable jewel.

This rippling expanse is the traditional source of Thailand's wealth, the intricately diked and dependably watered rice fields that have fed its people for more than 700 years. These are the Central Plains, the fertile heart of the country toward which the early Thais steadily, inevitably migrated from the mountains of the North and the jungles of the South, coming here to found their greatest cities.

If you drive across the Central Plains toward the end of the dry season in May, the fields are alive with blue-shirted, straw-hatted farmers plodding behind "iron buffaloes", the mechanical replacement for water buffaloes that turn the cracked and arid earth. A month or so later, when the rains have come, water flickers in the shallow paddies, and the young rice plants are of a vivid green that almost hurts the eye with its intensity.

In November, the rains trail off, the grain turns golden, and it is harvest time. The people reappear from the little hidden hamlets, from the temples where they have been passing the wet months as monks and from the city where they have been doing seasonal work. It is upon the harvest that their lives depend, upon which to a very real extent the whole country depends. And so to the fields come just about all the able-bodied members of every farming family.

Later, when the crop is in, there is time for festivals, for relaxation. Then, the air over the Central Plains will haze for hundreds of kilometers with smoke from burning fields, as the earth is prepared for another cycle of cultivation.

Several major rivers water this fertile heartland, most notably the Chao Phya which flows from the North to the Gulf of Thailand. On its way, it feeds the paddies through an incredibly complex network of streams and man-made canals.

Thai history has moved down these rivers, through these rich fields, and its remains are scattered about like an archaeological scrapbook: the Angkor-style towers of Lopburi, where the Khmers once ruled to reap the bounty of the Plains; the sprawling ruins farther south near Bangkok of once-great Ayutthaya, precariously leaning pagodas and the shells of palaces, half-submerged beneath the rampant vegetation that always lies in wait to take over when man turns his back (see "Bangkok Surroundings").

The smog-enshrouded immensity of Bangkok, latest of the capitals to be built on the prosperity of the Central Plains, shimmers on the horizon, half-threat, half-dream, tantalizingly near, yet in many ways as remote from the life of the farmers' fields as the moon.

Broad superhighways such as National Route 1 slice through the fields carrying flashy cars, roaring trucks, and air-conditioned tour buses to all parts of the country. Jumbo jets scream overhead on their way to and from Bangkok's Don Muang Airport, provincial towns and the cities of the world. Within the fields themselves the wail of the transistor radio breaks the traditional silence.

These 20th-century intrusions are changing this timeless quality of Thailand. Electrification has brought televisions and modern amenities; roads have brought trucks, iron buffaloes and the outside world to the doorstep of formerly remote farm communities. The farmers themselves have moved beyond the confines of their villages. It is a rare community that does not have at least one man who has spent a year or two as a construction worker in "Sa-oo" (Saudi Arabia) or elsewhere in the Middle East. Children study in faraway city schools or work in government offices and service industries. Women from disadvantaged families tell sad tales of lives in dark rooms in city back alleys earning money to support their families.

Yet the rhythms of life remain in the village. Though chemical fertilizers, mechanized equipment, and the necessity to double crop have altered some patterns, farm families retain their good humor and their trust in the traditional life. Buffaloes may disappear, children may move to the cities, more and more house walls are made of concrete rather than wood and the roofs sprout television aerials, but the tranquillity and pace of the countryside remains essentially unchanged.

In the hamlets of the Central Plains, more than any other part of the country you still see houses in the classic style of Thai architecture, the plain but elegant domestic equivalent of the magnificent temples that reached their full flowering at Ayutthaya. The paneled walls slant slightly inward to achieve an oddly graceful effect and the steep roof seems to strain toward the sky.

The faces of the people too, are less likely to show the imprint of the Chinese and the Lao, the Burmese and the Malay, all the races that have intermingled with the Thai in the cities and in the border regions. In the hamlets, with their extended families, their communal approach to farming, their reliance on the village temple as a source of social as well as spiritual sustenance, their deeply rooted sense of independence, the strongest, most enduring aspects of the Thai character can be seen more clearly here in the Central Plains than anywhere else.

Farmer in the heartland – good humor and a lasting trust in the traditional way of life.

ENTERING THE PLAINS

Reaching one's destination in the Central Plains, as in most other parts of Thailand, is generally quick and comfortable. The main cities in the center are linked to the capital by road, rail and air. Of these three modes, the most recently developed is travel by coach. A number of companies now offer rapid trips by air-conditioned coaches to most major destinations in Thailand. The standard of service on these vehicles is generally excellent. Snacks are served by hostesses, and soothing music is played on a tape deck; some coaches even screen videotapes. The "VIP" services are a welcome addition, offering reclining seats and ample leg room so one can sleep comfortably on overnight journeys.

The State Railways of Thailand takes the traveler at a more leisurely pace through the Central Plains on a line slightly to the east of Route 1. The railway passes through Ayutthaya, Nakhon Sawan, Phitsanulok, and Uttaradit on its way to Chiang Mai. On the Northern Express, air-conditioned first class sleepers are available, as well as couchettes in the first and second class. A restaurant car serves excellent Thai food and European breakfasts. National carrier Thai International provides frequent service to the Central Plains town of Phitsanulok.

Nakhon Sawan has always been an important commercial entrepot because of its location at the meeting of roads and rivers connecting North and Central Thailand. The Ping and Nan rivers, already swollen by their tributaries, the Wang and the Yom respectively, complete a journey of several hundred kilometers from the northern highlands to meet at Nakhon Sawan. Highway 1 divides here, sending a branch, Road 117, due north to Sukhothai and Phitsanulok while itself continuing northwest towards Tak.

Under its old name of Paknampoh, the town played a vital role in the teak trade. It was here that the great teak rafts, which had sometimes been traveling for two or three years from the northern forests, were broken up into smaller rafts for floating down to Bangkok on the Chao Phya River. Teak rafts may still be seen on the river below Nakhon Sawan, but they are not as numerous as they were in the heyday of Thailand's teak trade.

There are few traces of Nakhon Sawan's past in the modern commercial town. The most notable shrine is outside the town, across the bridge over the Chao Phya River. Here on a small hill stands **Wat Chomkiri Nagaproth**. The main structure dates from the 14th century Sukhothai period, but the Buddha image, seated on a throne supported by demons, is of the Ayutthaya period. Behind the main shrine is a massive, finely-adorned bronze bell, about 100 years old, supported on modern brick pillars.

A favorite outing for those living in and around Nakhon Sawan is a trip to **Bung Boraphet**, the lake located 2km to the east. This low-lying area acts as a catchment during the rainy season. Until they were hunted to extinction, Siamese crocodiles used to bask on its shores. At the height of the monsoon in September and October, the engorged lake covers an area of some 120sq km. The best time to visit is on a moonlit night in the cool season when you can picnic on the island in the middle of the waters.

The "new" city of **Kamphaeng Phet** lies 3km off Route 1, on the east bank of the Ping River about 120km northwest of Nakhon Sawan. This city was built by King Li Thai (1347–1368) of the Sukhothai dynasty to replace the older town of Chakangrao on the opposite bank. Both served as garrison towns for Sukhothai.

On the right-hand side of the approach road to Kamphaeng Phet are the remains of a laterite fort, **Phom Seti**, built to defend the earlier city. Farther along the road is the well-restored *chedi* of **Wat Chedi Klang Tung**, also a relic of the former city of Chakangrao.

Crossing a bridge over the Ping, you

ins of
mphaeng
et, a
iving city
the 14th
ntury.

come to the modern town. A short distance from the center, with its numerous rice and noodle eating-houses, is the well-designed **Provincial Museum** containing one of Thailand's finest bronze statues of the Hindu god Siva. This life-sized image was cast on the orders of the governor of Kamphaeng Phet in the first quarter of the 16th century.

Early in the reign of King Chulalongkorn (1868–1910), a German visitor removed the image's head and two hands. The governor at the time, too afraid to arrest a *farang* (foreigner), quickly sent word to Bangkok that the priceless fragments were on their way there by boat. Officials in Bangkok detained the German, who declared that he was going to give the fragments to the Berlin Museum.

King Chulalongkorn (whose skillful diplomacy saved Thailand from much more serious threats from the West) found a way to placate the German as well as keep the cultural treasures for his country. He promised to send an exact copy of the whole Siva image to Germany, so the fragments could remain in Thailand. And so it was done. The copy of the bronze is still in Berlin, while the head and hands of the image in the Kamphaeng Phet Museum have been skillfully restored. Other exhibits in the museum include pre-Sukhothai bronzes, stucco Buddha heads from monuments in the neighborhood, and some fine ceramics.

For a tour of the fortifications and temples, a car or coach is necessary since they are a considerable distance from the modern town. A visit to **King Li Thai's fortifications** reveals why the town was called Kamphaeng Phet or "Diamond Wall", the massive ramparts of earth topped by laterite rise 6m above the outer moat, now overgrown with water hyacinths.

It has been recently discovered that the moat was filled by a channel from the river itself; an irrigation system now being considered would utilize this old channel, another example of new technology still learning lessons from the past.

Folk dance at a local fair has crowd appeal.

The chief monuments of Kamphaeng Phet lie northwest of the walled city. The monks who built them were of a forest-dwelling sect, strongly influenced by teachers from Sri Lanka. Their temples, constructed of laterite, show Ceylonese influence. Most of them, however, underwent major changes during heavy restoration in the Ayutthaya period.

The familiar themes of Buddhist architecture are repeated in the ordination halls, *viharns* and *chedis* of these temples. Two temples are of special interest and should be visited even on a rapid tour.

Wat Phra Si Iriyabot derives its name from Buddha images which are depicted in four postures (*si* meaning "four," and *iriyaboth*, "postures") on the central square *mondop* (sanctuary). The standing image is largely intact, with the original stucco coating on its head and lower part of the body. This is an impressive and unaltered example of Sukhothai sculpture.

Unfortunately, the other images (in the sitting, walking, and sleeping postures) are in very poor condition. The whole temple stands on a platform encircled by the original laterite railing and walls.

The other temple, **Wat Chang Rob**, or Shrine of the Elephants, consists of the base of a great laterite stupa surrounded by elephant caryatids, a theme borrowed from Sri Lanka which claims that the universe rests on the backs of these beasts.

The row of elephants on the south side is almost complete, but several are missing on the other flanks of the stupa. Unfortunately, the spire of the great monument has vanished, but the ruins of a crypt on the upper level of the stupa can still be inspected. The pillars of the former *viharn* also remain. Repair work is currently underway which will restore their original lines but rob them of some of their mystery.

Hopefully, the teak forest setting will remain, as it is their presence which gives the Kamphaeng Phet monuments their charm.

Wat Phra Si Iyabot in amphaeng het – an naltered xample of ukhothai culpture.

OLD SIAM

As you head towards the ancient city of **Sukhothai**, northeast of Kamphaeng Phet, you pass through "new" Sukhothai, a bustling modern town of concrete shophouses. About 12km farther on, the road enters the city limits of old Sukhothai through the **Kamphaeng-hak ("Broken Wall") Gate**, the Highways Department having seen fit to run the road directly through the ruins rather than around them.

The remains of the massive walls reveal that the inner city was protected by no fewer than three rows of earthen ramparts and two moats. The city was begun by Khmers who left behind three buildings and the beginnings of a water system like that of Angkor Wat. After the Angkorian Empire began shrinking, the Khmers abandoned the city and the Thais moved in, building their own structures. They eschewed the intricate Khmer irrigation system, installing a much less complex one of their own. It is suggested that water, or the lack of it, in part contributed to the city's demise. It is thought that it was originally served by the Yom River which shifted course, depriving Sukhothai of a dependable source of water.

A short distance from Kamphaeng Hak Gate is the **Ramkamhaeng National Museum**, a good starting point for a tour of the enclave. The museum contains a fine collection of Sukhothai sculpture, ceramics and other artifacts, as well as exhibits from other periods. The entrance hall is dominated by an impressive bronze image of the walking Buddha. This style of image is regarded as the finest sculptural innovation of the Sukhothai period (1230–1440). There had been earlier essays in high and low relief, but the Sukhothai sculptors were the first to create walking Buddha images in the round. It also displays the elements which typify the Sukhothai style: fluid lines, a somewhat androgynous figure and strict interpretation of the 32 *raksanas* or characteristics by which a Buddha would be recognized:

wedge-shaped heels, arms hanging to the knees, fingers and toes of equal length, and others.

In this period, the Thais adopted Theravada Buddhism and invited monks from Sri Lanka to clarify points of scripture. While Buddhism was blossoming, Hindu influence remained strong as is revealed by the two bronze images of Hindu gods which flank the walking Buddha in the museum. The one on the right, with the combined attributes of Vishnu and Siva, is especially fine. Also worth noting is a stone torso of an *apsara*, or divinity, in the Khmer style. (Look behind the statue; in spite of ugly iron struts, you can still see the superb detail of its costume.)

An important object proudly displayed on the mezzanine floor is a copy of the famous stone inscription of King Ramkamhaeng; the original is the most prized exhibit of the National Museum in Bangkok. It was at the **Non Prasat** (Palace Mound), now merely a slightly raised terrace of earth and brick, that the inscription was found. In 1833, the future King Mongkut, then a monk, discovered the stone which had been inscribed in 1292. On it, King Ramkamhaeng had recorded his conquests in surrounding kingdoms, and the fact that in 1283 he devised the Siamese alphabet. However, some experts now doubt its authenticity and believe the inscription to be a much later work.

Once situated on the Non Prasat was the stone throne of King Ramkamhaeng, and although there is little to be seen now apart from the walled terrace, this was the numinous center of old Siam. Alexander Griswold notes: "The political significance of the throne can scarcely be exaggerated, for the king sat on it when he discussed affairs of state … and when he received his vassals who came to do homage." The stone throne, called the *Manangasila*, is now in the Temple of the Emerald Buddha in Bangkok.

Within the walls of Sukhothai are the ruins of some twenty *wats* and monuments, the greatest of them being **Wat Mahathat**. It is not definitely known who founded this shrine, which Griswold called "the magical and spiritual center of the kingdom," but it is presumed to have been King Sri Indradit (1220–1250), the first king of Sukhothai. Wat Mahathat owes its present form to a remodeling completed by King Lo Thai around 1345.

The original design, as the Fine Arts Department discovered a few years ago when making some repairs, was a quincunx of laterite towers standing on a laterite platform. The four axial towers, which can still be seen, are of the Khmer style but with stucco decorations added by King Lo Thai. The central tower is now hidden in the basement of Lo Thai's "lotus bud" tower. The axial towers were linked to the central tower by laterite buttresses which are still visible. The principal Buddha image, cast in bronze by King Li Thai (1347–1368) is now in Bangkok at Wat Suthat. The stucco frieze of walking monks around the base of the main tower is unusual.

Of the 20 other shrines within the walls, and some 70 more in the neighborhood, many repeat familiar architectural themes. The following shortlist, drawn up with the help of Professor Prince Subhadradis Diskul, an authority on the history and art of Sukhothai, indicates the monuments of special interest (for more detailed information, a guide to Sukhothai, published in English by the Fine Arts Department, is available at the museum).

Wat Sri Sawai, southwest of Wat Mahathat, was originally a Hindu shrine which contained an image of Siva. Triple towers remain, built in a modified Khmer style; the stucco decoration, added to the towers in the 15th century, showing mythical birds and divinities, is particularly fine.

Wat Sra Sri, on the way to the southern gate of the city has a spire (*chedi*) of the Sri Lankan type. The ordination hall (*bot*) lies on an island to the east of the spire. The ruins of the main shrine consist of six rows of columns, which lead to a well-restored seated Buddha image. Achille Clarac comments: "The detail, balance and harmony of the proportions and decoration of Wat Sra Sri, and the

A bullock cart, gaily decorated to celebrate *Lo Kratong*.

beauty of the area where it stands, bear witness to the unusual and refined aesthetic sense of the architects of the Sukhothai period."

Located immediately north of Wat Mahathat, **Wat Chana Songkhram** and **Wat Trakuan** have particularly fine Sri Lankan-style *chedis*, of which only the lower parts still stand. Wat Trakuan has revealed many bronze images of the Chiang Saen period.

Leaving the walled city by the northern San Luang, or the "Royal Shrine" gate, and traveling about a kilometer, you arrive at the important shrine of **Wat Phra Phai Luang**. It originally consisted of three laterite towers covered with stucco, probably built in the late 12th century when Sukhothai was still part of the Khmer empire. This shrine might have been the original center of Sukhothai, since Wat Mahathat is of a later period. A fragmentary seated stone Buddha image, accurately dated to 1191 in the reign of the Khmer King Jayavarman VII, was found here and is now in the grounds of the town's

Ramkamhaeng Museum. During restoration by the Fine Arts Department in the mid-1960s, a large stucco image of the Buddha in the central tower collapsed, disclosing numerous smaller images inside. Some date these images to the second half of the 13th century.

To the east of the main shrine lies a pyramidal brick *stupa* that originally contained seated stucco Buddha images dating from the late 13th century, on each story. Later the niches were walled up with bricks, which were removed during a restoration started in 1953. When heads of the stucco images began appearing on the antique market in Bangkok, authorities realized that the stupa was being pillaged. A team from the Fine Arts Department was dispatched to the site, but most of the damage had already been done. Those heads (facially of the Chiang Saen style) which have not left the country are in private collections in Thailand or in the reserves of the National Museum in Bangkok.

Beyond Wat Phra Phai Luang is **Wat**

Si Chum, which has one of the largest seated Buddha images in the kingdom. The *mondop*, or enclosing shrine, was built in the second half of the 14th century, but the image itself, called Phra Achana, or "The Venerable," is believed to be the one mentioned in King Ramkamhaeng's inscription. There is a stairway within the walls of the *mondop* which leads to the roof; largish persons should not attempt to ascend the narrow passage. The ceiling of the stairway is made up of more than 50 carved slate slabs illustrating scenes from Buddhist folklore. Their function is to turn the ritual climbing of the stairs into a symbolic ascent to Buddhahood.

There is a story that troops gathered here before a battle were inspired by an ethereal voice that seemed to come from the Buddha itself. Some suggest a brilliant ploy by a general who hid one of his men on the stairway and instructed him to speak through one of the windows concealed by the body of the image; the effect was magical, however, and the soldiers routed the enemy.

South of the walled city is another group of shrines and monasteries. One of the most interesting is **Wat Chetupon**, where the protecting wall of the *viharn* is made of slate slabs shaped in imitation of wood. The gates are also formed of huge plates of slate mined in the nearby hills. On a small scale, they resemble the megaliths of England's Stonehenge. The bridges across the moat which surrounds the temple are also made of stone slabs. On the central tower of Wat Chetupon are Buddha images in the standing, reclining, walking and sitting postures. The walking Buddha here is regarded as one of the finest of its type.

"To the west of the city of Sukhothai," says King Ramkamhaeng's inscription, "is a forested area where the king has made offerings. In the forest is a large, tall and beautiful *viharn* which contains an 18 cubit image of the standing Buddha." This is now identified as **Wat Saphan Hin**, "Monastery of the Stone Bridge." It is so-called because it is approached by a stairway of large stone

The ruins of Wat Chetupon.

slabs. The image is situated on the crest of a low hill and can be seen at a considerable distance. It is 12½m high, with its hand raised in the attitude of "giving protection." This is almost certainly the image described by King Ramkamhaeng.

Many other monuments are to be found in this western area. They were probably built by monks from Sri Lanka who preferred to locate their monasteries in the forest. Another monument worth visiting, near the road not far from the western gate of Sukhothai, is **Wat Pa Mamuang**, "Shrine of the Mango Grove," where King Li Thai installed a famous monk of the Theravada sect in 1361. Still standing are the foundations of the shrine and the ruins of the main *chedi*.

About 55km north of the modern town of Sukhothai along a new concrete highway lies the old city of **Si Satchanalai** on the banks of the Yom River. Founded, like Sukhothai, in the middle of the 13th century, it served as the seat of the viceroys of Sukhothai and was always mentioned as the twin city of the capital.

Whereas restoration, removal of trees, and the installation of lawns have removed some of the grandeur of Sukhothai, Si Satchanalai's bosky setting gives it an aura few other ancient sites have. It is a pleasure to wander through the wooded complex, rounding a corner and being surprised by a new *wat* or monument.

The first and most important monument to visit in Si Satchanalai is **Wat Chang Lom**. There can be little doubt that this is the "Elephant-girdled Shrine" described in King Ramkamhaeng's stone inscription. The great king records that he started to build it in 1285 to house some exceptionally holy relics of the Lord Buddha, and that it was finished six years later. It is the only surviving stupa which can be attributed with virtual certainty to King Ramkamhaeng. Built of laterite and stucco, it is a large bell-shaped spire of the Sri Lankan type standing on a two-storey, square basement. The upper tier contains niches for Buddha images, now mostly empty while the lower level

Below left, Wat Saphan Hin in Sukhothai, with its 18 cubic image of the standing Buddha". Right, Wat Chang Lom in Si Satchanalai, built in 1285 to house holy relics of Buddha.

contains 39 elephant caryatids, built of laterite blocks.

South of the Elephant Shrine are the ruins of **Wat Chedi Chet Thaew**, which include seven rows of stupas, believed to contain the ashes of the viceroys of Si Satchanalai. One of the stupas has a stucco image of the Buddha sheltered by the Naga (divine serpent), which is in unusually good repair.

Farther south still, and close to the massive walls of the city, are the remains of **Wat Nang Phya**, "Temple of the Queen." This has fine stucco decoration on one of the external walls. Dating probably from the 16th century, this stucco work has some affinities with European baroque.

Other temples worth visiting include **Wat Khao Phanom Pleung** and **Wat Khao Suwan Kiri**, set on two scenic hills linked by a walkway. **Wat Phra Si Ratana Mahathat** in Chalieng, one of the most beautiful temples, lies 2km southeast of the old city in a superb setting overlooking the Yom River.

Si Satchanalai is also associated with the famed Sawankhalok ceramics which were among Thailand's first export products. The brown bowls with their distinctive double fish design were sent to China aboard junks; remains of them have been found off the coast of Pattaya. It is still possible to buy genuine antique Sawankhalok ceramics in the area; most, however, are copies.

Phitsanulok now has only a few mementos of the past; a fire around 1960 razed most of the old town. The new city is a rather dull collection of concrete shop houses. However, nothing can detract from its superb location along the Nan River with its quays shaded by flowering trees, and its houseboats moored beside the steep banks. The great fire fortunately spared **Wat Mahathat**, the principal shrine in Phitsanulok. It remains a focus of piety, as it has for several centuries. The *Phra Buddha Chinaraj*, the image in the main *bot*, is venerated throughout Thailand. Regrettably, this has given rise to a busy traffic in religious objects and souvenirs. The seated image was cast in the Sukhothai style; a copy is at Wat Benjamabophit in Bangkok.

The *bot* which enshrines the *Phra Buddha Chinaraj* comprises a three-tiered roof that drops steeply to head-high side walls, focusing attention on the gleaming image at the end of the nave. Flanking the image are two wooden pulpits of superb late-Ayutthaya workmanship. The large one on the left is for monks who chant the ancient, Pali-language Buddhist texts; the smaller pulpit on the other side accommodates a single monk who translates the chants into Thai (since few of the congregation would understand Pali). Note the main doors inlaid with mother-of-pearl which date from the late 18th century.

The *prang* (spire) in the center of the temple complex was rebuilt in the Khmer style by King Boroma Trailokanath. The cloisters surrounding the *prang* contain Buddha images from several periods, some of them of great artistic value. A repository of art objects includes a collection of Thai and Chinese ceramics.

Left, the Phra Buddha Chinaraj, with its golden glow, is venerated throughout Thailand. Right, an old tree spreads its branches casting a cool shade over the ruins of the Wat Chedi Chet Thaew.

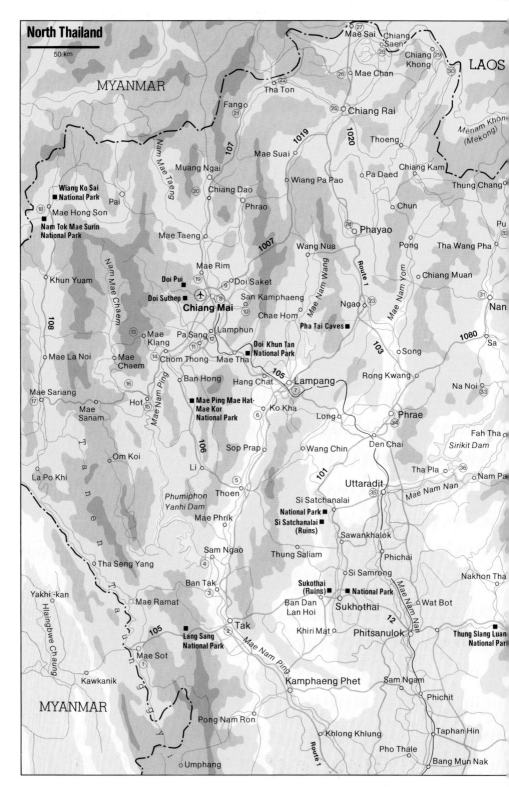

North Thailand

50 km

MYANMAR

LAOS

Mae Sai ⑳
Chiang Saen
⑱
Chiang Khong ㉙
⑱
Mae Chan ㉖
Tha Ton ㉒
Fang ㉑
Chiang Rai ㉕

Mènam Khong (Mekong)

107
1019
1020
Thoeng

Wiang Ko Sai National Park
Mae Suai
Chiang Kam
Thung Chang
Pai ⑱
Muang Ngai
Wiang Pa Pao
Pa Daed
Mae Hong Son ⑱
Chiang Dao ⑳
Nam Tok Mae Surin National Park
Phrao
Chun
Pu ㉜

Nam Mae Taeng

Mae Taeng ⑳
1007
Wang Nua
Phayao ㉔
Pong
Tha Wang Pha

Khun Yuam
Mae Rim
Doi Saket ⑨
Chiang Muan
⑱

108

Nam Mae Chaem

Doi Pui ⑲
Doi Suthep ⑧
Chiang Mai
San Kamphaeng
Chae Hom ⑩
Ngao ㉓
Route 1
Nan
㉛

Mae La Noi
Mae Klang ⑬
Pa Sang ⑫
Lamphun
Mae Nam Wang
Sa

⑪
Doi Khun Tan National Park
Pha Tai Caves ■
1080
Song

Mae Chaem ⑭
Chom Thong
Mae Tha
105
103

Mae Sariang ⑰
⑯
Ban Hong
Hang Chat
Lampang ⑦
Rong Kwang
Na Noi ㉝

Mae Sanam
Hot ⑮
Mae Ping Mae Hat-Mae Kor National Park
Ko Kha ⑥
Phrae

La Po Khi

Mae Nam Ping

106
Sop Prap
Wang Chin
Den Chai
Long ⑳
Phrae ㉞

Om Koi
Li
Fah Tha
Sirikit Dam

Thoen ⑤
101
Tha Pla
Nam Pa
㊱

Phumiphon Yanhi Dam
Si Satchanalai
Uttaradit ㉟
Mae Nam Nan

Mae Phrik
National Park ■
Si Satchanalai (Ruins) ■
Sawankhalok

Sam Ngao ④
Thung Saliam
Phichai

Tha Seng Yang
Ban Tak
Si Samrong
Nakhon Tha

Yakhi -kan
③
Sukothai (Ruins) ■
National Park ■
Wat Bot

Mae Ramat
Ban Dan Lan Hoi
Sukhothai
12

Hlaingbwe Chaung
105
Lang Sang National Park
Tak ②
Khiri Mat
Phitsanulok
Thung Slang Luan National Park ■

Mae Sot ①
Kamphaeng Phet
Sam Ngam

Kawkanik
Phichit

MYANMAR
Pong Nam Ron
Khlong Khlung
Taphan Hin

Route 1
Pho Thale
Bang Mun Nak

Umphang

190

Another group of simple houses, but different in architecture, and in atmosphere, than those on the Central Plains. Different in setting, too: this village is even more remote than the farming hamlets of the Central Plains. It is surrounded not by rice fields, but by craggy hills and mist-covered mountains, a wild and almost roadless terrain where distances are measured in walking hours rather than in kilometers.

In these jungled mountains, live unusual people: Meo tribesmen who wear vast, bulky turbans and clanking silver jewelry; Yao tribespeople who dress in finely-worked embroidery; several almost legendary small nomadic groups, like the Phi Thong Luang, "Spirits of the Yellow Leaves," who some thought to exist only in myth until an expedition discovered them.

Here, also, in lost valleys, fields of forbidden poppies grow, beginning a complex trail of illicit activity that ends on the streets of many Western cities. The poppies and the opium by-product were outlawed in Thailand more than 30 years ago, but the problem is far from simple. It is hard for the authorities to patrol adequately this wild terrain, but easy for smugglers to slip back and forth across the borders with Burma and Laos, which form the notorious "Golden Triangle" prominent in so many narcotics news stories.

The government has been trying a new tack. Two decades ago, King Bhumibol began an ambitious crop-substitution program aimed at weaning hillpeople away from their traditional dependence on opium cultivation. Additional government programs provide extension support and markets for the crops. Today, coffee, cantaloupes, brussels sprouts, apples, strawberries and other "foreign" produce are being harvested in abundance.

Missionaries and organizations, such as the royally sponsored Hill Tribe Foundation, are finding markets for the fine hilltribe handicrafts. And members of the elite Border Patrol Police are dropping by helicopter into the remote mountain villages not only to enforce the law but to set up schools and, for the first time, bring modern medicine and dentistry to villagers.

The hilltribes are still an exotic thread on the fringe of Thai life, but gradually they are being woven into the national fabric, venturing to the larger cities in the North. Some are forced there by increasing deforestation and land pressures; they sit on the streets of Bangkok selling their wares, lost amidst the alien din and traffic.

But the North has more to offer than strange hilltribes and jungled wilderness. It is also a place rich in history, with great kingdoms, legendary rulers, and artistic achievement that go back beyond the founding of the first Thai capital at Sukhothai in the 13th century. The celebrated Emerald Buddha, the most venerated of all the images in Thailand, was found in the North (most experts also

Preceding pages: for the Lisus, New Year is a communal festival; time stands still at Menam Kok, Chiang Rai.

believe it was made there) and spent much of its early existence in various northern temples.

According to a northern legend, King Mengrai of Chiang Saen, who ruled the North in the 13th century, was so powerful that when he decided to found a new capital, the future Chiang Mai, he was able to call on royal friends from other parts of the country, including Sukhothai, to assist him in the selection of a suitable location. The eminent surveyors knew they had found an auspicious site when they heard of a place where an extraordinary assembly of rare animals had been seen: two white sambar deer (a variety now extinct), two white barking deer and a white mouse with a family of five. King Mengrai, so the story goes, immediately ordered Chiang Mai to be built on the spot.

The North has been the scene of epic battles, of Burmese invasions, of the rise and fall of independent kingdoms, only distantly related to the ruling cities of the central part of the present-day country. Until the early part of this century, it was accessible from Bangkok only by a complicated river trip or by a journey of several weeks on elephant back. There are still old residents in the capital who remember the great day when the northern railway line was finally opened in the late 1920s, after more than ten years of tunneling and blasting through the mountains.

It is not surprising, then, that the region has retained a distinct flavor all its own, one still so strong that tourists from other parts of Thailand come here almost as if to another country. They marvel at the profusion and beauty of the temples with their splendid teak carvings and intricate Burmese-inspired decorations (there are more than a hundred in moderate-sized Chiang Mai alone), the splendor of the wild orchids that grow so profusely in the hills, the gentle good manners of the people (among whose hospitable habits it is to place a basin of cool water outside their gates for the benefit of thirsty passing strangers), the fabled good looks of the girls, and the novelty of having to bundle up in a sweater in the cool season.

Ancient handicrafts which have either succumbed to the machine or which never even existed in other regions still thrive here: delicate lacquerware, thin silver bowls pounded into complex designs over wooden molds, supple handwoven cottons and shimmering silk, expertly carved teak, paper umbrellas painted in bold designs and fine celadon stoneware.

Along with its manners, handicrafts and relative serenity, the North has also kept its love of festivals which are observed with greater frequency and enthusiasm than anywhere else in Thailand. A visitor who comes in the winter months between October and the end of January is almost certain to come across some kind of celebration ranging from the famous Loy Krathong water festival to localized affairs, like the gathering of the garlic crop in Lamphun when one of the local beauties is chosen "Miss Garlic".

The North is a region of great natural wealth and scenic beauty. Vast hardwood forests cover much of it, the working of which still

The Wieng Lakon parade in Lampang keeps the ancient history of Lanna alive.

require the services of trained elephants, which drag the huge logs downhill to the banks of rivers, to be floated down to mills below. Mines for minerals such as wolfram have been sunk in the mountains, producing booming new industries. The production of cut flowers is another new industry, and in the winter season, the florist shops of Bangkok are filled with unfamiliar gladioli, snapdragons, carnations and other blossoms which, like so many things in the North, seeem strange and special.

Getting to the North is now much easier than in the days of travel by boat and elephant. Thai International and Bangkok Airways offer regular scheduled flights to Chiang Mai, Chiang Rai and most of the major cities in North. Starting from mid-1994, Silk Air offers a direct flight from Singapore to Chiang Mai every Tuesday and Thursday.

Towns like Mae Hong Son high in the misty mountains dividing Thailand from Burma, like the Chinese town of Mae Salong and Loei can be reached by wide, paved highways.

Several trains and buses leave Bangkok daily for northern destinations. If you want to travel in style, take the "Nakorn Ping" Special Express. This offers first and second class cars cooled by air-conditioning or fan. A second class, fan-cooled sleeper is perfectly suitable for most travelers. Reservations for seats and sleepers should be made well in advance during school holidays and around the mid-April Songkran, the New Year holidays, Chinese New Year, and the Loy Krathong festival when hotels in Chiang Mai are full.

For travelers with cars, Route 1 leaves the Central Plains around Kamphaeng Phet, passes the northern gateway province of Tak, and follows the Wang River north-northeast to Lampang. From Lampang you can branch off on the all-weather road to Chiang Mai or continue on Route 1 to Chiang Rai. You should try to make several sidetrips on the North's scenic secondary roads.

Try to visit the North during the cool season (late November to February) when the days are usually bright and sunny but not too hot, and the nights cool enough for sweaters and jackets. Blue skies and clear air allow for good photography, and the evening chill makes you appreciate the warming effect of Chiang Mai's *kow tom* (hot rice porridge with egg and meat).

Travel beyond the North into Burma is not yet legally possible as the Burmese government does not issue visas for overland entry from Thailand. For years travelers were allowed to cross the Mekong River from Chiang Khong over to Ban Houei Sai in Laos. While relations between the two countries have improved considerably, the Laotians allow entry to the country only at Vientiane.

Akha tribesgirl with a head-dress of beads and baubles.

GATEWAY
TO THE NORTH

Tak is the gateway to Thailand's most scenic region: the North. This quiet town on the banks of the Ping River is but a ghost of its former brawling self. Once called Raheng, it was a logger's town. Just north of Tak was the confluence of the Wang and Ping, two of the four main tributaries of the Chao Phya River. Logs freed from the wild rapids on the upper Ping and those from the Wang were rafted and floated down river to Nakhon Sawan. The rapids have been buried under the Bhumibol Dam and, with them, the town's hurly-burly reputation.

During the 19th century, Tak was also a provisioning center for journeys west into Burma and north to Chiang Mai. Until the railway was completed in the 1920s, the only way north was by boat propelled by "polers" who set stout poles into the riverbed and then "walked" the boat upstream against the swift current. As the rapids were the most formidable obstacle on the river, it was in Tak that food stocks were replenished, polers hired, and boats readied for the pounding they would take through the narrow canyons.

Today, Tak is a prosperous but peaceful town just off Route 1. It is entered either by a direct route or the old route that threads through tiny manicured gardens and around a pond near the provincial offices. A broad, treeless esplanade separates the market from the Ping River; a high bund bars entry of the Ping's waters which used to swell over into the streets, flooding the town during the rainy season.

Other than the river at sunset and the orange suspension bridge that resembles San Francisco's Golden Gate, Tak offers few sights. North of its bustling market is **Wat Phrae** and **Wat Sibunruang**. The latter has a gold-topped *chedi* and contains the *Phra Buddhamon*, an early Sukhothai period image.

There are regular scheduled domestic flights to Tak. With the modern, air-conditioned Wiang Tak and Wiang

Tak 2 hotels, Tak is the point of departure for trips to Mae Sot and the Bhumibol Dam.

Road 105 leads west through rugged hills to the Burmese border town of **Mae Sot**. About 12km outside of Tak lies Luang Larn National Park whose waterfalls are hidden behind a screen of bamboo groves. If time allows, stop at the *nikhorn*, or "settlement," on Doi Mussu to view Lisu, Lahu and Meo hilltribes.

The road rises to Phawoh Mountain where truck drivers make offerings at the spirit house to ask for safe passage. Beyond the pass, the road drops through forests into a peaceful valley dotted with miniature farmhouses, white *chedis,* and ornate Burmese-style temples.

A fire in the mid-70s destroyed the core of the downtown area with its multitude of wooden shophouses, and refugee camps on the outskirts of town have changed much of Mae Sot's character. But with its confusion of short streets, sidewalk stalls, bicycles, and pedestrian shoppers, it retains the air of a Burmese town. It even boasts an airstrip. Shops advertise their wares in Thai, Chinese, Burmese, and English.

From Mae Sot, it is a 5-km drive to the Burmese border. Worth a visit is an ornate Burmese temple with tiers of red-tiled rectangular roofs fringed with silverwork that are piled heavenward into a tower. Within the sanctuary are four Buddha images, one of which has gold jewelry distending its earlobes. After a brief visit, drive to the Moei River which forms the border with Burma. This is the point at which the Asian Highway may someday enter Thailand, realizing an age-old dream of an unbroken ribbon of pavement linking Ho Chi Minh City with London.

Return to Tak and continue north on Route 1 and then onto Road 106 which describes an "S" and twines itself about Route 1. On the left, about 20km past Tak, the village of **Ban Tak** lies on the banks of the Ping. In the days when the river was the only road north, Ban Tak was a village of boatbuilders. Today it is quiet but picturesque with houses on stilts that teeter on the riverbank and a

itual
ancing
ccompanies
aditional
ffering made
t the Wat
ampang
uang.

rickety bamboo footbridge that looks down upon children swimming and splashing. At sunset the Ping turns silver, and boatmen drift like silhouettes in a shadow-play across the reflected light.

Bhumibol Dam (also called Yanhee Dam), sits 29km north of Ban Tak on the left of Route 1. The dam, one of Thailand's largest, generates enough power to help light Bangkok and a large number of Thailand's widely scattered 73 provinces. With permission, you can drive across the 154-m-high cement arch to view the reservoir which stretches 120km northwest to Hot District, not far from Chiang Mai. About 4km downstream is a planned town to house the dam's 10,000 employees and their families. Within it on the banks of the Ping is the air-conditioned Bhumibol Hotel which is open to outsiders.

About 63km north of the Bhumibol Dam turnoff, Route 1 arrives at **Thoen**. Although Thoen can be passed rapidly, it does enjoy a small claim to fame as the home of lucky *pohng kham* stones. Each *pohng kham* contains a variety of colors and encapsulated "scenes." Some of the clear pieces hold strange, crystalline formations resembling wisps of blue hair, jungle moss, or even a city skyline.

From Thoen to Lampang, Route 1 undulates over teak-covered hills and a mountain pass sprinkled with spirit houses before dipping into the broad, cattle country of the Yom River Valley dominated by the former kingdom of Lampang. Approximately 18km south of Lampang is the junction with the road to **Ko Kha**. Turn left past the town and cross the Wang River, bearing left for 1km, to reach one of treasures of the north, the elegant old temple, **Wat Lampang Luang**. Cherished by scholars for its antiquity and delicate artwork, the temple compound is all that remains of a fortressed city that flourished more than a millennium ago. It is said to have been founded by a 7th-century Lopburi princess, Chama Dewi, who bore two sons: one became king of Lampang, the other, king of Lamphun.

The *wat*, entirely rebuilt in the 16th century, played a key role in the golden

The 16th-century Vihar Namtan at Wat Lampang Luang is the oldest teak building in Thailand.

period of the Northern kingdoms. Nearly 200 years ago, Burmese invaders occupied the temple. According to legend, Thai attackers sneaked through a drain, surprising and routing their enemy. Monks will point to a hole in the balustrade which is said to have been caused by the cannon ball that killed a Burmese general.

The temple's museum features lacquered bookcases, jeweled Buddhas, and wooden *tong* banners that hang from poles like stiff flags. Most revered is a small "Emerald Buddha" believed to have been carved from the same jasper stone as its famous counterpart in Bangkok. It is displayed each November during the annual temple fair. The most important structures are the copper-plated *chedi* and the huge *viharn* with its low roofs.

About 18km past Ko Kha, Route 1 enters the provincial capital of **Lampang**. Half the size of Chiang Mai it has been developed nearly to the degree of its northern cousin. While much of its bucolic tranquillity has disappeared it retains one relic of the past found in no other city: horse-drawn carriages. These can be hired by the journey or by the hour. There are few more romantic pursuits than clip-clopping down a quiet, moonlit back street.

Two Burmese-style temples in the town are worth visiting. Seven chapels, one for each day of the week, stand at the base of the *chedi* in **Wat Pha Sang**, located on the left bank of the Wang River. On the right bank, **Wat Phra Keo Don Tau** is a lovely fusion of Burmese and Lanna (northern) architecture. In the pavilion, columns soar to ceilings covered in a kaleidoscope of inlaid enamel, mother-of-pearl, and cut glass depicting mythical animals and flowers. North of town stand the 20 chalky spires of **Wat Chedi Sao Phra** set in the rice fields.

There are regular scheduled domestic flights to Lampang from Bangkok as well as a rail service. For an overnight stay, there are the modern Thip Chang and Asia Lampang hotels. Approximately 100km north lies Chiang Mai.

eft, the nage of 'hze Choo hong Tip at Jat Phra Keo on Tau. ight, ornate aterior of Jat Phra Keo on Tau, a asion of urmese and anna rchitecture.

CHIANG MAI

Time and progress have wrought twin transformations on the once remote "Rose of the North". Concrete lamp standards have replaced trees, concrete rowhouses for teak houses, and noisy, piston-hammering *tuk tuks* for the silent but rapidly disappearing pedal *samlors* (pedicabs). They have also introduced that bane of modernity – traffic jams – to its once-tranquil streets. Yet even concrete and cacophony have failed to mask the captivating charm of **Chiang Mai**.

Chiang Mai has, for decades, been prized as a pleasant dry-season escape from the sticky humidity of Bangkok. Situated 305m above sea level in a broad valley divided by the picturesque Ping River, the city reigned for seven centuries as the capital of the Lanna (Million Rice Fields) kingdom. The city's remoteness ensured that the North remained outside the rule of Bangkok well into the 20th century.

In its splendid isolation, it developed a culture quite removed from that of the Central Plains, with wooden temples of exquisite beauty and a host of unique crafts including lacquerware, silverwork, wood carvings, ceramics and umbrella-making. Its dozen hilltribes only added to its luster as an exotic far-flung realm. Much of its other-worldly charm resides in its friendly people. Although their hospitality is being strained by the sheer numbers of visitors, they speak more softly, smile more readily and take the time to help strangers find their way more graciously than in many cities to the south.

Yet, the city is changing. The nation's second largest city (although some argue that Khon Kaen is bigger) this northern capital 710km from Bangkok has caught the eyes of the tourist and the businessman, both eager to flee the high prices, din and pollution of Bangkok. As a result, wasteland is being turned into modern farms producing crops unheard of two decades ago, paddy land is now sprouting factories and condomini-

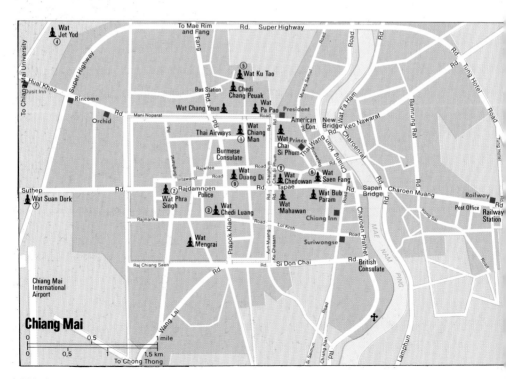

Chiang Mai

ums, and tall hotels are being erected in the downtown area to accommodate the hordes of visitors winging, railing and riding into the city.

Chiang Mai's history is as old as that of the Thais themselves. Its story begins farther north in the town of Chiang Rai. Its founder and king, Mengrai, ruled a large realm that ran as far north as Chiangsaen on the Mekong River. He founded Chiang Rai in 1281 but when the Mongol warlord, Kublai Khan, sacked the Burmese kingdom of Pagan in 1287, Mengrai realized that his realm was threatened and he formed a long-term alliance with the rulers of Sukhothai, then Thailand's capital. With his southern boundaries secure, Mengrai captured the old Mon Kingdom at Haripunchai (Lamphun) in 1292. To centralize his rule, he established a new base in the Ping River Valley in 1296. This new capital he named "Chiang Mai" or "new city".

Rather than building on the banks of the Ping which often floods, he erected his city half a kilometer to the west,

Chiang Mai is paying a price for its success with more highrise hotels and condominiums and factories cluttering its scenic beauty.

surrounding it with a stout brick wall.

Less than a century after its founding, however, Sukhothai had been supplanted as the capital by Ayutthaya. This new Siamese kingdom had its own expansionist dreams, ambitions which included designs on its neighbor to the north. Relations between the two cities became strained and for the next 400 years there was intermittent warfare. In the 16th century, Ayutthaya crushed an invasion by Chiang Mai, and in the century from 1550 to 1650 Chiang Mai's power began to wane. Then, to compound its troubles, the Lanna kingdom was invaded in the early 18th century by the same Burmese who were laying siege to Ayutthaya.

Fighting continued until 1775. Although the Burmese were finally defeated, the inhabitants of Chiang Mai were so exhausted and discouraged by the constant conflict that they abandoned the city. It remained deserted until 1796 when the back of the Burmese army had been broken and new Lanna nobles began restoring the city to

its former prominence. The present moat in Chiang Mai dates from soon after the re-establishment of the city. It continued to enjoy autonomy until the railway brought new ideas and administrators. Only in 1938 was it finally incorporated into the Thai nation.

Most visitors spend only two days in town before setting off to explore the cool air of the mountains, hilltribe treks, elephant camps and other delights of the northern hills. But there is much to see during those two days.

The town is dominated by the green mass of Doi Suthep. Its crown is the temple of Wat Prathat that appears with crystalline clarity through the chill December dawn air. While it is being warmed by the sun, the town is still in shadows. Near the moat, a minibus is filling with hardy trekkers setting off for Fang, 150km to the north, to begin a three-day jungle walk. At the edge of the lotus-filled moat, two young boys dangle lines in the water. Reflected in the water is a line of saffron-robed Buddhist monks on their morning alms walk. Padding silently on bare feet, they pause briefly before houses and shops whose inhabitants ladle rice and curries into their bowls. Another day begins in Chiang Mai.

The traveler soon discovers that despite its size, Chiang Mai is an easy city to navigate. Yellow or red buses ply such circuitous routes that the nominal fare buys a complete town tour. More expensive but still extremely cheap, *tuk tuks* convey passengers to any point around town. Pedal *samlors* provide a more leisurely way of seeing Chiang Mai.

Many travelers hire motorcycles or push bicycles. Agencies on Chang Klan Road and near the Tapae Gate do a thriving business renting motorcycles; most guest houses rent bicycles for as little as 10 baht per day.

Begin a Chiang Mai stay at the temple where the city's history began. **Wat Chiang Man**, whose name translates as "power of the city", was the first temple to be built by Mengrai. He resided there during the construction of the city in 1296. Two ancient and much venerated Buddha images are kept in the abbot's

quarters and can be seen on request. The crystal *Phra Sae Tang Tamani* is a small Buddha image taken by Mengrai to Chiang Mai from Lamphun where it had reputedly resided for 600 years. Apart from a short sojourn in Ayutthaya, the image has remained in Chiang Mai ever since. On Songkran, each April 13, it is ceremonially paraded through the streets to be propitiated by the town's residents.

The second image, a stone *Phra Sila* Buddha in bas-relief, is believed to have originated in India around the 8th century. Both statues are said to possess the power to bring rain and protect the city from fire. The only other important structure in Wat Chiang Man is a 15th-century square *chedi* buttressed by rows of sturdy stucco elephants.

Imperiously occupying the head of one of the city's principal streets is **Wat Phra Singh**, Chiang Mai's second most important temple after Wat Prathat Doi Suthep. Founded in 1345, its thick walls seem to shut out the bustle of traffic.

Wat Phra Singh is noted for three monuments: its library, *chedi* and Viharn Laikam. The Lanna-style wooden library, on the right side of the compound sits high on an older base decorated by lovely stucco angels.

Behind the main *viharn* is a beautiful wooden *bot* and behind it, a *chedi* built by King Pha Yu in 1345 to hold the ashes of his father, King Kam Fu.

Wat Phra Singh's most beautiful building is the small Phra Viharn Laikam to the left of the *bot*. Of all of Chiang Mai's temple buildings, it is the supreme representative of Lanna-style architecture. Built rather late in the Lanna period in 1811, the wooden building's front wall is decorated in gold flowers on a red lacquer ground. Intricate carved wood window frames compete with the doors.

The interior murals depict the life of Saengthong, one of the Buddha's last incarnations before he came to earth and achieved enlightenment. The building shelters an image said to have been created in Sri Lanka 1,500 years ago. Its

characteristics, however, suggest it was sculpted during the Sukhothai period. The original head was stolen in 1922; this one is a replica.

Portents of calamity are associated with **Wat Chedi Luang** built in 1401. In 1545, a violent earthquake shook its 86-m-high pagoda reducing its present height to 42m. It was never rebuilt but even in ruins, the colossal monument remains impressive. For 84 years the Emerald Buddha was housed in this *wat* before being moved to Vientiane, Laos. King Mengrai was reportedly killed nearby by a bolt of lightning. Close to the *wat* entrance stands an ancient tall gum tree whose longevity is tied to that of the city. When it falls, says a legend, so will the city. As if serving as counterbalance, the "lak muang" or city boundary stone in which the "spirit of the city" resides, stands near its base.

The *viharn* of **Wat Pan Tao**, next door to Chedi Luang, is a masterpiece of wood construction. Visible from the street, its doorway is crowned by a beau-

The well-preserved Wat Chiang Man, the first temple to be built by Mengrai, founder of Chiang Mai.

tiful Lanna peacock framed by golden *nagas* (mythical dragons).

Located outside the city walls, **Wat Chedi Jet Yod** was completed by King Trailokaraja in 1455. As its name ("seven spires") suggests, it is a replica of the Mahabodi Temple in India's Bodhgaya where Buddha gained enlightenment. The beautiful stucco angels which decorate its walls are said to bear faces of Trailokaraja's own family. Although similar to a temple in the contemporary Burmese capital of Pagan, it did not stop the Burmese from severely damaging it during their invasion of 1566.

Chiang Mai proper has still more temples worthy of a visit. **Wat Koo Tao**, hidden away behind the bus station, has a strange *chedi* resembling five pumpkins of diminishing size set one atop the other and decorated by flowers created from pieces of crockery.

One of the most impressive city temple complexes is **Wat Suan Dok**. At its northwest corner are whitewashed *chedis* that contain the ashes of Chiang Mai's royal family; the huge central *chedi* is said to hold no fewer than eight relics of Lord Buddha. **Wat Chedovan**, near the east gate, has three tiled *chedis* and a menagerie of mythical animals which seem to come alive in the slanting rays of the morning sun.

More difficult to reach is **Wat U-mong**. This forest retreat was created by King Mengrai as a Buddhist meditation center. Comprising a honeycomb of underground cells, the recently restored site sits among beautiful plane and teak trees and is one of the few quiet spots left in Chiang Mai.

A steep series of hairpin curves rise 12km up the flanks of Doi Suthep to Chiang Mai's best-known temple. The site was selected by an elephant which was turned loose with a Buddha relic strapped to its back; where it stopped, a temple would be built. It climbed the slopes of Doi Suthep, trumpeted and lay down. There, **Wat Prathat Doi Suthep** was built.

The road to the mountain sanctuary leaves the old city at its northwest corner. The road passes the North's most

The white-washed *chedis* of Wat Suan Dok hold the ashes of the royal family of Chiang Mai.

important educational institution, **Chiang Mai University**, officially opened in 1965 on a 200-hectare campus. It holds the **Tribal Research Center**, a small ethnographical museum where one can compare the costumes and implements of several hilltribes.

A bit farther on is an arboretum holding many species of northern Thailand's trees. Next to it is the **Chiang Mai Zoo**, started as a private collection by Mr. Harold Young and his son who donated it to the town. Given the extensive poaching in the North in recent decades, it probably contains more wild animals than the hills.

The road then begins its steep ascent, passing the entrance to the Huay Kaew waterfalls where you can find a minibus to take you to the top. Here, also, is a statue of the monk Krupan Srivichai, who in 1934 began constructing the road to the summit to make the temple more accessible to pilgrims. The scenery en route is spectacular, the road eventually ending at a parking lot and an entire town of souvenir stands.

Seven-headed *nagas* undulate down the balustrade of a 290-step stairway leading from the parking lot to the hill's 1,000-m summit. For the weary, a funicular makes the same climb for a few baht. From Wat Prathat Doi Suthep, Chiang Mai is spread at one's feet.

From the upper terrace, one climbs a few more steps through into the courtyard of the temple itself. In the late afternoon light, there are few sights more stunning than those which greet one at the final step. Emerging from cloisters painted rather clumsily with murals depicting the Buddha's life, one's eyes rise to the summit of a 24-m-high gilded *chedi* partially shaded by gilded bronze parasols. The *chedi* is surrounded by an iron fence whose pickets culminate in praying *devas* or angels. Thais clasp lotus flowers, incense and candles in their hands as they meditate on the teachings of the Lord Buddha and pray for guidance.

On the east and west ends of the compound are two *viharn*. At dawn, the one on the east holds chanting

nuns in their white robes. At sunset, the one on the west holds orange-robed monks chanting their prayers. Few sites have such an air of solemn devotion as this.

From the parking area of Wat Prathat, a road ascends a further 5km to **Phuping Palace**, the summer residence of the Royal Family. Situated at 1,300m, the palace holds audience halls, guest houses, dining rooms, kitchens and official suites to carry on the royal affairs at this remote hilltop retreat. It also serves as headquarters for royal agricultural and medical projects carried on among hilltribes and in nearby Thai villages. On Fridays through to Sundays and on holidays, when the royal family is absent, the public may stroll through the well-tended gardens aflame with roses, orchids, hibiscus and double-headed bougainvilleas.

From the palace entrance, the road continues through pine forests to the Meo hilltribe village of **Doi Pui**. The village has been on the tourist track for some time but recent improvements have brought real benefits to its inhabitants. It consists of a paved street hemmed by souvenir stands that wall-off hillltribe houses; with a bit of perseverance, it is possible to wander by the houses to see how the people live.

Once subsistence farmers, the tribesmen have learned that visitors come bearing gifts and the snap of a camera automatically triggers a hand extended for a donation. As the people, especially the children, in their bright red and black costumes are photogenic, a few baht is a worthwhile investment for a good photo.

Meos are nomadic people found here and in neighboring Burma and Laos. They once depended on opium cultivation for their livelihoods and despite government efforts to steer them towards more socially-acceptable crops, many still cultivate patches deep in the hills. An interesting insight into opium farming is provided by Doi Pui's Opium Museum which describes in detail the process of cultivation and harvest and displays the implements used. A hilltribe

Left, turbane children in rapt attention. Right, flower festival in Chiang Mai i a feast for th eyes.

206

museum presents artifacts and articles of clothing. For those who lack the time to go deeper into Thailand, this Meo village offers a typical example of hilltribe life. Doi Pui also has a beautiful flower garden.

Festivals and fetes: Chiang Mai is best during winter (late November through to early February). It is then that the "Rose of the North" is abloom with an astounding variety of beautiful flowers. Numerous resorts in nearby Mae Sa Valley carpet the hillsides in flower gardens and the annual **Chiang Mai Flower Festival** each February fills the streets with floral parades and the open areas with flower exhibitions.

Be careful on the streets of Chiang Mai on April 13 and for several days thereafter, for a sudden deluge of water can fall on you despite clear blue skies. **Songkran**, the traditional Thai new year is a time when one sprinkles water on one's friends to bless them. It rapidly degenerates into a water fight of gigantic proportions but coming at the hottest part of the dry season, nobody cares.

Prepare to be soaked a dozen times as you walk down the street.

Beware lest you are overtaken by the fate that befell Thomas Samuel at the start of the 17th century. One of the first Westerners to visit Chiang Mai, he was ordered by his employers, the East India Company, to leave the city but Samuel had fallen in love with the town. After ignoring several warnings, he was taken prisoner during the Burmese invasion of 1615, and died in Burma.

Mae Sa Valley: Once an agricultural region, the Mae Sa Valley cultivates a new moneyearner: tourism. Waterfalls, camps where one can watch elephants at work and take a long elephant-back ride into the hills, butterfly farms, orchid nurseries and a charming museum called Mae Sa House Collection contend for the visitor's attention. The valley also has a number of quiet resorts along its river. To reach it, drive 16km north of Chiang Mai past the Lanna Golf Course. Turn left onto Highway 1096 and the first of the attractions will begin to appear.

he Songkran stival in hiang Mai no wet ankets, ease.

HANDICRAFTS

What would anyone do with a half-life-size wooden elephant? There must be a good answer, for every other Chiang Mai handicrafts shop seems to have one. Chiang Mai's range of handicrafts is enormous, from matchbox sized dolls to gargantuan elephants.

Chiang Mai used to be divided into craft villages but except for isolated pockets, much of the production has moved to huge emporia along the Borsang-Sankamphaeng Road. In large studios, one can watch craftsmen at work and then select an item from the showroom. Carvers learn their skills at home since the company cannot afford to take risks on a novice. Craftsmen can also create works according to designs provided by the buyer.

Wood carving studios turn out excellent furniture and art objects along the Borsang Road. The supply of antiques has dwindled in recent years and has been replaced by replicas of old works as well as some imaginative decor items. Shops sell them as reproductions, making no attempt to pass them off as originals. The quality of carving and of painting varies but many are of superb design and execution and make excellent home decoration items and gifts.

There are several shops along the Borsang Road and in Borsang. One of the best known shops in Chiang Mai is Banyen on Wua Lai Road. It also has an excellent museum displaying originals. To get closer to the source, travel south along the Hot Road to Hang Dong. Down a road on the left is Ban Tawai where many of the wooden items are created and sold.

Wua Lai Road once resounded to the sounds of tapping as silversmiths pounded out jewelry and utensils. Now only a few are left. Others can be found on Borsang Road. Bare-chested, muscular smiths pound away at silver bowls propped on iron pegs. They hammer out intricate floral patterns or scenes from the familiar *Ramakien* epic and stories of the Buddha's many incarnations.

Silk shops and studios are found along the same road. Weavers at traditional looms demonstrate time-honored methods of turning silken skeins into shimmering cloth. Young girls frequently do the weaving and, with concentration, can produce about 6m of finished cloth per day. Silk can be purchased by the yard or as clothes, scarfs, pillowcases and other items. The same shops also sell printed and plain cotton fabrics.

Lacquerware is an old art in the North. There are two types – one of gold leaf on black lacquer and the other of red lacquer with green and black designs. Craftsmen also cover practical items such as trays and boxes with designs made from fragments of egg shells. Studios at the back of the shop demonstrate the techniques.

Chiang Mai's **umbrella-making** center is at the village of **Borsang**, 9km along the road to Sankamphaeng. Here, freshly-dyed paper and silk umbrellas and fans dry in front of every shop. They range in size from cocktail to 3m in diameter.

Umbrella production begins with a cane stem carefully cut and trimmed by young men deft with their cleavers. Young girls form bamboo strips into frames, over which translucent paper made from the pounded bark of the *sa* tree is meticulously pasted. On these canvases, scenes, bamboo groves, birds and other nature subjects are carefully painted.

Sankamphaeng is an ancient ceramics center where modern potters throw a variety of items including the famous **Thai celadon**, with its jade-green, crazed surface. Other pottery items are crafted here and in workshops near Hang Dong on the highway to Hot.

Hilltribe crafts include embroidered bags and jackets, silver jewelry and utensils, crossbows and knives.

For easy shopping in Chiang Mai, there are stores along Chang Klan Road and at open-air shops on the same street during the night market. The best place to buy exquisite celadon is Mengrai Kilns (show room is located in Chiang Mai, opposite the Gimkame Club).

Freshly-painted umbrellas are spread out to dry in the sun in the village of Borsang.

LAMPHUN

Several interesting sidetrips may be made from Chiang Mai to diverse sites like Lamphun, Mae Hong Son and Doi Inthanon, Fang, Chiang Rai, the northern border and the Golden Triangle.

To reach **Lamphun**, 26km south of Chiang Mai, leave Chiang Mai by crossing the Nawarat Bridge and then turning right to follow the Ping River. About 4km from the bridge, and beyond the Foreign Cemetery on the left, a fork to the right leads, after 1km, to an unusual *chedi* on the left called **Wat Chedi Liem**. This pyramidal *chedi* with its niches filled with standing Buddha images is similar to several in the kingdom, the most notable being at Wat Kukut in Lamphun.

Down the same road is the **McKean Leprosarium**, a pioneering institution founded by an American missionary to provide care for lepers shunned by their families. Modern medicine and education has eliminated or curtailed many of the more horrible effects of the disease so this sanitarium also treats patients with other diseases requiring long recuperation periods.

The road to Lamphun is one of the most beautiful in the north. It is lined on either side by tall dipterocarpus trees which were the gift to the community of two princesses, one of Lamphun and one of Chiang Mai who each planted 13km of these stately trees. Along the road is the town of Saraphi where shops overflow with wicker and rush baskets and other items. Along the road, one can also find small open-air shops that make the colorful funeral chariots into which a casket is placed for the journey to the crematorium.

Lamphun itself is famed for two old *wats*, attractive women, and young and prolific *lamyai* fruit trees. Located on the right bank of the Kuang, a canal leading off from the Ping, the provincial town was once situated on the main road to Chiang Mai. A new highway bypasses Lamphun, which is perhaps a blessing in disguise, because the town has managed to preserve a mellow up-country atmosphere, appropriate to its historical significance. Lamphun was once the seat of the Haripunchai kingdom. On the site of the original palace now stands Wat Prathat Haripunchai, on the left side of Lamphun's main street.

To gain the best perspective on **Wat Prathat Haripunchai**, enter it through its riverside gate, where large statues of mythical lions guard its portals. Inside the large compound, monks study in a large Buddhist school set among monuments and buildings which date as far back as the late 9th century making the *wat* one of the oldest in northern Thailand. The base of the 50-meter-high gold-topped *chedi* in the center of the courtyard is the oldest structure in the temple.

Ten centuries younger, but still respectably old, the gilded-roofed library stands to the left of a *sala* that shelters one of the largest bronze gongs in the world. The *sala* was restored after a 1915 fire damaged it. The somewhat disorganized temple museum contains a representative sampling of several styles of old Buddhist art, including a rather rare silver Buddha head. Another small building close by is garishly illustrated with frescoes depicting the good getting their reward and the bad their just desserts.

A kilometer west of Lamphun's old moat stands **Wat Kukut**, also known as Wat Chama Devi. Although generally uninteresting, the temple has a superb pair of unusual *chedis*. The larger *chedi* consists of five tiers, each of which contains three niches. Each niche holds a Buddha statue, making an impressive display of 15 Buddha images on each side, or 60 Buddhas in all gazing on the courtyard. This *chedi* is thought to have been built by Chama Devi, the fabled princess of Lopburi and queen of Lamphun.

The trip to Lamphun can also be combined with a visit to **Pa Sang**, about 12km southwest of Lamphun on Road 106. This cotton weaving center is also reputed to have some of the North's most beautiful women.

uddha
nage in a
che at Wat
ukut,
mphun.

MAE HONG SON

From Chiang Mai, regular domestic flights offer a bumpy, 40-minute flight over cloud-covered hills to **Mae Hong Son** several times a day. By land, a bus leaves Chiang Mai Gate daily at around 7am for the 11-hour, 368-km horseshoe journey, which passes through Hot and Mae Sarieng, then goes north through jungle and fields, past the Shan settlement of Khun Yuam, to arrive at Mae Hong Son by dusk. The trip is made more enjoyable by renting a car or a four-wheel drive jeep in Chiang Mai, driving to Hot, spending time in Mae Hong Son and then returning by the new northern route via Pai.

To reach Mae Hong Son by road, head south from Chiang Mai on Road 108. Just before the 57-km-stone, turn right and drive 10km to the entrance of **Doi Inthanon National Park**, named after its prime attraction, Doi Inthanon, the highest mountain in the country at 2,596m. Girls rush out to sell bead necklaces, and cold beer is served in small shops on the river's edge below **Mae Klang Waterfall**.

From the shops, walk up 20m to see this powerful cataract and its loud fusion of muddy brown water and white spray. Clearly marked footpaths branch into the rocky hills; one leads around a corner of boulders to a full view of a wider fall, **Pakauna**, which slides over its broad, craggy slopes for 120m like a liquid highway. The road continues to climb a further 25km to the peak of Doi Inthanon whose summit is dominated by an off-limits radar station. The views along the road of the surrounding valleys are spectacular.

The limestone knob of **Doi Inthanon** is a mere foothill in the southern extension of the Himalayan range that stretches southeast from Yunnan in southern China and resurfaces as far south as Irian Jaya. Although less than a giant, the mountain has a majesty of its own conveyed by the trumpeting of work-elephants who dwell on its slopes. Karen and Meo tribesmen also live in isolated villages but are slowly being re-located as the mountain is now a national reserve.

By making prior arrangements with park authorities in Chiang Mai, you can take a three-to-five-day hike on foot or by pony up the mountain. Several campsites maintained by the Wildlife Association afford simple accommodation for trekkers. During the climb you can observe rare birds and enjoy nature under a broad canopy of trees. Rather than a barren peak, the summit is lightly forested, complete with picnic tables and a Buddhist shrine.

At the 58-km-stone on Road 108, which is about 1km south of the park turnoff, lies **Chom Thong**. The town's pride is the elegant **Wat Phra That Si Chom Thong**, where glints of subdued light accentuate a beautiful collection of bronze Buddhas. The monastery creaks with old age, as do the slumping boughs of trees scattered about its courtyard. The brilliantly-gilded *chedi* dates from 1451, and the sanctuary, only 50 years later.

A large cruciform *viharn* built in 1516 is deeply carved with a profusion of floral patterns entwined with birds and *naga* serpents, dominates this temple compound. Four standing Buddhas, clothed like celestial kings, flank the *viharn*. Although much of the decoration in the temple reflects the Burmese penchant for elaboration, the central Buddha image with its protective *naga* seems eminently Thai, and resembles the famed image at Wat Phra Singh Luang in Chiang Mai. On either side of the *viharn* stand enshrined collections of miniature gold and silver Chiang Saen style Buddha images, some bejeweled and metallic, others carved of crystal.

Continuing south on Road 108, you will see many northern touches: rambling, stylized elephants carved on the backs of bullock carts; *lamyai* trees and green bean-patches; giant plaited baskets in which farmers thresh harvested rice; and shady, thatched-roof *salas* dotting the rice fields.

Hot, 88km southwest of Chiang Mai on Road 108, once lay 15km farther

south at the mouth of the Ping River, until the rising reservoir behind the Bhumibol Dam submerged it. Today, it has evolved into a fully-fledged town that seems to have been there forever.

Farther south on Road 1012 lies the site of ancient Hot. Cracked, rain-washed *chedis* dot the landscape like dignified relics from the time when Hot was part of the early kingdoms of the North. Excavations at these sites have unearthed gold jewelry, amulets and lively stucco carvings, which are now on display in the Chiang Mai Museum.

Road 1012 goes on to **Wang Lung**, a tiny village that earns its keep by selling dried fish caught in the catchment area created by Bhumibol Dam. Karen people have settled much of this area. Their necks hidden by a profusion of black beads, and their bodices covered with thick, colored patchwork, Karen tribeswomen walk into the tiny town to buy provisions.

You can hire a boat at Wang Lung for an hour's ride among the bamboo-and-reed-covered islands at the estuary of the Mae Ping and out onto the vast expanse of water at the upper end of the reservoir. Reflections of ruined *chedis* and strangely eroded cliffs enliven remote mountain scenes; but unless you speak Thai you will need a guide.

From Hot, Road 108 strikes out west across the Chaem River, following its right bank toward Mae Sarieng. About 17km from Hot, the road passes **Ob Luang Gorge**, called Thailand's version of the Grand Canyon, though it could be considered so only in miniature. Stop at the *sala* for a look into the deep, ragged incisions in the rock, cut over the ages by the river.

After the gorge, the road continues to wriggle like a snake through the hills. Butterflies and plumed blossoms brighten the way. Lovers of hot springs should turn left 4km after the gorge and drive another 5km to reach a lonely sulphur spring with a small campsite.

The drive to Mae Sarieng is more exciting than the town itself. The road runs like a roller coaster over the mountains. Not even motorbikes can reach

Spectacular display of rock formation at the Mae Klang waterfall, Doi Inthanon National Park.

some of the small leaf-and-bamboo huts tucked away in these hills.

Most of the villages belong to one of the largest hilltribe groups in Thailand, the Skaw Karen, who have settled along the Thai-Burmese frontier as far south as Chumphon. In the moist valleys they plant wet rice on steep terraces. The nomadic Karen burn away the forest to make clearings to plant new crops. This slash-and-burn technique has scarred the mountainsides and caused extensive erosion. On the slopes, black tree stumps stand out like whiskers on a green background of rice sprouts.

In places the road skirts high banks of red earth. Fresh mounds of mud on the asphalt show that landslides are not uncommon, because the banks cannot always hold back the runoff. The solution to this problem is the pine tree. Though it is not the tree one associates with tropical Thailand, the pine is well suited to rebuilding the soil. Its roots form an extensive earth-holding network, and its seeds do not easily burn. Before reaching the highest point on the road (at about 1,130m) on the way to Mae Sarieng, you pass the Thai-Danish Reforestation Camp which resembles a tropical Christmas tree farm.

Hemmed in by mountains, **Mae Sarieng** lies 103km west of Hot at the point where Road 108 bends to the north. Only a Burmese-style temple and Karen handicraft shops distinguish this small district seat and border trading post yet it may not be long before it can be reached by air.

Road 108 continues north on a rough track from Mae Sarieng through mountain scenery that is among the most breathtaking in Thailand, reaching **Mae Hong Son** 171km later. Secluded by jungle ridges and framed on the north and west by Burma, the province peacefully benefits from years of relative neglect by the outside world.

For years the place for seekers of old-world serenity, it is rapidly being developed with several major new hotels under construction. The presence of Karen, Meo, Lawa, Shan, Lisu, Lahu, and Burmese, all of whom easily outnumber the

The intertwined temples of Wat Chong Klang and Wat Chong Kum in Mae Hong Son.

ethnic Thais, adds intrigue to the ill-kept secret that Mae Hong Son lies on border smuggling routes. This air of illicit activity may well have been the reason it was selected as the site for the movie, "Air America", about the clandestine CIA airline that served in Laos during the Vietnam War.

Mae Hong Son lies in a valley between deep-green mountains, which accounts for its early morning fogs and its nickname, "The Vale of Mists". On particularly bad days, the peaks are obscured by heavy clouds or dark gray curtains of falling rain.

A commanding view of the town of Mae Hong Son and the surrounding countryside is afforded from Doi Kongmou which sits 250m above the town. At night, the two tall *chedis* of **Wat Phra That Doi Kongmou** atop the hill light up like timid beacons of civilization in this remote corner of Thailand.

A pond and a park at the center form a core of beauty and peace few other Thai towns possess. On the edge of the lake, across from a fitness park, are the intertwined temples of **Wat Chong Klang and Wat Chong Kum**. These Burmese-style *wats* with their pristine-white *chedi* look particularly moving in the dawn hours when reflected on the misty surface of the lake. Wat Chong Klang contains an interesting collection of carved wooden statues depicting figures from the *Phra Vessantorn* Jataka Tale. There is also a fine collection of Burmese glass paintings on the life of Buddha.

To return overland to Chiang Mai, retrace your steps on Road 108 via Mae Sarieng and Hot or continue north. Recent improvements have made the road negotiable even in the rainy season. It continues to the town of Pai, a settlement on the Pai River that looks from afar like a Swiss village.

Pai enjoys the remoteness once found in Mae Hong Son. As it is reached only after an arduous road journey, it is likely to remain that way for a few more years. From Pai, it is a picturesque journey on a winding road by bus or car back to Chiang Mai.

eft, a Shan child, resplendent in traditional attire. Right, poppies, with their illicit core of opium.

FANG

To reach the northern town of **Fang**, take Road 107 north from Chiang Mai (beginning at the Elephant Gate), towards Chiang Dao. The road passes through rice fields and small villages and then begins to climb past Mae Taeng and Mae Faek into the Mae Ping Gorge that forms the southern end of the Chiang Dao Valley. Ahead, on the left, one can see the outline of Chiang Dao Mountain as one follows the river's right bank through scenic countryside.

At the 56-km-stone is the Chiang Dao Elephant Camp on the bank of the Ping River. Twice each day at 9am and 10.30am, a line of elephants walks up the Ping River to be bathed by mahouts for the amusement of tourists who reward the baby elephants with bananas. The elephants then move to a dusty arena where they demonstrate how to make huge logs seem like toothpicks, picking them up or dragging them with great ease across the teak-shaded open space.

After the show, one can take a short elephant ride and then hire a small bamboo raft for a 45-minute trip down the Ping River.

About 60km from Chiang Mai on Road 107, a dirt road branches left and goes to **Doi Chiang Dao**, which, at an elevation of 2,186m, is Thailand's third highest peak. A jeep or a trailbike is needed to negotiate this 9-km-long track which emerges at a lookout point 1,000m up the mountainside.

From the government station there, officials trek out to assist hilltribes living on the slopes of Doi Chiang Dao and the neighboring mountains. At the nearby nursery, horticulturists experiment with new strains of tea that someday may be cultivated throughout the region. The government's agricultural aid on Doi Chiang Dao is aimed at eradicating opium cultivation.

Farther north, Road 107 enters the town of Chiang Dao, located 72km from Chiang Mai. Chiang Dao is little more than a provisioning post for surrounding villages but its wooden cafès and general stores are interesting to roam through. At the far end of town, a dirt road leads off to the left for 5km to **Chiang Dao Cave**. Boys with lanterns will lead one deep into the earth through high-ceilinged caverns with Buddha statues.

After visiting the cave, drive down a beautiful winding road through teak forests to the 118-km-stone. Three kilometers to the left are **Tab Tao Caves**. Climb the stairs to the so-called "light" cave on the left which contains a complete *viharn* lit by a shaft of light poring through a hole in the cave's ceiling.

The cave on the right is the "dark" cave through which a monk with a lantern will guide you 500m in. You must be fit and thin as some of the passages between the cave rooms require that you slither through a narrow opening. This is an activity that is certainly not for claustrophobics.

Fang, located 152km from Chiang Mai, is another one of those towns whose growth has blunted its reputation for wildness. During the 1950s the district witnessed a "black-gold rush," following a minor discovery of crude oil, but unfortunately, production never matched expectation.

Today, Fang enjoys a reputation as a natural conduit for opium smugglers although nothing in its non-descript appearance would suggest it. Sprawling both sides of the road in a flat valley, it is home to remnants of Chiang Kaishek's Kuomintang Army who settled in Fang and act as an auxiliary border patrol. The Yunnanese-speaking soldiers fled China after the Communist takeover in 1949.

Dressed in distinctively embroidered clothing, Yao hilltribes also live in the mountains around Fang. The women wear black hats decorated with red or magenta woolen balls, while babies carried on their mothers' backs sport little embroidered caps. Young girls may spend an entire year embroidering large pants – panels for their weddings. To appreciate the meaning and cultural context of this handicraft, read Jac-

Preceding pages, a journey through the caverns of Chiang Dao unearths a treasure trove of Buddha statues.

queline Butler's *Yao Embroidery*.

The government has worked extensively with the Yao, promoting crops as substitutes for the more lucrative opium. One Yao headman, leader of a 15-house village, proudly listed his new produce: potatoes, corn, garlic, chickens and pigs. His eyes widened as he happily described the size of the breeding pig presented to the village by the king. On the left about 8km northeast of Fang is an agricultural station near the hot springs of Baw Nam Rawn.

From Fang, a rough road leads north 24km to **Tha Thon** on the banks of the Mae Kok River. Here, you can rent a boat for an exciting three-hour journey down the Kok to Chiang Rai. It is now also possible to continue north to the town of **Mae Salong**.

The road is dusty but wide and has been paved since 1991. It swiftly climbs a ridge along the Burmese border to emerge at a small town which clings to the hillsides. At first, it seems one has taken a wrong turn and ended up in a Chinese village. The walls of Chinese houses are decorated by red banners covered in gold Yunnanese characters and everyone one meets speaks Yunnanese.

It quickly becomes apparent that these, too, are remnants of the Kuomintang Army who were given refuge in Thailand. Unfortunately, many soon became involved in the opium trade and were pacified only recently by the Thai army who renamed the town "Santakiri" which means "town of peace." Here, the inhabitants tend tea plantations and brew potent wines.

Of more recent vintage is Baan Hin Taek, a few kilometers east. It was only in 1988 that the opium warlord, Khun Sa, was routed out of his mountain stronghold. A 13-km paved road will soon lead to the village, allowing visits by outsiders. In the meantime, heavily-armed soldiers man bunkers labeled with the unreassuring sign, "Tourist Security Post".

The road east drops off the ridge, eventually entering the Chiang Rai Valley just above Mae Chan.

Bucolic vignettes in the North. Left, work elephants and below, cattle, bottle-fed by Akha women.

Chiang Rai lies only about 65km to the east of Fang; but at present Road 1001, which wriggles east from below Fang through Mae Suai toward Chiang Rai is unsurfaced and in poor condition. This means that a side trip to Chiang Rai begins in Chiang Mai, the focal point for the North.

Chiang Rai is linked to Chiang Mai by air; there are several domestic, daily flights directly to Chiang Rai from Bangkok or via Chiang Mai. Otherwise, the standard way to Chiang Rai is along Route 1, which continues north from Lampang or a highway that leads northeast from Chiang Mai via Doi Saket, cutting travel time by half over the old route through Lampang.

Route 1 twists around and over mountains on its way to **Ngao** 81km northeast of Lampang. At the highest point in the road, below twin rocky peaks, drivers stop, or if in a hurry just blow their horns or *wai* to pay respects to the *phis* believed to inhabit the pass. Scores of spirit houses, some simple like farmers' houses, others as elaborate as the Marble Temple, cluster along the roadside.

Teak saplings line Route 1 between Lampang and Ngao, thanks to the Forest Industry Organization (FIO). The FIO also runs the Lampang Young Elephants School. Here, 54km from Lampang and 1½km west of the highway behind Pang-la village, visitors can watch mahouts put their young pachyderms through mounting, marching and log-dragging drills until noon. If made to train beyond noon, the elephants stamp their feet in protest until they are allowed to lumber off to their stalls for a snack of sugar cane.

About 19km before the district town of Ngao, a left turn leads in less than 1km to a small grove of teak trees and a refreshment stand that mark the entrance to **Tham Pha Thai**, probably the most interesting cave in Thailand. Climb the 283 concrete steps up the hill to the bowl that contains several caves. Drop down into the mouth to the huge arched entrance to the grotto above which stands a gleaming white *chedi*.

Inside the main cave is a large bronze Buddha image, an object of great veneration, judging from the number of garlands and candles. Most striking, though, is the colossal stalagmite rising like a white explosion from a sea of limestone. Often a young novice monk will lead visitors down into the cave and point out bizarre limestone formations which, with a little imagination, can resemble a throne, a rabbit or a turtle. Slithering green snakes wrap themselves around electric wires or coil up in crevices. The guide explains that these snakes are protected and have never bitten anyone. The 400-m walk into the cave ends at a small mound of bat guano. Light streaks down from a jagged opening in the cave roof, projecting the silhouettes of flying bats onto the cavern walls.

About 12km before Ngao, on the left of Route 1, the Burmese-style **Wat Chong Kram** exudes charm in the face of alarming decrepitude. The ceiling is gradually becoming more crooked as its supporting pillars sink into the mud; as one guidebook has advised, "See it before it falls down!"

Route 1 continues through Ngao and then goes 49km farther to **Phayao**. Although quite small and outwardly undistinguished, Phayao holds great interest for archaeologists, as the town was rebuilt in the 11th century on a more ancient deserted site. Judging from the remains of a moat and eight city gates which enclose an area measuring about 2sq km, scholars believe the older site may predate the Bronze Age. Wat Li on the left of the road has a fine collection of terracotta Buddha heads of the Dvaravati period which were unearthed in the surrounding fields.

Between the lake and the road, as you leave Phayao, sits **Wat Si Khom Kham**, considered by scholars as the most important temple in the area for its 400-year-old, 16-m-high Buddha image inside a *viharn*. In a new ubolsot on the edge of the lake, modern Thai artist

Angkarn Kalayanapongsa has created a beautiful set of murals.

From Phayao, Route 1 continues north 94km to the provincial capital of **Chiang Rai**, located in Thailand's northernmost province, at an elevation of about 580 meters. King Mengrai who also established Chiang Mai as a walled city, founded it in 1281. Legend claims that the king, then ruler of Chiang Saen, decided to conquer regions to the south after his favorite elephant ran away in a southerly direction. The search for the elephant led to the banks of the Kok River, where the king decided to build Chiang Rai. A statue of the king stands north of Chiang Rai along the road to Mae Chan.

Like other cities of the north, Chiang Rai has undergone rapid development not only in the town itself but in the hills where vacation homes for Bangkok's affluent are rising. Near the busy streets are two of the town's most important temples: Wat Phra Singh and Wat Phra Keo. Both share the distinction of having once sheltered famous images. The *chedi* and *viharn* at **Wat Phra Singh**, where legend holds that an important Theravada image was located, have been restored too many times to allow accurate dating, but documents suggest the 15th century or earlier.

Wat Phra Keo, situated behind Wat Phra Singh, is believed to have been the original residence of the Emerald Buddha which is now in Bangkok at the royal temple of the same name. To the west of Wat Phra Keo rises Ngam Muang Hill. Inside the *wat* atop the hill, a reliquary is believed to contain the bones of King Mengrai, placed there by one of his sons.

From Chiang Rai, Road 110 goes 29km north to **Mae Chan**. Formerly a center for silverwork, the tiny district town now serves as a trading post for Akha and Yao hillpeople who sell their goods and buy manufactured items. You can still view some silver and other tribal handicrafts at the shops of Lao Tzan, a Yao merchant, and Lao Taa, who is half Lisu and half Haw Chinese (like the Kuomintang soldiers).

HILLTRIBES

About 2km beyond Mae Chan, a road on the left off Road 110 leads through a valley noted for its fragrant rice, and then ascends to Doi Thong (or "The Flag Mountain"). The tallest point in the region, the *wat* has an identical pair of *chedis* and enjoys an unparalleled view.

From the Mae Kam community development station and the Princess Mother Foundation on the mountain, government officials go out to assist local hillpeople in agricultural and village development projects.

The trail leading from the Mae Kam center continues on to Ko Saen Chai, an **Akha** village. The Akha, who inhabit Thailand only in Chiang Rai province, build wooden swings and hold swinging ceremonies around their New Year to bring good luck and to enhance the fertility of the soil. Akha women embroider their black shirts and hats with bright cloth beads and silver ornaments.

Chiang Rai province also hosts the Yao, the Blue and White Hmong, Lisu, Lahu, Lahu Shi, and Skaw and P'wo Karen. Each main group speaks its own language, and follows animist customs (based on a belief in spirits) as well as more recently adopted religious beliefs. Most of the tribes came to Thailand from China via Burma and Laos within the last 100 years. The Hmongs are probably the best known of these hillpeoples, partly due to the proximity of several Hmong villages to Chiang Mai, and also because of the tribal insurgency in the 1960s known as the Meo War.

Basically shy and clannish, the hillpeople settle at specific altitudes, some building villages only above 1,000m. Although members of some tribes have embraced Islam, Buddhism, or Christianity in response to missionary work, most retain strong animist convictions. They protect their homes and villages with altars, fertility symbols, totems and objects of sympathetic magic (including model airplanes).

Below left, Akha matriarch in the tribe's distinctive head-dress. **Below right** White Hmong beau

About 70,000 **Karen** in Thailand live in Mae Hong Son, Chiang Mai, Chiang Rai and Lamphun. They are of Tibeto-Burman stock. Many are Christians and have beliefs bearing some resemblance to early Christianity. The Karen are endogamous and matrilineal.

Nearly 20,000 **Lisu**, also of Tibeto-Burman origin, live in North Thailand as far south as Tak, where one group lives near a Black Lahu tribe. Different hilltribes often live peacefully in close proximity. They are patrilineal and have strong animist beliefs; each village has a folk healer and exorcist (*tongpa*). Along with the Hmongs, the Lisu have been major opium cultivators.

The **Lahu** are famed for their hunting skills. Some groups reportedly recognize a "man-god" who must qualify himself through physical and magical feats. **Yao** villages celebrate the Chinese new year by slaughtering a pig, drinking great quantities of rice wine, and making merry for days. The **Hmong** (Meo) practice a courting ritual in which boys and girls stand in separate lines throwing balls to each other to "break the ice."

Gradually all the tribes are assimilating Thai culture through trade contacts and education in *nikhorn* ("settlement") schools. The sale of their crafts has improved the economies of many of the tribes. Organizations like the Thai Hill-Crafts Foundation and the Border Patrol Police have found domestic and foreign markets for new agricultural produce introduced into the areas and for the colorful and distinctive tribal crafts. Many shops in Bangkok and other cities sell hilltribe jewelry, embroidery, bags and woven goods.

From Mae Chan, Road 101 continues 34km to **Mae Sai** at the northernmost point in Thailand. Mae Sai and Chiang Saen lie within the Golden Triangle formed by the borders of Burma, Laos and Thailand. This area does a thriving business selling many goods to Burmese who cross the border on shopping sprees. Many Thais from Chiang Rai *pai-tio* in Mae Sai and browse over smuggled items from Laos and Burma.

ovely Lisu
dies.

APEX OF THE GOLDEN TRIANGLE

There are two routes to the ancient capital of **Chiang Saen**. One can return south to Mae Chan, and then swing northeast on Road 1010. The other road begins in the middle of Mae Sai, running east from the Sin Wattana Hotel. This road takes one through beautiful countryside to the official point where the three countries meet. This Golden Triangle is demarcated by a gateway and a spacious modern hotel, the Golden Triangle Resort. Nine kilometers later, the road enters Chiang Saen.

Scholars believe the town was founded around the end of the 13th century and strongly fortified about 100 years later. The Burmese captured it in the 16th century, but Rama I recaptured it late in the 19th century. Fearing history would repeat itself with another Burmese invasion, however, Rama I ordered the town destroyed. It remained deserted until the reign of Rama V, and in 1957 the town became a district seat.

Chiang Saen's lovely setting on the Mekong River strongly enhances the charm of its old temples. Moreover, it is one of the few old towns in Thailand to have retained all its lovely old trees, giving it a rare claim to tranquillity. The remains of its stout wall and moat can clearly be seen at its perimeter and ruins of ancient monuments are scattered everywhere, popping up when one least expects them.

Just west of town stands **Wat Pa Sak**, whose name derives from the use of 300 teak (*sak*) trunks for the original enclosure. The temple's foundation was laid in 1295 during the reign of King Ramkamhaeng. Earlier Srivichaiya and Dvaravati influences, along with the predominant Sukhothai style, are evident in the *that* ("reliquary"), the clothing of the deities, and in the stucco walking Buddhas.

Located about 1km west of the town gate, **Wat Prathat Chom Kitti** occupies a hill commanding a good view of Chiang Saen. Chronicles suggest that the old *that* with a leaning top was first built around the 10th century and subsequently restored at least twice. Below this temple lies a ruined *chedi* in **Wat Chom Chang**. From there a staircase leads farther downhill toward town.

Close to the main street stand **Wat Chedi Luang** and a branch of the National Museum. The 60-m-tall 13th-century *chedi* stands out in style as well as size; its bricks rise from an octagonal base to a bell-shaped top. In the grounds of the museum one can see a good assortment of bronze Buddhas and other Chiang Saen art.

The most scenic return trip from Chiang Saen to Chiang Rai is via water in a long-tail boat down the Mekong River as far as **Chiang Khong**, a three-hour trip after the rainy season when the river is high. Be sure to check on security conditions before setting out. The river follows an approximately S-shaped course, first flowing southeast to the mouth of the Kok River, then curving north between beautiful hills and mountains, then finally south again for thrilling 20km down deep narrow sections, through rapids and eddies beneath steep, jungled mountain-sides.

At Chiang Khong, the river widens slightly. Set on left-bank hills, the Laotian town of **Ban Houei San** lies opposite the Chiang Khong district seat. Laotian government officials still work in fortifications built by the French. During the times when relations between Thailand and Laos are cordial, a ferry boat carries visitors across the river to Ban Houei San.

Chiang Khong town proper has few sights to offer other than watching the hilltribe people coming back and forth to visit the market and hospital here. Nevertheless, this trip used to be popular with visitors due to the availability of daily flights from Ban Houei San to the beautiful royal capital at Luang Prabang, with connections onward to Vientiane, and then back into northeast Thailand.

From Chiang Khong, Road 1021 goes to Thoeng, home of the lucky stones; Road 1021 then returns to the provincial capital of Chiang Rai.

he Wat
rathat Chom
itti in
hiang Saen
s believed to
ave been
uilt in the
0th century.

THE NAN VALLEY

To reach **Nan** from Chiang Rai, one must take a circuitous path, following Route 1 south through Phayao and Ngao, and then fork southeast onto Road 103 to Song and Rong Kwang districts of Phrae province. Phrae province, once notorious for its hired gunmen, is now better known for its tobacco plantations. At Rong Kwang, Road 101 heads northeast 96km to Nan. Taxis and buses convey passengers who disembarked from the train in Den Chai for Phrae and Nan. Nan is also linked by air with Bangkok by regular domestic flights that touch down at Phitsanulok and Phrae and continue on to Chiang Mai. It is also possible to fly directly from Chiang Mai.

Road 101 winds through sparsely settled hills and teak reserves. You may see some elephants dragging logs alongside the road. The government, through reforestation, is trying to re-duce the damage from overlogging but the trees take a long time to grow. Beyond Sa District, 24km before Nan, the road begins to parallel the Nan River that flows southward a few kilometers to the east. The fertile Nan valley supports rice and corn. The provincial capital, seat of an independent kingdom until this century, lies on the right bank of the river.

Nan's town walls were rebuilt in 1857 to replace the original walls destroyed in a severe flood 40 years earlier. The walls are roughly circular, a characteristic of Mon town planning, an influence which pre-dates the town's establishment in the late 14th century, and suggests habitation by an earlier group of people.

The first recorded settlement of Nan province dates from 1282 when Khun Fong, brother of the founder of Vientiane, set up a court in Wora Nakhon, 70km north of the present provincial capital. Nan's inaccessibility helped it remain relatively free, although it did fall occasionally under the sway of

Paddle power at the dragon boat race in Nan.

Chiang Mai, the Burmese (for 200 years), and other powers – until 1931 when the province came fully under the control of Bangkok.

The presence of Thai Army soldiers in Nan indicates that there are security problems in the remote districts. Nan town, though, is safe. The Thevarat Hotel has air-conditioned rooms although Nan is usually cool. Around 5am the main market begins to bustle; look for rattan products, famous Nan tangerines, and hand-crafted items sold by Yao women.

Just south of the *sala klang* government offices stands the town's most interesting temple, **Wat Phumin**, built in 1596 and extensively restored in the l9th century. The carved doors are nearly comparable to the famous doors of the *viharn* of Bangkok's Wat Suthat (now kept in the National Museum). Although the *wat*'s murals were inexpertly restored, they tell an interesting story of the kingdom, with scenes depicting the arrival of foreigners, and even some bawdy comic portrayals. Inside the unusual cross-shaped hall

are four gilded stucco images facing the cardinal directions.

Its most salient features are the twin *nagas* whose undulating bodies form balustrade railings for stairways on the east, running through the building itself and then down the stairway balustrade on the west. No other temple in Thailand is decorated in this manner. Unusual, too, are the northern and southern stairway finials which resemble giant flames.

The "Elephant-Supported Temple" or **Wat Chang Kham** is located in what was the center of the old walled city, now opposite the provincial administrative offices. Actually, it is an old *chedi* supported by elephant buttresses, seven elephants per side under the second tier of the base, a Sukhothai motif derived from Sri Lankan temples. A Nan prince built the *viharn* in 1547. Two walking and one standing Buddha images in front of the main altar are good examples of the Sukhothai style. An inscription dated 1547 records the installation of the

viharn's principal image in that year. On the reverse side is a prophecy about the fifth (future) Buddha, Sri Ariyametteya Bodhisattva.

Two life-size Sukhothai Buddhas, dated 1427, reside in **Wat Phya Phu**. One bears an inscription stating that it was cast in the fourth lunar month of that year. The total of five similar images at both *wats* was chosen to ensure that the then prince would be reborn as a man in the lifetime of the future fifth Buddha, and also to attest that Buddhism would last 5,000 years.

Wat Suan Tan, the only temple in the North with a *prang* (rounded ornate spire), also features an interesting 500-year-old bronze seated Buddha in its *viharn*. In 1450, the conquering King Tiloka of Chiang Mai gave the people of Nan seven days to collect enough metal for a new image, then he set a 100-day deadline for refugee Sukhothai artists to fashion it. The image is called *Phra Khao Thong Thip.*

Across the river from Wat Suan Tan, 3km southeast of town on a small hill, sits **Wat Chae Haeng**. There, during the fourth lunar month, Nan residents hold a boisterous fair, complete with fireworks. The temple's name, meaning "to soak the parched," refers to an incident in the life of Buddha which the pious believe predicted that this spot would shelter relics.

Southwest of town, down a dirt track off Road 101, **Wat Khao Noi** affords a good view of Nan from a small mountain. A golden parasol tops the old Chiang Saen *chedi* there. This temple hosts a colorful annual fair in the sixth lunar month.

Those who are not deterred by the sight of passing military convoys filled with weapon-toting troops can venture 60km north of Nan town to the district of **Phua**. There, missionaries and civil servants attend to the needs of several thousand people from the hilltribes and other ethnic minorities living in resettlement camps. The Thai government has relocated these people to isolate them from insurgents, but life in the Phua valley does not particularly suit hill people.

A more scenic and relaxed sidetrip goes south from Nan on Road 101 to Sa, then on the dirt road due south to Na Noi. A few kilometers beyond Na Noi lies **Sao Din Canyon**, a valley of wind-carved rock monuments used as a film setting in many Thai movies. From the canyon, return to Road 101, pass the junction with Road 103 at Rong Kwang and drive 31km to **Phrae**. The back streets of the town are filled with picturesque old wooden houses resting on stout columns. Also worth visiting is **Wat Phra That Cho Mae** which is set on a small hill surrounded by orchards and located on Road 1022 about 8km east of town. The high-ceilinged *viharn* and parts of the courtyard were recently renovated.

From Phrae, Road 101 follows the Yom River. Around Sung Men you may see hundreds of people digging and panning for gems, responding to news or rumors of new discoveries which send them scurrying in search of instant wealth.

About 10km beyond Sung Men lies Den Chai. You can reach Uttaradit, the next provincial town, by train or car.

If most of the buildings in **Uttaradit** seem new it is because the previous downtown area was hit by a calamity common among many of Thailand's towns: fire. A blaze in 1967 leveled most of the city and the concrete replacements have little to recommend them.

From Uttaradit town, which lies between the rail line and the Nan River, you can travel east 55km to **Sirikit Dam**, named after the queen. Completed in 1973, the dam generates power and provides great amounts of sorely needed water during the dry season to farms around Uttaradit. Below the dam, near Pak Pat village, stands the tallest teak tree in Thailand.

From Uttaradit, one can begin a trip to the Northeast by driving due south to Phitsanulok, then east on Road 12 to Lom Sak, and north on Road 203 to Loei. To return to Bangkok, drive south to Phitsanulok, picking up Road 117 to Nakhon Sawan and Route 1 for the remaining distance to the capital.

Sao Din Canyon – a valley of wind-carved rock monuments.

Northeast Thailand

50 km

NORTHEAST: AN AREA
IN TRANSITION

A Thai village of little romantic appeal: a tired-looking, dusty place where a few scrawny chickens peck in the shade of mean houses; not the sort of place likely to appear on any picture postcard. It is a picture characteristic of the Northeast.

Of Lao extraction, many Northeasterners' ancestors drifted across the great Mekong River which forms the natural border. Today, they retain the Lao quality of sweet passivity in the face of adversity. Historically, they have had ample opportunity to put the quality to use, for the Northeast has not been an easy place to live. The soil is thin and infertile, there is either not enough rain or too much, and the Mekong can be a terror at flood-time. Because of inadequate transportation few industries settle here, although many new ones are being drawn here by promises of cheap land and labor. Many Northeasterners go to Bangkok, leaving their poor villages to fill the most menial of unskilled jobs in the capital – servants, day-laborers, *tuk-tuk* and taxi drivers.

The Northeast is a high plateau on which about one-third of the country's population live. The basic agricultural products of the Northeast are poor-soil staples like cotton and jute. Mulberry trees, too, are grown to feed the worms that spin the silk that travels far away, to adorn a beautiful woman in New York or Paris. Small wonder that the Northeast also has a tradition of dissident politicians whose demands for social reform have been louder than those from most other parts of the country.

In the late 1950s, the modern Friendship Highway, a joint Thai-American undertaking, for the first time made this region accessible. In 1955, Their Majesties made the first-ever royal visit to the Northeast. In the 1960s, the establishment of several large American military bases during the Vietnam War, whatever their moral and political shortcomings, at least pumped new and needed money into the region and made boom towns out of once sleepy places like Nakhon Ratchasima (Korat), Ubon, Udon and Nakhon Phanom.

In April 1994, the first road bridge from Thailand crossing the Mekong River at Nong Khai into Laos was officially opened to traffic. At a cost of US$30 million, the bridge has generated an air of excitement and optimism into an area which had little to be optimistic about.

Today, there is a new drive to develop the Northeast. Numerous development projects have been initiated by the Royal Family and the government to create irrigation canals, village ponds and roads to transport agricultural produce to distant markets.

A northeastern university has been opened at Khon Kaen to serve the students of the area and introduce new ideas at the local level. A northeastern doctor, Krasae Channawong, a member of the new generation, won the Magsaysay Award (the Asian equivalent of the Nobel Prize) for his pioneering work in rural medicine and birth control in the impoverished village of Muang Phon where he grew up. There is a growing sense of achievement and purpose in E-san, and the day may not be far off when the name is no longer synonymous with poverty and problems.

For reasons that should be plain, the Northeast does not usually figure prominently on anybody's list of travel destinations in Thailand. But even this may be changing, too, thanks to some extraordinary discoveries being made at Ban Chieng concerning the region's distant past and recent efforts to restore some of the region's superb old monuments. The Northeast is a treasure trove of ancient monuments. Parts of the region were ruled by the Khmers during the great period when they built Angkor Wat, and colonized large areas of the Northeast, building temples and *stupas* in key cities. One, Phimai, not far from Nakhon Ratchasima (Korat), the largest city in the Northeast, has been carefully restored by the Department of Fine Arts; dubbed the "Angkor Wat of Thailand" it is already an important tourist attraction. If Angkor itself remains closed to outsiders, the Northeast may be the best available place in Asia to view the remains of this splendid culture.

Nor is the Northeast completely devoid of fine scenery. Among adventurous Thai tourists, a popular hot-season undertaking is a trip to Loei Province to climb 1,500-m Phu Kradung Mountain. The ascent is a mild endurance test, but the rewards are breathtaking views, a park-like plateau forested with pine trees, and a dramatic drop in temperature. During Thailand's cool season, Loei and Phu Kradung generally register the lowest temperatures in the kingdom.

The Northeast is a region in the midst of transition. The conventional traveler in search of the picturesque and the romantic would probably be best advised to miss it and concentrate on other areas of Thailand. For those who want to see something of contemporary problems, however, and thus get a more balanced view of the country as a whole, it is an essential part of the itinerary.

Travel in the Northeast today is generally fast and easy over a terrain that in most places slopes gently from an elevation of 250m above sea level in the northwest corner to less than 100m in the southeast.

There are domestic flights from Bangkok to Nakhon Phanom, Udon, Ubon, Khon Kaen and Loei in the Northeast. Overland, scores of buses depart Bangkok's Northern Terminal on Phaholyothin Road every day for direct trips to most northeastern provincial capitals with many stops along the way. Connections are available upcountry for buses to practically every town in the Northeast. Even remote villages can be reached by small, converted pick-up trucks, "baht buses". For luxury travel, there is an air-conditioned bus service to Nakhon Phanom and Surin.

The Khmer ruins of Phimai, dating from the same period of the Angkor Wat.

THE KORAT PLATEAU

The good roads of the Northeast invite travel by car, which undoubtedly is the best way to see the many out-of-the-way sights of this part of the country. Choose from two basic itineraries. Route 2 begins near Saraburi, north-northeast of Bangkok, and runs through the heart of the Northeast. Also called the Mitraparb or "Friendship" Highway, this road passes most of the big provincial capitals and ends at Nong Khai on the Mekong. For a more leisurely trip through rural Issan, take the "Elephant's Ear" route through Surin and Ubon for about four days along the scenic and ethnically interesting periphery of the Northeast.

The Friendship Highway, or Route 2, the main road through the Northeast, begins about 105km from Bangkok, just before the town of Saraburi. About 20km after the Saraburi turnoff on Route 2, a dirt road on the right leads to an experimental farm run by the Kasetsart Agricultural University of Bangkok and beyond to **Phra Ngam Cave** ("Beautiful Buddha Image" Cave) where a Dvaravati-era image may be seen. There are numerous other caves nearby, many of them unexplored.

Another 15km leads to **Muak Lek Valley**. Once known for malaria, Muak Lek has been transformed from an unhealthy jungle into dairy land that features a small Arboretum Garden Department where a wonderful variety of roses bloom around a blue stream and a roadside stand from which the Thai Danish Dairy sells fresh milk products, including yoghurt.

About 48km east of Saraburi, a sign points to **Wat Teppitakpunnaram** where a monumental white Buddha sits on a green mountain like an alabaster relic. The countryside in this area belongs to Khao Yai ("Big Mountain") National Park, hidden 40km to the south (see "Bangkok Surroundings").

Route 2 continues northeast up the Korat Plateau, passing the reservoir of **Lam Ta Kong Dam**.

Soon the blue lake disappears and scrub brush, typical vegetation of the dry Northeast, begins to dominate the scenery. Past the district town of Pak Chong 62km from Saraburi, travel another 86km to the provincial capital of Korat, now officially called Nakhon Ratchasima.

Richest and largest city in the Northeast, **Nakhon Ratchasima** (Korat) serves as a trade, communications and military center for the entire northeast region. It is also the capital of the most densely populated upcountry province in Thailand where over 1.5 million people live. Korat grew rapidly in the 1960s with the build-up of its Royal Thai Air Force Base where American fighter-bombers operated during the Indochina War.

Although a busy commercial center, Korat has not forgotten its past. A statue of national heroine Khunying Mo (Tao Suranari) presides over the town square and the whitewashed ramparts of the old city wall. Khunying Mo was the wife of an assistant provincial governor in the early 19th century, when Prince Anu of Vientiane led his army into Korat. After taking the city, the prince threatened to enslave its residents. Khunying Mo rallied the women of Korat who enticed many of the Laotian soldiers to a drunken revelry and then killed them. Prince Anu, who meanwhile had gone to attack Saraburi, was thus forced to withdraw his depleted forces to Vientiane.

With comfortable hotels such as the Chomsurang, Korat, Sri Pattana, Great Inn, Sakol, Sima Thani and Thai Pokaphan, which have air-conditioned rooms; a big night market; and at least five cinemas with films fresh from Bangkok; Korat makes a comfortable and convenient base for some interesting side trips.

To visit an important nearby silk production center, take Road 304 south towards Kabin Buri. After 27km lies the town of **Pak Thongchai** where Jim Thompson Co. has established a weaving cooperative to produce Thai silk. Road 304 also provides an alternative return route to Bangkok.

rth-eastern
oman with
pical
equered
adscarf.

KHMER RUINS

Korat's main nearby attractions are two sites created nine centuries ago by Khmer architects. Both Prasat Phanom Wan and Phimai lie north of Korat off Route 2. Drive north about 14km from the provincial capital to a dirt road that leads off to the right 4km to the isolated and peaceful monastery of **Prasat Phanom Wan**. Heavy stone galleries reveal the Khmer penchant for false windows with stone mullions, a method adopted to compensate for the soft stone.

Romantic zigzags cover the carved stones. An uncommon stillness pervades the place, broken only by the footsteps of resident monks. Unlike the majority of Khmer ruins, this one contains an active temple. Behind its well-preserved vaulted entrance, the original dark sanctuary is filled with many more recent Buddha images of different styles, most of them covered with patches of gold leaf. Full-grown trees sprout from the oldest chambers. The presence of older monks reminds visitors that donations are needed to help with the upkeep of the site.

Farther north 34km on Route 2, lies the turnoff on the right that goes about 10 km east to the ruins of **Phimai**, which along with the elephant roundup at Surin and the cool plateau of Phu Kradung, are the main tourist attractions of the Northeast. These are the only ruins in Thailand with hours; they close at 4.30pm to prevent plundering.

King Jayavarman VII, last of the great Angkor monarchs, who had his face chiseled in dozens of eerie angles on the towers of Angkor Thom, could easily have traveled from his palace along a 240-km road to Phimai, at the western extent of his kingdom. A string of 112 rest houses was constructed along the route to shelter other devotees making the long pilgrimage to Phimai.

During his reign (AD 1181–1201), Phimai prospered within a walled rectangular area 1,000m by 560m, situated on an artificial island created by linking the Moun River and one of its tributaries by means of a canal. Like the shrines at Angkor, the monuments at Phimai which endure in stone were never inhabited. Shops, shelters, libraries and houses were built of wood and have long since disintegrated.

The old city gate, probably the main entrance to the sanctuary, still stands at the end of Phimai's present main street. Along the street near the Moun River Bridge, the Fine Arts Department maintains an open-air museum displaying some of the more beautifully carved lintels and statues found in the area.

Before leaving Phimai, see *Sai Ngam*, "Beautiful Banyan Tree," 1km east of the temple on an irrigation reservoir. It has an extraordinary umbrella of dense leaves and roots which locals revere as a shelter for special spirits.

From Phimai you can continue north on Route 2 to Khon Kaen and beyond directly to the Mekong River town of Nong Khai. But for a better look at the rural Northeast, more Khmer temples, and folksy Issan atmosphere, journey along the road running roughly parallel to the Cambodian and Laotian borders.

For the longer route through the region, return to Korat and from there take Road 24 dipping south and then east at Chok Chai. Farther east about 80km Road 219 branches north to the town of Buri Ram. Stay on Road 24 for another 18km, to turn right at Ban Ta Ko at the sign for Prasat Phanom Rung. Follow the road to Ban Wan, bear left, and soon you reach Khmer hilltop temple ruins.

Three full ponds, essential elements of Khmer monumental architecture, and pretty farmland surround **Prasat Phanom Rung**. Historians believe this temple was an important station between Angkor and Phimai during the 11th and 12th centuries. Several generations must have elapsed during its construction, since several of the stone lintels resemble the early Baphuon style while the *nagas* date from the later Angkor Wat period. A stone inscription in Sanskrit mentions King Suryavarman II who built Angkor Wat.

The temple includes a stolen lintel spirited out of Thailand by art thieves and recently returned by the Chicago

Art Museum. The main *prang* of Phanom Rung and its galleries and chapels reflect the geometric precision of Angkor architecture; symmetrical doors and windows and antechapels face the four cardinal points. The monumental staircase, interrupted by landings, exudes the sense of mass and power typical of Khmer design. Look for the sandstone bas-reliefs of elephants and enthroned Hindu deities.

Monks of the Dharmayuti sect maintain the temple. During the Songkran festival in April, country folk walk in processions up the main staircase.

Going farther east on Road 24 to Prakhon Chai takes you near another site worth visiting. These second ruins can be reached by traveling south on Road 2075 about 1km to a smaller road which branches right near a modern temple. Follow it for 12km to Ban Chorake, "Village of Crocodiles," then another 1km to the Khmer temple ruins of Muang Tham.

Muang Tham or Lower Temple sits on a mossy lawn like an art historian's daydream. Older than Prasat Phanom Rung, its cornerstones were laid in the 10th century and the temple finished about a hundred years later. Thick jungle surrounded Muang Tham until recently, when a group of families migrated there from Ubon, cleared the area and founded a large village. The Fine Arts Department is now excavating the foundations preparatory to restoring this ancient site.

Five *prangs*, surrounded by galleries, protected by walls, and now shaded by trees, constitute Muang Tham. A beautiful lintel on the ground shows Krishna standing on the head of Kirtimukha and holding up Mount Govardhana. The central shrines have crumbled, but the temple retains hints of vivid detail. The huge rectangular stone blocks that form the outer walls contain drilled circular holes probably used for stone figures shaped like lotus buds. The outer rims of the ponds are lined with *nagas* whose many heads rise at the corners to mark the outer boundary.

Road 24 continues 38km to Prasat. To see more Khmer art, turn right on Road 214 and go about 4km south to the Mon-Khmer village of Ban Pluang. A track between the 30-and 31-km-stones (from Surin) branches east 500m to **Prasat Ban Pluang**, a small temple that features excellent carving. Drive back to Prasat and continue 29km north on Road 214 to the town of Surin.

Located on an old Mon-Khmer site, **Surin** was known primarily for silk raising until the T.A.T. began organizing an annual elephant roundup there each November. The people of Surin are famed for their skill at training elephants. During the well-publicized roundup, mahouts put their pachyderms through a variety of acts. Special buses and a train from Bangkok take tourists to the popular event.

A direct rail line connects Surin to the next province in the Northeast which borders on Cambodia, **Si Sa Ket**. Traveling by car is less direct. It requires driving south to Prasat, then left onto Road 24 to Khukhan and left again onto Road 220 for a short ride into Si Sa Ket town. On the way, you can detour to **Sik Oraphum** 31km northeast of Surin, via Roads 2077 and 2079, to see **Wat Ru Ngeng**, an 11th-century Khmer temple in a lovely natural setting. Four *prangs* are set at the corners of a square; a fifth graces the center and has beautifully carved pillars and a lintel which frame the door.

The province of Si Sa Ket's former main attraction no longer lies in Thailand. In 1963 the World Court awarded to Cambodia the splendid cliffside temple complex of **Khao Phra Viharn**. If relations between Bangkok and Phnom Penh allow, you may be able one day to visit Khao Phra Viharn, which can be reached from Si Sa Ket along a 63-km drive southeast to Kantharalak, then straight into the jungle on another 37-km leg to the border.

Khao Phra Viharn stretches almost a kilometer in length. Its stairs alternate between hewn bedrock and imported stones placed there before the days of Angkor Wat. Each layer is marked by an increasingly large *gopura* or gate, and ends at the topmost sanctuary that honors the god Siva.

To the east of the first *gopura,* a trail descends through the jungle to the Cambodian plains. Before the second *gopura,* a sacred pond cut in the rock was found to contain a 45-kg fish that now rests in Phnom Penh's National Museum.

The second *gopura,* shaped like a Greek cross, is superbly carved in the Khmer style of the 11th century. Its lintels show Vishnu in a scene from the Hindu myth of creation. The stairs continue in a symbolic ascent to heaven, past another purificatory basin, to the first courtyard with its two palaces and *gopura,* finally up to the second and third courtyards and the main sanctuary. At the end of the long ridge, one finds oneself on a breath-taking precipice, 600m above the Cambodian countryside, a stunning achievement in turning a natural site into a work of art.

Ubon (or Ubol) Ratchathani, "Royal Town of the Lotus Flower", lies 680km east of Bangkok. Its size and opulence contrast strongly with the surrounding countryside. Office buildings, construction sites, and some of the best endowed *wats* in the Northeast rise abruptly behind the banks of the Moun. The river flows eastward emptying into the Mekong about 100km downstream from Ubon.

Much of the town's growth coincided with the build-up of the Royal Thai Air Force Base during the 1960s when squadrons of American planes flew missions over Indochina from there. The Pathumrat, Bordin, Siam Wattana, and Ubon hotels offer air-conditioned rooms that are welcome in the hot season when the Northeast generally is hotter than the Bangkok area. The highlight of its festival year is the Wax Candle Procession each July in which huge mythical animals and legendary figures are brilliantly carved from beeswax and paraded through the streets.

Ubon province was the country's largest in area until its western half was split off to form Yasothorn. Ubon province still has a population well over one million, ranking third in that department after Bangkok and Korat.

uddha images of ifferent tyles are und in the anctuary of e Prasat hanom Wan.

FOLLOWING THE MEKONG RIVER

Allow a full day for the trip north from Ubon to Nakhon Phanom. First, drive 76km on Road 212 to Amnat Charoen. The dry land looks barely arable but somehow produces the rice that turns golden brown in late October and the kenaf that stands in bunches against the farmhouses.

Beyond Amnat Charoen about 2km on the left, shine the golden tiles of **Wat Phra Mongkol**. Behind an arbor, about 300m off the road the temple shelters a 4½-m high Buddha image.

Continuing north on Road 212 about 88km takes you to the district town of **Mukdahan** on the right bank of the wide and sluggish Mekong River, opposite the Laotian town of Savannakhet. Take the road to the river, turn right, and visit **Wat Sri Nongkran**, a buff-colored temple built by Vietnamese refugees in 1956. The gates present a curious mixture of Thai contours, Vietnamese script and Chinese-inspired dragons. Farther down the river bank stands the colorful Wat Jok Keo. An unsophisticated but vibrant mural enlivens its small *prang*.

From Mukdahan, 55km north lies **That Phanom**. The road is in good condition, straight and flat. You feel far upcountry, and you are. Uncultivated brush interspersed with rice fields rushes by. Black-shirted farmers balance produce-laden baskets from the ends of long poles. You drive close to the Mekong River all the way up to the village and temple of That Phanom.

Thousands of pilgrims from Northeast Thailand and Laos used to make an annual pilgrimage to **Wat That Phanom** to worship and make offerings at the base of the spire that was built around the 9th century and restored several times thereafter. In mid-1975, the spire collapsed after four days of torrential monsoon rains. But in 1979 the temple was restored again making it well worth a visit for those interested in history or simply seeking a beautiful riverside setting.

For a short and pleasant sidetrip into the countryside, 7km north of That Phanom and 8km inland is **Ban Renu**. Like several small weaving villages in North Thailand, Ban Renu is famous for pretty girls and cloth. Embroidered shirts, northeastern *ikat* sarongs (in which the material is pre-dyed in patterns), head rests and long dresses hang outside a dozen shops on the main street. The people are friendly bargainers. **Wat Prathat Renu**, the village's temple, features an extremely pretty spire covered with finely painted reliefs in bright blues, reds and yellows as well as in pastels. Portraits of elephant riders, angels, guardians and foot soldiers convey a vibrant realism that distinguishes such contemporary temple art in the Northeast.

Farther north about 45km on Road 212 lies **Nakhon Phanom**. On a fresh morning in Nakhon Phanom, a chain of powder-gray mountains can be seen behind the little Laotian town of Thakhek across the wide Mekong. Over 25,000 Vietnamese refugees crossed the river

A faithful guardian of Wat That Phanom.

248

during the 1950s and 1960s to settle in this province. Although security precautions complicated their resettlement, many Vietnamese have prospered financially in the town's own markets, and seem to have matched the overseas Chinese in business acumen.

During the Indochina war, American rescue and reconnaissance missions flew from the Royal Thai Air Force Base hidden behind grassy mounds 12km west of town. NKP, as the Americans dubbed the base, was also a listening post filled with sophisticated radios and electronic sensors. At that time you could buy at the market an appropriate symbol of such technologically sophisticated activity set in rural Thailand: fried bananas wrapped in discarded computer printouts listing traffic movements on the Ho Chi Minh Trail. Today, there is little to see in town. The Srithep, First, Chai Pattana, Windsor and Nakhon Phanom hotels all offer air-conditioned rooms if you decide to break your tour here.

From Nakhon Phanom, Road 22 runs west about 86km to Sakhon Nakhon. On the way you pass **Tha Rae** village, where a largely Catholic population, including many Vietnamese, supports a diocese complete with a seminary.

Sakhon Nakhon is spread out along a low plain that borders Nong Han, Thailand's largest lake; the town enjoys being the only northeastern province with plenty of water. The Araya, Somkiat and Charoensuk hotels have air-conditioned rooms.

The ancient Khmers left monuments whose significance is so minor that only those with keen archaeological interest should make a special effort to see them. The white *prang* of **Wat Choeng Chum** in the town center, hides a 10th century laterite *prang*; but you must peer through a crack in the door to see it. West of town on Road 22, 3km past the experimental rice station, a sign points to **Wat Narai Cheng Weng**, built by a princess in the 11th century. It holds a crumbling sandstone *prang* whose carved lintels beautifully exemplify the Khmer Baphuon style.

xquisite
hai silk in
he making.

ARCHAEOLOGICAL FINDS

From Sakhon Nakhon, Road 22 heads west toward Udon. About 110km from Sakhon Nakhon, in the dusty plateau of the Northeast, a small sign in Thai points to **Ban Chieng** located about 5km north of the highway. The Thai-Lao farm community in Ban Chieng and nearby Pulu Village sits on what may be the most significant archaeological find in Southeast Asia in many years.

The people of Ban Chieng, long used to encountering pots, beads, and even human bones when digging around their houses, paid little attention to the finds. Then in 1966, a young American named Stephen Young showed some of the finds to the Fine Arts Department. Subsequent excavations have unearthed pottery and other artifacts dated by thermoluminescence at between 4,500 and 5,700 years old.

At first, most archaeologists hesitated to venture broad theories about the Ban Chieng find. But further study, mainly conducted by a team from the University of Pennsylvania, has convinced many of the skeptics that an agrarian bronze-making civilization first appeared not in Mesopotamia or China, but in Southeast Asia.

Even were the claims of antiquity not authenticated, the beautiful whorl designs of the pottery and the intricacy of the bronze jewelry and implements would earn the Ban Chieng culture high marks among the early peoples of the earth.

The Thai government prohibits the illegal digging and sale of Ban Chieng artifacts, but enterprising villagers, hoping to earn a few baht, may approach visitors offering to sell green or dark blue beads, metal bracelets, pottery, and even human bones. Do not buy any of these items; you can be arrested for the unlicensed possession of antiques.

From Ban Chieng, Road 22 continues 47km west to **Udon Thani**, another town which grew quickly with the influx

Below left and right: pottery and other artifacts unearthed at Ban Chieng, believed to be between 4,500 and 5,700 years old.

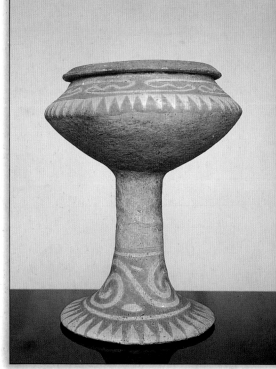

of American airmen during the 1960s. Today, instead of military convoys, noisy motorcycles and flashy new cars zoom over asphalt streets punctuated by increasing numbers of traffic lights.

From Udon, Route 2 runs north 53km to reach **Nong Khai** on the southern bank of the Mekong. Many buses and inter-province taxis travel to Nong Khai. With the opening of Thailand's first road bridge across Mekong River into Laos in April 1994, its days as a quiet town with few attractions other than a forgettable monument marking the end of the Friendship Highway are numbered. In some years, usually during September or October, monsoon rains swell the river, causing it to overflow its bank and damage crops and property in low-lying sections of the province. When the water level drops in the dry season, islands appear in midstream, and on weekends local residents take food, drink and radios out to *pai-tio* on the sandbars.

Road 210 runs west of Udon 143km to the rugged beautiful province of **Loei**.

What is now the traveler's delight was once the civil servant's nightmare; in the Thai bureaucracy, being assigned to Loei was like going to Siberia, for Loei in the old days was a jungle outpost that meant fever, cold weather, little comfort and poor security.

Enroute, stop at the **Elephant Cave** (*Tham Erawan*) about 54km before Loei and 2km off the road on the right. Despite its isolation, the monastery there is well organized. Signs in English entreat visitors "Please keep the law of Buddhist brother." A new and life-size statue of Erawan, the triple-headed elephant of Thai mythology, marks the steep stairway and rocky path to the cave's entrance. Prehistoric artifacts have been found here, but all that distinguishes the cave, apart from its size and an occasional cobra emerging from the rocks, is an elephant's skull. The climb up is rough.

Road 210 continues west to the town of Loei. A minor agricultural boom has not changed Loei's shy simplicity. The usually placid Loei River flows through

ower-
arlanded
ortheastern
llagers
erforming an
ncient ritual.

the center of town. At the Thai Udom and Phulaung hotels, you can find inexpensive rooms.

Plunge 50km west into the Loei wilderness of Road 203 to **Phu Rua** ("Boat Mountain"). The road cuts through heavy banks of red laterite, past a sawmill and fields of kenaf and cotton, the latter being the province's big money spinner.

About 30km west of town, on the way to Phu Rua, a *sala* refreshment area overlooks chains of bluish hills. In December, the mountains lie under thick blankets of smoke as farmers burn the forest undergrowth. Phu Rua itself is about 1,370m high. A rough road to the top affords a view of the surrounding national forest. From Phu Rua, hardy travelers can take a spine-jolting bus ride south on Road 203 to Lom Sak, then on to the provincial capitals of Phitsanulok or Phetchabun.

To see the Mekong near where it once again becomes the Thai-Lao border. drive 53km north of Loei to **Chiang Khan**. A boat can be hired for the 4-km ride downstream to the Kuang Kud Ku rapids, worthwhile if only for the sheer sense of being locked in the deeper heart of Southeast Asia. For the past decade, Chiang Khan has been the home of hilltribes displaced from Laos and living as refugees.

No experience in the Loei area can match the crisp beauty of **Phu Kradung National Park**, the most memorable escape in Northeast Thailand. Phu Kradung came to public attention only 50 years ago during the reign of King Rama VI. Today it is rarely visited on weekdays; students who have endured a 12-hour bus ride from Bangkok come on weekends to savor the invigorating cool, dry air.

Some say the mountain's name derives from the mysterious sound of a bell (*kradung*) that supposedly grows louder on holy days. Others believe the name is a corruption of *krating*, the wild bulls which used to inhabit the remote plateau until hunters killed them off.

The entrance to Phu Kradung lies about 50km southeast of Loei on Road 201 that goes to Chum Phae. About

Phu Kradung National Park with its cool invigorating air, is a popular weekend spot.

3km from the entrance, you arrive at the park office where you can arrange for porters, store excess equipment, and park your car. Take along tennis shoes, a wind breaker or sweater, packaged food (only one noodle shop operates on weekends), toilet articles, a camera, and a walking stick, if you are so inclined. Phra Kradung, a plateau lying between 1,200 and 1,500m, beckons the naturalist-at-heart to set out down the trail. The park provides bedding and blankets in cabins that hold up to eleven people. Unless you are a champion hiker, let the porters carry everything up the 5-km trail to the plateau. (You can even hire four porters and a sedan chair for the climb!)

It is by no means an easy climb but it is well worth the effort. After the fourth kilometer there is a cabin with cold water. Stop here, for the last kilometer is the toughest. Ladders negotiate the steepest boulders; views of the valley mitigate the strain. Once you make it up to the plateau you forget the tiring climb.

Atop Phu Kradung, clear and mostly level paths crisscross the 60-sq-km tableland. Rare birds, including hornbills, woodpeckers and pheasants, may be seen; and even wild elephants and panthers somehow manage to climb up. Most of the fauna is quite shy.

The park's cabins and upper offices are located 3km from a small radar station and a helicopter pad. Pick up a mimeographed map of trails and set off on nature walks. A good day begins before dawn with a chilly stroll to **Liem Pha Nok Hain** cliff to watch the sunrise. It is a long way down to the jungle where gibbons hoot. Spend part of the day finding the six waterfalls north of the cabins. About an hour before sunset, head for the serene setting of **Liem Pha Makdouk**, about 2km west of the radar station.

From Phu Kradung, you can take Road 210 to Khon Kaen and rejoin the Friendship Highway for the return trip to Bangkok; or return to Loei and cut across country on a rough road to Phitsanulok for a trip to the North.

shermen
e out a
ving from
e mighty
ekong river.

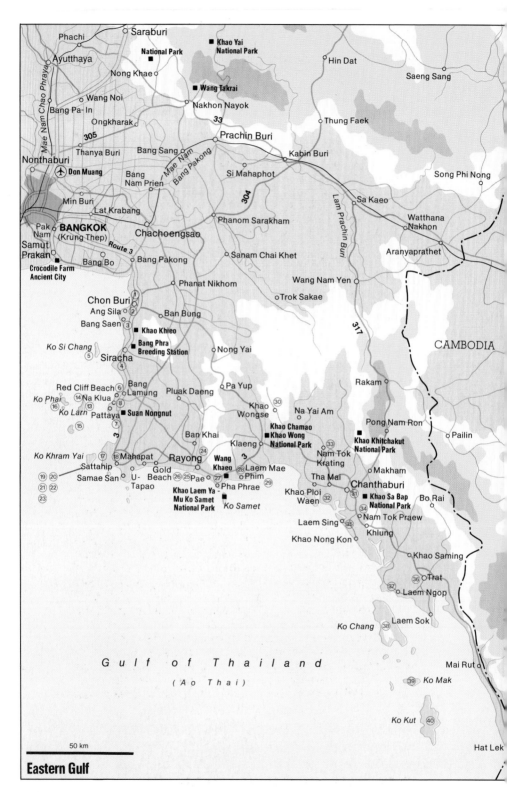

Phachi ○ Saraburi

Ayutthaya ○ ■ Khao Yai National Park National Park ○ Hin Dat

Nong Khae ○ Saeng Sang ○

Bang Pa-In ○ Wang Noi ■ Wang Takrai

Ongkharak ○ Nakhon Nayok Thung Faek ○

33

305

Nonthaburi Thanya Buri ○ Bang Sang ○ Prachin Buri Kabin Buri ○ Song Phi Nong ○

✈ Don Muang Bang Nam Prien Si Mahaphot ○ Sa Kaeo ○

Min Buri Lat Krabang *304* Watthana Nakhon ○

Pak Nam BANGKOK (Krung Thep) Chachoengsao Phanom Sarakham ○ Aranyaprathet ○

Samut Prakan *Route 3* Bang Bo ○ Bang Pakong ○ Sanam Chai Khet ○

Crocodile Farm Ancient City Phanat Nikhom ○

Chon Buri ○① Trok Sakae ○ Wang Nam Yen ○

Ang Sila ○② Ban Bung ○

Bang Saen ○③ ■ Khao Khieo

Ko Si Chang ○⑤ Bang Phra Breeding Station Nong Yai ○

Siracha ④

Red Cliff Beach ⑥ Bang Lamung Pluak Daeng ○ Pa Yup ○ Rakam ○ CAMBODIA

Ko Phai ⑭ Na Klua ⑧ Khao ③⓪ Pong Nam Ron ○

⑯ Ko Larn Pattaya ⑬ ■ Suan Nongnut Wongse Na Yai Am ○ Khao Khitchakut National Park Pailin ○

⑮ ⑦ Ban Khai ○ Khao Chamao ■ Khao Wong National Park Nam Tok ③③

Ko Khram Yai ⑰ ⑱ Mahapat Rayong ②④ Wang Khaeo Klaeng ○ Krating ○ Makham ○

Sattahip ○ Gold ②⑧ Laem Mae Tha Mai ○ Chanthaburi

⑲ ⑳ Samae San ○ U- Beach ㉖㉕ Pae ○ ㉗ ■ Pha Phrae ㉙ Khao Ploi Waen ○③② ③① ■ Khao Sa Bap National Park Bo Rai ○

㉑ ㉒ Tapao Khao Laem Ya - Mu Ko Samet National Park Ko Samet ○ ③④ Nam Tok Praew ○

㉓ Laem Sing ○③⑤ Khlung

Khao Nong Kon ○ Khao Saming ○

③⑥ ○ Trat

③⑦ ○ Laem Ngop

Ko Chang ③⑧ Laem Sok

G u l f   o f   T h a i l a n d Mai Rut ○

(A o   T h a i) ③⑨ Ko Mak ○

Ko Kut ④⓪

50 km Hat Lek

Eastern Gulf

256

THE EASTERN GULF: THAILAND'S PLAYGROUND

The "Elephant's Chin" has long reigned as the playground of Thailand. While it has few cultural attractions, its beaches and well-developed facilities have made it a magnet for fun-seekers. The focus of their attention has been the town of Pattaya some 120km southeast of Bangkok.

Few areas in Asia have undergone such a precipitous rise to fame and, some say, a plummet in popularity, as the beach resort of Pattaya. Barely more than two decades ago this huge resort was a beautiful, quiet beach known only to a handful of rather adventurous foreigners and Thais from Bangkok, who braved the drive over poor roads to spend a weekend by the sea. There were no hotels, just a few clusters of bungalows, a rough clubhouse for a group of sailing enthusiasts, a couple of good seafood restaurants and a small fishing village that gave the place its name. But it had all the ingredients for success: a graceful, 4-km-long crescent of golden sand lapped by gentle waves, warm tropical water, balmy breezes, tranquillity.

By the 1970s, others were beginning to discover its charms. A new road cut travel time to two hours and brought the resort within easy reach of Bangkok. Now, the big hotels began to rise along the beach and with them the ancillary services that would make Pattaya a full-fledged resort. By the 1980s, the visitors came flowing in from all directions. Europeans flocked to its beaches and in the capitals of Asia, a beach vacation anywhere but Pattaya was unheard of. Soon, it was being touted as Asia's Riviera, an area of abundant sea, sand and sun, making it one of the great success stories in Asian tourism. By the late 1980s, there were dozens of high-rise hotels not only on it but on Chomtien, the neighboring beach 4km south. Until then, Chomtien had been empty beach but it quickly developed to handle the overflow from Pattaya itself.

In recent times, Pattaya's lustre had begun to dull. There were disturbing signs that problems lurking beneath the surface had not been properly addressed and had grown to such proportions that they had robbed the resort of the very elements that made it so popular. Water shortages, polluted beaches and water, and inadequate roads discouraged many from visiting the resort. However, active steps have now been taken to remedy these problems which had also begun to spill over into Chomtien. The completion of the several new infrastructure projects will undoubedly return Pattaya to its former popularity.

But the Eastern region comprises more than Pattaya and many of the delights formerly sought there are available elsewhere. The Eastern Gulf Coast is an almost unbroken stretch of sand that runs from Chon Buri to Trat, the narrow finger of land that abuts Cambodia. Now that roads have been cut across the bulge of land that constitutes the Pattaya-Sattahip-Rayong area, Ban Phe, the clear waters and white sand beaches of southern coast and the islands off Trat are beginning to attract tourists.

Close to Bangkok, about half an hour before Pattaya, Bang Saen has long reigned as the favorite seaside place for Thai families. Pattaya now attracts Thai families as do the areas around Bang Saray. Around the "Elephant's Chin" at Sattahip, there are beaches at Samae San where the sea is crystal clear. Few beaches have been developed between Sattahip and Ban Phe southeast of Rayong. This is the center of a new industrial region with its center at Map Tha Phut where the underwater natural gas line from drilling platforms in the Gulf comes onshore. At the moment the land is subject to a tussle between tourism and industrial developers as the new Eastern Seaboard export processing zone begins to grow.

From Ban Phe east, there is an explosion of development with resorts one after the other reaching to Laem Mae Pim and including the island of Koh Samet. Again, there is a long stretch of uninhabited sand until one reaches Chanthaburi with its half dozen beaches.

Although tourism has brought the Eastern Gulf Coast new prosperity, it is far from being the region's sole source of income. Older industries in the area have long played an important part in the Thai economy. Much of the seafood consumed or exported by Thailand comes from Eastern Gulf ports, and some of the largest fruit orchards are located between Rayong and Chanthaburi.

Closer to Bangkok, towns like Si Racha and Chon Buri, if somewhat lacking in visual charm, are nonetheless important commercial centers, holding many factories for processing and canning the agricultural produce of the region. Si Racha, in particular, is noted as the home of a fiery hot chili sauce bearing its name that is a prominent feature of Thai dinner tables.

The most important development along the eastern coastline has been the construction of a new deepwater port at Laem Chabang to handle deep-draft ships unable to clear the bar into the Chao Phya River and proceed to Bangkok's port at Klong Toey. This new port, together with piers at the Thai Navy port at Sattahip, will serve the Eastern Seaboard Development project which may become the nation's industrial powerhouse. Already, a railway has been constructed from Bangkok to Chachoengsao and on to Laem Chabang and Sattahip to haul freight and containers into the capital and distribute them to regional centers upcountry.

All this industry notwithstanding, the Eastern Gulf Coast's main lure for the average visitor is its sun and sand and plentiful tourist facilities. Despite the naysayers, Pattaya and its sisters continue to thrive. To the average tourist, they seem vastly superior to the overcrowded resorts of America and Europe, and most visitors go home singing their praises.

A flurry of resort development in Koh Samet is rapidly changing the face of this pristine island.

ALONG THE COAST

A sprawling and industrious town of about a quarter million merchants, traders and craftsmen, **Chon Buri** for most tourists is but a lunch-stop on the way to Pattaya. Most of Thailand's oyster population breeds off the Chon Buri coast and farther south along the gulf.

The coast town is better known for its production of animal feed made from tapioca grown in the region. During the 1970s and early 1980s, the area around Chon Buri enjoyed a minor boom as a tapioca center, a success story that demonstrates the ability of the Thai agricultural and agro-business sectors to respond rapidly to new opportunities. When the animal feed markets of the Netherlands and West Germany identified a need for a new source of tapioca supply in the early 1970s, the Thai government encouraged plantations of this root which took well to the poor, dry soil of the area.

Plants to process the root into pellet form sprang up along the coast and the world's longest over-water conveyer belt was constructed to run the pellets from silos to deep-draft ships 3km offshore. Within a few years, this crop, formerly cultivated only for local use, became the country's number one foreign exchange earner. Moreover, Thailand became the world's number one producer, supplying fully 95 percent of the world's demand.

However, Chon Buri deserves to be more than just a lunch stop for the traveler on the move. It has its fair share of attractions. On the left, 3km before entering the town is **Wat Buddhabat Sam Yot**, "Buddha's Footprint Mountain of Three Summits." Built amid green trees by an Ayutthayan king and renovated during the reign of King Chulalongkorn, this hilltop monastery was once used to conduct the annual royal "Water Oath of Allegiance" during which princes and governors drank the waters of fealty, pledging unwavering loyalty to the throne.

Near the center of Chon Buri, a colossal gold-mosaic image of the Buddha dominates **Wat Dhamma Nimitr**. The largest image in the Eastern Gulf region and the only one in the country depicting the Buddha in a boat, the 40-m-high statue recalls the story of the Buddha's journey to the cholera-ridden town of Pai Salee. Through inspiration and compassion, the Buddha cured many of the afflicted. On the same hill is found the local Chinese Buddhist Society, surrounded by the burial shrines of prominent members.

Those interested in the historical arts will want to stop near the old market at a temple gate flanked by fruit sellers. The oldest and most important *wat* in the province, **Wat Intharam** is a mix of architecture and one of the best examples of Ayutthayan architecture in the Southeast. In the 18th century, this *wat* was the rallying point for soldiers recruited by King Taksin to drive the Burmese from Ayutthaya.

Within the *bot*, murals portray *devas* ("gods") and the Vessantara legend of the Buddha's life. The vitality of the frescoes, rendered to strict scenic formulas, belongs solely to the 18th century. Prince Naris, one of Thailand's most renowned artists, visited the *bot* at the turn of the century and told the abbot, "The workmanship is excellent. You must not allow anyone to restore it." His wish was kept.

Seven kilometers south of Chon Buri is the town of **Ang Sila**. Once favored by Thai royalty as a resort (the two old concrete houses on the shore were built by King Chulalongkorn to enjoy the sea air) the town takes its name of "Stone Basin" from the chain of rocks that forms an oval protrusion into the sea. The clang of hammers fills the air as artisans chip at granitic rock to make the mortars and pestles used for pounding chilies, grinding spices and mashing coconut. Wooden shop houses on the beachfront sell local beachwear, hats and baskets.

Farther south on the Ang Sila road, sits an unobtrusive yet unusual monastery called **Rua Sam Pao**. Facing seaward, its walls are shaped like the huge hull of a Chinese junk which some say

e Bay of Si
cha with
e inevitable
conut palm
the beach.

points to a shipwreck in which emigrants from China were lost. Symbolically, it represents a vessel carrying Buddhist faithful to nirvana.

The more than 300 meditation cells arranged around the main ship are also in the shapes of small boats. Many of the residents are very old and believe that to die at Rua Sam Pao brings good fortune. The old Chinese women believe that when they die their souls will be carried on the sea back to China.

Within the monastery are two miniatures of the giant Nakhon Pathom *chedi*. A Thai monk heads the monastery, in which the Chinese dialect of Teochew is commonly heard. The residents *kin jeh*, eat only vegetables and fruits.

South of Chon Buri, 18km on the road past Ang Sila, the beach at **Bang Saen** comes alive each weekend as hordes of Thai tourists descend on it in orange buses. A profusion of multicolored beach umbrellas, black inner tubes and wrinkled watermelon rinds quickly cover the sandy beach and the low surf is filled with bobbling heads.

The T.A.T. operates the Bang Saen Beach Hotel which has a swimming pool and comfortable, if not plush, rooms. Near the beach are bungalows under coconut palms. Across the main highway and somewhat inland just past the Bang Saen market is the **Bang Phra Golf Course** which has recently been renovated by a Japanese firm.

Beside it is the Bang Saen Reservoir bird refuge where, with permission, it is possible to sit in a blind and observe water birds. Up the hill behind the Reserve is the **Khao Khiew Open Zoo**. Operated by Bangkok's Dusit Zoo, it presents animals in their natural setting; in one section, visitors can wander among deer, elephants, donkeys and other wild animals. On the hill above are some simple but comfortable bungalows which can be reserved by contacting the Dusit Zoo.

Si Racha, 24km south of Chon Buri, descends from the hills and extends into the sea on tentacle-like piers. Its famous hot sauce can be enjoyed overlooking the water at the Si Racha Restaurant, where delicious fresh shrimp, crab, oyster, mussel or abalone can be dipped into the thick, tangy red liquid. An offshore rock supports a picturesque *wat* comprising Thai and Chinese Buddhist elements; shrines honor a monk who spent many years atop the seaside hillock. The inevitable footprint of the Buddha, cast in bronze, graces the *wat*, as do pictures of the goddess of mercy, Kuan Yin, and the Monkey God.

The *wat* overlooks arrow-shaped fish traps made of nipa palm stakes – a mode of construction so functional that it has endured for centuries throughout Southeast Asia. From the longest pier at Si Racha, boats ferry passengers to nearby **Koh Si Chang** island. If you haven't the patience to wait for the regular ferry, a weather-beaten diesel fishing boat rents for around 500 baht per round trip and takes less than one hour to reach the island.

Koh Si Chang's waters, clear from November through January, offer snorkelers and scuba divers a glimpse of abundant sea life. On the southern end of the island are deserted beaches and a house built by King Chulalongkorn for use during his periodic retreats from Bangkok's heat.

The Eastern Gulf: It lies within easy reach of Bangkok. Air-conditioned and fan-cooled buses leave regularly from the Eastern Bus Terminal opposite Soi 63 on Sukhumvit Road for Chon Buri, Si Racha, Sattahip, Rayong, Chanthaburi, and Trat; air-conditioned buses leave half-hourly for Pattaya. Although the railway to Pattaya may provide an interesting way in theory to reach the resort, in practice it is slow and erratic. There is no public domestic flight service.

The main route along the Eastern Gulf Coast is Sukhumvit Highway, which becomes Route 3 outside of Bangkok. Route 3 officially originates at Bangkok's busy Rajprasong intersection at the Erawan Shrine Hotel on Ploenchit Road. Past the railway tracks and the expressway, Ploenchit's name changes to Sukhumvit.

Beyond the crowded shops and sois of Sukhumvit, traffic thins and, after the bridge over the Phra Kanong Canal, the highway reaches Bangna suburb. From there a new shortcut to Bang Pakong cuts 25km off the journey south, bypassing Paknam (or Samut Prakarn) at the broad mouth of the Chao Phya River. Branching left and heading southeast, the shortcut offers fewer sights, more factories and less upcountry atmosphere than the old road. For a slower but more interesting journey, continue due south to Paknam. The road follows a scenic *klong* for 75km passing the Ancient City, the Crocodile Farm and Klong Dan.

The traditional tranquillity of the *klong* is shattered only by the occasional roar of a long-tailed boat and the silent sprouting of another television antenna. Framed by coconut trees, nipa palms and bougainvillea, square-shaped fishing nets on the end of long counter-weighted bamboo poles hang above the canal's waters.

Huge water jars sit at the feet of the stairways which climb up stilts to the thatched-roof huts above. Boys in tucked-up sarongs play *takraw*; girls shampoo in the *klong*. Old ladies sell fruit and the chestnut-like *lukjak*. Along the right-hand side of the highway, stretch mangrove flats where villagers gather wood to make into charcoal, while their children catch crabs.

On the old Sukhumvit Road, about 12km past Paknam and 3½km past the Crocodile Farm turnoff, a seafood restaurant beckons from a marshy bank. Years ago, when the single good road south from Bangkok went just this far, the restaurant's fresh breezes, tangy food and seclusion drew the capital's high society. Today you can share in the local nostalgia by ordering splendid dishes of shrimp (*gung*), crab (*poo*), and oyster (*hoy nang lom*).

At the 56-km-stone, Route 3 arrives at the busy fishing port of Klong Dan. The old highway then curves east to merge with the main highway and the town of Bang Pakong. The four-lane highway swings south once more and heads for the distant hills of Chon Buri.

n exhilarat-
ng canter
cross the
each in
attaya.

PATTAYA, THE THAI RIVIERA

Pattaya has long reigned as Thailand's premier beach resort; only now is its dominance being challenged by Phuket and islands of the South. Its long prominence is odd because Pattaya really does not have much of a beach. What it does have in abundance is a bewildering range of facilities that add up to a complete vacation.

Pattaya's two busiest main roads run parallel to the 4km bay. The northern portion of Beach Road is dominated by first class hotels, a scattering of restaurants and some open air bars. Second Road also has many hotels and restaurants interspersed between bars, discotheques, two transvestite shows and other night spots. Numerous sois connecting the Beach Road and Second Road hold small hotels, restaurants and a significant number of bars.

The area known as South Pattaya, from the South Pattaya Road to the base of a tall hill, is the entertainment, dining and shopping section. This is where the rowdier aspects of nightlife can be found: the bargirls who cruise the streets or sit in open-air bars watching a highly-doubtful version of Thai boxing and video movies, or chatting with friends and potential clients. The area also holds gay bars, a transvestite cabaret show and discos.

South Pattaya is the main shopping and dining area. Scores of food stalls and itinerant vendors selling Buddhas and leather belts, amulets and bracelets line the streets. Fruit and flower stalls further brighten the scene. Jewelers do a brisk trade in sapphires and rubies. Tailors cajole customers into having a dress or safari suit created in 24 hours. Music blares from bars and stores selling pirated cassettes.

The hill, dominated by a huge cement-seated Buddha and a radio station, provides a splendid view of the entire resort. In the evening, the bay is studded with trawlers which catch either fish or tourists, transporting the latter to the island of Koh Larn.

Koh Larn, identified in brochures as "Coral Island", but whose name translates as "Bald Island" used to be known for its coral reefs. These have long since been blasted out of existence by fishermen who used dynamite to stun the fish. Yet, glass-bottomed boats are still used to ferry visitors from the trawlers to the shore, their passengers peering in vain at the dead gray coral in hopes of seeing something alive.

Koh Larn has the wide, soft sand beaches Pattaya lacks and is a wonderful place to spend a leisurely day. The shore is covered with good seafood restaurants and there are water sports facilities for those who want to stir from their beach chairs. The island also has a golf course.

Pattaya's hill separates the main resort area from an area of luxury hotels and private beaches including the Royal Cliff and Asia hotels. Farther south is the new resort of Chomtien whose beaches are only marginally better than Pattaya's. Here are found bungalow

eft, Pattaya as the cilities to ffer the unseeker a omplete oliday. elow, it lso has one f the finest olf courses the ountry.

complexes, hotels and a host of good seafood restaurants.

Pattaya and Chomtien are a paradise for water sports lovers. Windsurf boards and sailboats, snorkeling and scuba-diving equipment, jetskis, water scooters and water skiing equipment can be rented. The adventurous may try parasailing wherein one is strapped into a parachute harness and towed aloft by a speedboat. Be extremely careful when riding water scooters or motorcycles as accidents can happen at the most innocuous moments and have been known to take a heavy toll on visitors to the resort. The overhead cable-ski facility on a man-made lake just outside Pattaya on the way to Nong Nooch Village is an excellent new facility.

The keen angler can test his skill at landing groupers and red snapper, mackerel and bonito, sailfish and barracuda. Fishing expeditions can be arranged at local shops and at Bang Saray farther down the coast.

Land sports facilities are also available. Nearly all the large hotels have immaculate tennis courts and swimming pools.

Ten kilometers east of Pattaya is the Siam Country Club which boasts one of the finest golf courses in the kingdom. Along the same road is the Reo Ranch where one can rent Appaloosa horses for canters across the countryside. Bowling alleys, a shooting range and snooker parlors complete the sports picture.

Excursions can be organized to sapphire mines, orchid farms and an elephant kraal. For non-sybarites, evenings can be spent watching movies on the in-house channel provided in big hotel rooms.

Pattaya offers a wide range of dining opportunities. At several restaurants, you choose fresh seafood arrayed on ice and the chef cooks it to your liking. There are also numerous outdoor restaurants where one can dine on superb Thai food. Most Continental and Asian cuisines are represented at the resort as are the fast food and ice cream parlors found in most American cities. Beer, whiskeys and fine wines can also be ordered.

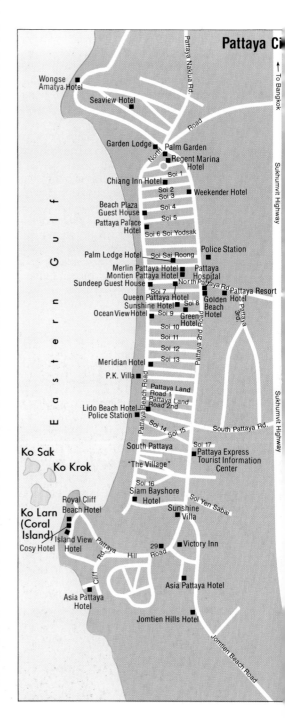

ISLAND HOPPING

Some of Pattaya's prime attractions lie hidden underwater in the reefs of offshore islands. The resort offers the possibility to explore them, in-depth as it were. Scuba diving shops like Seafari and Steven's Dive Shop, have a full range of equipment. Their professional instructors offer courses leading to internationally-recognized NAUI or PADI certification up to Divermaster level and including specialized courses such as underwater photography. The courses are reasonably priced.

Although the waters off Pattaya are generally murky, there are some good diving opportunities at nearby islands. Diving expeditions can be arranged by a number of dive shops. Among the favorite nearby islands are **Koh Larn** and **Koh Sak**.

Among the tropical sea life to be seen are tube worms, clownfish, soldierfish, damselfish, green parrot wrasse, polka dot grunts, batfish and huge friendly groupers. Beware of stepping on stonefish or sea urchins and take care during the monsoon season not to brush against jellyfish carried in by storm winds. One advantage of diving in Pattaya is that the water is warm and one can swim unconstricted by a wet suit.

Southwest of Koh Larn, about another hour or so by boat, lies **Koh Lin**. Although quite small, this island has many good diving spots. On the sea bottom are a relatively recent wreck, good coral formations and fascinating sea life. Due west of Koh Larn, about the same distance away as Koh Lin, is **Koh Pai**. Here are strikingly beautiful fish, coral and shells. You share the area with anglers trying to hook huge sailfish, marlin, groupas, and, if you are not careful, you.

Snorkeling opportunities are few in the Pattaya area but one can travel farther south to Samae San with its clear waters. It is best to wear a T-shirt when snorkeling as the hot sun can quickly burn tender skin.

An exotic underwater world awaits the diver and snorkeller.

SOUTH OF PATTAYA

Year by year, visitors have been exploring farther and farther south of Pattaya, discovering new resort areas on land and sea that offer greater degrees of peace and isolation. One popular resort is **Nong Nooch Village**. This bungalow complex situated in parkland around a lake, offers a wide variety of activities including an elephant show, an orchid nursery and a cactus garden.

Just beyond Nong Nooch on the right is a new area dominated by the SeaSand Club on its own private beach. The next resort south is Bang Saray, better known as a fisherman's haven than as a sun spot. Weekend fishermen rent boats for expeditions to catch deep sea fish which abound in the offshore waters. The area is one of the premier spots in the world for marlin and sailfish.

Overlooking a scenic bay sprinkled with small islands, the little fishing town of **Sattahip** about 20km south of Pattaya grew up overnight to become an attractive, busy deep-water port. In the heart of town a large, modern temple rests on turquoise pedestals, while in the commercial center, a boisterous market teems with fish, fruit and vegetables.

Sattahip offers little more to do than stroll past the shops or sit in an open-front coffeeshop sipping an *o liang* (the great local version of sweet iced coffee that came from French Cambodia). Enjoy a spicy curry near the market, or browse over teak elephants in the souvenir shops.

Six kilometers past Sattahip, a broad modern road on the right leads to a large Thai military base that once served the US Air Force as its only mainland Asian B-52 airstrip. At the base, turn right again and then, after 1km, turn left along the fence at the side of the base. The road again turns right and 8km further on ends at Samae San.

Jetties poke out from the hill-backed fishing town of **Samae San** into the translucent turquoise bay dotted by five islands. Cream and mauve squid dry in the sun near the long wooden piers which have floating gasoline stations.

From Sattahip, the road follows the coastline but offers only occasional glimpses of the sea. The land is flat and arid, providing little scenic beauty until one approaches the town of Rayong.

Situated 221km from Bangkok, **Rayong** is divided by an estuary which cuts through the commercial district of sundries stores, coffee shops and a forest of tall TV antennas. A right turn at the stop light just past the air-conditioned O-Tani Hotel leads across a dilapidated bridge to an old but industrious fishing village that occupies a strip of land between the beach and the estuary.

Rayong is famed for its *nam plaa*, or "fish sauce," the source of salt in Thai diets and the *sine qua non* of Thai condiments. Producing the sauce is a cottage industry in Rayong, and many homes have backyard factories. A small silver fish that abounds in the Gulf is allowed to decompose for about seven months to produce a ruddy liquid that is filtered and bottled on the spot.

The resorts associated with Rayong occupy a strip of beach to the southeast of Rayong. About 20km east of Rayong, a turn to the right takes you to **Ban Pae** whose shores are covered with quiltwork created by Poseidon. Dressed in weathered black shirts, straw hats and sarongs, women carpet the ground with tangerine-colored shrimp, allowing them to dry in the sun. Though the sight is compelling, the stench is overwhelming as the sun quickly decomposes the scraps and leftovers that will be used for chicken, duck and crocodile feed.

This scenic fishing port is sheltered on the west by a rocky outcrop, and by the island of **Koh Samet** to the south. The island is remembered by students of Thai literature as the place where Sunthorn Phu, a flamboyantly romantic court poet, retired to compose some of his works. Born in nearby Klaeng, Sunthorn called the island "Koh Kaew Phisadan" or "island with sand like crushed crystal". His assessment was as practical as it was poetic; the island and the beaches of the mainland produce some of the finest sand in the world, a fact appreciated by glass makers.

From a quiet poetic retreat, the island has gained popularity as a superb resort. Cheap bungalow complexes are quickly being razed to build small hotels and while the loss of budget accommodation is to be regretted, the garbage which had begun to mar the island's beauty will not be.

The coastal road leading east from Ban Pae, passes fish sellers and barber shops before entering the kilometer-long pine forest of **Ban Pha Phrae** national park, a refreshing change in scenery from the scrubland which precedes it. To the south one can see the rocky islets east of Koh Samet.

Seven kilometers farther down the road is the first of several lovely resorts. **Wang Kaew** offers small "villages" of bungalows set among seaside gardens.

Resorts stretch the 10km from Wang Kaew to the peninsula of **Laem Mae Phim**. In front of the fishermen's shacks along the shore, women sell sweets and roasted squid. Just offshore are two jagged islands called **Khi Plaem**, "Fish Droppings." Here weathered fishermen unload the small silver fish used to make *nam plaa*. To the left of a small promontory are three islands. The nearest and largest, the privately-owned **Koh Man Nai**, offers a sheltered beach, small bungalows and seafood restaurants.

To return inland to Route 3, fork left after Laem Mae Phim, passing through dense rubber plantations and bamboo groves. Three kilometers farther the small village of Ban Kram is arranged around a large old tree wrapped with colorful sacred cloths. Beneath the tree is an animist shrine and nearby stands a spirit house. Farther down Route 3 is the town of **Klaeng**, birthplace of the poet, Sunthorn Phu, who lived during the reigns of Rama II and Rama III. Three kilometers before entering the town, a small memorial etched with a number of his verses honors his work. The figures in the pond are characters from his most famous work "Phra Apaimani and Sri Sisuwan". The lady in the water is the giant ogress Pi Sua Samut who, charmed by Phra Apaimani's flute playing, is on her way to abduct him.

Past Klaeng on Route 3 at the 288-km-stone, a turn left along a small town street leads to a road that 13km later leads to the caves of **Khao Wong** in the Khao Chamao National Park.

A mystery prevails at this cavern-riddled mountain. Villagers claim photographs shot from the mystic jagged peaks invariably turn out blank when processed. Nothing in the gray-streaked outcrop suggests magical power; it dominates a valley of red laterite dust and farmlands.

Khao Wong is filled with caverns. One old woman, her face powdered white to cool her skin after bathing, has lived there since childhood, but claims she has not yet seen all the caves. In Tam Plak, a hollow near the *wat*, water drips on the brow of a stalagmite image of Lord Buddha. Worshipers visit the cave to offer prayers and light yellow candles. They shake divining sticks and learn their fortunes. Villagers claim that crocodiles live in underground streams, and that some of the cave walls gleam with diamonds.

shermen turning with e day's tch.

CHANTHABURI AND SURROUNDINGS

Further south along the Eastern Gulf, about 330km south of Bangkok lies **Chanthaburi**, a town with a past as exciting as its present. Gems, delicious fruits, handicrafts, beaches, an air of quiet antiquity, and relics of the past make this a prime tour spot for Thais, despite its distance from Bangkok.

Its history begins as much as 6,000 years ago. Skeletons suggest habitation by an advanced race of people. The pages are blank until the 17th century when Ayutthaya's King Narai moved communities of Chiang Mai and Lao residents to the town to defend it against incursions by Khmer and Vietnamese forces.

Its recent history is contained in a hill and a jail. About 5km south of town stands Khai Nern Wong, "Camp on a Small Circular Hill." King Taksin retreated here after the fall of Ayutthaya in 1767 to regroup his forces, recruit new soldiers and construct a fleet of warships. From this staging point, he returned to Ayutthaya to rout its Burmese occupiers.

On the same hill are the remains of a fortress built by King Rama III. At several points around the hill derelict cannons point at the now silent jungle. Several of the pieces are of great size; locals claim they could protect the mouth of the Chanthaburi river about 11km away. Today, spirits are believed to keep watch in the ruined stronghold. To reach it, drive down Road 3346 for 4.2km and turn right onto Road 3147. About 250m farther on is the fortress entrance.

Nearby is Laem Singh, site of a confrontation with colonial powers. Around the turn of the century, the Thais were embroiled in a territorial dispute with the French occupiers of Cambodia. The French invaded and for 11 years stationed a garrison force at Laem Singh. The Tuk Daeng (Red Building) Customs House and the Kook Khi Kai (Chicken Dung Prison) attest to their presence. To reach it, turn off Route 3 at the 348-km-stone and drive for 16km.

The area between Chanthaburi and the border lies in a climate pattern somewhat different from the rest of Thailand. This corner of the kingdom receives the southwest monsoon which makes it wetter but greener. The clouds water rubber plantations and a luscious rambutan crop, reputedly the best in the kingdom.

The town sits amid rolling hills, beside the winding Chanthaburi River. Motorcycles clog the streets, another immediately noticeable sign of the town's wealth. Shops along the river and elsewhere are open in the front, revealing rows and rows of grinding stones where artisans patiently cut facets on precious stones mined nearby.

Across the river is the French-style Church of the Immaculate Conception, the largest Catholic church in Thailand. Built around 1880, its congregation comprises Thai-Vietnamese who migrated to Thailand over the last two centuries. The descendants of these immigrants engage in a number of businesses, foremost of which is the weaving of reed mats, handbags and purses in attractive shapes and patterns. Many items are made in homes; some excellent products can be ordered from the nuns of the church.

Chanthaburi now has several air-conditioned hotels, such as the Eastern, Chanthaburi, Kasemsarn and Travel Lodge to cater to the growing number of visitors to the town.

The area's prime activity is mining for sapphires and other precious stones. The red soil of the rubber plantations is pitted with holes up to 12m deep as each miner stakes his claim and begins to dig, hauling out the muck by the bucketful. It is back-breaking work with meager rewards but occasionally a giant gemstone is found, instant riches that prod the other miners to continue their labors.

The nearest gem mining area is at **Khao Ploi Waen** ("Hill of the Sapphire Ring"). To reach it, return to Khai Nern Wong, the fortified town. About 2km past it is the Precious Stone Purchasing

m-mining
back
eaking
rk
h uncertain
urns.

Junction where the stones are traded. Another 1km up the road is Khao Ploi Waen. The open pits gouged out of the hillside are 2m to 10m deep.

Organized tours are conducted of the Chanthaburi mining areas, including a find-it-yourself tour in which visitors can prospect on their own, keeping whatever gems they unearth. Check with the local tour agencies.

Once out of Chanthaburi, head down the road to its waterfalls. At the 324-km-stone of Route 3, directly opposite the Chanthaburi turnoff, a dirt road leads inland for 22km through orchards of rambutan, durian, oranges and lychees. Turn right and go another 3km to reach **Nam Tok Krating** ("Bull Waterfall") a cascade of small falls tumbling 400 meters across a granite face.

Farther down Route 3, near the 347-km-stone, is another popular waterfall, **Nam Tok Praew**. Beyond makeshift stalls where women sell sticky rice and durian jam, is an oddity, a pyramidal *chedi* overlooking the falls.

The *chedi* commemorates a consort of King Chulalongkorn who drowned while being rowed up the Chao Phya River to Bang Pa-in. Her death was particularly tragic, since her attendants could have saved her had they not been forbidden by custom to touch the body of a royal person.

The falls and pools are seldom deserted in daylight. While boys in shorts and sarongs do flips into the cool water, modest girls sit fully covered under the spray. The fish are more daring and come nibbling at feet dangling in the water. During the durian season, busloads of Thais from as far as Bangkok roar in to see the falls and bargain for the seductive fruit.

The road to Trat passes through rubber plantations, paddy and marshlands. It arrives at Trat 400km from Bangkok and the last major town before the Cambodian border.

Trat itself is undistinguished, but serves as a starting point for trips to beautiful offshore islands. Stock up on provisions and head 19km from the clocktower to the port of **Laem Ngop**.

The waterfall of Nam Tok Praew tumbles into a pool which is a popular place for bathing and picnicking.

There you can rent a boat to **Koh Chang**. At 8km wide and 30km long, Thailand's third largest island is famed for wild boar and the **Mai Yom Waterfall**. Off the northern tip of Koh Chang some of the largest sharks in the gulf cruise near a rocky outcrop. Nearby, **Koh Mark** and **Koh Kut** offer clear lagoons and good diving. Accommodation consists of a few simple bungalows.

From Trat, drive down the narrow finger of Thailand to the town of **Klong Yai**, built over the water. From the main street, rows of houses run into the sea; between them, parked like cars on a side street, moored the fishing trawlers that earn the inhabitants their income.

For a roundabout but scenic drive back to Bangkok, return to Chanthaburi and head north on Road 317. It hugs the Cambodian border all the way to Sa Kaeo and the former Cambodian refugee camp of Khao-I-Dang. About 66km from Chanthaburi is Khao Soi Dao, "Mountain of the Harvest of Stars," with its lovely waterfalls. During the monsoon season, the open areas and riverbanks shimmer with the iridescent wings of tens of thousands of butterflies. Farther on is Wat Tham Lek Khaw Chaka, a cave monastery about 140km north of Chanthaburi.

At Sa Kaeo, you can turn right and drive 57km on Road 33 to **Aranyaprathet**. Situated on the border with Cambodia, the town was the administrative center for a huge effort to aid Cambodian refugees. A dozen international volunteer agencies and United Nations organizations have offices here. Until recently, the area was ringed by refugee camps. Although most of the refugees have now returned to the new democratic Cambodia, sporadic fighting between Cambodian government forces and remnants of the Khmer Rouge results in frequent spills across the border. There is no danger to those town, but one should be cautious from venturing too far into the countryside.

If you have been traveling by local transport, you can catch a train or air-conditioned bus from Aranyaprathet to Bangkok.

e villagers Klong Yai pend on ese fishing awlers for eir elihood.

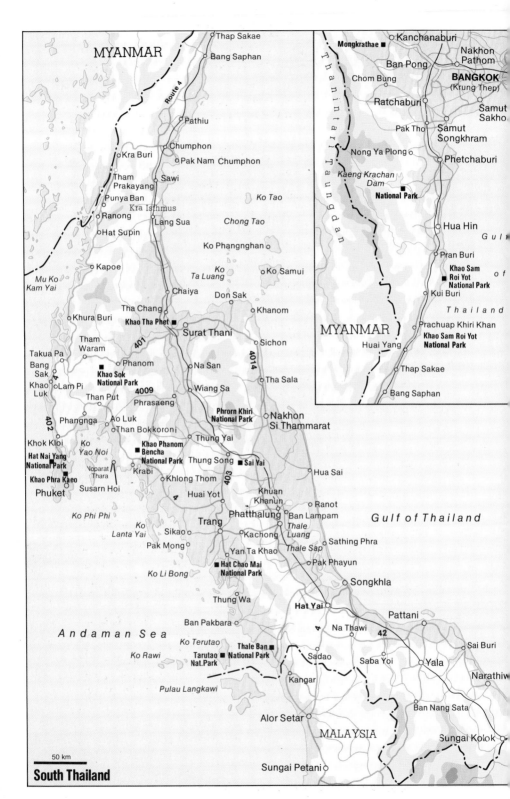

South Thailand

50 km

THE SOUTH:
BEAUTY AND THE BEACH

A stretch of pure white sandy beach lies, this time, on an island off the west coast of southern Thailand. On one side of the island, sheer limestone cliffs rise from the indigo waters of the Andaman Sea like prehistoric monsters. On the other side, a simple fishing village looks suspiciously like a postcard of tropical paradise.

The island is prized, not for its beauty, but for its bounty. Lithe young men who have never heard of vertigo, climb rickety bamboo ladders to the ceilings of enormous caves to harvest glutinous nests built by tiny swifts. The nests are prized by Chinese the world over as the principal ingredient of the delicacy known as bird's nest soup. South Thailand is reputed by connoisseurs to have the purest and tastiest of this delectable gourmet delight.

While farmers gather coconuts, fishermen set out in boats to net a tasty dinner; both lives as inexorably paced by the rhythms of nature as those of the farmers in the Central Plains, more than 1500km away.

Countless large and small islands like this one are scattered down the narrow strip of land that leads to Malaysia. Its eastern coast faces the Gulf of Thailand, the other shore lies on the Andaman Sea and Indian Ocean. Other than the larger islands like Koh Samui (*koh* in Thai means "island") and Phuket which have been developed as a major tourist center, few are ever seen by visitors; their tropical beauty is known only to those who live and work on them.

Thailand's South, a long arm of land, the "Elephant's Trunk", contains 14 provinces and is rich in stunning scenery. Wild jungles alternate with rocky mountains and broad beaches of powdery sand. Offering excellent recreational facilities, seafood, skindiving and spectacular scenery, the region has now been discovered by the outside world which has placed it firmly on the tourist map.

In many ways the South is a world far removed from the rest of the country, especially the farther south you go. A different climate, religion and type of farming makes it unique among Thailand's regions. Groves of rubber trees are more common than fields of rice. Once the visitor enters the southernmost provinces of Betong, Pattani, Narathiwat and Yala, the gilded dome of a Muslim mosque becomes a more familiar sight than the sloping orange roof of a Buddhist temple.

In the provinces near the border, the people speak Malay as well as Thai, and throughout the region, there is a distinctive southern dialect, as well as a southern cuisine resembling that of Malaysia. Products like *yan lipao*, pewter, batik and shadow puppets are found only in the South. The southern rainy season – two of them, in fact – is wetter and longer than in the rest of the country, the wettest months of all being December and January.

Preceding pages, a spectacular sunset in the south.

Like the North, the South was for many years semi-autonomous, governed by its own princes who ruled far from the culture and seat of power at Bangkok. Only in the present century has the South become integrated into the Thai kingdom.

It has had its own problems too. Many of its people have felt cut off from the mainstream of Thai culture, misunderstood by the rulers in far-off Bangkok. One result of this has been a small but worrying separatist movement composed of radical Moslems who would like to see the distant provinces joined to Malaysia.

After long neglect of this problem, the government is now taking positive steps to relieve the sense of alienation. Officials assigned to the South are now encouraged to learn the local customs and dialect and a southern university and a number of teachers' colleges and vocational schools have been established throughout the South. The royal family has built a palace at Narathiwat, not far from the border. It uses it as a base for travels around the region to oversee royal projects to develop water resources and new crops that will benefit farmers.

Rich in natural resources, the South is Thailand's most prosperous region after Bangkok. Rubber, the country's second largest agricultural export product after rice, thrives so well in the humid climate that Thailand is one of the world's largest exporters. On the upper peninsula, pineapple is grown and canned in such quantities that Thailand is also one of the world's principal exporters. There are also thousands of hectares planted in coconut and palm oil. Tin, mined in the South and refined in Phuket's huge smelters, is exported in such quantities that Thailand ranks as the world's number three exporter.

Haadyai, the railway terminus of the South, is one of the fast-growing cities in Thailand. A brash, brassy boom town, it attracts not only businessmen seeking to profit from local industry, but also thousands of Malaysian tourists lured by its free-swinging night life. Malaysians constitute the largest single group of tourists coming to Thailand; the majority of them come for the pleasures Haadyai offers.

Tourism is a fairly new industry in the South but already it is becoming a major foreign exchange earner. For many years, the principal means of getting to the area was the railway, and that was convenient to only a few of the more scenic spots along the peninsula. The only dependable way of getting to the lovely islands of the Gulf was to take a Thai Navigation Department freighter. Getting to Phuket in the Andaman Sea was a major undertaking over rough roads and crossing the open water by ferry. Only the really adventurous attempted it even after the Sarasin Bridge was built.

New highways and air services have changed the picture. Several daily domestic flights to Phuket have brought its superb beauty within the reach of tourists and the face of the island is changing rapidly. *Time* Magazine once listed Phuket among a small number of destinations still unspoiled by package tours. With 10,000 hotel

Koh Phi Phi offers unspoilt beaches, crystal-clear waters and a bewitching seascape.

rooms, its isolation has been compromised but it is still one of the most beautiful places in Asia.

There are daily flights from Bangkok to Phuket, Trang, Haadyai, Nakhon Si Thammarat, Suratthani, Pattani and Narathiwat.

Late each afternoon, the State Railways of Thailand offers daily express service to the South from Bangkok's main Hualampong Station. For those rushing through to Malaysia, it arrives in Butterworth (the terminal for the Malaysian island of Penang) about 17 hours later. Connections can then be made with trains to Kuala Lumpur and Singapore. Although designated "express," this is no scenery-blurring train; its leisurely pace affords a good view of green rice paddies, *klong*-side villages, craggy mountains and busy towns. Each stop provides a sampling of local food. Hawkers rush to the train's windows selling fresh fruits, *khanoms* ("sweets") wrapped in banana leaves, barbecued meats, dried squid and the ubiquitous iced soft drinks and coffee served in plastic bags.

Travelers in no particular hurry are encouraged to break their journeys at several points in order to see attractions the train normally passes after dark. Note, however, that on a journey of under 200km you can break your journey only once and for no longer than 48 hours. Railway stations swarm with buses, taxis and boats bound for outlying towns. When booking a seat do not underrate second-class passage, which on many trains equals the comfort of first-class. Comfortable berths can be reserved for the overnight portions of the journey.

The young and hardy might prefer to board an air-conditioned coach for the run from Bangkok to the South. Bangkok to Phuket takes about 14 hours; Bangkok to Haadyai about 20 hours.

Alternatively, South Thailand may be approached from Malaysia. There are daily scheduled international flights serving Phuket from Singapore, Kuala Lumpur and Penang, as well as regular international flights to Haadyai from Singapore and Kuala Lumpur. There is also an air service to Phuket directly from Hong Kong.

Trains depart Butterworth daily for Haadyai en route to Bangkok at 1.40pm, arriving at Haadyai after a 4½-hour journey. Quicker by far are the buses from Butterworth to Haadyai and faster still are the "shared" taxis. The latter depart Butterworth when they have a full load of five persons; fares are very reasonable. Those approaching the South from Malaysia's east coast (Kota Bharu) cross the Thai-Malaysia border to the station of Sungai Kolok; from there it is a two-hour journey to Yala.

An ancient locomotive permanently parked on an unused track.

ENTERING THE SOUTH

Route 4, the main road west from Bangkok leads to the South's first attractions: Phetchaburi and its palace, and the beaches of Hua Hin. This route allows you to include a visit to the Rose Garden and Nakhon Pathom. If you want to plunge directly into the South, head southeast down the Thon Buri-Pak Tho Highway that cuts across the countryside and joins Route 4 just south of Ratchaburi.

There is little to distinguish **Ratchaburi** but in recent years it has become a ceramics center with some innovative work being created in its studios. One can happily spend a day wandering from shop to shop to browse among a wide variety of styles, shapes and types.

Phetchaburi, 165km south of Bangkok, has far more to offer. As you approach the town on Route 4, take the left fork and continue past a rocky hill on the right. Cross the railroad tracks and stop under the shady trees for a visit to **Khao Luang Cave**. Around midday, huge stalactites and dozens of Buddha images are bathed in a shaft of soft light that pours through the cave roof.

As Route 4 enters the town, *naga*-topped walls frame the pathway to **Khao Wang Palace** built by King Mongkut in the 1860s. Ascend the fragrant frangipani fringed path, past the royal stables to the recently-restored palace at the summit. The gleaming white palace that blinds one in full daylight is dominated by an observatory the king constructed to pursue his favorite pastime of astronomy. The view from the parapet is superb; one can survey the entire city, its river, rice fields and the mountainous Burmese border to the west.

Four temples worthy of a visit are Wat Yai Suwannaram east of the river and Wat Kamphaeng Laeng just southeast of it. Wat Yai Suwannaram, built in the 17th century, holds murals that are among the oldest in the country. Wat Ko Keo Sutharam contains fading but beautiful Ayutthayan-period murals dating from 1734. Wat Mahathat in the middle of town is marked by the huge prang which

towers over it. Much of the decor is new but it is a magnet for the town's Buddhists, and festivals or rites are usually in progress there. Wat Kamphaeng Laeng, a Khmer temple, is thought to delineate the westernmost frontier of the Angkorian empire. About 16km east of town is the beach of Haad Chao Samran.

Some 17km south of Phetchaburi on Route 4, a road on the right leads to **Kang Krachan Dam** (also called Ubol Ratana Dam after King Bhumibol's eldest daughter). The road first follows a canal, then passes an older dam, and finally arrives at the earthen walls of Kang Krachan. The Irrigation Department usually grants tourists permission to stay at its bungalow overlooking the scenic reservoir and to take boats up the reservoir to the river.

Continue 35km south of Phetchaburi to **Cha-am**, the first of several beach resorts along the peninsula. Long favored by Thais, it has recently been discovered by foreigners.

About 30km farther south lies **Hua Hin**, Thailand's oldest major beach resort. It was put on the map in 1910 by

Prince Chakrabongse, brother of Rama VI, who led a party of European and Thai royalty down the peninsula to hunt game. Here, King Prachadipok (1925–1935) built a palace called Klai Klangwan, meaning "far from worries." Fittingly, he was vacationing here on June 24, 1932, when a bloodless coup toppled him, replacing 700 years of absolute monarchy with a constitutional one.

A 1932 *Guide to Bangkok* called the resort, "the most popular with travelers…longing for a game of golf." In those days, golf traps were imprinted with tiger pawprints. Today, Hua Hin's well-tended 18-hole golf course is considerably tamer.

Remnants of the 1930s linger at the Sofitel Central Railway Hotel. Recently renovated, it has retained its air of gentility, with ceiling fans and gardens filled with a menagerie of animal topiary. A bit south, the Royal Garden Hotel offers modern amenities. The Hua Hin beach is wide but unremarkable.

Hua Hin town lacks the charm of the Railway Hotel. Its shops sell plastic blow-up porpoises and ducky tubes, seashells artfully fitted into vases and ashtrays, beachwear and floppy hats. For some lively local color, stroll down to the pier in the morning or evening to watch fishermen unload their catches and women examine and bargain for a wide variety of fresh seafood, including an occasional shark or stingray.

Leave Hua Hin by heading south again on Route 4. About 22km from the town, the highway crosses Pranburi River, then enters a town by the same name. A road to the left leads to Pak Nam Pranburi situated 8km away at the river-mouth. Children play under stilt-houses while fishermen hang their nets to dry on wooden racks.

On Route 4 south of Pranburi you begin to glimpse the jagged outline of the **Khao Sam Roi Yot** (300 Peaks Range) National Park. Turn left at Pranburi main intersection, and drive for about 2km, at which point the road forks right, continue for 2km. Turn right at the police sub-station. Drive 19km to the park check post, and then another

14km to the headquarters. The gorges and caves here used to shelter highwaymen who robbed unwary travelers; their haunts were cleared out long ago. Now deers, monkeys and numerous species of birds roam the park.

The sky above Khao Sam Roi Yot is fondly remembered in the annals of the Chakri Dynasty. On August 18, 1868, King Mongkut, an astute mathematician and astronomer, took the governor of Singapore and members of the Bangkok court to this place to view a total eclipse of the sun which he had foretold. The king's prediction, to the astonishment of local astrologers, was only four minutes off. News of this event helped to discredit the superstition that an eclipse occurred when a giant swallowed the sun and disgorged it when impelled by gongs and general noise-making. Unfortunately, King Mongkut contracted a fever and died a week after his return to Bangkok.

About 90km south of Hua Hin, down a road that branches left just before the 323-km-stone, **Prachuap Khiri Khan** faces a scenic little harbor enclosed by knob-like hills. As you enter Prachuap, a hill rises to the left and seems, in certain light, to reflect a patch of sky. In fact, a natural arch at **Khao Chong Krachok** ("Mirror Mountain") frames the sky. Steps, 395 in all, lead up the hill to a small monastery surrounded by frangipani trees. Within the *chedi* are special Buddha relics bequeathed to the state by Rama I and Rama IV and used in the coronation of Chakri kings.

Continue on the road to town, pass the administrative offices, then turn left down the road to the northern end of the beach. Bungalows shaded by trees serve as a pleasant stopover if you wish to break your journey here. Otherwise, dine on seafood at one of the restaurants along the beach before driving on.

From Prachuap, continue 27km south on Route 4 and at the 350-km-stone, turn right for 7km to **Huay Yang Waterfall**. The waters cascade over 120m of boulders in a jungle not far from the Burmese border. The waterfall is located in an area called Thap Sakae District which is famous as a trading spot.

Precarious dwellings do the hillside (Hua Hin.

CROSSING THE ISTHMUS

About 35km beyond Thap Sakae District lies the town of **Bang Saphan** which is divided in two by the tracks of the southbound railway. As you enter the town, turn left and 12km later arrive at a wide bay rimmed by a pretty, 6-km-long beach. The green hill, Khao Mae Pamphung, is to the north; Koh Thalu Island is to the south. Here you can enjoy seafood and drinks served on wooden tables right on the beach.

Back on Route 4, south of Bang Saphan, the countryside becomes lush and mountainous. Rubber plantations spread beneath limestone cliffs that erupt from the Isthmus of Kra and far south down the Malay Peninsula.

Around 490km south of Bangkok, Route 4 comes to an important junction where it branches right and goes to the Andaman Sea on the west coast. The left branch leads to Chumphon, Lang Suan and the east coast town of Surat Thani, Nakhon Si Thammarat and Songkhla.

Turn left 8km at this junction to reach **Chumphon** noted for its inexpensive bird's nest soup. East of it lies **Paknam Chumphon**. Situated at the mouth of the Chumphon River, this fishing port rents boats by the hour for trips to nearby islands where swallows build their nests. During the mating season from March through to August, authorized collectors climb high up the cliffs to fetch the delicacies.

The island of Lanka Chio is especially famous. Merchants bid for concessions to take the nests, and even hire gunmen to guard their stake. It is fascinating to watch the gathering of nests, but let the guards know you are just looking. The island-dotted coastal waters make for exciting sailing too for those inclined to do so.

Head directly south on Road 41 to Surat Thani. The more scenic Route 4 strikes west across the narrowest point on the Kra Isthmus, then veers south and follows the Pak Chan River through Kra Buri on the way to Ranong.

About 12km beyond Kra Buri, turn left just before the 504-km-stone to reach **Tham Prakayang**, a temple in a cavern. If you have no flashlight the monks may lend one for the dark ascent into the image-filled cave. One completely black Buddha gazes upon you through mother-of-pearl eyes. A limestone and wooden staircase leads up and out of the cave to well-worn paths trodden by monks who meditate amid the foliage atop the outcrop.

South of Tham Prakayang, the highway winds through jungled hills and crosses a wide river. Soon after the 597-km-stone, **Punyaban Waterfall** appears next to the road. Truck drivers stop, don *sarongs*, and take a quick dip in the cool water. This is a popular spot for Thai tourists who stop for snacks at the teahouse near the falls. Climb a path to the left of the falls for a good view of the Pak Chan estuary, nearby islands, and the mountains on the southern tip of Burma. At the 612-km-stone, turn right near the Thara Hotel to enter **Ranong**. The hotel itself holds one of

Ranong's main attractions: hot mineral water piped from nearby thermal springs.

To reach the springs, travel up the road behind the hotel which runs along the left-hand side of the river. One kilometer on is a small shrine to the spirit of the springs. A well encloses the main outlet which pours forth 500 liters per minute of 70° C sparkling mineral water. Cross a suspension bridge to a little park or climb the hill behind the shrine to a small *wat* enclosed in a lovely, secluded grove.

The road past the hot springs takes you to the village of **Hat Supin**. This is tin-mining country; stark landscapes of white silt, bamboo scaffolding, deep dark pits and gouged-out cliff faces are everywhere. In open-cast mining, water from high-pressure hoses carves holes in the earth.

The mineral-laden water is filtered through a sieve which separates the tin ore from the mud and sand. In the morning you can watch sturdy women use wooden bowls to pan tin in the river, while their husbands work in the chalk quarry behind the village. One of Thailand's major exports, tin is mined all along the Indian Ocean coast of the Kra Isthmus. Much of the ore comes from private holdings like those around Hat Supin. A small sign with fish painted on it points the way to **Wat Hat Supin** where children rush up to sell you sweet popcorn. Visitors feed the popcorn to hundreds of carp that swarm in a pool by the side of the temple.

Drive back to Ranong, then take the 3-km road to **Pak Nam Ranong** on the sea where boats unload fish at a modern wharf and trucks dump tons of crushed ice on emptied decks. From this port some boats sail the Indian Ocean as far as Bangladesh in search of fish.

Directly opposite Pak Nam Ranong is Ranong Island, with its stilt houses and fishing boats. You can rent a boat for trips to the island. Return to Route 4 and continue south past Kapoe and Khuraburi. About 4km north of Takua Pa is the junction with Road 401 leading east to Surat Thani and Chaiya.

Eclectic paintings cover the walls of Suan Mok, a modern Buddhist retreat in Chaiya.

288

A great drive full of ups, downs and sharp corners, Road 401 zigzags over and around the cloud-cloaked limestone pinnacles of the Kra Isthmus. For the first 37km, it traverses the wide valley of the Takua Pa River, passing tin mining camps flanked by mountains. Then the road enters the hills and plunges through a remarkable series of streaked limestone precipices and splintered rocks.

For a midway rest, stop 59km beyond the start of Road 401 at **Wat Thamwaran**, just to the left of a small river. The *wat* provides a simple shelter for monks who meditate near a cave.

Approaching Surat, as the Thais call it, Road 401 leaves the hills and enters dense rubber plantations. About 120km from the Route 4 turnoff, Road 401 bends right for the final 12km into the town of **Surat Thani**. This busy ship-building, fishing and mining center lies on the right bank of the Tapi River. Surat itself has little worth seeing, but is the point of departure for interesting sidetrips. The first is for those interested in ancient history. To reach it, drive north on Road 41 for 20km to Chaiya.

A small, sleepy town of unpainted wooden buildings – a 60-second pause for the Bangkok express – **Chaiya** could be any small town of South Thailand. But the area is the subject of a dispute claiming it to be the capital of a once-great empire.

A group of historians now believe that the capital of the Srivijaya empire, described by the wandering Chinese monk, I Ching, in AD 671, was not Palembang in Sumatra, but Chaiya. In fact, they claim, the date previously accepted as the founding of the empire in Palembang was actually the date it was conquered by Chaiya. Even the name Chaiya, they believe, is a contraction of Srivijaya.

Only a few traces remain of this mighty empire, which once stretched from Java through Malaysia to Thailand. Less than 2km out of town stands **Wat Mahathat**, one of the most revered temples in Thailand. Its central *chedi* is thought to be over 1,300 years old and is a direct visual link between

sing the Isthmus,

owest t on the hern nsula, ighway s its way ugh mist-uded stone acles.

Chaiya and the Srivijaya period. A small museum adjoining the *wat* has on display, some interesting relics found in the vicinity.

Closer to town is **Wat Wieng**, where an inscription dated AD 755 is ascribed to a King Vishnu. It was the erroneous attribution of this inscription, 50 years ago, to a different location that led to the hypothesis that Palembang was the Srivijayan capital.

Two other *wats*, **Wat Long** and **Wat Kaeo**, equidistantly spaced from Wat Wieng, mark the sites of the Srivijaya edifices. Today only Wat Kaeo holds a dim reminder of a forgotten past in the crumbling wall of a once-great stupa. All that is known is that it was built to commemorate a victory. Perhaps the shattered remains of a Buddha, peering through a mist of cobwebs from his lonely niche, know the truth.

A few kilometers west of these historic remains, a small hillock rises from the flat countryside. Here stands a Buddhist retreat named **Suan Mok**, as new as Chaiya's past is old. The walls and columns inside the central building are covered with an eclectic series of paintings that run the gamut from the history of Buddhism to Aesop's fables.

Suan Mok owes a surrealistic touch to a wandering Zen Buddhist, Emanuel Sherman, whose search for enlightenment led him from the United States to Japan and Thailand, eventually ending on the island of Phangan off the Thai coast. After his death local artists covered one wall with illustrations to portray Sherman's epigrams.

Bas-reliefs telling the story of the Buddha decorate the outer walls. They were modeled locally from photos of the Indian originals. Suan Mok's quirky touch continues into its adjoining structures. The *bot* is a large concrete ship that serenely sails the sea of suffering to eventual nirvana.

Suan Mok's abbot, Phuttathat, is a much respected man whose followers flock here from all over Thailand and the world. His lay brother is one of the chief proponents of the Chaiya capital theory.

PHUKET AND OTHER RESORTS

Fifty kilometers south of Takua Pa is the town of Khok Kloi; the road to the left leads to Phang-nga. The right-hand road heads south and, 30km later, crosses the Sarasin Bridge onto **Phuket**, one of Asia's most beautiful islands.

Unlike many islands, Phuket's beauty is not limited to its beaches. About the size of Singapore, its beaches sprawl along the foot of a range of hills covered in jungle, coconut groves, rubber plantations and picturesque villages. Beyond the beaches are reefs teeming with marine life. Thus, Phuket offers more than beach lounging, it offers the opportunity to explore a tropical world of surpassing beauty.

Yet for decades, Phuket was known only to a few. The long road south from Bangkok to reach it, the lack of a bridge across the causeway, bad roads on the island itself and a seeming disinterest in developing it for recreation meant that it languished in isolation for decades. Besides, Phuket had enough on its plate. With its rich tin deposits, rubber and coconut crops, it ranked as Thailand's second wealthiest province.

By the 1970s, it began to show up on backpacker's maps. They stayed in fishermen's bungalows or camped out on the beach at Patong on the western shore. Then the word spread and developers descended on the island. Its airport was expanded to handle jets, dirt roads were paved and the ancillary services necessary to a beach resort were installed. Today, visitors wing in on direct flights from Vienna, Singapore, Hong Kong and Sydney as well as several daily wide-bodied aircraft flights from Bangkok. With 150 hotels, the visitors threaten to outnumber the locals.

The road from the mainland crosses the Sarasin Bridge, heading for the town of Phuket 30km to the south. Along the way, it passes the airport before arriving at the intersection with the roads to Surin Beach and Phak Chit. Here stand two bronze women warriors, drawn swords in hands. The pair are the sisters, Chan and Muk, who in 1785 led an army of villagers to repel Burmese invaders and preserve Phuket's independence.

Phuket's wealth comes from four principal sources. Its waters and the interior areas are rich tin lodes that are major contributors to Thailand's position as the world's third largest tin exporter. Rubber is also a major moneyearner as are coconuts and rice.

Tin built the town of Phuket, home for some 60,000 Thais. Unlike many provincial towns, Phuket has an identity of its own. The style is set by the beautiful colonial-style houses built by tin and rubber barons at the end of the 19th century following a disastrous fire which destroyed the downtown area. This style is being repeated in many of the buildings now being erected, a rare attempt to give some architectural unity to a unique area.

The streets in the inner city are lined with Sino-Portugese-style shophouses. Three stories high, the rowhouses were built by middle-income Chinese to house their extended families. The ground floor normally serves as a shop and reception hall; the upper floors are the living quarters. Large signs with big characters etched in gold are hung over and alongside the doors to identify the family and clan residing within.

Phuket's history is as momentous as it is tumultuous. It nearly became an important outpost of the British Empire. In 1786, Captain Light of the East India Company, who had married a Phuket woman, sought to secure the island for British interests. The Thai government's claim of suzerainty as well as a British government decision to seek a more strategic island to guard the important Straits of Malacca led Light to drop the endeavor. He went on to found Penang which subsequently became the chief British island colony on the Malay peninsula until the founding of Singapore in 1819. Phuket lapsed into the backwater of history.

In 1876, a miner's rebellion shook the island. Rampaging immigrant Chinese laborers – some say they were protesting harsh conditions in the mines, others say they were involved in a war between rival factions – threatened the island's stability. Only after a long struggle was the rebellion quelled. It brought to fame the two monks at Wat Chalong whose images are covered in gold leaf.

The two, would-be colonists and Chinese, have left their imprint on Phuket's architecture. The Chartered Bank building, Thai Airways office and others with their arched loggias resemble the buildings of colonial Singapore and Penang. The charm of these old buildings is complemented by the many Chinese shrines that accent the city with bright splashes of color. Of note is the brightly-painted **Put Jaw Temple** and its companion **Jui Tui** next door which sit just past the market on Ranong Road. Like many similar Chinese shrines elsewhere in Asia, its central altar is dedicated to Kuan Yin, the goddess of mercy.

Outside of the town, the only building worthy of note is **Wat Chalong**. It sits 6km further south on the Phuket Bypass, a ring road of sorts that runs west of Phuket town. The opulently-decorated temple is famed for the gold leaf covered statue of Luang Pho Chaem, the *wat's* abbot who gained fame as a bone setter, a skill he put to good use in the Miner's Rebellion of 1876.

Phuket's glory, however, lies in its beaches and it has a wealth of them. All are located on the western side of the island; the eastern shore is comprised primarily of rocky shoals.

The most developed is **Patong** west of Phuket town. In the early 1970s, Patong was little more than a fishing village on a wide crescent of sand. It has however made up for lost time, with a vengeance. Gone is the village, replaced by an entire town with hotels, supermarkets, shopping arcades, entertainment centers and a range of amenities.

The beach is dotted with colorful parasols and the bay with yachts. Unlike most of the other Phuket beaches, Patong has a wide range of water sports facilities including windsurfing, water skiing, parasailing, jetskis, sailing and boogie boards. One can rent scuba gear and even take lessons leading to PADI

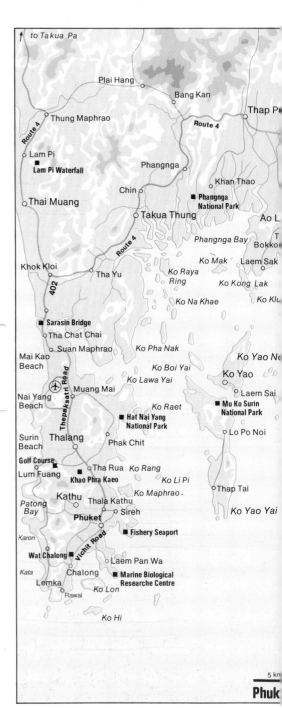

certification. These shops offer diving trips into the bay or west to the Similan Islands, considered one of the best diving areas in Asia with crystal clear blue water and a multitude of marine life. One can also snorkel at Kata Noi, two beaches to the south, or Phi Phi island four hours east of Phuket.

Patong also has the most developed land sports facilities on the island. Most large hotels have pools and many have tennis courts. A beautiful 18-hole golf course and driving range have been built in the rolling hills along the road between Phuket town and Patong.

Patong has many restaurants specializing in Thai seafood. The prize item on the menu is the giant Phuket Lobster weighing up to 3g and with enough meat to feed two. There are also Continental and Asian restaurants.

Patong has open-air bars with hostesses along Soi Bangla in the middle of the resort. These "barbeers" as they are called, are open, roofed squares with the bartenders inside and the patrons on stools outside. They offer bargirls and

videos but are crammed into such a small area that the din can be deafening. So far Patong has been able to avoid the excesses of Bangkok nightlife and the seediness of Pattaya's night scene perhaps because the clientele is primarily couples rather than bachelors. There are also three discotheques, a snooker parlor, and a night bazaar.

It is possible to rent cars, jeeps and motorcycles to explore the island. A valid driver's license is all that is necessary. The rental price normally includes insurance and unlimited mileage.

A coastal road links Nai Yang near the airport with Rawai on the southern tip of the island. Just to the north of Patong are Kamala, Surin and Laem Singh beaches.

Kamala beach is a small fishing village set in a coconut plantation. There are a few bungalows but the strong undertow mitigates against the creation of a large-scale resort here. Similarly, **Surin** beach is beset by bad currents so no development has taken place there. Instead, there is a nine-hole golf course

Kata Noi beach offers a less crowded alternative to the other more popular beaches in Phuket.

kept cropped to the proper height by a herd of water buffaloes who, by being moving hazards, wreck havoc with any serious golfer's game. **Haad Singh** is a lovely cove, the private preserve of the Pansea and Amanpuri resorts.

The long **Bang Thao** beach is dominated by a single resort, as is the beautiful **Nai Yang** beach just south of the airport. Set in the heart of Nai Yang National Park, it is cooled by casaurina trees. Besides the large major hotel there are a few bungalows rented by the park headquarters.

Beyond Nai Yang is Phuket's longest beach, **Mai Khao**. The 9-km beach is as yet undeveloped in spite of attempts by entrepreneurs wishing to cover it in resorts have been thwarted by environmentalists. Here, each December through to February night, giant sea turtles lay their eggs in deep holes they laboriously dig in the sand with their powerful flippers.

South of Patong is **Relax Bay** with its single hotel, Le Meridien Phuket. Beyond it is **Karon** beach and, past a small ridge running a finger into the sea, Kata beach. Karon has several large and medium-sized hotels but is otherwise occupied by small villages of bungalows. Not as developed as Patong, Karon and Kata both have clean, wide beaches. Karon even has enough wave action to allow surfing; boards are available for rent. The two beaches appeal to the holidaymaker interested in relaxing, soaking up the sun, swimming and enjoying excellent seafood. Both have their own restaurants and are developing a nightlife.

Kata is the site of Asia's second Club Med, a tribute to its beauty. There are other bungalow complexes as well as some good restaurants. Water sports facilities are limited to windsurf boards and sailboats but a stable hires horses for canters down the beach or safaris into the jungled hills above the resort that offer stunning views of the islands.

Over the hill from Kata is **Kata Noi** (Little Kata). It has a large hotel, white sand and a superb snorkeling area at the southern end of the beach.

A new road leads along a ridge to **Nai Harn**, providing spectacular views for several kilometers along the coast. At the southwestern edge of Phuket, Nai Harn is one of the island's prettiest beaches. A strand of sand nestled between two tall hills, fronted by a calm sea and backed by a lagoon, it is an idyllic setting if there ever was one. It boasts the island's most expensive hotel and cheapest bungalows, all on the same beach. Water sports facilities are limited but the beach is so beautiful no one cares. Nai Harn is renowned for its sunsets.

Within sight of Nai Harn is a stunning vantage point for viewing the sunset: **Promthep Cape**, a tall hill dotted with date palms and bright yellow grasses, plunging into a sea hissing against its rocky shore. Around the corner from Promthep, at the end of the highway from Phuket town is Rawai whose foreshore is a mass of rocks that lie exposed during low tide. It is then that shell hunters venture out, turning over the stones in search of specimens.

Rawai holds one of the island's two *Chao Lay* or sea gypsy villages. The sea gypsies were once nomadic fishing families, roaming from island to island. They are skilled fishermen both above and below the water. From a young age they dive to great depths in search of giant lobsters, staying there for up to three minutes. They are a simple people who adhere to animistic beliefs.

Their village, and that at **Koh Siray** east of Phuket town, are not terribly clean. Most families live in thatched huts set on stilts and protected by tin roofs, with the livestock living beneath the floor. There is not a lot to see in either village. East of Phuket town, the Phuket Aquarium houses a variety of colorful, well-displayed Andaman Sea fish and coral. Near it is the only major beach on the western shore, **Cape Phanwa** with one large hotel, the Cape Phanwa Sheraton.

A word of warning about Phuket: during the monsoon season (May–October), many of the beaches develop a particularly vicious undertow.

Transportation around the island is by blue-and-white wooden buses that leave the Phuket market for every point on the island. Small, four-wheeled vehicles called *tuk-tuks*, carry four passengers in comfort. Buses and *tuk-tuks* are very affordable.

Here, as in Samui, the preferred vehicle is the motorcycle. Phuket has numerous roads that lead into picturesque little villages (the town itself is reputed to have had the first paved road in the kingdom).

In the waters off the eastern coast are numerous pearl farms. Most grow what are known as "half pearls" but one, on Koh Naka Noi, grows the full-sized South Sea pearls worth thousands of dollars. It also claims to have produced the world's largest pearl. Visitors are welcome on the island if they arrive in an organized tour; these can be arranged in Phuket town or at the mainland port of Ao Po from which tour boats leave.

Phuket is the departure point for journeys to the beautiful Phi Phi a few hours east by boat and amazing Phang-nga Bay to the north of Phuket.

e Meridien
huket, one
f the many
otels that
ave mush-
oomed on
ie island to
ater to a
rowing
umber of
isitors.

IDYLLIC ISLANDS

Several times daily, buses make the one-hour journey from the railway station at Surat Thani to Ban Don. Speedboats leave Ban Don at 9am and 11am for a three-hour journey to Samui. Another leaves at 12.30pm for Samui and Pha-ngan, 45 minutes further on.

A quaint variation is to take the overnight boat which leaves Ban Don at 11pm, arriving at Samui at 6am. An express boat takes just two hours and leaves at 8.30am and 10.30am.

The newer, faster route is to take a one-hour, 70km bus ride from Surat Thani to the Lame Kula Pier at Don Sak. Ferries depart at 9am and 4pm, on a one-hour trip to Na Thon, the biggest town on Koh Samui.

The fastest route of all is to fly from Bangkok on Bangkok Airways which lands at a new airstrip in the middle of the island.

About 250sq km or the size of Pe-nang, Samui is one of the prettiest islands in the Gulf. Superb beaches, hills, jungles and waterfalls provide scenic variety rivaled by few other islands. For over a decade it has been the domain of the backpackers but its natural beauty has drawn a new clientele and is now in transition to more comfortable (and expensive) lodgings.

Despite the changes, Samui's lifestyle is still relaxed. Coconuts are the mainstay of the island's well-developed economy that utilizes labor-saving devices like monkeys trained to climb the tall trees and pluck the coconuts. The smell of roasting coconut meat, rich and savory, pervades the island.

Aside from a hotel on Yai Noi Bay, Na Thon Bay and others at Chawaeng Bay, accommodation comes in the form of simple bungalows costing less than US$4 per night. There's no shortage of them; they can be found on all of the island's dozen beaches.

Simple Thai food is cheap and delicious on Koh Samui. At the Na Thon's morning market you can breakfast on

Preceding pages, fishing vessels etched out i the after-glc of sunset on Phang-nga Bay. **Below**, golden statu of Buddha dominates t coast line o Koh Samui.

noodles and mild coconut curry for a few baht. Hawkers sell an endless variety of rice and coconut sweets. Try the coconut and date paste balls wrapped in sweet dough and deep fried. Fruits grown on the island – coconuts (the main export), papayas, bananas, mangoes (in season), pineapples and jackfruit – are remarkably cheap.

The main activity for visitors on Koh Samui is "beaching." The beaches have long stretches of dazzling white sand littered with cowries and crawling with tiny wind crabs; warm, clear water; and bright sunshine that is blotted out only in December when the rains pour down.

A fleet of *song tao* – small pickup trucks converted to taxis with two parallel rows of seats at the back – serve Koh Samui. Cheap and fast, they never refuse a fare and load up until passengers are hanging off the tailgate and roof. Visitors can organize a "do-it-yourself" island tour. For about 50 baht a head, half a dozen persons can pile into a *song tao* and ride the 52-km road that runs along the coast, the entire circumfer-

perfect hide-
way island
Krabi.

ence of the island. You can do the trip yourself by renting a motorcycle which gives you the option of stopping or turning off onto sideroads wherever you want. Alternatively, make a similar round-the-island tour by boat for about the same price.

Worth visiting are **Na Muang Falls**, **Hin Ngu Temple** with its huge seated Buddha, and a tiny beach near Lamai with "grandmother" and " grandfather" rocks, whose names are a tribute to Thai observation and wit.

An excursion worth making is to the small villages scattered around Koh Samui that are home to the island's more than 32,000 inhabitants. Near the mountains are coconut plantations and lush forests where hidden paths penetrate to clusters of simple, yet beautiful, wooden homes.

There is a remarkable sense of peace on Koh Samui. The island and the sea produce an abundance of food and the forests provide bamboo and wood for shelter. Life seems easy. There are several schools and the wealthier families

send their bright children to universities on the mainland. Those not aspiring to an intellectual or commercial career in the big city know there are coconuts to feast on just outside their doors.

To the north of Samui is **Koh Phangan**, with the same type of bungalow accommodation.

Gather some friends and, for 400–500 baht, hire a fishing boat to explore nearby islands. One of the most popular is Angthong National Park, a one-hour boat journey northwest of Samui. From the dock, you climb a steep stairway to a rocky bowl that holds a huge inland lake with water the pale green of glacial lakes.

If you are not heading south to Nakhon Sri Thammarat, cross the peninsula from Surat Thani back to **Takua Pa**. Over a thousand years ago, Takua Pa was a port for Indian traders who settled along the Malayan coast when the region was called Suvannabhumi, Land of Gold.

Some scholars think the Indians sought shortcuts to the South China Sea.

Unearthed statues have helped trace caravan routes across the Kra Isthmus to Surat Thani. Two 7th-century Dvaravati statues found on an island in the mouth of the yellowish Takua Pa River, add to the archaeological evidence. Today, Takua Pa has little claim to fame except as the district center of a rich tin mining area. Travelers can stop here for a bite to eat on the way to Phuket.

About 13km south of Takua Pa, a road branching off Route 4 to the right leads to **Bang Sak Beach** which rims a wide bay. Behind a refreshment stand, a thatched palm screen encloses a freshwater well for bathing and changing clothes. With its turquoise waters and white sand, isolated Bang Sak Beach lacks only Tahitian drums to complete an idyllic Polynesian setting. Soon after Bang Sak, the road rises from sea level and meanders along jungled cliffs. In gaps between the trees, wide, white beaches and small fishing fleets appear below. Farther out at sea, barges are engaged in small-scale mining.

About 36km from Takua Pa, as the

A solitary *sampan* glides through Phang-nga Bay.

highway completes a twisting descent back to the sea, **Khao Luk Beach** lies immediately to the right. About 30 families live most of the year in the natural shelter of this cove. The men do not fish; with the aid of air pumps and goggles, they dive for tin. Like nautical prospectors, they stay under water one or two hours at a time, loading tin-bearing sand into buckets. Workers hoist the full buckets onto bamboo rafts and sieve their contents.

Every June, the powerful monsoon churns up the ocean and halts the tin diving off Khao Luk. The mining families abandon their huts to the destructive lashing of wind and sea until the monsoon relents.

Returning to Route 4, about 69km south of Takua Pa, a reddish dirt road to the left just before a small school marks the entrance to **Lam Pi Waterfall**. Follow the road 2km through a rubber plantation to the three-tier fall and a clear pool perfect for bathing.

Island interlude: Turquoise waves caress a beach so dazzlingly white it is almost painful to the eye. Colorful fishing boats seem suspended in mid-air, so crystal-clear is the pale blue water. With palm-fringed beaches and lofty limestone mountains as a backdrop, **Koh Phi Phi** rivals Phuket as one of the most beautiful islands in Asia.

The islands lie three hours east of Phuket's Ao Makham Bay and three hours west of Krabi on the mainland. Phi Phi comprises two islands: the smaller Phi Phi Ley, a craggy limestone monolith reminiscent of the peaks of Phang-nga Bay, and Phi Phi Don which, unlike its sister, is filled with bays and beaches.

Phi Phi Don is shaped like a barbell with two limestone karsts joined by a narrow spit of land. Its small population lives in a scattering of fishing villages that are rapidly being nudged farther into the jungle by the burgeoning resorts. Two resort complexes dominate Ton Sai Bay, the docking point for the island. Here, too, are clustered the restaurants and travel agencies offering boat and diving tours of the waters around Phi Phi.

A half dozen beaches divided by rocky headlands run to the southeast; Haad Yao or "Long Beach" is the largest and most popular. In these bays, accommodation is limited to thatched bungalows. Sports facilities are limited but there are excellent snorkeling waters off Haad Yao. It is also possible to climb to the highest point on the island for a spectacular view of the bays.

The nearby **Phi Phi Ley** is renowned as a site for swifts who build their nests on the ceilings of rocky caverns. A web of bamboo scaffolding reaches up, disappearing into the gloomy upper recesses. Men climb up these precarious ladders to collect the nests which are sold as delicacies to Chinese gourmets.

The cave's other inhabitants produce the guano that coats the cave floor and fills the air with its distinctive odor. On the cave wall close to the entrance are mysterious paintings depicting a variety of sailing ships. Some have likened them to Viking ships.

From Phi Phi, regular boat service allows one to continue one's journey to

rrealistic
ang-nga
y.

Krabi without back-tracking through Phuket and Phang-nga.

About 30km northeast of Khok Kloi on the mainland north of Phuket, a road on the left leads to **Suan Ku** with a limestone cave filled with dozens of Buddha images. Light streaming through an opening gives the cave a mystical aura.

Route 4 soon enters the small town of Phang-nga where several small hotels provide simple accommodation. There is also the Phang-nga Bay resort from which boats depart on an exciting journey to one of the wonders of the world, Phang-nga Bay. This is a collection of enormous limestone mountains that rise straight out of the sea and, at points, can remind you of the fjords of Norway. The boat winds among these on its way to the outer islands, leaving one's imagination to drift and dream up animals and mythical beasts the contorted shapes suggest. In some instances, the Thais have done the job for you, as at one which they have named Koh Ma Chu or "Puppy Island".

Just before the mouth of Phang-nga River, the boat approaches the base of **Khao Kien** mountain where a cavern contains primitive paintings depicting human and animal forms like the cave drawings of Lascaux. To the right lies a large rock island called **Koh Pannyi** where an entire Muslim fishing village stands on stilts over the water.

The boat proceeds through a maze of islands, each more astonishing than the last. Highlights of this "lost world" setting include:

Tham Lawd: On a seeming collision course with a huge limestone outcrop, the boat slips into a barely discernible, overgrown entrance to a cave. For more than 50m you slide under giant stalactites. Rocks protruding from the water appear to have been sliced by a sword-wielding god.

Tham Nak: A twisted stalagmite at the entrance resembles a *naga* serpent, giving this cave its name. Green stalactites burst from the ceiling like a frozen waterfall. The whole mountain-island seems from the outside to drip with

Exploring Tham Khaev, one of the many fascinating caves in Phang-nga Bay.

streaked limestone. Scenes from numerous Thai movies have been filmed here.

Koh Thalu: *Thalu* means to pass from one side to the other, in this case not over the mountain, but under it. The boat squeezes through a cave filled with stalactites.

Koh Khao Ping Gun is perhaps the most spectacular of Phang-nga's islands. Behind the beach, the mountain seems to have split in two and the halves to lean against each other. Locals say they are two lovers. A small staircase leads to a cavern above the water where limestone formations look like large mounds of spilled glue. This was the setting of part of the James Bond movie, "The Man with the Golden Gun". A small beach overlooks another island, **Koh Tapoo**, (Nail Island) which looks like a thorny spike driven into the sea.

The return journey is usually through mangrove swamps whose prime residents are small lungfish. These evolutionary beasts, halfway between amphibian and reptile, bask in the slick mud, breathing air but flopping back into their watery home if disturbed.

Several onshore caves in Phang-nga are worth visiting. Approached from town, **Tham Russi** or "Hermit Cave" lies on the left 2km before the Customs House turnoff. A stalagmite resembling a hermit has been embellished by human hands which have fashioned a long white beard, a saffron cloth around the shoulder, and a cane. Many believe the *russi* has power to cure the sick and predict winning lottery numbers.

Unusual labyrinthine grottoes weave through Tham Russi. In a parklike atmosphere, lovers stroll over bridges crossing pools within the cave. The area is well-lit with neon tubes; it even has toilet facilities.

Continuing 500m down the road, passing the governor's office on the left, you see a blue sign down a trail towards *Wat Tham Pong Chang*, "Temple-Cave in the Elephant's Stomach." A claustrophobic tunnel to the left of a pool leads into a small shrine adorned with statues of three sacred elephants.

ck slabs, ade of trified ells 25 llion years d, jut out of h Phi Phi.

THE SOUTH-WEST COAST

Two kilometers past Phang-nga on Route 4 is a fork where a sign points right, 85km to Krabi. Beyond the fork the road rises into a winding pass through giant limestone hills and fertile valleys as you enter one of the most spectacular drives in Thailand. At the foot of the pass on the right, the humble visage of a Buddha statue at **Wat Kirirong** greets you at the entrance to a hollow carved from huge cliffs.

South of Wat Kirirong the horizon resembles the graph line of a seismic tremor, with huge jutting rocks thrusting out of the jungle. About 45km from Phang-nga the road squeezes between two gargantuan rocks and flows into the town of **Ao Luk**, 40km before Krabi. Turning right at the main junction in town you go 2km to reach **Than Bokkoroni National Park**, one of the most beautiful in Thailand. Like a scene from

Lost Horizon, the park is dominated by lofty cliffs. In one spot, an underground stream rises amid lush vegetation at the base of a mountain. Gravel paths snake beneath cliff faces covered in green vines punctuated by red hibiscus.

Returning to Route 4 you can stop at **Ban Thong Agricultural Station** where botanists breed new strains of rubber, coffee and tea. Continuing along Route 4, you wind through dense stands of rubber trees. Strips of white latex dry like laundry on bamboo poles placed in front of small houses.

About 25km south of Ao Luk, beneath and around unpredictable limestone "eruptions," is **Naichong Rubber Experimental Station** where new varieties of high-yielding rubber trees are being created. By taking Route 4 all the way toward Krabi (the highway actually passes 5km north of it), you miss a scenic sidetrip. If you have an extra few hours, turn right about 7km beyond the Naichong Station. Continue for 6½km, then left for 11½km through small farming villages not far from the sea. A

Tiny crabs weave a fine lace network on a deserted stretch of Krabi beach

white sign points to Hat Noparat Thara Beach 7km down a dirt road.

Hat Noparat Thara faces rocky islands half a kilometer off-shore that can be reached on foot at low tide. Along the beach, casaurina trees provide shade for food vendors and vacationers. Dungalows can be rented at the Hat Noparat Thara Park headquarters. The nearby **Poda** and **Chicken** islands offer superb snorkeling.

Farther down the coast is the new resort area of **Ao Phra Nang**. A few hotels have been built on the beach but the principal accommodation is found in bungalow complexes. This is being touted as the beach resort of the future with plans being mooted for air service from Bangkok.

The road continues to **Susarn Hoi** ("Shell Cemetery") **Beach**. Natural rock slabs comprising thousands of petrified shells 25 million years old, jut at odd angles along the shore. It is worth examining these frozen pieces of the past, comparing pre-historic shell shapes with those found today.

The road eventually enters **Krabi**, a non-descript town on the banks of the Krabi River. Myriad off-shore sandbars block the view of the distant sea. Old black junks with yin and yang talismans painted on their bows often berth at Krabi. From the docks you can catch boats to Koh Phi Phi.

As you head southeast from Krabi on Route 4, the land gradually flattens. Dike-enclosed rice fields appear on both sides of the road. Seemingly abandoned suitcases and boxes on the roadside designate bus-stops; passengers wait patiently under banana trees.

Only fanatical spelunkers will venture off Route 4 to investigate the small caves at **Khao Pina**. To reach them, turn left 92km from the Krabi junction down a side road. It leads, after 1½km, to a small temple at the base of a tall staircase climbing to two caves. Take your own flashlight. A strange statue of a Thai official dressed in a white medal-festooned jacket and blue pants poses stiffly before a chapel.

Back on Route 4, you pass through Huai Yot, 108km from Krabi and after 28km enter **Trang**, an industrial town inhabited primarily by Teochew-speaking Chinese immigrants who originally sought work here panning tin but wound up running the rubber trade.

Trang's Chinese heritage is reflected in monuments at the northern approach to the city. At **Ban Bangrok**, 3km north on Route 4, a Teochew shrine honors Kwan Tee Hun, a red-faced, bearded god believed to have the power to prevent or start war. Farther south on Route 4 a dragon gate guards the city.

From Trang you can take a number of interesting sidetrips. **Pak Mong Beach** lies on the Indian Ocean off Road 4046 (the Sikao Road) just after the 28-km-stone from Trang. It is a long bumpy trip but the scenery and sunsets are memorable. **Surin**, which lies a short distance west of Trang on Route 4, has a large, beautiful pond surrounded by well-kept gardens. Continuing northeast from Trang through Huai Yot you pass through a beautiful winding valley and arrive at Nakhon Si Thammarat.

he hinter-nd of Krabi ith its lush opical egetation in ontrast to ark outcrops f limestone oulds.

THE DEEP SOUTH

A long main street runs like a spine through the long and narrow ancient city of **Nakhon Si Thammarat**. Lining either side are undistinguished provincial town buildings plus a museum, a store selling shadow-play puppets and several temples. The Thai, Thaksin, Neramit, Montien and Bualuang hotels have air-conditioned rooms.

Nakhon was an important city in the Dvaravati and Srivichaya empires. A few Dvaravati sculptures remain in **Wat Mahathat**, one of the oldest temples in Thailand. On the south end of town, the *wat*'s prime attraction is a 77-m-high *chedi* whose spire is covered by 270kg of gold. To the right of the *chedi*, a temple museum houses an assortment of delicate gold and silver offerings. Next to the *wat*, the Viharn Luang, with its inward-leaning columns, is a fine example of Ayutthaya period design.

Thailand's nielloware industry began in Nakhon 60 years ago. You can observe craftsmen at work at the original Nakhon shop on Chakrapetch Road. While niello resembles enamelware, it is more durable. A design rendered in silver or gold wire is laid down on a metal base. A black alloy is then poured into the spaces, leaving the precious metal to glow in an ebony sky. Objects range from ashtrays to royally-commissioned jewelry.

The road north takes you to the Gulf coast town of **Sichon** which offers scenic views and Srivichayan artifacts. You can also visit the cave that reputedly sheltered King Taksin when he fled from the Burmese. Take the road across the railroad tracks to Lan Saka Village, turn right at the first fork, and go 9km to the cave where the view of the countryside is magnificent.

An all-weather highway linking Nakhon to Songkhla runs through numerous lime orchards and past several dusty arenas where fighting bulls are trained. But an alternative to the new

Below left, the opulent interior of Wat Mahatha in Nakhon Si Thammarat; and right, th crowing glor of the *wat* is its gracefull, 77-m-high *chedi*.

road is the older Route 4 which leads, via Trang, to Phatthalung.

Enroute to Phatthalung on Route 4, about 20km east of Trang, the **Khao Wang Nature Reserve** encompasses jungle, a rocky creek and a waterfall. Drive into the reserve but do not panic if you encounter soldiers brandishing weapons; the reserve also hosts a military camp.

Khao Chong represents part of Thailand's nascent conservation and ecology movement. Students at its Nature Education Center study southern animals in their natural rain forest environment. The small zoo houses local fauna, like the Binturong civet, Prevost squirrel, Brahminy kite, hog badger and some endangered species including the white-handed gibbon which poachers usually capture at a young age by killing its mother.

The hog badger has an interesting connection with southern bull fighting, which is the region's prime entertainment and draws gamblers from far and wide. The long-clawed mammal is oc-

casionally shot for the fat on its nose. A bull with this wild-smelling fat rubbed on its horns, it is claimed, can intimidate and defeat any opponent. Naturally, the use of this fat is regarded as cheating.

From the Khao Chong Nature Reserve, drive 34km to **Phatthalung**. Along this stretch of Route 4 motorists used to be relieved of their cash and valuables by bandits but such occasions are now rare. You will likely only see Thai Army soldiers camped in tents between rows of rubber trees.

Route 4 to Phatthalung zigzags under towering trees, past pink earthen rock, up and down the mountainous watershed along the spine of the isthmus. About 3km before Phatthalung, the highway branches south to Haadyai. Continue straight, past the provincial administrative offices, and then bear left on a road to Khuan Khanun ("Jackfruit Hill") and **Wat Ku Ha Sawan**.

This antiquated temple was recently renovated, but behind its yellow buildings a staircase climbs up to a large grotto lighted by a natural arch. A delightful

elebrating
e *Chok Phra*
stival in
ongkhla.

obese laughing Buddha marks the entrance. Around a copper-leafed Bodhi tree are gathered dozens of Buddha images. Light from the arch glints off the gold leaf on the statues.

To the right of the *wat* lies another cave formerly inhabited by a hermit monk. His personal collection of images is kept there.

To visit another temple and the northern end of the Thale Sap inland sea, take the road leading east. **Wat Wang** ("Palace Temple") is 8km from the city on the left side of the road. An attractive *chedi* graces the temple courtyard. Inside the temple proper you will find unrestored frescoes dating back about 200 years.

Continue down the road another 7km to Ban Lampam where the water of the inland sea, 70km from its entrance to the Gulf of Thailand, is fresh.

A short boat trip from Phatthalung town leads to **Tham Malai**, a cave lying between the province's two famous peaks: Broken-Hearted Mountain and Broken-Headed Mountain. Legend says these represent two women turned to stone as punishment for jealousy. Catch the boat behind the train station for the 15-minute ride to Tham Malai. A monk caretaker will turn on a generator to light up the stalactites.

Phatthalung offers the Ho Fah and Thai hotels but you may wish to continue without stopping. If so, head back to Route 4 and turn south for Haadyai.

Haadyai, the commercial capital of south Thailand, is a boom town. Rubber and tin have been its traditional income earners but they are rapidly being overshadowed by an active nightlife and commercial center geared towards the thousands of sybaritic Malaysian men who pour over the border each month to enjoy its illicit bounty. Nightclubs with singers, massage parlors and brothels are the magnets for men for whom such activity is illegal in their own country and whose religion prohibits dalliance. They play and purchase for a few heady days before returning to a sober life.

Haadyai has several cultural points

Winsome Songkhla smiles.

of interest for those turned-off by its nightlife. Wat Haad Yai Nai in the middle of town has the third largest reclining Buddha in the world. Do not just admire the exterior of this giant atop its three-meter high base. Ascend its pedestal and enter the Buddha's innards where lungs and shrines sit side by side.

On the outskirts of the town, en route to Songkhla, is the **Rubber Research Center**. It serves all of Thailand, testing grafting and tapping methods, and studying how to induce the rubber trees to be more bountiful in their production of latex. Small-holding farmers study at the center where there is a rubber processing laboratory. If the subject interests you, telephone one day in advance to request a tour.

Next to the research center is the **Songkhla Nakharin University**, a splendid complex set on 120 hectares. A pumpkin-shaped building containing the auditorium and laboratories is surrounded by a moat. Arched windows in the pumpkin catch breezes from all directions and funnel them through the building to provide natural air-conditioning. An exhaust pump in the center sucks the warm air out.

Sunday is the day for bullfights. Do not envisage a *corrida* with *matadors* and *picadors*; bull fighting Thai style is a contest which pits one humpbacked bull against another. Two animals are brought face to face. They lower their heads, clash horns and paw the ground, each pushing against the other like sumo wrestlers. The fight may last minutes or a couple of hours. It ends when one bull "bulldozes" the other to the edge of the ring or when one simply turns and takes flight.

People come all the way from Bangkok to savor the shark's fin soup at Haadyai's restaurants. Other specialities are poached duck and fried pigeon. Several large open-air restaurants serve superb seafood to the accompaniment of raucous live music.

Haadyai has *tuk-tuks* to take you anywhere in town. Taxis transport you to Songkhla.

SONGKHLA AND ON TO MALAYSIA

If Haadyai is brash then **Songkhla** is discreet. Like the name of the inexpensive restaurant in Paris (now alas no more) that one passes on to a friend with the promise not to tell anyone lest it be spoiled, Songkhla is a well-kept secret from the pleasure-seekers who visit Haadyai. Indeed, Songkhla is the main reason for the non-reveler to visit Haadyai. Trains, buses and taxis cover the 25km between the two towns in half an hour.

Built on a peninsula, Songkhla is an old Chinese city sunning peacefully on a leg of land hemmed on three sides by water. Of the three, only the seaward (eastern) shore is suitable for sunning and swimming. The north portion of the beach is backed with lush casaurina trees and here one finds monks in saffron robes walking past humpbacked bulls being prepared for the bullfights.

The focal point of the beach is a bronze statue of a little bronze mermaid looking wistfully seaward like her sister on Copenhagen's shore. She perches on a rock immediately opposite the Samila Hotel, the only hotel of distinction in Songkhla.

Immediately northwest of the mermaid, a score of seafood restaurants occupy the sandy strand. Select your ingredients from fresh seafood displayed on ice including 35-cm-long tiger prawns. While waiting for them to be cooked, relax in colorful deck chairs alongside low tables.

Across the road from the Samila Hotel is **Khao Noi**, a topiary garden with realistic fighting bulls, birds in flight and an elephant, sculpted out of a living yew. Around the corner, on Sukhum Road, a group of monkeys gathers in the late afternoon to scratch, screech and scowl. They sit, hands on knees, looking like crotchety members of a debating society.

Songkhla boasts two museums. The chock-a-block museum in **Wat Majimawat** (popularly called **Wat Klant**) is in marked contrast to the spic-and-span, recently renovated **Old Governor's Palace**, a beautifully-proportioned Chinese mansion built in 1878. The latter contains an excellent collection of ceramics and documented relics recovered by scuba divers from an ancient wreck in the Gulf of Thailand. The Majimawat museum collection ranges from early Thai Bencharong (five-color) pottery and 200-year-old shell boxes to a pre-electric fan that operates on gas. You are on your own, though, because there are no labels and the monk in charge speaks only Thai.

The 200-year-old marble Buddha gracing the altar inside the *viharn* is minus its gold lotus crown which is now preserved in a vault to protect it from thieves. Stone lions, a gift of a rich 19th-century Chinese merchant, guard the doorway which opens on to a set of interesting murals. Some show scenes of Songkhla's history while others depict European sailors and a steam boat. Lift your eyes as you walk along Nakhon Nawk Road and Nakhon Nai

Left, a close-up view of a colorful fishing boat of the south, with a bright-painted prow. Right, Songkhla is still a well-kept secret.

Street; old Chinese families living in these lovely Sino-Portuguese shophouses are reputed to be extremely rich and conservative.

Continue towards the lake to Vichienchom Road. A steep path leads, 20 minutes later, to the summit of **Mount Tangkuan** and the ruins of an ancient *chedi*. The panorama is superb and the bustle at the wharves along the lake give credence to Songkhla's claim to being the busiest fishing port in Asia.

A pleasant excursion can be made to **Koh Yor** situated in **Thale Sap** or **Songkhla Lake**, one of the largest lakes in Southeast Asia. The lake is, in fact, a deep inlet rather than a proper lake, and, being connected to the sea, its waters are rather brackish. En route to Yor Island, stop at the Fisheries Station where enormous white *plaa kapong* (white snappers) are bred. Koh Yor is renowned for its locally woven cotton, ancient Buddhist monuments and its tranquillity.

The lake is also home to tens of thousands of water birds which mi-grate here to settle among its rushes. With special permission, it is possible to take a boat into this huge lake to observe their habits. To one's surprise, the water, even in the middle of the lake, is no more than 1m deep, making the grassy bottom with its darting fish easy to see.

Another excursion by boat is to the offshore islands of **Maew** and **Nu** (Cat and Rat). Nu is the larger of the two and has some pleasant picnic spots and swimming beaches.

Three kilometers south of the Samila Hotel is a small, extremely active fishing village inhabited mainly by Muslims. It is the fishing boats rather than the fisher people that are the most colorful. It would be difficult to beat these brightly-painted *gorlae* for imaginative themes and execution.

Beyond the fishing village sits the rocky beach of **Khao Seng** whose fame rests on a precariously poised giant boulder called **Nai Bang's Head**. Legend says that if you succeed in pushing it over you will uncover the millionaire's **Off to work.**

treasure buried beneath it. Inland from the beach is the **Banloa Coconut Plantation** where you can watch monkeys trained to climb trees and toss down selected coconuts.

Wat Kho Tham is built among enormous boulders on a nearby hilltop. The cave contains the inevitable Buddha's footprint and a reclining Buddha sheltered by an overhanging rock. Around the corner is **Wat Mae Che**, a charming sandy spot inhabited by Buddhist nuns. The shaven-headed nuns, often quite young, dress in white robes, grow flowers and rise at 4am to meditate and read philosophy before setting out to collect alms.

From Haadyai, there are two rail and three road routes to Malaysia. The more frequently used railway line runs southwest, crossing the border to Alor Setar and Butterworth, opposite Penang. The second heads southeast through Yala and ends at the border town of Sungai Kolok. From there, it is a short walk and taxi ride to Kota Bharu on the east coast of Malaysia.

For those eager to explore more of the

e Silpa
ves near
la are a
grimage
e for
uthern
ais.

south, there is the beautiful island park of **Tarutao** in the Andaman Sea. To reach it, drive Route 4 north of Haadyai for 40km to Rattaphum and then turn almost due south for 65km to Satun. In Satun, you can hire a boat to cross the sea to Tarutao.

Tarutao National Park is a collection of islands that form the northern portion of the Langkawi island group of northern Malaysia. There are accommodations on the Tarutao itself.

Down the east coast from Songkhla are the provincial capitals of Pattani, Yala and Narathiwat. Many residents of these towns are Chinese but the majority of the people are of Malay descent. The towns hold little interest except to students interested in ethnic diversity. For them, there are mosques to visit and Malay speakers to talk to.

Of interest near Yala are the Silpa caves. The large cave of **Tham Koo Hu Pimuk** contains a 25-m-high Buddha, considered a holy pilgrimage site by southern Thais. It is an apt place to conclude your Thai adventure.

INSIGHT GUIDES
Travel Tips

OYSTER *GLX*

◈ Samsonite[*]

Our Strengths Are Legendary[*]

[*]Trademarks of Samsonite Corporation

TRAVEL TIPS

Getting Acquainted

THE PLACE

Lying between 7° and 21° latitude, Thailand has a total land area of 514,000 sq km (198,000 sq miles), nearly the size of France. The country is said to resemble an elephant's head with its trunk forming the southern peninsula. Bangkok, its capital, is sited at its geographic center, approximately at the elephant's mouth. The country is bordered by Malaysia on the south, Myanmar on the west, Laos across the Mekong River to the northeast and Cambodia to the east.

The north is marked by low hills and contains the country's tallest peak, Doi Inthanon, standing 2,590m (8,490ft) tall. A range of hills divides Thailand from Myanmar and forms the western boundary of the broad alluvial Central Plains which is the country's principal rice-growing area. To the east, the Plains rise to the Korat Plateau which covers most of the Northeast. The spine of the southern peninsula is the same range of hills that separate Thailand from Myanmar, sloping down to the Andaman Sea on the west and the Gulf of Thailand on the east. Thailand has a total of 2,600km (1,600 miles) of coastline.

Bangkok is situated at 14° north latitude. Like Hungary's Budapest, Bangkok is a city divided into halves by a river, the Chao Phya which separates Bangkok and Thonburi. The city covers a total area of 1,565 sq km (602 sq miles) of delta land of which no natural area is more than 2 m (7 ft) above any other. Its population totals 5.8 million although a semi-permanent migrant population, has in recent years, swelled that number to an unofficial 8 million. Bangkok functions as the epicenter of the country's political, business and religious life, a primate city some 35 times larger than Thailand's second and third largest cities of Chiang Mai and Korat.

Time Zones

Thailand Standard Time is 7 hours ahead of Greenwich Mean Time. Hence when it is +7 hours GMT in Bangkok, it is:

Hong Kong	+ 1 hour GMT
Tokyo	+ 2
Sydney	+ 3
Honolulu	- 17
Los Angeles	- 14

CLIMATE

There are three seasons in Thailand – hot, rainy and cool. But to the tourist winging in from anywhere north or south of the 30th parallel, Thailand has only one temperature: hot. To make things worse, the temperature drops only a few degrees during the night and is accompanied 24 hours by humidity above 70 percent. Only air-conditioning makes Bangkok and other major towns tolerable during the hot season. The countryside is somewhat cooler, but, surprisingly, the northern regions can be hotter in March and April than Bangkok.

Adding together the yearly daytime highs and the nighttime lows for major world cities, the World Meteorological Organization has declared Bangkok to be the world's hottest city. When the monsoon rains fall, the country swelters.

The following temperature ranges give a reliable guide to the degree of heat you can expect:

- **Hot season** (March to mid-June): 27–35°C (80–95°F)
- **Rainy season** (June to October): 24–32°C (75–90°F)
- **Cool season** (November to February): 18–32°C (65–90°F) but with less humidity.

THE PEOPLE

Thais are remarkably tolerant and forgiving of foreigners' foibles but there are a few things which will rouse them to anger.

For one, they regard the Royal Family with a reverence paralleled in few other countries, they react strongly if they consider any member of royalty has been insulted. Ill-considered remarks or refusing to stand for the Royal Anthem before the start of a movie will earn some very hard stares.

A similar degree of respect is accorded the second pillar of society, Buddhism. Disrespect towards Buddha images, temples or monks is not taken lightly. Monks observe vows of chastity which prohibit their being touched by women, even their mother. When in the vicinity of a monk, a woman should try to stay clear to avoid accidentally brushing against him. When visiting a temple, it is acceptable for both sexes to wear long pants but not shorts. Unkempt persons are frequently turned away from major temples.

From the Hindu religion has come the belief that the head is the fount of wisdom and the feet are unclean. For this reason, it is insulting to touch another person on the head, point one's feet at him or step over him. Kicking in anger is worse than spitting at him.

A Wise Man Never Thinks How Far He's Come. He Thinks How Far He Can Still Travel.

FINE CHAMPAGNE COGNAC
REMY MARTIN
XO
SPECIAL

REMY XO BECAUSE LIFE IS WHAT YOU MAKE IT

Pack your trunks for a holiday that's smooth as sil

Few countries can provide such a choice of exotic holiday experiences as Thailand.

Elephants still roam wild in Thai forests and have played an important cultural and working role since the early days of the Kingdom.

Today, you can enjoy the unforgettable thrill of a trek atop your own private elephant, on trails that lead through lush northern forests.

If riding a two-ton elephant isn't the holiday you had in mind, how about sailing aboard a traditional seventeen metre junk in the Andaman Sea?

Or relaxing in a luxury hotel and swimming in crystal blue waters at one of Thailand's famous beach resorts?

ROYA
ORCH

Holida

Then there's the shopping - but that's another story.

The first thing you need is our Royal Orchid Holidays brochure. In it you'll find every holiday imaginable in this exotic and mystical land.

Pick up a free copy from your travel agent or nearest Thai office and discover the treasures of the Kingdom.

And, of course, the best way to fly to Thailand is on Thai International, where you'll enjoy our world renowned Royal Orchid Service while you fly there smooth as silk.

Swatch. The others just watch.

seahorse/fall winter 94-95

shockproof
splashproof
priceproof
boreproof
swiss made

swatch✚
SCUBA 200

When wishing to pass someone who is seated on the floor, bow slightly while walking and point an arm down to indicate the path to be taken. It is also believed that spirits dwell in the raised doorsills of temples and traditional Thai houses and that when one steps on them, the spirits become angry and curse the building with bad luck.

Greetings
The Thai greeting and farewell is *"Sawasdee"*, spoken while raising the hands in a prayer-like gesture, the fingertips touching the nose, and bowing the head slightly. It is an easy greeting to master and one which will win smiles.

Dress & Hygiene
Thais believe in personal cleanliness. Even the poorest among them bathe daily and dress cleanly and neatly. They frown on those who do not share this concern for hygiene.

Public Behaviour
Twenty years ago, Thai couples showed no intimacy in public. That has changed due to Western influence on the young, but intimacy still does not extend beyond holding hands. As in many traditional societies, displaying open affection in public is a sign of bad manners.

Terms of Address
Thais are addressed by their first rather than their last names. The name is usually preceded by the word *"Khun"*, a term which honors him or her. Thus Silpachai Krishnamra would be addressed as Khun Silpachai when someone speaks to him.

You will find some Thais referred to in newspapers with the letters M.C., M.R. or M.L. preceding their names. These are royal titles normally translated as "prince" or "princess". The five-tier system reserves the highest two titles for the immediate Royal Family. After that comes the nobility, remnants of the noble houses of old. The highest of these three ranks is Mom Chao (M.C.), followed by Mom Rachawong (M.R.) and Mom Luang (M.L.).

The title is not hereditary, thanks to a unique system which guarantees that Thailand will never become top-heavy with princes and princesses. Each succeeding generation is born into the next rank down. Thus, the son or daughter of a Mom Chao is a Mom Rachawong. Soon, Thailand will be a nation of Nai, Mr., and Nang, Miss or Mrs. – a truly democratic realm.

Concepts
A few Thai concepts will give not only an indication of how Thais think but will smooth a visitor's social interaction with them. Thais strive to maintain equanimity in their lives and go to great lengths to avoid confrontation. The concept is called *"kriangjai"* and suggests an unwillingness to burden someone older or superior with one's problems. In many cases,

it means not giving someone bad news until too late for fear it may upset the recipient.

"Jai yen" or "cool heart", an attitude of remaining calm in stressful situations, is a trait admired by Thais. Getting angry or exhibiting a *"jai ron"* (hot heart) is a sign of immaturity and lack of self-control. Reacting to adversity or disappointment with a shrug of the shoulders and saying *"mai pen rai"* (never mind) is the accepted response to most situations.

"Sanuk" means "fun" or "enjoyment" and is the yardstick by which life's activities are measured. If it is not *"sanuk"*, it is probably not worth doing.

Thais converse readily with any stranger who shows the least sign of willingness. They may be shy about their language ability but will struggle nonetheless; speak a few words of Thai and they respond even more eagerly. Be prepared, however, for questions considered rude in Western societies such as: How old are you; how much money do you earn; how much does that watch (camera, etc) cost? Thais regard these questions as part of ordinary conversation and will not understand a reluctance to answer them. If, however, one is reticent about divulging personal information, a joking answer delivered with a smile will usually suffice; for e.g., to the above question of "How old are you?" with "How old do you think?" (out of politeness, they will usually guess a lower age and one can agree with them).

THE ECONOMY
Nearly 70 percent of Thailand's 55 million people are farmers who till alluvial land so rich that Thailand is a world leader in the export of tapioca (No. 1), rice (No. 2), rubber (No. 2), canned pineapple (No. 3) and is a top-ranked exporter of sugar, maize and tin.

THE GOVERNMENT
Thailand is a constitutional monarchy headed by His Majesty, King Bhumibol. His power has been reduced considerably from the period before the 1932 Revolution. However, he can, by the force of his personality, influence the direction of important decisions merely by a word or two.

Although he no longer rules as an Absolute Monarch of previous centuries, he is still regarded as one of the three pillars of the society – monarchy, religion and the nation. This concept is represented in the five-banded national flag: the outer red bands symbolizing the nation; the inner white bands the purity of the Buddhist religion; and the thick blue band at the center representing the monarchy.

The decades he has spent in the countryside working with farmers to improve their lands and yields has influenced others to follow his example in serving the people. His mother, the Princess Mother, Her Majesty, Queen Sirikit, and other members of the royal family have also been active in promoting the interests of Thais in the lower economic strata. Thus, the photographs of Their Majesties which hang in nearly every home, shop and office, have been placed there, not out of blind devotion, but out of genuine respect for the Royal Family.

The structure of the government is defined by the 1932 Constitution and the 11 ordinances that have followed it (the last, in 1991). Despite the many revisions, the Constitution has remained true to the spirit of the original aim of placing power in the hands of the people, although the exercising of it has favored certain groups over others.

Modeled loosely on the British system, the Thai government comprises three branches: legislative, executive and judiciary, each acting independently of the others in a system of checks and balances. The legislative branch is composed of a Senate and a House of Representatives. The Senate consists 270 leading members of the society including business people, educators and a heavy preponderance of high-ranking military officers. They must be over 35 years of age and must not be members of political parties. Members serve for life and new ones are selected by the Prime Minister and approved by the King. The House of Representatives comprises 360 members elected by popular vote from each of the 76 provinces of Thailand.

The executive branch is represented by a Prime Minister who may or may not be an elected Member of Parliament. He is selected by a single party or coalition of parties and rules through a cabinet of ministers, the exact number dependent on his own needs. They, in turn, implement their programs through the very powerful Civil Service. The present Prime Minister, Chuan Leekpai, the leader of the largest party in the ruling coalition government, was selected in 1992 following national elections.

The Judiciary comprises a Supreme Court, an appellate court, and a pyramid of provincial and lower courts. It acts independently to interpret points of law and counsels the other two branches on the appropriateness of actions.

PLANNING THE TRIP

WHAT TO BRING

Bangkok, Chiang Mai and Phuket are modern cities with most of the modern amenities found in similar large cities in Europe or North America.

Chapstick and moisturizers are needed in the north during the cool season. Sunglasses and hats are useful items to protect eyes and sensitive skin from tropical glare.

Clothes should be light and loose; natural blends that breathe are preferable to synthetics. Open shoes (sandals during the height of the rainy season when some Bangkok streets get flooded) and sleeveless dresses for women, short-sleeved shirts for men, are appropriate. Suits are worn for business and in many large hotels but, in general, Thailand lacks the formal dress code of Hong Kong or Tokyo. Casual but neat and clean clothes are suitable for most occasions.

The cool season in the north can be chilly. A sweater or sweatshirt will be welcome, especially when traveling in the hills.

One exception is the clothing code for Buddhist temples and Muslim mosques. Shorts are taboo for women and for men wanting to enter some of the important temples. Those wearing sleeveless dresses may also be barred from certain temples. Improperly dressed and unkempt visitors will be turned away from large temples like the Temple of the Emerald Buddha. Dress properly in deference to the religion and to Thai sensitivities.

MAPS

Bangkok
Bookshops carry a variety of maps of Thailand. Among the best are those printed by APA and several local publishers. The most accurate map of Bangkok is published by Siam Book Store with no title other than *Especially for Tourists*. It details the routes for ordinary and air-conditioned buses and sells for 60 *baht*. There are also a number of specialized maps. The Association of Siamese Architects publishes a series of four colorful hand-drawn *Cultural Maps* with details and information on Bangkok, the Grand Palace, the Canals of Thonburi and Ayutthaya.

D.K. Books issues an English-language book of canal maps by Geo.-Ch. Veran under the title *50 Trips into the Canals of Thailand*. Detailed maps outline journeys using the express and long-tailed commuter boats which operate along Bangkok's river and canals. There is also a French-language edition.

Nancy Chandler's *Market Map* has colorful cartoon maps of all of Bangkok's major markets. This well-traveled lady has filled the margins with useful information designed to make a market trip fun. For historians, the Jim Thompson House sells old maps of Siam; they make handsome home decor items when framed.

Chiang Mai

The best maps are those included as part of a free monthly guide called *Welcome to Chiang Mai*. P&P 89 Promotions' *Tourist Map of Chiang Mai, Rose of the North* has a very good map of the North but a rather muddled map of Chiang Mai. Many interesting items have been left out and the bus map is very difficult to figure out. It costs 40 *baht*.

Like her Bangkok *Market Map*, Nancy Chandler's Chiang Mai map is filled with useful tips as well as precise directions on how to find the best shopping bargains in the city.

Phuket

The best, *Phuket Planner*, is printed by Compass Publishing Co. and costs 35 *baht*. It includes detailed maps of the island, town and Phi Phi island.

ENTRY REGULATIONS

All foreign nationals entering Thailand must have valid passports. Foreign nationals holding valid passports from the following countries will, at the point of entry, automatically and without formality be granted a free transit visa valid up to 15 days, provided that they have a fully paid ticket which enables them to travel out of the kingdom within the stipulated time:
Africa: Kenya and Senegal.
Americas: Argentina, Brazil, Canada, Mexico, and USA.
Asia: Brunei, Indonesia, Japan, Malaysia, Myanmar, Philippines, Republic of Korea, Singapore, and Turkey.
Europe: Austria, Belgium, Denmark, Finland, France, Germany, Greece, Iceland, Ireland, Italy, Luxemburg, Netherlands, New Zealand, Norway, Portugal, Spain, Sweden, Switzerland, UK, and Yugoslavia.
Pacific: Australia, Fiji, Papua New Guinea, Vanuatu, and Western Samoa.
It has been mooted that in the near future the validity of the free Transit Visa will be increased to 30 days. Visitors to Thailand from the countries listed here, arriving at Don Muang, Chiang Mai, Phuket and Haadyai International Airports, may apply for a 15 day tourist visa upon landing at the airport. The application for such a tourist visa must be accompanied by two photographs as well as the necessary fee.
Americas: Antigua & Barbuda, Bahamas, Barbados, Belize, Bolivia, Chile, Colombia, Costa Rica, Domi-

nica, Ecuador, Grenada, Guatemala, Haiti, Honduras, Jamaica, Panama, Paraguay, Peru, St. Kitts & Nevis, St. Lucia, St. Vincent & the Grenadines, Surinam, Trinidad & Tobago, Uruguay, and Venezuela.
Asia: Bangladesh, Bhutan, Cyprus, India, Maldives, Nepal, and Pakistan.
Africa: Burkina Faso; Burundi, Cameroon, Cape Verde, Central African Republic, Chad, Comoros, Djibouti, Equatorial Guinea, Gabon, Gambia, Guinea, Guinea Bissau, Ivory Coast, Lesotho, Liberia, Malawi, Mali, Mauritania, Mauritius, Morocco, Niger, Rwanda, (Republic of) South Africa, Sao Tome and Principe, Seychelles, Sierra Leone, Somalia, Swaziland, Tanzania, Togo, Uganda, Zaire, Zambia and Zimbabwe.
Pacific: Kiribati, Nauru, Tonga, Solomon Islands, and Tuvalu.
Europe: Albania, Andorra, Bulgaria, Liechtenstein, Malta, Monaco, San Marino, and the Vatican.

Visa Extensions

If planning a longer stay, a transit visa valid for 30 days or a tourist visa valid for 60 days must be obtained from a Royal Thai Embassy or Consulate abroad by filing an application, supplying three passport-sized photographs and paying a fee of 200 *baht* (US$7.90) and 300 *baht* (*US$* 11.80) respectively. Visas can be extended by applying at the Immigration Division on Soi Suan Plu (8.30am– 4pm, Monday–Friday) before the visa's expiration date. The fee is 500 *baht*.

Re-Entry Visa

Visitors wishing to leave Thailand and return before the expiry of their visas can apply for a re-entry permit prior to their departure at immigration offices in Bangkok, Chiang Mai, Pattaya, Phuket and Haadyai. The fee is 500 *baht*. An exit visa, however, is not required.

Customs

The Thai government prohibits the import of drugs, dangerous chemicals, pornography, firearms and ammunition.

Foreign tourists may freely bring in foreign banknotes or other types of foreign exchange. For travelers leaving Thailand, the maximum amount permitted to be taken out in Thai currency without prior authorisation is 50,000 *baht*.

Foreign guests are allowed to import without tax, one camera with five rolls of film, 200 cigarettes, and one litre of wine or spirits.

On Departure

Tax: On departure from Bangkok's international terminal, travelers must pay an airport tax of 200 *baht* (US$8) at the check-in counter. Those on international flights from Phuket are charged 150 *baht* (US$6). Domestic airport departure tax is 20 *baht* (US$0.80).

HEALTH TIPS

Visitors entering the kingdom are no longer required to show evidence of vaccination for smallpox or cholera. Persons arriving from Africa must show certificates indicating vaccination against yellow fever.

Concerned about the spread of AIDs, the government, in late 1987, passed a new regulation barring the entry into Thailand of persons with the disease. However, the regulation has not been known to have been enforced.

Hygiene

Thais place high value on personal hygiene and are aware of the dangers of germs and infections. They do not, however, place such a high priority on keeping the environment clean. Establishments catering to foreigners are generally careful with food and drink preparation.

Bangkok water is clean when it leaves the modern filtration plant; the pipes that carry it into the city are somewhat less than new and visitors are advised to drink bottled water or soft drinks. Both are produced under strict supervision as is the ice used in large hotels and restaurants. Most streetside restaurants are clean, a quick glance should tell you which are and which are not.

Precautions

With its thriving nightlife and transient population, Bangkok is a magnet for the types of diseases one would expect to find in red light districts anywhere. The women (and men) in these service industries are aware of the consequences of carelessness and of not insisting that their partners take precautions, but economic necessity coupled with a Thai reluctance to offend anyone means that there is a great risk of taking home a souvenir one would rather not show to friends and loved ones.

The rule is to assume that there is a good chance of picking up something and to take appropriate measures. With the spread of AIDS worldwide, there is even more reason to be careful. Some massage parlors, mindful of the dangers, now bar foreign patrons and cater only to Thais in the belief that they reduce their risks.

Malaria and dengue fever persist in the rural areas. When in the hills – especially in the monsoon season – apply mosquito repellent on exposed skin when the sun begins to set.

MONEY MATTERS

Currency

The *baht* is the principal Thai monetary unit. It is divided into 100 units called *satangs*. Banknote denominations include the 1,000 (grey-pink), 500 (purple), 100 (red), 50 (blue), 20 (green) and 10 (brown) notes.

While the banknotes are easy to decipher, the coinage is a confusing matter with a variety of sizes and types for each denomination. There are 10 *baht* coins (brass center with a silver rim), two different 5 *baht* coins (silver pieces with copper rims), three varieties of 1 *baht* coin (silver; usually only the smallsize will fit in a public telephone), and two small coins of 50 and 25 *satang* (both are brass-colored).

Exchange Rates

The very stable Thai currency is tied to a basket of international currencies heavily weighted in favor of the US dollar. The rate at time of press was 24.9 *baht* to one dollar. For daily rates, check the *Bangkok Post*, the *Nation Review*, or *Thailand Times* newspapers. There is no currency black market.

Both cash and traveler's checks can be changed in hundreds of bank branches throughout the city; rates are more favorable for traveler's checks than for cash. Banking hours are 8.30am–3.30pm, Monday–Friday, but nearly every bank maintains money-changing kiosks. These kiosks may be found in Bangkok as well as Thailand's other major cities. Hotels generally give poor rates in comparison with banks whose rates are set by the Bank of Thailand.

Exchange Control

Foreign tourists may freely bring in foreign bank notes or other types of foreign exchange. Upon leaving Thailand, a foreign tourist may freely take out, without prior authorization, foreign means of payment in any amount. The maximum amount that may be taken out of Thailand without prior permission in Thai *baht* is 50,000 per person.

BANKING SYSTEM

Thailand has a sophisticated banking system with representation by the major banks of most developed foreign countries. Money can be imported in cash or traveler's checks and converted into *baht*. It is also possible to arrange telex bank drafts from one's hometown bank. There is no minimum requirement on the amount of money that must be converted. Money can be reconverted into the currency of your choice at bank counters at the airports in Bangkok, Chiang Mai, Phuket and Haadyai.

Bangkok

Banks in Bangkok include Thai institutions and branches of foreign banks. Most are equipped to handle telegraph and telex money transfers and a wide range of money services. Banking hours are 8.30am–3.30pm. Up-country the services are much more restricted. If you have overseas business to conduct with a bank, it is better to do it in Bangkok.

THAI BANKS
Bank of Asia, 191 Sathorn Thai Road. Tel: 2872211/3.
Bank of Ayuthya, 550 Ploenchit Road. Tel: 2550022, 2550033.
Bangkok Bank, 333 Silom Road. Tel: 2343333

Bangkok Bank of Commerce, 99 Surasak.
Tel: 2342930.
Bangkok Metropolitan Bank, 2 Chalermkhet 4.
Tel: 2230561/89
First Bangkok City Bank, 20 Yukoi 2.
Tel: 2230501.
Krung Thai Bank, 35 Sukhumvit Road.
Tel: 2552222.
Nakornthon Bank, 90 Sathorn Nua Road.
Tel: 2332111/9.
Siam City Bank, 1101 New Petchaburi Road.
Tel: 2530200-9.
Siam Commercial Bank, 1060 New Phetchburi
Road. Tel: 2561234.
Thai Danu Bank, 393 Silom Road. Tel: 2305000.
Thai Farmers Bank, 400 Paholyothin Road.
Tel: 2731191, 2701122.
Thai Military Bank, 34 Phyathai Road.
Tel: 2460020, 2457503.
Union Bank of Bangkok, 1600 New Petchaburi
Road. Tel: 2530488.

OVERSEAS BANKS
Bank of America NT. & SA, 2/2 Wireless Road.
Tel: 2516333.
Bank of Tokyo, Thaniya Bldg., 62 Silom Road.
Tel: 2360119, 2369103
Banque Indosuez, 142 Wireless Road. Tel: 2533616/
9, 2530106
Banque Nationale de Paris, Dusit Thani Bldg., 5th
floor, 946 Rama I Road. Tel: 2334310, 2381655.
Chase Manhattan Bank N.A., Silom Centre Bldg.,
965 Rama I Road. Tel: 2521141/50.
Citibank N.A., 127 Sathorn Thai Road.
Tel: 2132441.
Deutsche Bank AG, Thai Wah Tower, 21 Sathorn
Thai Road. Tel: 2850021.
Hongkong & Shanghai Bank, Hongkong Bank
Bldg, 64 Silom Road. Tel: 2331904/17.
Mitsui Taiyo Kobe Bank, Boonmitr Bldg., 138
Silom Road. Tel: 2343841/8.
Standard Chartered Bank, 946 Rama IV Road.
Tel: 2340820/9.
United Malayan Bank, 149 Suapa Road.
Tel: 2219191/5.

Chiang Mai
Bangkok Bank, Head office: 53-59 Ta Pae Road.
Tel: 233452. Branches: 164-12-5 Chang Klang
Road. Tel: 233528, 252881; 125 Chotana Road.
Tel: 222383, 221306. (Kiosk open 8.30am–8.30pm)
Bank of Asia, 149/1-3 Chang Klang Road. Tel:
234535, 234755. (Kiosk open 8.30am–8pm)
Bank of Ayuthya, Head office: 222-6 Ta Pae Road.
Tel: 236509, 252446. Branch office: 70 Chotana
Road. Tel: 211700/1. (Kiosk open 8.30am–8pm)
Krung Thai Bank, 298/1 Ta Pae Road. Tel:
235038, 235380. (Kiosk open 8.30am–4.30pm)
Siam Commercial Bank, 17 Ta Pae Road. Tel:
235667, 234519. (Kiosk open 8.30am–7pm)
Thai Farmers Bank, Head office: 136/9 Moo 3,

Chotana Road. Tel: 211672, 212013. Branch office:
169-71 Ta Pae Road. Tel: 236025, 233778. (Kiosk
open 8.30am–6pm)
Thai Military Bank, 207 Chang Moi Road.
Tel: 234867-8. (Kiosk open 8.30am–6pm)

Phuket
Bangkok Bank, 22 Pang-nga Road. Tel. 211292.
(Kiosk open 8.30am–8.30pm)
Bank of Asia, 206 Phuket Road. Tel: 211566.
(Kiosk open 8.30am–8pm)
Bank of Ayuthya, 64 Rasda Road. Tel: 211577.
(Kiosk open 8.30am–8pm)
Krung Thai Bank, 61 Rasda Road. Tel: 211586.
(Kiosk open 8.30am–4.30pm)
Siam Commercial Bank, 66 Rasda Road.
Tel: 212254. (Kiosk open 8.30am–6pm)
Thai Farmers Bank, 14 Pang-nga Road.
Tel: 212061. (Kiosk open 8.30am–6pm)
Thai Military Bank, 76/3 Ranong Road.
Tel: 212123. (Kiosk open 8.30am–6pm)

CREDIT CARDS

American Express, Diner's Club, Mastercard and
Visa are widely accepted throughout Thailand.
Many stores will levy a surcharge on their use, the
highest (3–5 percent) of which is for American
Express cards. Credit cards can be used to draw
emergency cash at most banks.

Credit Card Warning: Credit card fraud is a major
problem in Thailand. Don't leave your credit card in
a safe deposit box and when making a purchase, make
sure that you obtain the carbon copy receipt.

Each card has a local representative office, their
addresses and telephone numbers are listed below:

Bangkok
American Express, 388 Phaholyothin Road.
Tel: 2730033. Hours: 8.30am–5.30pm, Monday–
Friday.
Diner's Club, 11th floor, Dusit Thani Bldg., 946
Rama IV Road. Tel: 2383660. Hours: 8.30am–5pm,
Monday–Friday.
VISA and Mastercard, Thai Farmers Bank (Head
Office), 400 Paholyothin Road. Tel: 2701122.
Hours: 8.30am–3.30pm, Monday–Friday.

Chiang Mai
American Express, Head Office: Bangkok Bank, 53-
59 Ta Pae Road. Tel: 233452. Branch: 164-12-5
Chang Klang Road. Tel: 233528, 252881.
VISA and Mastercard, Thai Farmers Bank (Head
Office), 400 Paholyothin Road. Tel: 270112. Hours:
8.30am–3.30pm, Monday–Friday.

Phuket
American Express, Seatours, 95/4 Phuket Road.
Tel: 216979.
VISA and Mastercard, Thai Farmers Bank 14 Pang-
nga Road. Tel: 211558.

PUBLIC HOLIDAYS

The following dates are observed as official public holidays:

New Year's Day	January 1
Magha Puja	February (Full Moon)
Chakri Day	April 6
Songkran	April 12–14
Labor Day	May 1
Coronation Day	May 5
Ploughing Ceremony	May (variable)
Visakha Puja	May (Full Moon)
Asalha Puja	July (Full Moon)
Khao Pansa	July (Full Moon)
H.M. Queen's Birthday	August 12
Chulalongkorn Day	October 23
H.M. King's Birthday	December 5
Constitution Day	December 10
New Year's Eve	December 31

Chinese New Year in February is not an official public holiday but many shops and businesses are closed for several days.

FESTIVALS & FAIRS

To the host of traditional festivals have been added a number of local celebrations which have been elevated to a new status through promotion by the TAT to draw tourists. Festivals to celebrate a successful fruit or vegetable harvest are marked by the selection of a beauty queen as in Miss Banana, Miss Garlic, Miss Rambutan, Miss Grape and a host of other odd titles.

Temple fairs up-country are great fun to attend. They are usually held in the evenings during the cool season to raise money for repairs to temple buildings. There are carnival rides, freak shows, halls of horror, *rumwong* dances, food vendors and deafening noise – the one element without which a fair would not be a fair. If you see one in progress, stop, park and enjoy yourself.

The dates for these festivals and fairs change from year to year. Check the exact dates by calling the TAT in Bangkok at 2801305.

January
New Year's Day is a day of relaxation after the festivities of the night before. It is a public holiday.

Phra Buddha Chinarat Fair is held in late January or early February. Enshrined in Phitsanulok's Wat Phra Si Ratana Mahatat, Phra Buddha Chinarat is one of Thailand's most sacred and delicately-cast Buddha images of the Sukhothai style. The fair includes a display of giant birds made from straw, folk performances and various entertainment.

Don Chedi Memorial Fair in Suphanburi (late January) commemorates the decisive battle won by King Naresuan the Great at Don Chedi, the fair features historical exhibitions, entertainment and local handicraft stalls.

Bo Sang Umbrella Fair in Bo Sang near Chiang Mai is held in the main street and it celebrates the traditional skill of making gaily painted umbrellas and other handicrafts.

February
Flower Festival is held in Chiang Mai during early February. This annual event features flower displays, floral floats, beauty contests and it coincides with the period when the province's temperate and tropical flowers are in full bloom.

Dragon and Lion Parade is held annually between January and February in the central Thailand town of Nakhon Sawan by people of Chinese ancestry. The Dragon and Lion procession is a traditional homage-paying rite to the golden dragon deity in gratitude for his benevolence to human beings. The lively parade comprising marching bands, golden dragon and lion dances, and a procession of deities, takes place along the downtown area of the city.

Chinese New Year is not celebrated with the boisterousness of other Asian countries. The temples are a bit busier with wishes made for good fortune in the coming year but otherwise there is nothing to mark the period. Shops close and behind the steel grills, private family celebrations go on for three or four days.

Magha Puja, a public holiday in Bangkok and a Buddhist holiday on the full moon night of February marks the spontaneous gathering of 1,200 disciples to hear the Lord Buddha preach. In the evening, Thais gather at temples to hear a sermon by the chief monk of the *wat*. Then, when the moon is rising, they place their hands in a praying position before their faces and, clasping candles, incense and flowers, follow the chanting monks around the *bot* of the *wat* three times before placing their candles and incense in trays at the front of the *bot*. It is a most solemn and moving ceremony.

March
Kite flying is not a festival but it would be difficult to convince kite enthusiasts otherwise. They gather on Sanam Luang in Bangkok in the afternoons as the brisk winds haul their large kites aloft, filling the sky with bright colors.

Barred Ground Dove Festival. Dove lovers from all over Asia come to Yala for this event. The highlight is a dove-cooing contest involving over 1,400 competitors.

April
Chakri Day on 6th April celebrates the founding in 1782 of the dynasty which presently rules Thailand. It is celebrated in the palace but there are no public ceremonies. An official holiday, most Thais celebrate it as a day off from work.

The **Phra Chedi Klang Nam Fair** in April is one of the larger temple fairs. It is celebrated at the *wat* on the river's edge at Prapadaeng, 15 km (9 miles) south of Bangkok on the Thonburi side of the river.

Songkran is a public holiday which in the past was the traditional Thai New Year until royal decree shifted the date to January 1 to accord with the rest of the world. It most closely resembles the Indian festival of "Holi" which occurs at the same time. Songkran is a time of wild revelry, a chance for the normally placid Thais to let off steam. The central event is the sprinkling of water on one's friends to bless them but this usually turns into a boisterous throwing of buckets of water on passersby.

The celebration of Songkran in Bangkok is a little more subdued than in the north, and while it may be safe for a visitor to ride in an open-windowed bus down the street, he is advised to be prepared when walking in the street, riding a *tuk tuk* or visiting the night life areas in Patpong, Nana Entertainment Plaza and Soi Cowboy.

To see Songkran at its most riotous, travel down the western bank of the Chao Phya River to the town of Phrapadaeng. There, no one is safe but in the April heat, who cares – a dousing is cool relief from the burning rays of the sun.

Songkran in the north of Thailand, particularly in Chiang Mai, is fervently celebrated over several days and attracts many visitors from Bangkok.

Turtle Releasing Fair. At Nai Yang beach in Phuket, young turtles are released for their journey to the sea. The festival begins early in the morning with alms offered to monks and is accompanied by music, dancing, sports and food.

May

Labor Day (May 1) is a public holiday.

Coronation Day (May 5) is a private royal affair and a public holiday.

The **Rocket Festival** in Yasothon in the northeast of Thailand is held in early May. Well worth the trip to witness the launching of the locally designed and made missiles of all shapes and sizes, some as tall as a man.

The Plowing Ceremony is a colorful ancient tradition celebrated only in Bangkok. Held at Sanam Luang, it is presided over by His Majesty King Bhumibol and marks the official start of the rice planting season. Crimson-clad attendants lead bullocks, drawing an old-fashioned plow, around a specially prepared ground. The lord of ceremonies, usually the Minister of Agriculture, follows behind, scooping rice seed out of baskets held by pretty maidens and sowing it in the furrows left by the plow, all to the accompaniment of blaring conch shells and drums.

Visakha Puja is a public holiday on the full moon night of May that commemorates the birth, enlightenment and death of Buddha. The three things are all said to have happened on the same day. Visakha Puja is celebrated like Magha Puja with a triple circumambulation around the temple as the moon is rising.

Fruit Fairs. Their are annual fairs in Chiang Mai, Rayong, Chantaburi, Trat and several other locations throughout Thailand to celebrate the harvest of lychees, durian, mangosteen, rambutan, jack fruit and zalacca. Besides stalls selling the produce of the surrounding orchards, there are beauty pageants, cultural shows and local entertainment.

June

Sunthorn Phu Day. This annual celebration in late June commemorates the birth of the Thai poet Sunthorn Phu. The festivities include dramatic performances and puppet shows depicting his literary works, poetry recitals and folk entertainment.

July

Asalaha Puja on the full moon night of July is the third most important Buddhist holiday and marks the occasion when Buddha preached to his first five disciples. It is celebrated on the full moon night in similar manner to Magha Puja and Visakha Puja. It also marks the beginning of the three-month Lenten season. Tradition says that Buddha was approached by farmers who asked that he bar monks from going on their morning alms rounds for a period of three months because they were trampling on the rice shoots they had just planted. They offered instead to take food to the monks at the temple during this period, a practice which has been followed ever since.

Khao Phansa is celebrated immediately following Asalha Bucha and marks the commencement of the annual three-month Rains Retreat.

Candle Festival takes place during Khao Phansa in the northeast town of Ubon. It celebrates the commencement of Phansa with a lovely spectacle where some beautifully embellished beeswax candles are ceremoniously paraded before being presented to temples.

August

Her Majesty Queen Sirikit marks her birthday (August 12) by religious ceremonies and private celebrations. It is a public holiday.

September

On the first day of the eighth lunar month, Chinese celebrate the **Moon Festival.** They place small shrines laden with fruit, incense and candles in front of their houses to honor the moon goddess. It is a lovely festival, the highlight of which are the utterly scrumptious cakes shaped like a full moon. They are specially prepared, often by chefs flown in from Hong Kong, and found no other time of the year.

Phichit Boat Races. A regatta featuring long boat races. Similar events are held in Phitsanulok and all over Thailand at this time of year. The low slung, wooden boats are raced with great gusto.

October

The **Chinese Vegetarian Festival** held in mid-October, is a subdued affair by comparison with the firewalkers of Phuket island version. Enormous amounts of vegetarian food, Chinese operatic performances and elaborate offerings are made at various Chinese temples around the city. A superb photographic opportunity. Only those wearing all white attire are allowed in the area of the altar, so dress appropriately.

Ok Pansa marks the end of the three-month Lenten season and the beginning of the Kathin season when Buddhists visit *wats* to present monks with new robes and other necessities. Groups will rent boats or buses and travel long distances to spend a day making gifts to monks of a particular *wat*. If you are invited, by all means go because it is a day of feasting and fun as well.

Chulalongkorn Day (October 23) honors King Rama V (1868–1910) who led Thailand into the 20th century. On this public holiday, students lay wreaths before his statue in the plaza at the old National Assembly building during an afternoon ceremony.

Lanna Boat Races. If you miss the Pichit Boat Races, this regatta is just as exciting.

The **Buffalo Races** held in late October in Chon Buri rival the excitement of the Kentucky Derby.

November

Golden Mount Fair held the first week of November in Bangkok is one of the noisiest of temple fairs. Carnival rides, food concessions, variety performances and product stalls are the main attractions. Buddhist temple fairs all over Thailand are held throughout the cool season to raise money for reparations.

The **Little Royal Barge** Festival at Wat Nang Chee in Phasi Charoen early in November is a smaller version of the grand Royal Barge procession but it is marked by more gaiety in small towns.

Loy Krathong, one of the most beautiful festivals anywhere in Asia, is on the full moon night of November. It is said to have been started in Sukhothai in the 13th century. A young queen, Nang Nopamat, is said to have floated a small boat laden with candles and incense downstream past the pavilion where her husband was talking with his friends. Whatever the origins, it has grown to be one of the country's most enchanting festivals, a night when Thais everywhere launch small candle-laden boats into the rivers and canals to ask blessings. The tiny dots of light and shimmering water are mesmerizing.

Long-boat races have become increasingly popular in the past few years and it is not unusual to open a newspaper during November and find that yet another race is being staged somewhere in Thailand. They are colorful and exciting and provide superb photo opportunities for someone with a telephoto lens.

The **Elephant Round-Up** in Surin is held in mid-November and attracts visitors from all over Thailand.

The **Phra Pathom Chedi Fair** at the world's biggest stupa in Nakhon Pathom, 56 km (35 miles)

west of Bangkok is another temple fair, and is regarded as one of the most exciting.

Khon Kaen Silk Fair. Silk weaving demonstrations and a chance to buy lustrous silk in a major center of production.

River Kwai Bridge Week. A sound and light presentation recaptures this dark period of recent history when Asians and Europeans died in their thousands at the hands of the Japanese to build the infamous Death Railway during World War II.

Sunflower Fair. The photogenic sight of Mexican sunflowers in bloom is best seen in the hills of Doi Mae U-Khor as Mae Hong Song holds a three-day festival of ox-carts decorated with the beautiful flowers. When the flowers fade, the seeds are used to make insecticides.

December

Trooping of the Colors (December 3). The royal regiments dressed in brilliantly-colored costumes pass in review before the King. Held on the plaza before the old National Assembly building, the Trooping of the Colors is the most impressive of martial ceremonies equivalent to the Changing of the Guard in London.

His Majesty King Bhumibol celebrates his birthday (December 5) with a ceremony at Wat Phra Kaew only for invited officials and guests and with a private party. It is a public holiday.

King's Cup Regatta. Long distance yacht racing from Nai Harn Bay in Phuket with entries from around the world.

Constitution Day (December 10) is a public holiday in Thailand.

Christmas will soon be a Thai holiday if the merchants have any say in the matter. If endless repetitions of Christmas carols in department stores bludgeon everyone into acceptance of it, it may not be long before it becomes an official holiday.

But **New Year's Eve** on December 31 is a public holiday.

GETTING THERE

By Air

Bangkok is a transportation center for Southeast Asia with service provided by more than 40 regularly scheduled airlines. There are four international airports at Chiang Mai, Phuket, Haadyai and Bangkok with service to the capital either direct or via a stopover at one of the other cities.

Thailand's flag carrier, Thai Airways International Ltd. serves 51 destinations in 34 countries on four continents and enjoys a high reputation for excellence and superb inflight service. Within Thailand it operates a network of daily flights to Thailand's major towns aboard a fleet of sleek modern aircraft.

Thailand's principal airport, Don Muang, is located 22 km (14 miles) north of Bangkok. In September 1987, it opened a modern new extension with airbridges which doubled handling capacity and now speeds visitors through immigration formalities, baggage collection and customs. At the airport, are currency exchange counters paying bank rates, transportation desks, and a desk of the Thai Hotels Association where it is possible to book a hotel room in the city. An airport tax of 200 *baht* (US$5) is levied.

AIRLINE OFFICES

Bangkok
Bangkok International Airport (Don Muang).
Tel: 5351111

Aeroflot Soviet Airlines, Mezzanine floor, 183 Regent House, Rajdamri Road. Tel: 2511223/4/5, 2510617/8.
Air France, Ground floor, 942/51 Charn Issara Tower, Rama IV Road. Tel: 2339477, 2341333.
Air India, 16th floor, Amarin Plaza Bldg., 500 Ploenchit Road. Tel: 2569614/9.
Air Lanka, Ground floor, Charn Issara Tower, 942/34-35 Rama IV Road. Tel: 2369292/3, 2364981.
Air New Zealand, 1053 New Road.
Tel: 2371560/2.
Alitalia, 8th floor, 138 Boonmitr Building, Silom Road. Tel: 2334000/4.
All Nippon Airways, Federal Transport Co., Ltd., 2nd floor, 313 C.P. Tower, Silom Road.
Tel: 2385121, Tktg: 2385141.
Aom French Airlines, Adat Sales (T) Co.,Ltd., 8th floor, 518/5 Maneeya Centre Building, Phloenchit Road. Tel: 2511393, 2559966/8.
Asiana Airlines, 14th floor, 54 B.B. Building, Asoke Road. Tel: 2607700/7.
Balkan Bulkarian Airlines, Far East Travel Center Ltd., 20/18 Soi Bangkok Bazaar, Rajdamri Road. Tel: 2533063/4.
Bangkok Airways, 140 Pacific Place Building, Sukhumvit Road. Tel: 2534014, 2534004.
Biman Bangladesh Airlines, Ground floor, 56 Chongkolnee Building, Surawongse Road.
Tel: 2357643/4, 2333896/7.
British Airways, 2nd floor, 942/81 Charn Issara Tower, Rama IV Road. Tel: 2360038, 2380886/7.
Cambodia International Airlines, Queen Sirikit National Convention Centre, Ratchadapisek Road. Tel: 2293389/93.
Canadian Airlines International, 6th floor, Maneeya Building, 518/5 Ploenchit Road. Tel: 2514521, 2555862/6.
Cargolux Airlines, 295/29-31 GSA Wallem Shipping (Thailand), Surawongse Road.
Tel: 2377830/7.
Cathay Pacific Airways, 5th floor, 942/136 Charn Issara Tower, Rama IV Road. Tel: 2339825, 2336105/9, 2354330/9, 2376161/70.
China Airlines, 4th floor, Peninsula Plaza Building, 153 Rajdamri Road. Tel: 2534241/4, 2535733, 2534436/8.

China Southern Airlines, 134/1-2 Silom Road. Tel: 2355250/4.
Czechoslovak Airlines, Air People Tour & Travel Co., Ltd., 2nd floor, Regent House, 183 Rajdamri Road. Tel: 2543921/5.
Delta Airlines, 7th floor, Patpong Road, 1 Surawongse Road. Tel: 2376838.
Druk Airlines, 405 Silom Road. Tel: 2333012/0, Tktg: 2343100/19.
Egypt Air, 3rd floor, C.P. Tower, 313 Silom Road. Tel: 2310505/8.
Emirates, 2nd floor, B.B. Building, 54 Soi 21, Sukhumvit Road. Tel: 2607400/4.
Ethiopian Airlines, Oriole Travels & Tours Co., Ltd., 2nd floor, S.S. Building, 10/12-13 Convent Road. Tel: 2334038, 2334714, 2336744.
Eva Airways, Soon Hua Seng Building, 122-122/1 North Sathorn Road. Tel: 2382479.
Federal Express, 5th floor, Panawong Building, 104 Surawongse Road. Tel: 2353564, 2351443, 2335449, 2351445.
Finnair, Pacific Leisure, 6th floor, Maneeya Center, 518/5 Ploenchit Road. Tel: 2553860, 2515012, 2515075.
Garuda Indonesia Airways, 27th floor, Lumpini Tower, 1168 Rama IV Road. Tel: 2856470.
Gulf Air, Ground floor, Maneeya Center Building, 518/5 Ploenchit Road. Tel: 2547931/4.
Indian Airlines, 2/1-2 Dejo Road, Surawong Road. Tel: 2333890/2.
Iraqi Airways, 2nd floor, J.J. Tower, 325-329 Silom Road. Tel: 2355950/5, 2333271/4.
Japan Airlines, Mezzanine floor, Wall Street Tower, 33/33-34 Surawongse Road. Tel: 2332440, Tktg: 2337503.
KLM Royal Dutch Airlines, 2 Patpong Road, Surawongse. Tel: 2355150/9, 2366542.
Korean Air, 699 Kong Bunma Building, Ground floor, opp. Narai Hotel, Silom Road.
Tel: 2359221/6.
Kuwait Airways, 10th floor, C.T.I. Tower Building, Ratchadapisek Road. Tel: 2615062/9.
Lao Aviation, c/o all branches of Thai Airways International Offices.
Lauda Air, 14th floor, Wall Street Tower, 33/67-68 Surawongse Road. Tel: 2332544, 2332565/6.
Lot Polish Airlines, 485/11-12 Silom Road. Tel: 2352223/7, 2357092/4.
LTU International Airways, The Rama Garden Hotel, 9/9 Vibhavadi Rangsit Road. Tel: 5613784/6.
Lufthansa German Airlines, 1st floor, Bank of America, 2/2 Withayu Road. Tel: 2550370, Tktg: 2550371.
Malaysia Airlines, Ground floor, Panawong Building, 98-102 Surawongse Road. Tel: 2364705/9, Tktg: 2365871/5.
Martin Air, Associated Cargo Systems Co., Ltd., 15th floor, CTI Tower, 191/69 Ratchadapisek Road. Tel: 2611045/6.
Myanmar Airways, 48/5 Pan Road, Silom. Tel: 2349692, 2333052.

Nippon Cargo Airlines, 3rd floor, C.P. Tower Building, 313 Silom Road. Tel: 2313080/2.

Northwest Airlines, 4th floor, Peninsula Plaza, 153 Rajdamri Road. Tel: 2540781/9.

Olympic Airways, 4th floor, Charn Issara Tower, 942/133 Rama IV Road. Tel: 2376160.

Pakistan International Airlines, 52 Surawongse Road. Tel: 2342961/5, 2342352.

Philippine Airlines, Chongkolnee Building, 56 Surawongse Road. Tel: 2332350/2, 2342483, 2352584.

Qantas Airways, 11th floor, Charn Issara Tower, 942/51 Rama IV Road. Tel: 2360102, Tktg: 2360307, 2367493/4.

Royal Bhutan Airlines, c/o Thai Airways International Co., Ltd., 485 Silom Road. Tel: 2333810, 2343100/19.

Royal Brunei Airlines, 20th floor, Charn Issara Tower, 942/52 Rama IV Road. Tel: 2330056, 2330293.

Royal Jordanian, Ground floor, Yada Building, 56 Silom Road. Tel: 2368609/17, 2360030/9.

Royal Nepal Airlines, Ground floor, Sivadon Building, Ground floor, 1/4 Convent Road. Tel: 2333921/4.

S.K Air, 57/16 Wireless Road. Tel: 2548550/1.

Sabena Belgian World Airlines, 3rd floor, C.P. Tower, 313 Silom Road. Tel: 2382201/3.

SAS Scandinavian Airlines System, 412 Rama I Road, Soi 6, Siam Square. Tel: 2538333.

Saudi Arabian Airlines, Ground floor, C.C.T. Tower, 109 Surawongse Road. Tel: 2369395.

Silk Air, 12th floor, Silom Centre Building, Silom Road. Tel: 2360303, 2360440.

Singapore Airlines, 12th floor, Silom Centre Building, Silom Road. Tel: 2360440/50, Tktg: 2360303.

South African Airways, 6th floor, Maneeya Centre Bldg., 518/5 Ploenchit Road. Tel: 2559968/9.

Swiss Air, 2nd floor, F.E.Zuellig Bldg., 1 Silom Road. Tel: 2332935/8, Tktg: 2332930/4.

Tarom Romaniam Air Transport, 89/12 Bangkok Bazaar, Rajdamri Road. Tel: 2531681/5.

Thai Airways International Ltd., Head Office: 89 Vibhavadi Rangsit Road, Tel: 5130121; Silom Office: 485 Silom Road, Tel: 2333810; Yaowaraj Office: 45 Anuwong Road, Tel: 2249602/8; Lan Luang Office: 6 Lan Luang Road, Tel: 2800070, 2800080; Charn Issara Office: 4th floor, Charn Issara Tower, 942 Rama IV Road; Tel: 2354588, 2354595; Asia Hotel Office, 296 Phyathai Road. Tel: 2152020/1.

Trans Mediterranean Airways, 15th floor, CTI Tower, 191/69 Ratchadapisek Road. Tel: 2611039/40.

Tropical Sea Air, Building 302, Bangkok International Airport, Vibhavadi Rangsit Road. Tel: 5353466/7.

Turkish Airlines, Gulf Express Transport Agency, 3rd floor, C.P. Tower Bldg., 313 Silom Road. Tel: 2310300/7.

Union De Transport Aeriens, Ground floor, Charn Issara Tower, 942/51 Rama IV Road. Tel: 2341330/9, 2369080/2.

United Airlines, 9th floor, Regent House, 183 Rajdamri Road. Tel: 2530558, Tktg: 2530559.

Vietnam Airlines, 584 Ploenchit Road. Tel: 2514242.

Chiang Mai

Thai Airways International, 240 Prapoklao Road. Tel: (053) 211541, 210043.

Phuket

Phuket International Airport. Tel: 311511.

Bangkok Airways, 158/2-3 Yaowaraj Road, Phuket. Tel: (076) 212341.

Dragon Airlines, 37/52 Montri Road, Phuket. Tel: (076) 215300.

Malaysian Airlines, 1/8-9 Choomporn Road, Phuket. Tel: (076) 216675, 213749

Thai International, (international and domestic), 41/33 Montri Road, Phuket. Tel: (076) 212400, 212644, 212880, 212855 and 78 Ranong Rod, Phuket. Tel: (076) 212195, 212499, 212946. Airport: (076) 311194.

By Sea

The days when travelers sailed up the Chao Phrya River to view the golden spires of Bangkok are long gone. Luxury liners now call at Pattaya and Phuket but have ceased serving Bangkok. Check with a travel agent or shipping company to find those which depart from your city.

By Rail

Trains operated by the State Railways of Thailand are clean, cheap and reliable albeit a little slow. There are only two railroad entry points into Thailand, both from Malaysia on the southern Thailand border. The trip north to Bangkok serves as a scenic introduction to Thailand.

Express trains, some with sleeping car accommodation, leave Kuala Lumpur throughout the day and arrive about seven to nine hours later at Butterworth, the port opposite Malaysia's Penang island. A train leaves Butterworth at 1.40pm everyday, crossing the border into Thailand and arriving in Bangkok at 8.35am the next day. Air-conditioned first and second class sleepers are available. Dining cars serve local food.

First class Butterworth-Bangkok tickets are US$61 (1,555 *baht*) while second class tickets are US$25 (635 *baht*). Trains leave Bangkok's Hualampong Station everyday at 3.15pm for the return journey to Malaysia arriving the next day at 12.10pm.

A second, somewhat less convenient but more entertaining train travels from Kuala Lumpur up Malaysia's east coast to the northeastern town of Kota Bharu. A taxi crosses the border to catch the SRT train from the southern Thai town of Sungai Kolok. Trains leave Sungai Kolok in the morning, arriving in Bangkok in the early morning on the following day. First-class sleeper tickets are US$45 (1,158 *baht*); second-class sleepers are US$24.25 (618 *baht*).

Non-residents of Thailand may purchase a rail pass from the State Railway of Thailand at specially reduced rates, entitling them unlimited trips and distances for a period of 20 days. Contact the Advance booking Office at Hua Lampong Station, Bangkok (Tel: 2333762, 2447788) for full details.

If you like to travel in style and prefer not to fly, the newly introduced Eastern & Oriental Express (Tel: 2168661) is Asia's most exclusive travel experience. Traveling once a week between Singapore, Kuala Lumpur and Bangkok, the 22 carriage train with its distinctive green and cream livery passes through spectacular scenery. The one-way fare begins at 28,600 *baht* per person.

By Road

Although Thailand borders four countries, until recently only that with Malaysia was open to road traffic. In April 1994, the new Thai-Lao Friendship Bridge opened up a Thailand's first road link to Laos. Drivers will find that most Thai roads are modern and well maintained by comparison with those of its neighbors. The Malaysian border closes at 6pm so plan your itinerary accordingly.

SPECIAL FACILITIES

Left Luggage

There are two left luggage facilities at Don Muang Airport. One is on the 1st floor on the northern end of the Arrival Hall after passing through customs. The second is in the Departure Hall on the 3rd floor near the currency exchange counter. The fee is 20 *baht* (US$0.80) per bag per day.

Porter Services

There are no porters as such but luggage carts are available free for both arriving and departing passengers. Upon request, the airport can also provide wheelchairs and other assistance for disabled persons.

Reservation

Hotel reservations can be made in the airport arrival lounge once you have passed through customs. It is recommended that you book a room in advance during the Christmas-New Year and Chinese New Year Holidays and outside of Bangkok for Songkran in mid-April.

SPECIAL INFORMATION

DOING BUSINESS

Most hotels have business centers with communications and secretarial services in several languages. Elsewhere in Bangkok, it is possible to lease small offices with clerical staff.

Business Organizations

American Chamber of Commerce, 140 Wireless Road. Tel: 2511605, 2519266. Open from 8.30am–noon, 1–4.30pm on Monday–Friday.

British Chamber of Commerce, Room 604 Bangkok Insurance Bldg., 302 Silom Road. Tel: 2341140, 2341169. Open from 8am–noon, 1–4.30pm on Monday–Friday.

British Council, 428 Soi 2 Siam Square, Rama I Road. Tel: 2526136, 2526111. Open from 8.30am–4pm on Monday–Friday. In Chiang Mai: 198 Bamrungrat Road. Tel: 242103.

Franco-Thai Chamber of Commerce, 104 Wireless Road. Tel: 2519385. Open from 8.30am–noon, 2–5pm on Monday–Friday.

German-Thai Chamber, 699 Klongboonma Bldg., Silom Road. Tel: 2342396, 2347190. Open from 9am–noon on Monday–Friday.

Goethe Institute, 18/1 Soi Ngamduplee, Rama 4 Road. Tel: 2869002/3. Open from 8am–5pm on Monday–Friday; and from 8am–noon on Saturday.

Japanese Chamber of Commerce, 4th fl., Panunee Bldg., 513/3 Ploenchit Road. Tel: 2569170/1. Open from 9am–5pm on Monday–Friday; and from 9am–noon on Saturday.

CHILDREN

Bangkok offers few activities for children. Department stores like the Chidlom branch of Central Department store and Thai Daimaru devote their top floors for electronic games arcades and miniature carnival rides like bumper cars.

Children enjoy the unusual animals of **Dusit Zoo** or paddling boats in its lake or in **Lumpini** or **Chatuchak Park**. **Magic Land** at 72 Paholyothin Road near the Hyatt Central Plaza Hotel is an amusement park with a ghost house, bumper cars and carnival rides. On weekdays, the 70-*baht* ticket covers an unlimited number of rides. On weekends, it is limited to 2 hours. Open 10am–5.30pm, Monday to Friday; 9.30am–7pm, Saturday and Sunday.

East of town at 101 Sukhapiban 2 Road, **Siam Park** is a theme park with water slides and flumes. It is open 10am–6pm, Monday to Friday; and 9am–7pm, Saturday and Sunday. Adults: 80 *baht*, children: 50 *baht*. **A word of warning**: The park prohibits the wearing of T-shirts in the swimming areas so take plenty of suntan oil for tender young skins.

GAYS

Gays find Thailand a very tolerant country. For entertainment there are gay bars at the following places:

Bangkok

Gays quickly discover that Thailand is one of the most tolerant countries in the world. Most of the gay bars are on Patpong 3 or the upper end of Silom

Road. They are much like their female counterparts in mixing dancing and drinking with opportunities for pick-ups. Unfortunately, there is an unsavory side to it involving very young boys; but generally, if it is socializing and companionship you are seeking, you will find it here.

Chiang Mai
The Butterfly Room, 126 Loi Kroa Road. Tel: 249315, 213584. Nightly cabaret, 11pm–midnight. **The Coffee Boy**, 248 Toong Hotel Road. Tel: 244458, is in an old Lanna house. Classical music with cabaret on weekends at 11pm.

Pattaya
Transvestite shows originated in Pattaya and the oldest two are still here. At **Tiffany's** and **Alcazar** on the Second Road, men dressed in gorgeous costumes mime the megastars, mouthing the words to hit songs.

Phuket
Black and White on Soi Bangla presents a cabaret show with transvestites each Tuesday and Friday at 11pm. A second gay bar, **My Way**, is on Soi Patong Post office. Phuket's best known transvestite show is Simon Cabaret on the Patong/Karon Road.

Special Clubs
Alliance Francaise, 29 S. Sathorn Road. Tel: 2863879, 2863841. Open Monday–Friday, 8am–7.30pm; Saturday, 9–7pm. In Chiang Mai: 138 Charoenprathet Road. Tel: 235277.
American University Alumni (AUA), 179 Rajdamri Road. Tel: 2511606. In Chiang Mai: 24 Rajdamnern Ave. Tel: 211377.
Foreign Correspondents Club of Thailand, 21st fl. Dusit Thani Hotel. Tel: 2331130 ext. 206. Open Monday–Saturday, 9am–midnight.
Lions Chaophaya (Bangkok) Association, 10 Soi Soomvijai, New Petchburi Road. Tel: 2589037. Meetings on the last Thursday of the month. Foreign members are welcomed.
Rotary Club, Bangkok Rotary, Hilton Hotel. Tel: 2511360. Meetings on Thursdays at 12.30pm. Bangkok South Rotary, Montien Hotel, Tel: 2348060 ext. 260. Meetings on Fridays at 12.30pm. Bangkapi Branch, Siam Inter-Continental Hotel, Tel: 2530355. Meetings on Tuesdays at 12.30pm. Foreign members welcome; English is the medium.

PHOTOGRAPHY

Shimmering temples, beautiful scenery, people willing to be photographed, and no restrictions on photographing ceremonies and festivals make Thailand a photographer's delight. Pack far more film than you would for other destinations. If you don't, you will find all the major brands – Kodak, Fuji, Konica, Agfa – on sale in most towns. Slides can be processed within a day and there are mini-labs to process print film in as little as 23 minutes.

Thailand's tropical light tends to be rather harsh at midday, so pack a polarizing filter as well as a slight warming filter (81A) to take the blue tint out of shots, especially during the monsoon season. It is also advisable for slide photographers to set their ASA (ISO) meters one stop higher (i.e. instead of 64, set it at 80) to give a bit more color saturation. A fill flash is also useful. Thais are not like silly tourists; when the sun is bright, they sit in the shade or wear hats. A flash will highlight faces that would normally be in shadowy areas.

· USEFUL ADDRESSES

Tourist Information
Planning a trip to Thailand can be made easier if you contact a travel agent or an office of the Tourism Authority of Thailand. These offices offer promotional brochures, maps and videotapes of the country's many attractions.

The Tourism Authority of Thailand is the Thai government's official tourism promotion organization. The Head Office at 372 Bamrung Muang Road (Tel: 2260060, 2260072, 2260085) will provide you with essential tourist information, but for a more complete service, the Information Office at 4 Ratchadamnern Nok Avenue (Tel: 2801305) has a wealth of brochures on various attractions and personnel to answer questions.

Numerous publishers issue travel magazines that give current information on events and attractions that is usually reliable. Listed below are some of the offices of the Tourism Authority of Thailand.

THAILAND

Central
Kanchanaburi: Saeng Chuto Road.
Tel: (034) 511200, Fax: (034) 511200.
Phra Nakhon Si Ayutthaya: Si Sanphet Road.
Tel: (035) 246076/7, Fax: (035) 246078.
Lop Buri: H.M. The Queen's Celebration Building, c/o Lop Buri Provincial Hall, Narai Mahart Road. Tel: (036) 422768, 422769, Fax: (036) 422769.
Pattaya: 382/1 Chaihat Road, South Pattaya. Tel: (038) 428750, 427667, Fax: (038) 429113.
Rayong: 153/4 Sukhumvit Road. Tel: (038) 655420/1, Fax: (038) 655422.
Cha-Am: 500/51 Phetkasem Road.
Tel: (032) 471005/6, Fax: (032) 471502.

North
Chiang Mai: 105/1 Chiang Mai-Lamphun Road. Tel: (053) 248604, 248607, Fax: (053) 248605.
Chiang Rai: 448/16 Singhakhlai Road.
Tel: (053) 717433, Fax: (053) 717434.
Phitsanulok: 209/7-8 Surasi Trade Center, Boromtrailokanat Road. Tel: (055) 252742, 252743, Fax: (055) 252742.

Northeast

Nakhon Ratchasima: 2102-2104 Mittraphap Road. Tel: (044) 213666, 213030, Fax: (044) 213667.
Ubon Ratchathani: 264/1 Khuan Thani Road. Tel: (045) 243770/1, Fax: (045) 243771.
Khon Kaen: 15/5 Prachasamosorn Road. Tel: (043) 244498/9, Fax: (043) 244497.
Nakhon Phanom: c/o Provincial Administration Office, Abhibanbancha Road. Tel: (042) 513490, 513491, Fax: (042) 513492.
Udon Thani: c/o Provincial Education Office, Phosi Road. Tel: (042) 241968, Fax: (042) 241968.

South

Haadyai: 1/1 Soi 2 Niphat Uthit 3 Road. Tel: (074) 243747, 238518, 231055, Fax: (074) 245986.
Phuket: 73-75 Phuket Road. Tel: (076) 212213, 211036, Fax: (076) 213582, 217138.
Surat Thani: 5 Talat Mai Road, Ban Don. Tel: (077) 281828, 288818/9, Fax: (077) 282828.
Nakhon Si Thammarat: Sanam Na Muang, Ratchadamnoen Road. Tel: (075) 346515-6, Fax: (075) 346517.

ASIA PACIFIC

Australia: 7th floor, Royal Exchange Bldg, 56 Pitt St., Sydney 2000. Tel: (02) 2477549, 2477540, Fax: (612) 2512465.
Hong Kong: Room 401, Fairmont House, 8 Cotton Tree Drive, Central. Tel: (852) 8680732, (852) 8680854, Fax: (852) 8684585.
Japan: Hibiya Mitsui Bldg, 1-2, Yurakucho 1-Chome, Chiyoda-ku, Tokyo 100, Tel: (03) 5806776/7, Fax: (813) 35807808; Hirano-machi Yachiyo Bldg, 5th floor, 1-8-13 Hiranomachi Chuo-ku, Osaka 541, Tel: (06) 2314434, Fax: (06) 2314337; Hakata Pal Bldg, 2nd Floor, 2-63 Gokushu-Machi, Hakata-Ku, Fukuoka 812, Tel: (092) 2623031, Fax: (092) 2623032.
Malaysia: c/o Royal Thai Embassy, 206 Jalan Ampang, Kuala Lumpur. Tel: (093) 2480958, Fax: (093) 2413002.
Singapore: c/o Royal Thai Embassy, 370 Orchard Road, Singapore 0923. Tel: 2357694, 2357901, Fax: 7335653.
South Korea: Room 2003, 20th Floor, Coryo Daeyungak Center Building, 25-5, 1-Ka. Chungmu-Ro, Chung-Ku, Seoul. Tel: (02) 7795417, 7795418, Fax: (02) 7795419.
Taiwan: Thailand Trade and Economic Office, 2B Central Commercial Building, 16-18 Nanking East Road, Section 4, Taipei. Tel: (02) 5796111, Fax: (886 2) 5779914.

EUROPE

France: 90 Avenue des Champs-Elysees, 75008 Paris. Tel: 45628656, 45628748, Fax: (331) 45637888.

Italy: Ente Nazionale per il Tourismo-Thailandese, Via Barberini 50 00187, Rome. Tel: (06) 4873479, (06) 4818927, Fax: (396) 4873500.
England: 49 Albemarle St., London WIX 3FE. Tel: (01) 4997670, (71) 4997679, Fax: (44 71) 6295519.
West Germany: Bethmannstr, 58/IV., D-6000, Frankfurt/M.I. Tel: (069) 295704, (069) 295804, Fax: (49 69) 281468.

AMERICA

5 World Trade Center, Suite 2449, New York, N.Y. 10048. Tel: (212) 4320433, Fax: (1 212) 9120920. 3440 Wilshire Blvd, Suite 1101, Los Angeles, CA 90010. Tel: (213) 3822353, 3822354, Fax: (1 213) 3897544. 303 East Wacker Drive, Suite 400, Chicago, IL 60601. Tel: (312) 8193990, Fax: (1 312) 5650359.

PRACTICAL TIPS

EMERGENCIES

Security & Crime

When in Thailand, **avoid** the following:

• Touts posing as Boy Scouts soliciting donations on Bangkok's sidewalks. The real Boy Scout Foundation obtains its funds from other sources.

• Touts on Patpong offering upstairs live sex shows. Once inside, one is handed an exorbitant bill and threatened with mayhem if he protests. Pay, take the receipt, and go immediately to the Tourist Police to gain restitution.

• Persons offering free or very cheap boat rides into the canals. Once you are well into the canal, you are given the choice of paying a high fee or being stranded.

• Persons offering to take you to a gem factory for a "special deal". The gems are usually flawed and there is no way to get your money back.

• Persons on buses or trains offering sweets, fruits or soft drinks. The items are often drugged and the passenger is robbed while unconscious. This is unfortunate because Thais are generous people and it is normal for them to offer food to strangers. Use your discretion.

If you do run into trouble in Bangkok, the police emergency number is 191. There are also Tourist Police assigned specially to assist travelers. They are located at the Tourist Assistance Center at the Tourism Authority of Thailand headquarters at No.

4 Rajdamnern Nok Avenue and can be reached by telephoning 195 or 2828129. They also maintain a booth on the Lumpini Park corner of the Rama 4 and Silom roads intersection. Most members of the Force speak English.

Their offices can be found in Chiang Mai and Phuket as well. In Chiang Mai, they are located below the Tourist Authority of Thailand office at 105/1 Chiang Mai-Lamphun Road. Tel: 232508, 222977. In Phuket, find them at the TAT office at 73-75 Phuket Road. Tel: 212213, 211036.

MEDICAL SERVICES

HOSPITALS

First-class hotels in Bangkok, Chiang Mai and Phuket have doctors on call for medical emergencies. The hospitals in these three cities are the equivalent of those in any major Western city. Intensive Care Units are fully equipped and staffed by doctors to handle emergencies quickly and competently. Nursing care is generally superb because there is a higher staff to patient ratio. Many doctors have been trained in Western hospitals and even those who have not speak good English.

Most small towns have clinics which treat minor ailments and accidents. In the unlikely event that you suffer a criminal attack in Bangkok, you must go to a Police Hospital, normally the one at the Rajprasong intersection. Up-country, most hospitals will treat you.

Bangkok
Bangkok Adventist Hospital, 430 Phitsanuloke Road. Tel: 2811422, 2821100.
Bangkok Christian Hospital, 124 Silom Road. Tel: 2336981/9, 2351000.
Bangkok General Hospital, 2 Soi Soonvijai, New Petchaburi Road. Tel: 3180066.
Bangkok Nursing Home, 9 Convent Road. Tel: 2332610.
Bamrungrad Hospital, 33 Soi 3, Sukhumvit Road. Tel: 2530250/69.
Deja General Hospital, 346 Sri Ayutthaya. Tel: 2460137.
St. Louis Hospital, 215 Sathorn Thai Road. Tel: 2120033.
Samitivej Hospital, 133 Soi 49, Sukhumvit Road. Tel: 3920010/9, 3920061/5.
Siam General Hospital, 15/10 Soi Chokchai 4, Lardprao. Tel: 5142157/9.
Sukhumvit Hospital, 1411 Sukhumvit Road. Tel: 3910011.

Chiang Mai
Lanna Hospital, off the Superhighway on the northeast side of town. Tel: 211037.
McCormick Hospital on Kaew Nawarat Road, also on the northeastern edge of town. Tel: 241311/2.
Suan Dok Hospital on the corner of Boonruangrit

and Suthep roads across from Wat Suan Dok. Tel: 221122.

The city's biggest hospital is part of Chiang Mai University on Suthep Road.

Phuket
Mission Hospital on the northern end of Phuket town on Thepkrasatri Road. (Highway 402 to the airport). Tel: 212396.
Andaman Hospital, half a kilometer south of Patong on the road to Karon. Tel: 7230108. Ambulance is available.

Medical Clinics

For minor problems, there are numerous clinics in all the major towns and cities. There are many polyclinics in Bangkok with specialists in several fields. The **British Dispensary**, located at 109 Sukhumvit Road (between Sois 3 and 5), Tel: 2528056 has British doctors on its staff. In Chiang Mai, you can go to Chuang Pak Polyclinic at 52/2 Chang Puak Road, Tel: 210213. Similar clinics are to be found in major towns and cities.

VD Clinics

These doctors have seen it all so there is no reason to be shy or embarrassed. Very professional, very thorough treatment ensures you return home with a clean bill of health.

Dental Clinics

Dental clinics are almost as numerous as medical clinics.

In Bangkok, one clinic with a long-standing reputation is the **Dental Polyclinic** at 211-3 New Petchburi Road, Tel: 3145070. The **Dental Hospital**, 88/88 Soi 49, Sukhumvit Road, Bangkok, Tel: 2605000-15 looks more like a hotel than a dental hospital and has the latest and most sophisticated imported dental equipment in Thailand.

In Chiang Mai, there is Dr Thavorn's Clinic at 156 Chang Moi Road. Tel: 236443.

In Phuket Town, the Dental Care Clinic is located at 62/5 Rasda Center. Tel: 215025.

Chiropractor

Bangkok has only one chiropractic clinic and it utilizes the Japanese method (no bone cracking as practised in the West but firm massages to ease pinched nerves back into place). It is open 9am–6pm. Monday to Saturday, 9am–noon on Sundays. Down Soi Vichan at No. 51, off Silom Road. across from the Victory Hotel. Call 2342649 for an appointment.

Snake Bites

There is little chance of being bitten by a poisonous snake in Bangkok or its environs but should it occur, most clinics have anti-venom serum on hand. If they cannot acquire any, travel to the **Saowapha Institute** (Snake Farm) on Rama IV Road. They maintain sera against the bites of six types of cobras and vipers. Up-country clinics maintain a constant supply of anti-venom serum supplied by the Saowapha Institute.

OTHER SERVICES

Counseling: The Community Services of Bangkok is a volunteer organization made up of foreigners to provide information to families living in Bangkok. They operate a hotline and are always willing to help travelers with problems who have nowhere else to turn. They also have a Counseling Service for those in mental distress. Telephone them at 2585663.

Pharmaceuticals are produced to the highest standards and pharmacies must have a registered pharmacist on the premises. Most pharmacy personnel in the shopping and business areas speak English.

Emergency Repairs: Shoe repairs and key grinding services are available in most of the larger department stores.

WEIGHTS & MEASURES

Thailand uses the metric system of meters, grams and liters.

ELECTRICITY

Electrical outlets are rated at 220 volts, 50 cycles and accept either flat-pronged or round-pronged plugs.

BUSINESS HOURS

Government offices are open from 8.30am–4.30pm on Monday–Friday. Business hours are from 8am or 8.30am–5.30pm on Monday–Friday. Some businesses are open half days from 8.30am–noon on Saturdays. Banks are open from 8.30am–3.30pm, five days a week but operate money-changing kiosks throughout the city which are open until 8pm, seven days a week.

The Central Post Office in Bangkok is located on New Road between Suriwongse and Siphya Roads. It opens at 8.30am and closes at 4.30pm on Monday–Friday, and from 8.30am–12.30pm on Saturdays, Sundays and holidays.

Branch post offices are located throughout the city and many of these usually stay open until 6pm. Kiosks along some of the city's busier streets sell stamps and aerograms and ship small parcels. Hotel reception counters will send letters for their guests at no extra charge.

Most department stores are open from 10am–9pm seven days a week. Ordinary shops open at 8.30am or 9am and close between 6pm and 8pm, depending on the location and type of business. Some pharmacies in the major cities remain open all night.

Small open-air coffee shops and restaurants open at 7am and close at 8.30pm though some stay open past midnight. Large restaurants generally close at 10pm. Most coffeeshops close at midnight; some stay open 24 hours.

TIPPPING

Tipping is not a custom in Thailand although it is becoming more prevalent. A service charge of 10 percent is generally included in restaurant bills and is divided among the staff. A bit extra for the waitress would not go unappreciated. Do not tip non-metered taxi or *tuk-tuk* drivers unless the traffic has been particularly bad and he has been especially patient, 10 *baht* would suffice for a long journey over 60 *baht*. Hotel room boys and porters are becoming used to being tipped but will not hover with hand extended if you do not.

RELIGIOUS SERVICES

• ANGLICAN
Christ Church, 11 Convent Road. Tel: 2343634. Services: 8am, 10am.

• INTERDENOMINATIONAL
International Church of Bangkok, 67 Soi 19, Sukhumvit Road. Tel: 2608187. Services: 8am.
International Christian Assembly, 196 Soi Yasoop 1, Ekamai Road. Tel: 3914387. Services: 10.30am, 6pm.

• BAHAI
Bahai Faith, 77 Soi Langsuan, Ploenchit Road. Tel: 2525355. Services: 8am, 5pm.

• BAPTIST
Calvary Baptist Church, 88 Soi 2, Sukhumvit Road. Tel: 2518278. Service: 10.45am.

• CATHOLIC
Holy Redeemer Church, 123/19 Soi Ruam Rudi, Wireless Road. Tel: 2566305. Sunday Mass: 8.30am, 9.45am, 11am, 5.30pm.
Assumption Cathedral, 23 Oriental Lane, New Road. Tel: 2348556. Sunday Mass: 10am.
St. Louis Church, 215/2 South Sathorn Road. Tel: 2110220. Mass: 6am, 8am, 10am, 5.30pm.
Evangelical Church of Bangkok, 42 Soi 10, Sukhumvit Road. Tel: 2519539. Services: 9.15am, 11am.

• MORMON
Mormon Church, 72 Chulintr Lane, Soi 21, Sukhumvit Road. Tel: 2583585, 2583586. Services: 9am, noon.

• HINDU
Thamsapha Association, 50 Soi Wat Prok, New Road. Tel: 2113840. Services: 7am–10pm.

• JEWISH ASSOCIATION OF THAILAND (ASHKENAZI)
121 Soi Sainam Thip 2, Soi 22, Sukhumvit Road. Tel: 2582195. Service: 6.30pm on Friday. Please contact Rabbi Kantor.

- **EVEN CHEN SYNAGOGUE (SEPHARDIC)**
The Bossotel, 55/12-14 Charoen Krung Road, (near Shangri-La Hotel). Tel: 2349409. Services: 9.30am on Saturday.

- **MUSLIM**
Sha-Roh-Tal Islam Mosque, 133 Soi I Sukhapiban Road. Tel: 3288950. Services: 12.30pm–2pm.

- **SEVENTH-DAY ADVENTIST**
Seventh-Day Adventist Hospital Church, 430 Phitsanuloke Road. Tel: 2821100. Services: 8am, noon.
Seventh-Day Adventist Ekamai Church, 12 Soi Kasempanichakam, Klongton. Tel: 3913594/5. Services: 8am, noon.
Seventh Day Adventist Chinese Church, 1325 Rama 4 Road. Tel: 2154529. Services: 10.30am, noon.

- **SIKH**
Wat Sirikurusing Saha, 565 Chuckrapetch Road. Tel: 2211011. Services: 6am, 5pm.

MEDIA

Press
The English language morning newspapers are one of the foreigner's lifelines to the outside world. There are three national English language dailies – *Bangkok Post, The Nation* and *Thailand Times*. The *Asian Wall Street Journal* and the *International Herald Tribune* dailies are available at most bookstalls after 4pm. Newsstands in major hotel gift shops carry air-freighted, and therefore expensive (at least 50 *baht* per copy), editions of British, French, German and Italian newspapers. Newsagents on Sukhumvit Soi 3 also offer Arabic newspapers.

Radio
AM radio is devoted entirely to Thai-language programs. FM frequencies include several English language stations with the latest pop hits. Radio Thailand offers 4 hours of English-language broadcasts each day on the 97 MHZ frequency. Of value to visitors is an English-language program of travel tips broadcast regularly throughout the day.

Television
Bangkok has five Thai language color television channels. In addition, there are now two cable television networks in Bangkok. I.B.C. has five channels, four of which covering news, entertainment, sports and movies are broadcast in English. Thai Sky TV has three channels, all in English. As well as the two cable television networks, all the major hotels and many of the smaller ones also receive satellite television from around the world. Keeping in touch with what is happening in the rest of the world is not a problem wherever you are in Thailand.

POSTAL SERVICES

Thailand has a comprehensive and reliable postal service. Major towns offer regular air mail service as well as express courier service that speeds a package to nearly every point on the globe.

In addition to the postal service, Bangkok offers a number of international courier agencies including Federal Express, Purolater, DHL and Skypak.

Main post offices in Bangkok, Phuket and Chiang Mai have special facilities where stamp collectors can browse and buy from a wide selection of beautiful Thai stamps. In Bangkok, the Central Post Office on New Road between Suriwongse and Siphya roads opens at 7.30am and closes at 4.30pm on Monday–Friday; and from 9am–noon on Saturday, Sunday and holidays. At the right side of the lobby is a packing service with boxes in various sizes. A department on the right end of the building is open 24 hours and sells stamps and sends telegrams.

Branch post offices are located throughout the country. Hours vary but they generally close at 4pm. Some stay open as late as 6pm. Post office kiosks along some of the city's busier streets sell stamps, aerograms (8.50 *baht* each) and ship small parcels. Hotel reception desks will also send letters for no extra charge.

TELECOMMUNICATIONS

Thailand has a sophisticated communications system, not that it always works; the lines have a way of getting jammed, like the traffic, especially after a heavy rain. Most hotels have telephones, telegrams, telexes and fax facilities. Hotel operators can place international telephone calls within minutes; many hotel rooms have installed IDD for convenience.

There is a serious shortage of telephone lines in Bangkok and the position is now being addressed by the installation of an additional 2 million telephones. The modernisation has meant that some existing telephone numbers have changed, often upon short notice, so if you have a problem getting through, try telephoning 13 to verify the number. The operators speak English.

Telephone
Bangkok has a sophisticated communications system with most overseas calls handled by operators. Most hotels have telephones, telegrams, mail, telex and fax facilities. Hotel operators can place international telephone calls within minutes; luxury Bangkok hotel rooms have IDD phones. If the hotel lacks such facilities, place your long distance calls at the General Post Office annex on the ground floor of the Nava Building on Soi Braisanee, just north of the GPO itself. It is open 24 hours.

Telegrams & Fax
Main post offices in nearly every city offer telegram and telex services to all parts of the world. Fax

services are now available throughout the country. Fax operations are generally run by small shops which also offer long-distance telephone service. They ask a nominal service charge in addition to the normal long-distance rates. Look for their signs along main streets of provincial towns.

EMBASSIES & CONSULATES

All of the embassies are open from Monday through to Friday unless otherwise stated.

Embassies

Apostolic Nunciature Embassy, 217/1 Sathorn Tai Raod. Tel: 2175853/4. Visas: 8.30am–5pm.

Argentine Embassy, 20/85 Prommitr Villa, off Sukhumvit 49/1. Tel: 2590401/2, 2599198. Visas: 8am–1pm.

Australian Embassy, 37 Sathorn Tai Road. Tel: 2872680. Visas: 8.15am–12.15pm.

Austrian Embassy, 14 Soi Nantha, Sathorn Tai Road. Tel: 2873970/2. Visas: 9am–12am.

Bangladesh Embassy, 727 Sukhumvit Soi 55 (Thonglor). Tel: 3929437. Visas: 8.30am–12am.

Belgium Embassy, 44 Soi Pipat, off Silom Road. Tel: 2367876, 2360150. Visas: 8.30am–1pm.

Brazilian Embassy, 239 Soi Sarasin, Rachadamri Road, Lumpini. Tel: 2626023, 2526043. Visas: 9.30am–1.30pm.

Brunei Embassy, 19 Soi 26, Sukhumvit Road. Tel: 2605884/7, 2611877/9. Visas: 8.30am–noon and 1–4pm.

Bulgarian Embassy, 3/44 Ladprao Soi 31, Chatuchak. Tel: 5139781/2. Visas: 8am–2pm.

Canadian Embassy, 138 Boonmitr Bldg., 11 & 12th floors, Silom Road. Tel: 2374126. Visas: 8am–11am.

Chilian Embassy, 15 Soi 61, Sukhumvit Road. Tel: 3918443, 3914858. Visas: 8.30am–2pm.

Chinese Embassy, 57 Ratchadaphisek Road, Dindaeng. Tel: 2457032. Visas: 9am–noon.

Commonwealth of Independent States (Russia) Embassy, 108 Sathorn Nua Road. Tel: 2349824, 2343939. Visas: 7.30am–12am.

Czechoslovakian Embassy, Building 1, 16th floor, 99 Wireless Road, Pathumwan. Tel: 2566663. Visas: 9am–noon (Monday, Wednesday, Friday).

Danish Embassy, 10 Soi Atthakan Prasit, Sathorn Tai Road. Tel: 2132021/5. Visas: 9am–3pm (Friday 9am–12am).

Egyptian Embassy, 49 Soi Ruam Rudi, Phoenchit Road. Tel: 2530161, 2538138. Visas: 9am–1pm.

Finnish Embassy, Amarin Plaza, 16th floor, 500 Ploenchit Road. Tel: 2569306/9. Visas: 7.30am–3.15pm.

French Embassy, 35 Soi 36 (Soi Rong Phasi Kao), Charoen Krung Road. Tel: 2340950/4. Visas: 8.30am–noon issued by Consular Section, 29 Sathorn Tai Road. Tel: 2132181/4.

German Embassy, 9 Sathorn Tai Road. Tel: 2132331/6. Visas: 8.30–11.30am.

Greek Embassy, 99 Thanakul Bldg., 3rd floor, Rama 9 Road. Tel: 2473551, 2467974, 2471068. Visas: 8am–2pm.

Hungarian Embassy, 28 Soi Sukchai, off Sukhumvit 42. Tel: 3917906, 3912002/3. Visas: 9am–noon.

Indian Embassy, 46 Sukhumvit Soi 23 (Soi Prasanmit) Sukhumvit Road. Tel: 258 0300-6. Visas: 9am–noon.

Indonesian Embassy, 600-602 Phetchaburi Road. Tel: 2523135/40. Visas: 8.30am–noon and 1.30–3.30pm.

Iranian Embassy, 602 Sukhumvit (between Sois 22-24) Sukhumvit Road. Tel: 2590611/3. Visas: 8am–4pm.

Iraqi Embassy, 47 Pradipat Road. Tel: 2785335/8. Visas: 10am–noon.

Israeli Embassy, 31 Soi Lang Suan, Ploenchit Road. Tel: 2523131/4. Visas: 8am–noon.

Italian Embassy, 399 Nang Linchi Road, Tung Mahamek. Tel: 2872054/7. Visas: 9.30am–11.30am.

Japanese Embassy, 1674/4 New Phetchaburi Road. Tel: 2526151/9. Visas: 8.30am–noon at Asoke Tower, Sukhumvit 21. Tel: 2590234/7.

Korean Embassy, 23 Thiam-Ruammit Road, Huay Kwang, Samsaennork. Tel: 2477537/9. Visas: 8.30am–noon and 1.30pm–4.30pm.

Laotian Embassy, 193 Sathorn Tai Road. Tel: 2132573/4, 2131203, 2873963. Visas: 8am–noon.

Malaysian Embassy, 35 Sathorn Tai Road. Tel: 2861390/2. Visas: 8.30–11.30am.

Mexican Embassy, 44/7-8 Convent Road. Tel: 2356367, 2340935. Visas: 8.30am–12.30pm.

Myanmar Embassy, 132 Sathorn Nua Road. Tel: 2332237, 2344698. Visas: 8.30am–noon.

Nepalese Embassy, 189 Soi 71, Sukhumvit Road. Tel: 3917240. Visas: 8.30am–noon.

Netherlands Embassy, 106 Witthayu Road. Tel: 2547701/5. Visas: 8.30am–noon.

New Zealand Embassy, 93 Witthayu Road. Tel: 2518165. Visas: 8.30am–11.30am.

Norwegian Embassy, Bank of America Bldg., 11th floor, Witthayu Road. Tel: 2530390/2. Visas: 9am–noon.

Pakistan Embassy, 31 Soi 3 (Soi Nana Nua), Sukhumvit Road. Tel: 2530288/90. Visas: 9am–noon.

Philippines Embassy, 760 Sukhumvit Road. Tel: 2590139/40. Visas: 8.30am–noon and 1.30pm–4pm.

Polish Embassy, 61 Soi 23 (Soi Prasanmit), Sukhumvit Road. Tel: 2584112/3. Visas: 9am–noon.

Portugese Embassy, 26 Captain Bush Lane, Si Phaya Road. Tel: 2340372. Visas: 9am–1.30pm.

Romanian Embassy, 150 Soi Charoenpon, Pradipat Road. Tel: 2797902, 2797872. Visas: 9am–noon (Monday, Wednesday, Friday).

Saudi Arabian Embassy, Sathorn Thani Bldg., 90 Sathorn Nua Road. Tel: 2371938/41. Visas: 10am–noon.

Singapore Embassy, 129 Sathorn Tai Road. Tel: 2862111, 2861434. Visas: 8.30am–noon.

Spanish Embassy, 93 Witthayu Road. Tel: 2526112, 2528368. Visas: 8.30am–1pm.

Sri Lankan Embassy, 48/3 Soi 1, Sukhumvit Road. Tel: 2512788/9. Visas: 8.30am–noon and 1pm–3.45pm.

Swedish Embassy, 20th floor, Pacific Place, 140 Sukhumvit Road. Tel: 2544954/5. Visas: 8am–noon.

Swiss Embassy, 35 Witthayu Road. Tel: 2530156/60. Visas: 9am–noon.

Turkish Embassy, 153/2 Soi Mahadlek Luang 1, Ratchadamri Road. Tel: 2512987/8. Visas: 8.30am–2.30pm.

United Kingdom Embassy, 1031 Ploenchit Road. Tel: 2530191/9. Visas: 8am–11am, (Friday 8am–noon)

USA Embassy, 95 Witthayu Road. Tel 2525040/9, 2525171/9. Visas: 7.30am–10am.

Vietnamese Embassy, 83/1 Witthayu Road. Tel: 2515835/8. Visas: 8.30am–11.30am and 1.30pm–4pm.

Yugoslavian Embassy, 28 Soi 61, Sukhumvit Road. Tel: 3919090/1. Visas: 9am–noon.

Consulates

Chilian Consulate, Bangkok Bank Bldg., 18th floor, 333 Silom Road. Tel: 2332177, 2360151, 2356780. Visas: 8.30am–noon and 2pm–5pm.

Columbian Consulate, c/o TTMC Ltd., 222 Than Settakij Bldg., 7th floor, Vipavadee Rangsit Road. Tel: 2784386, 5130459/63.

Danish Consulate, EAC Bldg., 53-55 Oriental Avenue. Tel: 2360220. Visas: 7.30am–3pm (Monday–Thur), 7.30am–12.30pm (Friday).

Dominican Consulate, 96/9 Chakkaphatdiphong Road. Tel: 2814345/6, 2814745. Visas: 9am–3pm.

Gambian Consulate, 610/5-6, Songwad Road, Samphantawongse. Tel: 2240091. Visas: 8.30am–5pm.

Greek Consulate, President Tour Bldg., 3rd floor, Siam Square Soi 6. Tel: 2515111/7, 2521686. Visas: 9am–noon and 1–3pm.

Icelandic Consulate, 59 Soi Nawin, Chuaphloeng Road. Tel: 2491300. Visas: 1pm–5pm.

Irish Consulate, United Flour Mill Bldg., 11th floor, Ratchawong Road. Tel: 2230876. Visas: 9am–noon and 1pm–4pm.

Iraqi Consulate, 1139 Charoen Krung Road, Si Phaya, Bangrak. Tel: 2371443. Visas: 9am–4.30pm.

Jordanian Consulate, 47 Soi Ekamai, Sukhumvit Road. Tel: 3917142. Visas: 9am–noon.

Kenyan Consulate, 568 Soi Panich Anand, Sukhumvit 71, Klongtan. Tel: 3918294, 3918370, 3918857. Visas: 8.30am–noon and 1pm–3.30pm.

Mali Consulate, Orakarn Building, 12th floor, 26-42 Chidlom Road, Pleonchit. Tel: 2541490. Visas: 8am–3pm.

Maltese Consulate, 106/1 Soi 53, Sukhumvit Road. Tel: 2590035/8. Visas: 9.30am–5pm.

Mexican Consulate, 1 Soi Annopnarumitr Samsennai, Dindaeng Road. Tel: 2460206/5. Visas: 8.30am–noon and 1pm–3.30pm.

Monaco Consulate, 302/81-83 Rama 9 Road, Huay Kwang. Tel: 2482094/9. Visas: 8.30am–noon.

Oman Consulate, Aswinwichit Bldg., 7th floor, 134/1-2 Silom Road. Tel: 2367385-6. Visas: 9am–noon.

Papua New Guinea Consulate, Sino-Thai Tower, 30th floor, 32/56 Soi Asoke, Sukhumvit Road. Tel: 2601321, 2583436. Visas: 9am–11am.

Panamanian Consulate, Sarasin Bldg., G.P.O. Box 1168, 14 Surasak Road, Bangrak. Tel: 2360250 ext. 239. Visas: 8.30am–4.30pm.

Peruvian Consulate, 10 Soi 3, Ramkhamhaeng 24, Seri 2 Road, Huamark. Tel: 3141054, 3143752. Visas: 9am–11am.

Senegalese Consulate, Regent House, 12th floor, 183 Rajadamri Road. Tel: 2525692-7. Visas: 8.30am–4.30pm.

Sri Lankan Consulate, 1/7-8 Soi 10, Sukhumvit Road. Tel: 2510803, 2518062. Visas: 8.30am–5.30pm.

Taiwanese Consulate, Far East Trade Office, Kian Nguan Bldg., 10th floor, Witthayu Road. Tel: 2519274/6, 2519393/7. Visas: 9–11am and 2pm–4pm.

Tunisian Consulate, Siwikon Bldg., 10th floor, 18/8 Soi 21, Sukhumvit Road. Tel: 2593170/6. Visas: 8.30am–4.30pm.

Uruguayan Consulate, 267 Sing Sian Yit Pao Bldg., 267 New Road. Tel: 2253718/9. Visas: 10am–noon.

GETTING AROUND

FROM THE AIRPORT

FROM BANGKOK AIRPORT

The journey along the expressway into the city can take from 30 minutes to one hour or more, depending on the traffic conditions. The new expressway from the airport into Bangkok currently under construction will be completed by the end of 1994 to alleviate the congestion. Some hotels have limousines to pick up guests.

Oriental Bangkok, Shangri-La and Royal Orchid Sheraton Bangkok have together launched an express airport service to transfer their guests to and from the airport by catamarans.

Air-Conditioned Mini-Buses

The Authorized Transportation Service at the Arrival Hall in Don Muang Airport operates a transport service into the city to hotels or private residences on a round-the-clock basis. Air-conditioned limousines are the most convenient transportation to town and cost between 350–400 *baht*. The official air-conditioned mini-buses cost 100 *baht* per passenger and leave the airport every 30 minutes.

Because they have to fight traffic to deliver their passengers at various hotels around the city, they can take considerable time to get you to your hotel. It might be worth shelling out extra for a limousine if you arrive at the airport during the rush hour. There is also a shuttle minibus that operates between the Airport and the City Terminal at the Asia Hotel on Phya Thai Road at 30-minute intervals between 7am and 9pm. It costs 60 *baht* per person.

Thai international also operates a shuttle service between the airport and Pattaya. The three hour journey costs 180 *baht* and will deliver you and collect you from most of the major hotels in Pattaya.

Taxis

Air-conditioned public taxis charge 200 *baht* to nearly every point in the city. A clerk at a counter near the door between the Arrival Lounge and the street issues written instructions on your destination and the price. Hand this paper to the taxi driver and pay him the price noted on it. If you think the price is too high or are going a shorter distance, you can walk out to the main highway and flag down a taxi. Remember, some taxis are not metered, one must bargain for the fare. A sharp bargainer can ride to town in air-conditioned comfort for as little as 150 *baht*. The new metered public taxis obviate the necessity of bargaining and if the traffic is not congested will usually be less expensive than non-metered public taxis.

For economy minded travelers, five air-conditioned buses – Nos. 3, 4, 10, 13, and 29 – stop in front of the airport. The trip into town costs just 15 *baht*. The last buses leave about 8pm (except for No. 4 which stops running at 7pm).

For the very economy-minded, a train leaves from the station across the highway every hour until 8.13pm for Hualampong Station in the center of Bangkok. The 40-minute journey costs 5 *baht*.

For the return trip to the airport, the Authorized Transportation Service has in-town offices at 485 Silom Road (Tel: 2354365, 2354366), Montien Hotel (Tel: 2337060), and Asia Hotel (Tel: 2150780). Most major hotels have air-conditioned limousines. Non-metered taxis make the trip for 150–250 *baht* depending on traffic conditions. Metered taxis will be less expensive if there are no traffic jams on the way.

International and Domestic Transfer

The 500-m (547-yd) trip between Bangkok's International and Domestic Airports is by way of a free shuttle bus at 10–15 minute intervals.

FROM CHIANG MAI AIRPORT

Chiang Mai's airport is a 10-minute drive from the city center. There is a frequent bus service but it runs a circuitous route and visitors with a lot of luggage might prefer the following modes of transportation:
Limousines: Major hotels have limousines to ferry

guests with reservations (one can make a reservation at airport) to their premises. They charge about 50 *baht* per person.

Mini-Van: Thai International operates a mini-van between the airport and its town office on Prapoklao Road. The cost each way is 20 *baht* per passenger. You must then find your own way from the office to the hotel.

FROM PHUKET AIRPORT

Limousines: THAI Ground Services offers air-conditioned limousines to each beach. The price is computed per vehicle and each vehicle holds four persons. Prices per vehicle (no extra charge for luggage) range from 250 to 450 *baht* (US$10–18).

Mini-Vans: Major hotels maintain mini-vans to ferry guests with reservations (it is possible to make a reservation at the airport) to and from the airport. They charge up to 500 *baht* (US$20) per car. Thai International's mini-van runs hourly between the airport and its Phuket town office on Ranong Road. The cost each way is 50 *baht* (US$2) per passenger. You must then find your own way from the office to the beach.

DOMESTIC TRAVEL

By Air

Thai Airways International (THAI) operates a domestic network serving 22 towns, offering seven daily services to some of them, such as Chiang Mai and Phuket.

Bangkok Airways is Thailand's first privately owned domestic airline and provides a highly efficient, first class service to most of the major resort destinations in Thailand as well as Phnom Penh in Cambodia. The present destinations from Bangkok covered by their fleet of modern aircraft are Koh Samui, Phuket, Hua Hin, Trang, Mae Hong Son, U Taphao, Loei and Phnom Penh.

If you are planning a trip to the tropical island of Koh Samui from Bangkok, you will save much traveling time by air, which by road and boat may amount to a 14-hour journey.

By Rail

The State Railways of Thailand operates three principal routes from Hualampong Railway Station. The northern route passes through Ayutthaya, Phitsanuloke, Lampang and terminates at Chiang Mai. The northeastern route passes through Ayutthaya, Saraburi, Nakhon Ratchasima, Khon Kaen, Udon Thani and terminates at Nong Khai. The southern route crosses the Rama 6 bridge and calls at Nakhon Pathom, Petchburi, Hua Hin and Chumphon. It branches at Haadyai, one branch running southwest through Betong and on down the western coast of Malaysia to Singapore. The southeastern branch goes via Pattani and Yala to the Thai border opposite the Malaysian town of Kota Bharu.

In addition, there is a line from Makkasan to Aranyaprathet on the Cambodian border. Another leaves Bangkok Noi Railway Station for Kanchanaburi and other destinations beyond along the old Death Railway. There is also a short route leaving Wongwian Yai station in Thonburi that travels west along the rim of the Gulf of Thailand to Samut Sakhon and then to Samut Songkram.

Express and Rapid services on the main lines offer first-class air-conditioned or second-class fan-cooled cars with sleeping cabins or berths and dining cars. There are also special air-conditioned express day coaches which travel to key towns along the main lines.

TRAIN STATIONS IN BANGKOK
Hualampong: Rama 4 Road. Tel: 2330341.
Bangkok Noi: Tel: 4113102.

By Road
Air-conditioned bus service is available to most destinations in Thailand. VIP coaches which allow extra leg room are the best for overnight journeys to Phuket and Chiang Mai. Air-conditioned coaches also leave half-hourly from the Eastern bus terminal on Sukhumvit Road (opposite Soi 63) for Pattaya and other points beyond. For the very adventurous, there are fan-cooled buses filled with passengers and chickens and tons of luggage that are used by poorer Thais for their journeys across the country.

To reach a small town from a large one, there are smaller buses or *baht* buses – pick-up trucks with a passenger compartment on the backs.

PUBLIC TRANSPORT

Taxis, *Tuks-Tuks* & Motor-Cycles
There are two types of taxis available in Bangkok, metered and non-metered. Both are air-conditioned and reliable, but the drivers' command of English is often less than perfect. This presents a problem not only in conveying to him your destination but in the case of non-metered taxis, bargaining the price as well.

Do not step into a non-metered taxi without having first agreed on a price. The price can fluctuate depending on the hour of the day and the amount of traffic, rain, and the number of one-way streets he must negotiate. A sample fare for 9am between the Dusit Thani Hotel and the Grand Palace or between the Oriental Hotel and the Jim Thompson House would be 70 *baht*. The base fare for all journeys is 30 *baht*. Taxi drivers do not charge you an extra fee for baggage stowage or extra passengers and there is no tipping.

The recently-introduced metered taxis are a much better choice if you do not know the precise distance to your intended destination. If you know Bangkok well, you might be able to negotiate a price below that which you would pay for a metered taxi, but taxi drivers are experts at outwitting their less knowledgeable passengers, so if you are just a casual tourist

stick to the metered taxis. The minimum basic fare is 35 *baht*.

If the English fluency of taxi drivers is limited, that of *tuk-tuk* (also called *samlor*) drivers is even less. *Tuk-tuks* are the brightly colored three-wheeled taxis whose name comes from the noise their two-cycle engines make. They are fun for short trips but choose a taxi for longer journeys. A *samlor* driver on an open stretch of road can seldom resist racing and the resultant journey can be a hair-raising experience. For very short trips, the fare is 20 *baht*.

The side roads leading off the major roads are called *sois*. At the entrance to many *sois*, there are motor-cycle taxis that for around 5 *baht* will take you into the soi perched on the back. Crash helmets provided by the drivers must be worn on the major roads. To some, this form of transport is the answer to Bangkok's traffic, but in the case of an accident, which is not a rare occurrence, the driver will not hold any insurance cover.

Buses & Mini-Buses
Bangkok buses come in four varieties: executive, air-conditioned, ordinary, and the green mini-buses. They operate every two or three minutes along more than 100 routes and are an excellent way to see the outer areas of the city. Bus maps give the routes for all types of buses.

Buses are especially useful during rush hours when traveling up one-way streets like parts of Sukhumvit Road because they can speed along specially-marked bus lanes going against on-coming traffic. Conductors prowl through the aisles collecting fares and issuing tickets. Unfortunately, destinations are only noted in Thai so a bus map is needed. Most routes cease operating around midnight though some (Nos. 2 and 4) run all through the night.

The newly introduced air-conditioned executive micro-buses with red and grey livery hold 20 seated passengers with a flat rate fare of 20 *baht*, but serve fewer routes. The more common, big blue and white air-conditioned buses serve a dozen routes through the city and the fares start at 6 *baht*.

Fares for the green mini-buses are 2 *baht* 50 *satang*.

Ordinary buses come in two varieties: red and white (3 *baht* 50 *satang*) and blue and white (2 *baht* 50 *satang*). Aside from the price, there is no difference in service routes. Both can be very crowded (it is a sight to see one listing heavily to one side while students cling to the open doors). Their route numbers correspond with those of ordinary buses since they ply the same routes. Their drivers are the cowboys of the road and usually drive in very colorful fashion. Some drivers deck out their buses with stereo sets; others even have television sets, though on bumpy roads the reception is less than perfect.

Bus Stations
For bus and coach journeys to destinations outside of Bangkok, the major terminals are:
Eastern: Opposite Soi 63 (Ekamai), Sukhumvit

Road. Tel: 3912504, 3922521.
Northern and North-Eastern: Moh Chit, Phaholyothin Road. Tel: 2710101/5, 2794484/7
Southern: Boromrat Chonnani Road. Tel: 4350511, 4345558.

Boats

White express boats with red trim run regular routes at 20–30 minute intervals up and down the Chao Phya River, going all the way to Nonthaburi 10 km (6 miles) north of the city. The service begins at 6am and ceases at 6.30pm. Fares are 6 *baht* for short distances.

Ferries cross the river at dozens of points and cost 1 *baht* per journey. They begin operating at 6am and stop at midnight.

Bangkok is not one of the easiest cities to find your way around but, luckily, there is plenty of help.

Chiang Mai

Buses: Chiang Mai has two types of buses, the yellow and the red minibuses which carry passengers along five routes through the town. Fares are 2 *baht* each. Consult city maps for routes.

Tuk-tuks, the motorized three-wheel taxis, charge according to distance, starting at 10 *baht*. You must bargain for the price before you get in.

Samlors, the pedal trishaws, charge 5 *baht* for short distances. Bargain before you board.

Phuket

Buses: Picturesque wooden buses ply regular routes from the market to the beaches. They depart every 30 minutes between 8am and 6pm between Phuket town market and all beaches except Rawai and Nai Harn. Buses to Rawai and Nai Harn leave from the traffic circle on Bangkok Road. They prowl the beach roads in search of passengers. Flag one down. Fares range from 10 to 20 *baht*.

Tuk-tuks operate between Patong and Karon/Kata and between Kata and Nai Harn for up to 40 *baht*, depending on distance. Intracity *tuk-tuks* charge 10 *baht* per person regardless of distance for trips within Phuket town or Patong.

Motorcycle taxis leave from the market on Phuket town's Ranong Road. Drivers in maroon vests convey passengers anywhere in the downtown area for 5 *baht* per ride. It is a convenient way to get around.

PRIVATE TRANSPORT

Limousines

Most major hotels operate air-conditioned limousine services. Although the prices are about twice those of ordinary taxis, they offer the convenience of English-speaking drivers and door-to-door service.

Rental Cars

Thailand has a good road system with over 50,000 km (31,000 miles) of paved highways and more are being built every year. Road signs are in Thai and English and you should have no difficulty following a map. An international driver's license is required.

Driving on a narrow but busy road can be a terrifying experience with right of way determined by size. It is not unusual for a bus to overtake a truck despite the fact that the oncoming lane is filled with vehicles. It is little wonder that when collisions occur, several dozen lives are lost. Add to that, many of the long-distance drivers consume pep pills by the bucketful and have the throttle to the floor because they are getting paid for beating schedules. One is strongly advised to avoid driving at night for this reason. When dusk comes, pull in at a hotel and get an early start the next morning.

Avis, Hertz and numerous local agencies offer late model cars with and without drivers and with insurance coverage for Bangkok and up-country trips. Prices for a chauffeured Mercedes Benz (Bangkok only) average 4,000 *baht* per day (2,500 *baht* for self-drive) and 2,200 *baht* for a chauffeured Toyota (1,800 *baht* for self-drive) plus gasoline costs (8.90 *baht* per liter for Premium at the time of going to press). A deposit of 2,000 *baht* or more is required.

Up-country, agencies can be found in major towns like Chiang Mai and Phuket. These also rent four-wheel drive jeeps and mini-vans. When renting a jeep, read the fine print carefully and be aware that you are liable for all damages to the vehicle. Ask for First Class insurance which covers both you and the other vehicle involved in a collision.

Bangkok

Unfortunately, there are no car rental desks at Bangkok Airport. Contacted by telephone, agencies will deliver the car to your hotel and you can fill out the rental forms there.

Avis, 2/12 Wireless Road. Tel: 2555300/4.
Hertz, 987 Ploenchit Road. Tel: 2536251.
Grand Car Rent, 233-5 Asoke-Dindeng Road. Tel: 2482991/2.
Klong Toey Car Rent, 1921 Rama IV Road. Tel: 2519856.
SMT **Rent-a-Car**, 931/11 Rama 1 Road, (opp. National Stadium). Tel: 2164436, 2168020.

Chiang Mai

Avis, Head office: 14/14 Huay Kaew Road, Tel: 222013, 221316. Open from 8am–6pm. Branches: Dusit Inn, Tel: 251033, 251034; Chiang Inn. Tel: 235655. Open from 8am–5pm.
Hertz, 12/3 Loi Kroa Road, Tel: 235496, 249473; Novotel Suriwongse, Tel: 236789, 236673; Chiang Mai Plaza. Tel: 252-Aod Car Rent; 49 Chang Klang Road. (opposite the Night Bazaar). Tel: 249197.

Phuket

Avis, Airport. Tel: 311358; Le Meridien Phuket, Relax Bay, Tel: 321480; Holiday Inn Phuket,

Patong, Tel: 321020; Phuket Cabana Hotel, Patong, Tel: 321138; Dusit Laguna Phuket, Bang Thao, Tel: 311174; Phuket Arcadia Hotel, Karon, Tel: 381038; Phuket Island Resort, Rawai, Tel: 215950; Club Med, Kata, Tel: 214830.

Hertz, Airport. Tel: 311162; Pearl Hotel, Montri Road. (Phuket town), Tel: 211044; Pearl Village Resort, Nai Yang, Tel: 311378; Patong Merlin Hotel, Patong, Tel: 321070; Thara Patong Hotel, Patong, Tel: 321520.

Motor-Cycle Rental

Motorcycles can be rented in Pattaya, Chiang Mai and Phuket for economical rates. Remember that when you rent a motorcycle, you must surrender your passport for the duration of the rental period; so change money first.

Motorcycles range in size from small 90cc models like Honda Dreams and similar brands to giant 750 cc behemoths. The majority are 125cc trailbikes. Rental outlets can be found along beach roads and main roads in each town. Prices run between 100 and 400 *baht* per day.

It is not uncommon for rental motor-cycles to be stolen, especially in Pattaya, so you are well advised to lock them up when not in use and only park them in areas with supervision.

ON FOOT/HITCH-HIKING

There are not many places one can walk in Thailand other than national parks like Khao Yai and Phu Kradung. It is possible to hitch a ride on ten-wheel trucks but it is not advisable simply because the drivers often drive in a manner designed to frighten the life out of you; if you are female, you are only asking for trouble. It is strongly recommended that you do not travel at night on trucks as the drivers are often tanked up on amphetamines and cause some of Thailand's most horrendous accidents.

WHERE TO STAY

HOTELS

The hotel accommodation in all the major tourist destinations in Thailand is equal to the very best anywhere in the world. The facilities in the first-class hotels may have as many as 10, or more different restaurants serving Western and Asian cuisine, coffee shops, swimming pools, exercise rooms, business centers, banqueting halls, shopping arcades, and cable & satellite television. The service is second to none. Indeed, most of the moderately priced hotels rival what in Europe would be considered a first-class hotel. Even the budget and inexpensive hotels will invariably have a swimming pool and more than one food outlet.

If you are on a limited budget, there are numerous guesthouses offering clean, economical accommodation. Once of primary interest only to backpackers because of their sparse facilities, many have now been upgraded to include fans, air-conditioning and bathrooms in the rooms rather than down the hall. As such, they afford a viable alternative to more up-market travelers. Prices range from 80 to 250 *baht*. Generally possessing no more than a dozen rooms, they are more like pensions than hotels and appeal to travelers who like personalised service, friendly staff and a more relaxed pace. Their numbers are legion and to list them would fill several books. In Bangkok they are to be found along Khaosarn Road and Soi Ngam Duphli off Rama 4 Road. In Chiang Mai, check along the river and in the area of Chaiyaphum Road. Phuket and Pattaya are much less common.

BANGKOK

First-class (3,000 *baht* up)
Airport, 333 Choet Wutthakat Road. Tel: 5661020/1, 5662060/9. 300 rooms.
Amari Boulevard, Soi 7, Sukhumvit Road. Tel: 2552930, 2552940. 310 rooms.
Arnoma Swissotel, 99 Ratchadamri Road. Tel: 2553411/9. 380 rooms.
Bel-Aire Princess, 16 Soi 5, Sukhumvit Road. Tel: 2534300/30. 160 rooms.
Central Plaza, 1695 Phahonyothin Road. Tel: 5411234. 607 rooms.
Delta Grand Pacific, Soi 17-19, Sukhumvit Road. Tel: 2552440. 400 rooms.

Dusit Thani, 946 Rama IV Road. Tel: 2360450/9, 2380032. 533 rooms.

Emerald, 99/1 Ratchadapisek Road. Tel: 2764567. 640 rooms.

Evergreen Laurel, 88 North Sathorn Road (at the intersection with Soi Pipat). Tel: 2349829. 158 rooms.

Grand Hyatt Erewan, 494 Ratchadamri Road. Tel: 2541234. 400 rooms.

Hilton International, 2 Witthayu Road. Tel: 2530123. 343 rooms.

Holiday Inn Crowne Plaza, 981 Silom Road. Tel: 2384300. 662 rooms.

Imperial Queen's Park, 36 Soi 22, Sukhumvit Road. Tel: 2619000. 1,400 rooms.

Imperial, 6 Witthayu Road. Tel: 2540023/100, 2540111. 370 rooms.

Indra Regent, 120/126 Ratchaprarop Road. Tel: 2521111. 439 rooms.

Landmark, 138 Sukhumvit Road. Tel: 2540404, 2540424. 415 rooms.

Le Meridian President, 135/26 Gaysorn Road. Tel: 2530444. 387 rooms.

Mandarin, 662 Rama IV Road. Tel: 2380230/59. 343 rooms.

Mansion Kempinski, 75/23 Soi 11, Sukhumvit Road. Tel: 2532655, 2557200. 127 rooms.

Menam, 2074 Charoen Krung Road. Tel: 2891148/9, 2890352/3. 718 rooms.

Monarch Lee Gardens, 188 Silom Road. Tel: 2381991. 448 rooms.

Montien, 54 Suriwongse Road. Tel: 2348060, 2337060. 496 rooms.

Narai, 222 Silom Road. Tel: 2370100/39. 500 rooms.

Novotel Bangkok, Soi 6, Siam Square. Tel: 2556888. 429 rooms.

Oriental, 48 Oriental Avenue. Tel: 2360400/39. 393 rooms.

Rama Gardens, 9/9 Vipavadi Rangsit Road (8km from Airport). Tel: 5610022. 364 rooms.

Regent Bangkok, 155 Ratchadamri Road. Tel: 2516127. 415 rooms.

Rembrandt Hotel, 19 Sukhumvit Road 18. Tel: 2617100/4. 407 rooms.

Royal City, Boromratchonni Road, (Pinklao-Nakhonchaisri Road). Tel: 4330200, 4330300. 400 rooms.

Royal Garden Riverside, 257/1-3 Charoen Nakhon Road. Tel: 4760021/2. 427 rooms.

Royal Orchid Sheraton, 2 Captain Bush Lane, Si Phraya Road. Tel: 2345599. 776 rooms.

Shangri-La, 89 Soi Wat Suan Plu, Charoen Krung Road. Tel: 2367777. 694 rooms.

Siam City, 477 Si Ayutthaya Road. Tel: 2470130, 2470120/30. 530 rooms.

Siam Inter-Continental, 967 Rama 1 Road. Tel: 2530355/7. 400 rooms.

Sol Twin Towers Bangkok, 88 Soi Rong Muang, New Rama VI Road. Tel: 2169544. 700 rooms.

Sukhothai Bangkok, 13/3 Sathorn Tai Road. Tel: 2870222. 190 rooms.

Swissotel, 3 Convent Road. Tel: 2335345, 2343729. 57 rooms.

Tara, 18/1 Soi 26, Sukhumvit Road. Tel: 2592900/19. 196 rooms.

Tawana Ramada, 80 Surawongse Road. Tel: 2360361. 265 rooms.

Moderate (2,000 baht up)

Alexander, 3303 Soi 85, Ramkhamhaeng Road. Tel: 3771740/1, 3750300/30. 308 rooms.

Ambassador, 171 Soi 11-13, Sukhumvit Road. Tel: 2540444, 2550444. 946 rooms.

Asia, 296 Phaya Thai Road. Tel: 2150808. 640 rooms.

Baiyoke Suite, 130 Ratchaprarop Road. Tel: 2530362, 2550330/41, 2550150/62. 240 rooms.

Bangkok Cadet Movenpick, Soi 15, Sukhumvit Road. Tel: 2540228. 108 rooms.

Bangkok Palace, 1091/336 New Phetchaburi Road. Tel: 2550305, 2530510/50. 692 rooms.

Classic Place, 1574-1598 New Petchaburi Road. Tel: 2554444/9, 2550404/9. 267 rooms.

De-Ville Palace, 474 Soi 39, Ramkhamhaeng Road. Tel: 5300560/79. 235 rooms.

First, 2 Phetchaburi Road. Tel: 2550111. 350 rooms.

Fortune Blue Wave, Ratchadapisek Road. Tel: 2476333. 429 rooms.

Four Wings, 40 soi 26, Sukhumvit Road. Tel: 2602100. 325 rooms.

Holiday Mansion, 53 Witthayu Road. Tel: 2550084/90. 94 rooms.

Impala, 9 Soi 24, Sukhumvit Road. Tel: 2588612/6, 2590053/4. 200 rooms.

Jade Pavilion, 30 Soi 22, Sukhumvit Road. Tel: 2594675/89, 259 9270-79. 215 rooms.

Manora, 412 Suriwongse Road. Tel: 2345070-29. 240 rooms.

Maruay Garden, 1 Soi 40, Phahonyothin Road. Tel: 5610510/29. 315 rooms.

New Peninsula, 295/3 Surawongse Road. Tel: 2343910/7. 150 rooms.

Plaza, 178 Surawongse Road. Tel: 2351760/79. 191 rooms.

Quality Hotel Pinnacle, 17 Soi Ngam Dupli Rama IV Road. Tel: 2873411/5, 2870123/31. 170 rooms.

Regency Park, 12/3 Soi 22, Sukhumvit Road. Tel: 2597420/39. 124 rooms.

Royal Lake View, 649/76 Asoke-Din Daeng Road. Tel: 2460227, 2460229, 2466682. 176 rooms.

Royal Princess, 269 Lan Luang Road. Tel: 2813088. 170 rooms.

Royal River, 670/805 Charansanitwong Road. Tel: 4330200/9, 4330300/19. 404 rooms.

Siam Beverly, 188 Ratchadapisek Road (opp. Robinson Dept. Store). Tel: 2754046/8, 2900170/9. 200 rooms.

Silom Plaza, 320 Silom Road. Tel: 2368441/84, 2360333, 2347795/6. 209 rooms.

Somerset, 10 Soi 15, Sukhumvit Road. Tel: 2548500/24. 78 rooms.

Sunroute Bangkok, 288 Rama IX Road, Asoke-Din Daeng Road. Tel: 2480011/80. 408 rooms.
Swiss Park, 155/23-28 Soi 11, Sukhumvit Road. Tel: 2529191, 2540228, 2529358/9. 108 rooms.
Tai-Pan, 25 Soi 23, Sukhumvit Road. Tel: 2609888, 2609898. 150 rooms.
Tantawan Place, 119/5-10 Surawongse Road. Tel: 2382620/39. 75 rooms.
Tong Poon, 130 Soi 4 Rong Muang Road. Tel: 2160020/39. 160 rooms.
Trinity Place, 150 Soi 5, Silom Road. Tel: 2380052, 2382662. 110 rooms.
Winsor, 8-10 Soi 20, Sukhumvit Road. Tel: 2580160/5, 2581524/6. 212 rooms.

Budget (1,000 *baht* and up)
Ariston, 19 Soi 24, Sukhumvit Road. Tel: 2590960/9. 160 rooms.
Bangkapi Royal Rose, 3191 Ladphrao 127, Bangkapi. Tel: 3750020. 215 rooms.
Bangkok Centre, 328 Rama IV Road. Tel: 2384848/57, 2384980/99. 250 rooms.
Bossotel, 55/12-14 Charoen Krung Road, (near Shangri-La Hotel). Tel: 2349409, 2358001. 69 rooms.
Carlton Inn, 22/2-4 Sukhumvit 21, Asoke Road. Tel: 2580471/3. 20 rooms.
Chaleena, 453 Soi 65, Ramkhamhaeng Road. Tel: 5397111, 5397122, 5397101/14. 309 rooms.
Chaophya Park, 229-229/1-2 Ratchadapisek Road. Tel: 2759601/11. 404 rooms.
China Town, 526 Yaowarat Road. Tel: 2261267/92. 80 rooms.
Collins International House (YMCA), 27 Sathon Tai Road. Tel: 2872727, 2871900. 250 rooms.
Continental, 971/16 Phahonyothin Road. Tel: 2781385, 2797567. 122 rooms.
Crystal, 65 Soi Nathong, Ratchadapisek Road. Tel: 2761871/9, 2778823, 2771012, 2778221. 92 rooms.
Elizabeth, 169/51 Pradipat Road, Saphan Kwai. Tel: 2795342/3, 2795304/5. 272 rooms.
Eurasia Mungkorn Wing, 33/2 Soi Wattana Niwet, 7 Sutthisan Road. Tel: 2750060/77. 208 rooms.
Euro Inn, 249 Soi 31, Sukhumvit Road. Tel: 2599480/7. 82 rooms.
First House, 14/20-29 Soi 19, Phetchaburi Road. Tel: 2540300/13. 133 rooms.
Golden Horse, 5/1-2 Damrongrak Road. Tel: 2801920. 96 rooms.
Grand De Ville, 903 Mahachai Road. Tel: 2257554/92, 2550050. 219 rooms.
Grand Palace Bangkok, 522/163 Asoke-Dindaeng Road. Tel: 2487580/98. 410 rooms.
Grand Tower, 22/1 Soi 55, Sukhumvit Road. Tel: 2590380. 600 rooms.
Inter Place, 118/92 Ramkhamhaeng Road. Tel: 3190330/45. 259 rooms.
Jasmin, 2082 New Phetchaburi Road. Tel: 3192421/8. 72 rooms.
Jim's Lodge, 125/7 Soi Ruam Rudi, Ploenchit Road. Tel: 2553100, 2550190/9. 75 rooms.

La Residence, 173/8-9 Surawongse Road. Tel: 2333301, 2354795. 23 rooms.
Majestic Palace, 97 Ratchadamnoen Klang Road. Tel: 2815000, 2805610/22. 65 rooms.
Manhattan, 13 Soi 15, Sukhumvit Road. Tel: 2550166, 2550188. 196 rooms.
Mido, 222 Pradipat Road. Tel: 2798944, 2794561/6. 200 rooms.
Naza Garden, 84 Soi 20, Sutthisan Road. Tel: 2772329, 2772305, 2750050/9. 167 rooms.
New Fuji, 299-301 Surawongse Road. Tel: 2345365/6, 2338270/2. 60 rooms.
New Trocadero, 343 Surawongse Road. Tel: 2348920/9. 130 rooms.
Niran Grand, 61 Soi 103 (Udomsuk), Sukhumvit Road. Tel: 3990405/7, 3939485/7. 390 rooms.
P.R. Union Inn, 296/1-9 Soi 10, Issaraphap Road. Tel: 4380111, 4370420/38. 150 rooms.
Park, 6 Soi 7, Sukhumvit Road. Tel: 2554300/9. 139 rooms.
Rajah, 18 Soi 4, Sukhumvit Road. Tel: 2550040/83. 450 rooms.
Regina Palace, 1 Soi Soontornsiri, Ratchadapisek Road. Tel: 2750088/95. 310 rooms.
Rex, 762/1 Sukhumvit Road, (opp. Soi 49). Tel: 2590106/15. 131 rooms.
River Side Plaza, 753/45 Ratchawithi Road. Tel: 4340090/3. 262 rooms.
Royal Pacific Plaza, 335 Rama IX Road, Bangkapi. Tel: 3199621/4. 212 rooms.
S.D. Avenue, 1672/124 Boromratchonni Road. Tel: 4340400/24. 325 rooms.
Sariya House, 13 Soi 40, Ramkhamhaeng Road, Huamark. Tel: 3780019, 3781965. 60 rooms.
Siam Orchid Inn, 109 Soi Ratchadamri, Ratchadamri Road. Tel: 2552119, 2553140/3, 2514417. 40 rooms.
Silom Street Inn, 284/11-13 Silom Road. Tel: 2384680. 30 rooms.
Stella Palace, 120/359 Ratchaparop Road. Tel: 2518255/8. 220 rooms.
Suriwongse Tower Inn, 410/3-4, Suriwongse Road. Tel: 2351206/9, 2351350/3. 81 rooms.
Thai, 78 Prachathipatai Road. Tel: 2822831/3, 2822835. 100 rooms.
Tower Inn, 533 Silom Road. Tel: 2344051, 2344053. 140 rooms.
Union Tower, 2355 New Phetchaburi Road. Tel: 3141964/73. 183 rooms.
Viangtai, 42 Tani Road, Banglampu. Tel: 2805392/9, 2805434/45. 240 rooms.
Vital House, 39 Soi 8, Sukhumvit Road. Tel: 2533410/1, 2535122. 40 rooms.
Wall Street Inn, 37/20-24 Soi Surawongse Plaza, Surawongse Road. Tel: 2334144, 2334164/7, 2354650. 80 rooms.
White Orchid, 409-421 Yaowarat Road. Tel: 2260026. 340 rooms.

Inexpensive (400 *baht* and up)
A One Inn, 13-15 Soi Kasemsan 1. Tel: 2164770, 2153029. 22 rooms.

Asoke Place, 4/49 Soi 21, Sukhumvit Road.
Tel: 2583742, 2583733. 20 rooms.
Bangkok City Garden, 12/1 Soi 10, Pradipat Road.
Tel: 2711159, 2796285. 30 rooms.
Bangkok Noorie, 178/7 Soi Wuttiphan, Ratchaparop
Road. Tel: 2523340, 2515171, 2510723/4. 48
rooms.
Baron, 544 Ratchadapisek Road. Tel. 2464525/39,
2460250. 160 rooms.
Boran House, 487/48 Soi Wattanasin, Ratchaparop
Road. Tel: 2533639, 2532252. 30 rooms.
Burapa, 160/14 Charoen Krung Road.
Tel: 2213545/9. 168 rooms.
Business Inn, 155/4-5 Soi 11, Sukhumvit Road.
Tel: 2547981/4, 2557155/8. 70 rooms.
Cadena Palace, 72/54 Soi Indramara 1/1 Sutthisan
Road. Tel: 2700514/8. 145 rooms
Century, 9 Ratchaparop Road. Tel: 2467800/9. 96
rooms.
China Inn, 19/27-28 Soi 19, Sukhumvit Road.
Tel: 2557571/3, 2533439. 27 rooms.
City Inn, 888/37-39 Ploenchit Road. Tel: 2521552,
2542070/1. 30 rooms.
City Lodge 1, 8/7 Soi 19, Sukhumvit Road.
Tel: 2544783/5, 2537096. 34 rooms.
City Lodge 2, 137/10 Soi 9, Sukhumvit Road. Tel:
2537680, 2537705, 2537759, 2554670. 28 rooms.
Classic Inn, 120/51-54 Ratchaprarop Road.
Tel: 2080496/7. 41 rooms.
Comfort Inn, 153/11 Soi 11, Sukhumvit Road.
Tel: 2519250, 2543559/60. 60 rooms.
Crown, 503 Soi 29, Sukhumvit Road. Tel: 2580318/
9, 2584438. 63 rooms.
Dynasty Inn, 5/4-5 Soi 4, Sukhumvit Road.
Tel: 2501397, 2521386, 2524522. 55 rooms.
Embassy, 21 Pradipat Road. Tel: 2798441, 2792641/
2. 80 rooms.
Federal, 27 Soi 11, Sukhumvit Road. Tel: 2530175/
6, 2534768/9. 90 rooms.
Florida, 43 Phayathai Road. Tel: 2470990, 2470995,
2470103. 107 rooms.
Fortuna, 19 Soi 5, Sukhumvit Road. Tel: 2515121/
6, 2532593. 110 rooms.
Golden Dragon, 20/21 Ngam Wong Wan Road,
(10km from Airport). Tel: 5890130/41. 114 rooms.
Golden Gate, 22/3 Soi 2, Sukhumvit Road.
Tel: 2528126, 2515354. 55 rooms.
Golden Palace, 15 Soi 1, Sukhumvit Road.
Tel: 2525115/6, 2525169. 65 rooms.
Grace, 12 Soi 3, Sukhumvit Road. Tel: 2530651/
79. 555 rooms.
Grand Inn, 2/7-8 Soi 3, Sukhumvit Road.
Tel: 2549021/7. 24 rooms.
Honey, 31 Soi 19, Sukhumvit Road. Tel: 2530646/
9, 255 6795-6, 255 7172. 75 rooms.
Inn Town, 40/6-7 Soi 3, Sukhumvit Road.
Tel: 2535475, 2535575. 19 rooms.
Krung Thai, 4 Rang Nam, Phayathai Road.
Tel: 2453261, 2450347. 77 rooms.
Liberty, 215 Pradipat Road. Tel: 2710880/1,
2710150. 202 rooms.

Malaysia, 54 Soi Ngam Dupli, Rama IV Road.
Tel: 2863582, 2871457/8. 120 rooms.
Metro, 1902 New Phetchaburi Road. Tel: 3144741/
3. 73 rooms.
Miami, 2 Soi 13, Sukhumvit Road. Tel: 2535611/
3, 2530369. 123 rooms.
Middle East Sahara Mansion, 21/22 Soi 3/1,
Sukhumvit Road. Tel. 2520575, 2547790/2,
2527490. 161 rooms.
Mirama, 777 Mahachai Road. Tel: 2224191/5,
2211711, 2211720, 2211724. 156 rooms.
Morakot, 2802 New Phetchaburi Road.
Tel: 3140761/3, 3191461. 121 rooms.
My House, 14 Soi 7, Phahonyothin Road.
Tel: 2781350/5. 109 rooms.
Nana, 4 Soi 4, Sukhumvit Road. Tel: 2520121,
2558383. 334 rooms.
New Empire, 572 Yaowarat Road. Tel: 2346990/
6. 140 rooms.
Newrotel, 1216/1 Charoen Krung Road.
Tel: 2371094, 2331406. 30 rooms.
Opera, 16 Soi Somprasong 1, Phetchaburi Road.
Tel: 2524031/2, 2557771. 56 rooms.
President Inn, 155/14-16 Soi 11, Sukhumvit Road.
Tel: 2554230/4. 25 rooms.
Prince, 1537/1 New Phetchaburi Road.
Tel: 2516171/6. 211 rooms.
Rajah Palace, 234 Ratchadapisek Road.
Tel: 2761841/54. 80 rooms.
Ramada, 1169 Charoen Krung Road. Tel: 2348971/
5. 60 rooms.
Reno, 40 Soi Kasemsan 1, Rama I Road.
Tel: 2150026/7. 67 rooms.
Rio Residence, 88/2-3 Nanglinchi Road.
Tel: 2870041/9. 77 rooms.
Rose, 118 Surawongse Road. Tel: 2337695/7,
2334888, 2335076. 99 rooms.
Royal Garden Home, 63/1-4 Soi 3, Sukhumvit
Road. Tel: 2535458/61. 60 rooms.
Royal, 2 Ratchadamnoen Klang Avenue.
Tel: 2229111/20. 297 rooms.
Ruamchit Travel Lodge, 11/1 Soi 10, Sukhumvit
Road. Tel: 2526403, 2510284. 72 rooms.
Sathon Inn, 37 Soi 9, Silom Road. Tel: 2344124.
90 rooms.
Siam, 1777 New Phetchaburi Road. Tel: 2524967/
8, 2525081. 120 rooms.
Star, 31/1 Soi Kasemsan 1, Rama I Road.
Tel: 2150020/1. 60 rooms.
Suda Palace, 24 Sutthisan Road. Tel: 2700601/2,
2700585/87. 130 rooms.
Sukhumvit Crown, Soi 6, Sukhumvit Road.
Tel: 2538401, 2535672/3. 150 rooms.
Super, 49 Soi Ruamsirimit, Phahonyothin Road.
Tel: 2710786, 2710791. 200 rooms.
Suriwong, 31/1 Surawongse Road. Tel: 2333223/
5, 2338751. 102 rooms.
Swan, 31 Custom House Lane, Charoen Krung
Road. Tel: 2338444, 2348594, 2135198. 80 rooms.
Swiss Inn, 1/29 Soi 11, Sukhumvit Road.
Tel: 2554522/3, 2536261. 20 rooms.

Trang, 99/8 Wisutkasat Road. Tel: 2822141/4. 80 rooms.

Warirat Pavilion, 6/54 Soi Wat Thewasunthon, Ngamwongwan Road. Tel: 5809625/6, 5892817. 30 rooms.

Welcome Palace, 30 Naret Road. Tel: 2345402/4, 2377920/46. 422 rooms.

White Inn, 41 Soi 4, Sukhumvit Road. Tel: 2511662, 2527090. 24 rooms.

World Inn, 131/5-7 Soi 7-9, Sukhumvit Road. Tel: 2557274/5, 2535391/2, 2537727. 50 rooms.

World, 1996 New Phetchaburi. Tel: 3144340/6. 100 rooms.

YWCA, 13 Sathorn Tai Road. Tel: 2861936, 2867331, 2863310, 2862329. 58 rooms.

GUESTHOUSES & APARTMENTS

A. A., 84-86 Phra Sumen Road. Tel: 2829631/2, 2829520. 200 rooms.

A.T. 90/1-11 Rambuttri Road, Banglampu. Tel: 2826979, 2812507. 8 rooms.

Amara Court, 645/44-51 Phetchaburi Road, (opp. Indonesian Embassy). Tel: 2518980/1. 16 rooms.

Apple 1, 10/1 Phra Athit Road, (opp. Unicef). Tel: 2816838. 20 rooms.

Apple 2, 11 Soi Khai Chae, Phra Sumen Road. Tel: 2811219.

Asoke Place, 4/49 Soi Asoke, Sukhumvit Road. Tel: 2583733, 2583742. 19 rooms.

Atirach, 813/32-33 Soi 21, (City Center), Phetchaburi Road. Tel: 2545414, 2517424. 36 rooms.

B.K., 11/1 Soi Surao, Chakraphong Road, Banglampu. Tel: 2815278, 2813048. 25 rooms.

Ban Sabay Inter Hostel, 8/137 Soi Sahakorn 15, Ladphrao 71. Tel: 5390150. 42 (dormitory).

Bangkok Christian, 123 Soi Saladaeng 2, Convent Road. Tel: 2336303, 2332206. 36 rooms.

Bangkok Inn, 155/12-13 Soi 11, Sukhumvit Road. Tel: 2544834/7. 18 rooms.

Bangkok Youth Hostel, 25/2 Phitsanulok Road. Tel: 2824236/7, 2810361. 22 (dormitory).

Banglampoo Square House, 131-133 Phra Sumen Road. Tel: 2824236/7, 2814962. 60 rooms.

Beer, 22 Phra Athit Road, Banglampu. Tel: 2800744. 25 rooms.

Bonny, 132 Khaosan Road, Banglampu. Tel: 2819877. 12 rooms.

Boston Inn, 4 Soi Si Bamphen, Rama IV Road. Tel: 2861680, 2860726. 70 rooms.

C & C, 12 Wisutkasat Road, (by Wat In). Tel: 2801974, 2824941. 40 rooms.

C.H., 216-216/1 Khaosan Road, Banglampu. Tel: 2822023. 22 rooms.

Central, 10 Trok Bowonrangsi, Tanao Road. Tel: 2820667. 18 rooms.

Charasri, 59/3 Wisutkasat Road, (opp. June 42 Hotel). Tel: 2829305, 2819528. 16 rooms.

Chart, 61 Khaosan Road, Banglampu. Tel: 2803785, 2801481. 15 rooms.

Eastin Lakeside, 50/492 Muang Thong Thani 3,

Chaeng Wattana Road. Tel: 5740174/80. 144 rooms.

Ekalerk, 119 Soi Viang Fah, Ratchaprarop Road. Tel: 2471905, 2471920. 200 rooms.

Golden Bangkok, 641/1-2 Chakrapet Road, (near Merry King Dept. Store). Tel: 2253786, 2214237. 42 rooms.

Grand Tower, 22/1 Soi 55, Sukhumvit Road. Tel: 2590380. 400 rooms.

Green House, 88/1 Rambuttri Road, Banglampu. Tel: 2810323, 2819572. 70 rooms.

Hello, 63-65 Khaosan Road. Tel: 2818579, 2813551. 29 rooms.

Home & Garden, 16 Soi Wat Samphraya. Tel: 2801475, 2819845. 15 rooms.

J. House, 1 Trok Mayom, Chakrapong Road. Tel: 2812949. 32 rooms.

James, 116/1 Prachatipatai Road. Tel: 2800362. 20 rooms.

Joe, 77 Trok Mayom, Chakrapong Road. Tel: 2815547. 23 rooms.

K.C., 58-64 Soi Khai Chae, Phrasumen Road. Tel: 2820618. 14 rooms.

Krit Thai Mansion, 931/1 Rama Road, (opp. National Stadium). Tel: 2153042, 2152370, 2152582. 50 rooms.

Lee, 21/38-39 Soi Ngamdupli, Rama IV Road. Tel: 2862069. 24 rooms.

Lek, 125-127 Khaosan Road, Banglampu. Tel: 2812775, 2825223. 20 rooms.

Little Home, 23/12 Soi Thewarat (near National Library), Sri Ayutthaya Road. Tel: 2813412, 2821574 18 rooms.

Mango, 64 Soi Rambuttri, Phra Athit Road. Tel: 2814783. 30 rooms.

Merlin, 33 Soi 8, Ramkamhaeng Road. Tel: 3190043/7. 55 rooms.

Mermaids' Rest, 6/1 Soi 8, Sukhumvit Road. Tel: 2535123/4, 75 rooms.

Mery V, 35 Soi Chanasongkhram, Phra Athit Road. Tel: 2829267/8. 60 rooms.

Miami, 1629/7 New Phetchaburi Road. Tel: 2521004/6. 120 rooms.

Muangphon Building, 931/8-9 Rama I Road, (opp. National Stadium). Tel: 2150033/4, 2153056. 75 rooms.

My House, 37 Soi Chanasongkhram, Phra Athit Road. Tel: 2829263/4. 30 rooms.

N.P. (Ngamphit), 28/2 Trok Rongmai, Phra Arthit Road. Tel: 2828114. 40 rooms.

Narai Inn, 5/7 Soi 53, Sukhumvit Road. Tel: 2580601/4. 79 rooms.

New Siam, 21 Soi Chanasongkhra, Phra Athit Road. Tel: 2824554. 60 rooms.

New World House, 2 Soi 2, Samsen Road, Banglampu. Tel: 2815596/605. 65 rooms.

Nut, 217-219 Khaosan Road. Tel: 2826401. 16 rooms.

P., 151-157 Trok Sa-Ke, Tanao Road. Tel: 2241967. 28 rooms.

P.S., 9 Phra Sumen Road. Tel: 2823932/3. 50 rooms.

Paradise, 57 Sri Ayutthaya Road, (behind National Library). Tel: 2824094. 12 rooms.
Peachy, 10 Phra Athit Road. Tel: 2816471, 2816659. 50 rooms.
Ploy, 2/2 Khaosan Road. Tel: 2821025. 40 rooms.
Prasuri, 85/1 Soi Phrasuri, Dinsor Road. Tel: 2801428. 15 rooms.
Pro, 90/16 Rambuttri Road, Banglampu. Tel: 2828277, 2811494. 20 rooms.
R.S. Mansion, 69/10 Soi Ratchaprarop, Ratchaprarop Road. Tel: 2452801, 2453029, 2468468, 2468861. 60 rooms.
Rachada Residence, 6/11 Soi Sueyaiutis, Ratchadapisek Road. Tel: 5124933/4. 45 rooms.
Ranee, 84/73-74 Soi 80, Charoen Krung Road. Tel: 2917377/8, 2920722. 80 rooms.
Red Stone, 11/1 Soi Thantawan, Surawongse Road. Tel: 2360108, 2369324, 2362857/8. 80 rooms.
River View, 768 Soi Panurangsi, Songwat Road, (near River City complex). Tel: 2358501, 2345429. 40 rooms.
River, 18/1 Soi Wat Samphraya, Samsen Road. Tel: 2800876. 12 rooms.
Roof Garden, 62 Soi Chanasongkhram, Phra Athit Road. Tel: 2801423. 32 rooms.
Royal Mansion, 69/299 Soi Mahatthai, Lad phrao Road. Tel: 5300391/8. 140 rooms.
S.T., 72/2 Nakhon Chaisi Road. Tel: 2431107, 2434763. 27 rooms.
S.V., 19/35-36 Soi 19 Sukhumvit Road. Tel: 2531747, 2530606. 20 rooms.
Safety, 1036/6 Rama IV Road. Tel: 2868904, 2871542. 17 rooms.
Santi Lodge, 37 Sri Ayutthaya Road, (behind National Library). Tel: 2812497. 15 rooms.
Sawatdee, 71 Sri Ayutthaya Road, (behind National Library). Tel: 2825349, 2810757. 28 rooms.
Scout Hostel, Physical Education Dept, Rama I Road. Tel: 2153533. 3 rooms (40 beds).
Silom City Court, 35/1 Soi Pipat 2, Silom Road. Tel: 2339031, 2347924, 2356821. 37 rooms.
Sri Prommin, 1 Soi 38, Sukhumvit Road. Tel: 3919057, 3811309. 30 rooms.
Sweety, 49 Ratchadamnoen Klang Road, (opp. Post Office). Tel: 2816756. 23 rooms.
T.T. 1, 138 Soi Wat Mahaphrutharam, Si Phraya Road. Tel: 2363053/4. 30 (dormitory).
T.T. 2, 516-8 Soi Sawang, Si Phraya Road. Tel: 2362946. 30 rooms.
Tavee, 83 Soi 14, Sri Ayutthaya Road, (behind National Library). Tel: 2801447, 2825983. 16 rooms.
Tic, 105 Buranasat Road (off Tanao Road). Tel: 2246269. 10 rooms.
Top, 126/1 Khaosan Road. Tel: 2819954. 35 rooms.
Truly Yours, 242-246 Soi 1, Samsen Road, Banglampu. Tel: 2800371. 18 rooms.
Uncle Rey, 7/10 Soi 4, Sukhumvit Road. Tel: 2525565. 24 rooms.

V.I.P., 168 Khaosan Road. Tel: 2825090. 10 rooms.
Venice House, 546/1-548 Krungkasem Road, (near Wat Sommanat). Tel: 2818262, 2818762. 40 rooms.
Vorapong, 39 Soi 6, Samsen Road. Tel: 2811992/3. 69 rooms.
Waranchai, Soi 31, Samakkhi Road, Thasai, Nonthaburi, (8 km/5 miles from Airport). Tel: 5894165. 20 rooms.
We-Train, 501/1 Moo 3, Dechatungka Road, (opp. Airport). Tel: 5662288, 5661774. 38 rooms.
White, 30 Soi Arsawin 1, (behind 35 Bowl), Boromratchonni Road. Tel: 4352966. 27 rooms.

THE CENTRAL PLAINS & EAST COAST

AYUTTHAYA

(500 *baht* and over)
Ayutthaya Grand Hotel, 55/5 Rochana Road. Tel: (035) 244484. 122 rooms.

(100 *baht* and over)
Phara in Racha, 136 Mu 7, Tambon Chiang Rak Noi, Bang Pa-In. Tel: (035) 361081. 53 rooms.
Si Samai, 12/19 Naresuan Road, Phra Nakhon Si Ayutthaya. Tel: (035) 251104, 251228. 78 rooms.
Thai Sena, 268 Sena-Navin Soi 2, Sena. Tel: (035) 201032. 17 rooms.
Thai Thai Bungalow, 13/1 Naresuan Road, Phra Nakhon si Ayutthaya. Tel: (035) 251505. 20 rooms.
Thai Thai Palace, 19/1 Mu 2, Asia Highway, Km 72-73, Uthai. Tel: (035) 241980. 32 rooms.
U-Thong Hotel, 86 U-Thong Road, Tambon Ho Rattana Chai, Phra Nakhon Si Ayutthaya. Tel: (035) 251136. 65 rooms.
U-Thong Inn, 210 Mu 5, Rochana Road, Phra Nakhon Si Ayutthaya. Tel: (035) 242236/9. 96 rooms.
Wiang Pha, 1/8 Rochana Road, Phra Nakhon Si Ayutthaya. Tel: (035) 241353. 22 rooms.

CHACHOENGSAO

(100 *baht* and over)
Happy Home, By Pass Road. Tel: (01) 3210133. 40 rooms.
Happy Inn, Chachoengsao-Panom Sarakham Road. Tel: (038) 512236. 24 rooms.
Jai Inn, Bang Pakong Road. Tel: (038) 512236. 33 rooms.
Mitsamphan, 76-92 Kuakoon Road. Tel: (038) 511079. 38 rooms.
Panom Garden, 333 Mu 4, Phanomsarakham Road, Phanom Sarakham. Tel: (038) 551145. 44 rooms.
Rim Fung Bangpakong, 61/5 Bangna-Trat Road. Tel: (038) 531855, 531512. 22 rooms.
River Inn, 122/1 Marupong Road. Tel: (038) 511921. 70 rooms.
Rungreung Bungalow, 999 Phanomsarakham Road, Phanom Sarakham. Tel: (038) 551200. 13 rooms.

Yenchit, 203 Maha Chakkaphat Road.
Tel: (038) 511200. 29 rooms.

CHANTHABURI

(1,500 *baht* and over)
Caribou Highland Hotel, 14 Shavana-utit, Wat
Mai. Tel: (039) 321584.

(500 *baht* and over)
Eastern, 899 Tha-Chalab Road. Tel: (039) 312218/
20. 142 rooms.

(100 *baht* and over)
Ban Kaew Hotel, 41/210 Raksak-Chamun Road.
Tel: (039) 312507.
Bungalow Buthsaracome, 5/6 Thachang.
Tel: (039) 321563. 27 rooms.
Bungalow Che Vu, Tha Chalab Road.
Tel: (039) 311949. 20 rooms.
Bungalow Holiday, Tha-Chalab Road.
Tel: (039) 313204. 24 rooms.
Chai Lee, 106 Kwang Road. Tel: (039) 311075.
Chantanimit, 116-118 Rimnam Road.
Tel: (039) 312388. 57 rooms.
Chanthaburi Hotel, 42/6 Tha-Chalab Road.
Tel: (039) 311300. 70 rooms.
Kasem San 1, 98/1 Benchama-Rachuthit Road.
Tel: (039) 311100. 60 rooms.
Kasem San 2, 23 Sri Rongmuang Road.
Tel: (039) 311173. 119 rooms.
Kiat Khachon, 27/28 Tha-Luang Road.
Tel: (039) 311212, 313139. 63 rooms.
Muang Chan, 257-259 Sri Chan Road.
Tel: (039) 312909, 321073. 99 rooms.
Paradise Hotel, 759/2 Amphoe Muang.
Tel: (039) 313723.
Paris Inn, 3/15 Thungdon Daeng Road.
Tel: (039) 321214, 321473.
Travel Lodge, 14 Raksak-Chamun Road.
Tel: (039) 311531, 311647. 212 rooms.

CHONBURI

(3,000 *baht* and over)
Royal Cliff Beach Resort, 353 Mu 12, Banglamung.
600 rooms.
Royal Garden Resorts Pattaya, 218 Beach Road,
Pattaya. 300 rooms.

(2,000 *baht* and over)
A-One The Royal Cruise, 499 Soi 2, Beach Road,
North Pattaya. Tel: (038) 424242, 424874/9. 200
rooms.
Asia Pattaya, 325 Cliff Road, South Pattaya. Tel:
(038) 428602/6, 423491/5, 428557. 314 rooms.
Dusit Resort, 240 Pattaya Beach Road, North
Pattaya. Tel: (038) 429901/3, 428541, 425611/
21. 474 rooms.
Grand Jomtien Palace, 356 Jomtien Beach, Jomtien.
Tel: (038) 231405/8. 252 rooms.

Montien Pattaya, 369 Mu 9, Pattaya Second Road.
Tel: (038) 428155/6, 428255, 428332. 300 rooms.
Pattaya Lodge, 43 Mu 5, Naklua Road, Naklua.
Tel: (038) 428014. 103 rooms.

(1,500 *baht* and over)
A.A Villa, 288 Mu 5, Naklua Soi 12, Pattaya City.
Tel: (038) 428313, 422515/8. 51 rooms.
Ban Suan, 14/1 Mu 12, Jomtien Beach, Pattaya
City. Tel: (038) 231072. 36 rooms.
Bangphra Resort, 45 Mu 6, Tambon Bangphra,
Sriracha. Tel: (038) 311149, 311321. 55 rooms.
Dongtarn Villa, 405 Mu 12, Jomtien Beach, Pattaya
City. Tel: (038) 231049. 23 rooms.
Natural Park Beach Resort, 412 Mu 12, Jomtien
Beach, Pattaya City. Tel: (038) 231561-70. 116
rooms.
Nong Nooch Village, Sukhumvit Road, Sattahip.
Tel: (038) 429342, 429321. 62 rooms.
Orchid Lodge, 240 Mu 5, Beach Road, North
Pattaya. Tel: (038) 428161, 428175, 428323,
428133. 236 rooms.
Pattaya Leben, 124/7 Mu 9, Soi 4 North Pattaya.
Tel: (038) 427434, 427430. 76 rooms.
Pattaya Palace, Opp. Shinnawatra Thai Silk,
Pattaya Second Road. Tel: (038) 428409, 428487.
428066, 428319. 270 rooms.
Pattaya Park Beach Resort, 345 Jomtien Beach,
Pattaya City. Tel: (038) 423000/6, 429786. 240
rooms.
Ramada Pattaya Beach, 144/81 Mu 10, Pattaya
Second Road. Tel: (038) 428755/9. 360 rooms.
Royal Jomtien Resort, 408 Mu 12, Jomtien Beach,
Pattaya City. Tel: (038) 231350-69. 390 rooms.
Siam Bayshore, 559 Mu 10, Beach Road, South
Pattaya. Tel: (038) 428678/81. 270 rooms.
Siam Bayview, Soi 10, Pattaya Second Road.
Tel: (038) 423871/9. 260 rooms.
Sol Jomtien, 37/2-11 Mu 2, Na Jomtien, Sukhumvit
Road. Tel: (038) 231490/4. 137 rooms.
The Resort House, 396/1 Mu 12, Cliff Road,
Pattaya City. Tel: (038) 427479. 18 rooms.
Town In Town, 206 Mu 9, Central Pattaya Road.
Tel: (038) 426350/4. 360 rooms.
Tropicana, 98 Mu 9, Pattaya Second Road. Tel:
(038) 428645/8, 428516, 428566, 428158. 186
rooms.
Tropicana, 427 Mu 12 Jomtien Beach, Pattaya City.
Tel: (038) 231701/16, 232044/5. 400 rooms.
Wong Amat, 277-8 Naklua Soi 18, Pattaya City.
Tel; (038) 426990/9. 207 rooms.
Woodlands Resort, 164/1 Naklua Road, Pattaya
City. Tel: (038) 421707, 425661/2. 80 rooms.

(1,000 *baht* and over)
Ambassador City Jomtien Hotel, 21/10 Sukhumvit
Road, Km 155, Najomtien, Sattahip, 4,500 rooms.
Astoria Resort, 38/5 Soi Pingpa, Naklua Road,
Pattaya City. Tel: (038) 427061/9. 53 rooms.
Beverly Plaza, 59/35 Mu 10, Pratamnak Road,
Pattaya City. Tel: (038) 421278/9. 210 rooms.

Chomtalay, 321/6 Mu 12, Jomtien Beach, Pattaya City. Tel: (038) 231070. 49 rooms.

Dongtarn Resort, 45/7 Mu 12, Jomtien Beach. Tel: (038) 231191. 30 rooms.

Golden Cliff House, 352-55 Cliff Road, South Pattaya. Tel: (038) 424810/2, 423133. 48 rooms.

Grand Sole, 370 Mu 9, Pattaya Second Road. Tel: (038) 427555. 253 rooms.

Jomtien Garden, 44/14 Mu 12, Jomtien Beach. Tel: (038) 231001/4. 105 rooms.

Jomtien Palace, 401 Mu 12, Jomtien Beach. Tel: (038) 429149.144 rooms.

Mountain Beach, 378/16 Mu 12, Cliff Road, Pattaya City. Tel: (038) 426520/4. 320 rooms.

Nipa Lodge, 137 Mu 9, Central Pattaya Road. Tel: (038) 428321/2, 429185/6. 139 rooms.

Ocean View, 382 Mu 10, Beach Road, Pattaya City. Tel: (038) 428084, 428434. 112 rooms.

Pattaya Center, 224/27 Mu 10 Soi 12, Beach Road, South Pattaya. Tel: (038) 425877/8, 428692. 260 rooms.

Royal Classic, 129/16 Mu 9, Central Pattaya Road. Tel: (038) 427800/9. 272 rooms.

Royal Palace, 215/2 Pattaya Second Road, South Pattaya. Tel: (038) 425656/9, 426262/8. 350 rooms.

Royal Twins Palace, 213 Mu 10, Pattaya Second Road. Tel: (038) 420260/4. 350 rooms.

Sala Jomtien, 351 Mu 12, Jomtien Beach, Pattaya City. Tel: (038) 231074/8. 30 rooms.

Sunbeam, 217/27 Soi 8, Pattaya Second Road. Tel: (038) 427123/7. 270 rooms.

Swan Beach Resort, 132/3 Mu 12, Jomtien Beach, Pattaya City. Tel: (038) 231266. 126 rooms.

The Pattaya Garden, 157/77 Naklua Road, Pattaya City. Tel: (038) 426782/4. 416 rooms.

Villa Navin, 350 Mu 12, Jomtien Beach, Pattaya City. Tel: (038) 231065/7. 74 room.

White House Resort, 75/135-141 Jomtien Beach, Pattaya City. Tel: (038) 231184, 231310. 116 rooms.

(500 *baht* and over)

A-A Pattaya Hotel, 182 Pattaya Soi 13, Beach Road, Pattaya City. Tel: (038) 428656, 429057, 429444. 82 rooms.

Aqua Marina Cabana, 62/2 Na Jomtien Road, Pattaya City. Tel: (038) 231290/1. 29 rooms.

Baiyok Pattaya, 557 Mu 10, Cliff Road, South Pattaya. Tel: (038) 423300/2, 426024/6. 136 rooms.

Bangsaen Beach Resort, 55-150 Bangsaen Beach, Bangsaen. Tel: (038) 381675/7, 381628/9, 383236/8. 170 rooms.

Bangsaray Fishing Inn, Bangsaray, Sattahip. Tel: (038) 436095. 16 rooms.

Bay Breeze Hotel, 503/2 Opp. Soi 10, Pattaya Second Road. Tel: (038) 428384. 70 rooms.

Beach View, 389 Soi 2, Beach Road, North Pattaya. Tel: (038) 422660/2. 135 rooms.

Best House, Soi Pattaya Land 3, Pattaya City. Tel: (038) 423515. 20 rooms.

Bungalow 55555, 555/5 Mu 5, Naklua Soi 12, Pattaya City. Tel: (038) 421297. 72 rooms.

Ceasar Palace, 176 Mu 10, Pattaya Second Road. Tel: (038) 428607, 427684, 425724. 219 rooms.

Central Inn, 161/1 Soi Sukrudee, Central Pattaya Road. Tel: (038) 424697. 60 rooms.

Chalord Hotel, 60/1 Mu 10, South Pattaya. Tel: (038) 428651. 218 rooms.

Coral Inn, 411 mu 12, Jomtien Beach, Pattaya City. Tel: (038) 231283/7. 36 rooms.

Cosy Beach, 400 Mu 12, Cliff Road, South Pattaya. Tel: (038) 429344, 429334, 421802. 260 rooms.

Day Night Hotel, 20 Mu 2, South Pattaya Road. Tel: (038) 427620/1. 600 rooms.

Diamond Beach, 373/8 Mu 10, South Pattaya. Tel: (038) 428071, 429885/6. 118 rooms.

East Sea Resort, 170/1 Pattaya Naklua Road. Tel: (038) 426524/5. 90 rooms.

Flipper Lodge, 520/1 Soi 8, Beach Road, South Pattaya. Tel: (038) 426401/3. 72 rooms.

Furama Beach, Central Pattaya Road. Tel: (038) 428580/1. 51 rooms.

Furama Jomtien Beach, 125/16-17 Mu 12, Jomtien Beach, Pattaya City. Tel: (038) 231869/73. 32 rooms.

Garden Square, 131/8 Mu 5, Naklua Soi 12, Pattaya City. Tel: (038) 428929, 424929, 424180. 400 rooms.

Gardenia, 240/5 Pattaya Naklua Road. Tel: (038) 426356/7. 17 rooms.

Golden Beach Resort, Na Jomtien Road, Pattaya City. Tel: (038) 428205, 231590. 50 rooms.

Golden Beach, Opp. Soi 9, Pattaya Second Road. Tel: (038) 429960, 428891. 339 rooms.

Golden Town, Naklua Soi 12, North Pattaya, 23 rooms.

Grand, 103 Mu 10 Soi 14, South Pattaya. Tel: (038) 428286, 428249, 429696. 115 rooms.

Holiday Corner, 175/51 Soi 15, South Pattaya. Tel: (038) 426072. 39 rooms.

Island View, 401 Mu 14, Cliff Road, Pattaya City. Tel: (038) 429817/8, 428818. 209 rooms.

Jomtien Cosy Inn, 29/14 Soi Amnuaythip 2, Jomtien Beach, Pattaya City. Tel: (038) 231925/7. 28 rooms.

Jomtien Hotel, 403/34 Mu 12, Jomtien Road, Pattaya City. Tel: (038) 426600/1. 50 rooms.

Julie Complex, 235/5 Mu 10, Beach Road, South Pattaya. Tel: (038) 429968, 429918. 51 rooms.

King Resort, 112-113 Mu 7, Sattahip. Tel: (038) 231825. 120 rooms.

Knight Inn, 334/118 Jomtien Beach, Pattaya City. Tel: (038) 231475/6. 40 rooms.

Lek, 284/5 Mu 10 , Pattaya Second Road. Tel: (038) 425550/2. 76 rooms.

Little Duck Pattaya, 336/22 Mu 9, Central Pattaya Road. Tel: (038) 428104/5, 428065. 176 rooms.

Loma, 193 Mu 5, Naklua Road, Pattaya City. Tel: (038) 426027. 120 rooms.

Marine Beach, 131/62 Mu 12, Jomtien Beach. Tel: (038) 231129/30. 65 rooms.

Mermaid's Beach Resort, 75/102 Mu 12, Jomtien Beach, Pattaya City. Tel: (038) 231907. 103 rooms.
Mike, 339 Mu 9, Pattaya Second Road, South Pattaya. Tel: (038) 422222/9. 60 rooms.
Moonlight On Sea, 207-214 Mu 5, Naklua Road, Pattaya City. Tel: (038) 428128, 428150. 40 rooms.
Namfon Lodge, 388 Mu 9, Soi 2 North Pattaya. Tel: (038) 421296. 25 rooms.
Nautical Inn, 10/10 Mu 10, Beach Road, Pattaya City. Tel: (038) 428110, 429890. 80 rooms.
North Pattaya View, 256/24 Pattaya-Naklua Road. Tel: (038) 428093, 428215. 90 rooms.
On Hill Luxury House, 144/81 Mu 10, Jomtien Road. Tel: (038) 423844. 25 rooms.
Opal House, 75/182 Mu 12, Jomtien Beach, 21 rooms.
P.K. Villa, 595 Beach Road, South Pattaya. Tel: (038) 429107. 103 rooms.
Paradise Inn, 12 Mu 10, Cliff Road, Pattaya City. Tel: (038) 423300/2, 426024.6. 136 rooms.
Pattaya Inn Beach, 380 Soi 2, North Pattaya. Tel: (038) 428718/9,428400. 120 rooms.
Peace Resort, 179/40 Mu 5, North Pattaya. Tel: (038) 425706, 426605, 426608. 80 rooms.
Regent Marina, Srinakorn Center, North Pattaya. Tel: (038) 429977/8, 428015, 429298. 210 rooms.
S.S. Bangsaen Beach, 245/52 Mu 13, Bangsaen. Tel: (038) 383575/6, 381670, 371670. 76 rooms.
Sea Breeze, 374/12 Mu 12, Jomtien Beach. Tel: (038) 231056/9. 105 rooms.
Sea Sand Club, Km 163 Sukhumvit Road, Bangsaray, Sattahip. Tel: (038) 435163. 46 rooms.
Seaview Resort, 444 Mu 10 Soi 18, Naklua Road. Tel: (038) 429317, 429189. 247 rooms.
Serene, 564 Mu 10, Pattaya Second Road. Tel: (038) 422952, 423304, 428737. 45 rooms.
Siam Country Club, 500 Mu 9, Pornprapanimit, Pattaya City. Tel: (038) 428002, 428 062. 30 rooms.
Silversand Villa, 97 Mu 12, Jomtien Beach. Tel: (038) 231288, 231030. 107 rooms.
Skaw Beach, 519/97 Mu 10, Pattaya Second Road. Tel: (038) 421489. 60 rooms.
Sriracha Lodge, 4 Choemjomphon Road, Sriracha. Tel: (038) 311647, 311609. 113 rooms.
Sugar Palm Beach, 45/5 Mu 12, Jomtien Beach, Pattaya City. Tel: (038) 231386. 41 rooms.
Surf House, 44/45 Mu 12, Jomtien Beach. Tel: (038) 231029. 55 rooms.
Thai Garden Resort, 179/138 Mu 5, North Pattaya Road. Tel: (038) 426009, 422612. 183 rooms.
V.C. Pattaya, 492 Mu 10, South Pattaya. Tel: (038) 424504/8. 100 rooms.
Weekender, 78/20 Pattaya Second Road, North Pattaya. Tel: (038) 428720, 429461, 202 rooms.
Welcome Plaza, 213 Mu 10, Pattaya Second Road. Tel: (038) 424765/7, 426241. 268 rooms.
Windmill Resort, 665 Mu 5, Naklua Road, Pattaya City. Tel: (038) 425930. 101 rooms.
Wonder Land, 378/311 Cliff Road, Pattaya City. Tel: (038) 428366. 50 rooms.

KANCHANABURI

(3,000 *baht* and over)
River Kwai Resort, 9/1 Mu 3, Tambon Thamakham. Tel: (034) 515094/5. 256 rooms.

(1,500 *baht* and over)
Home Phu Toey, Tambon Thasao, Sai Yok. Tel: (02) 2803458/9, 2824043. 51 rooms.
Pung Waan Resort, 123/1 Tambon Thasao, Sai Yok. Tel: (034) 591017/8. 69 rooms.
Resotel Kanglawa Resort, 55 Mu 5, Tambon Wangkachae, Sai Yok. Tel: (034) 591036. 30 rooms.

(1,000 *baht* and over)
Kwai Yai Garden Resort, 99/9 Mu 3, Tambon Thamakham. Tel: (034) 523611/2. 60 rooms.
M.N. Kwai River Side, 64 Mu 2, Tambon Gaeng Seant. Tel: (034) 513167-8. 23 rooms.
River Kwai Hotel, 284/3-16 Saeng Chuto Road. Tel: (034) 511184, 511565. 127 rooms.
River Kwai Village Hotel, 72/ Mu 4, Tambon Thasao, Sai Yok. Tel: (034) 591055. 114 rooms.
Sinsomboon Resort, Tambon Tha-Khanoon, Thong Phapoom. Tel: (034) 511045, 513507. 40 rooms.

(500 *baht* and over)
Ban Chai Daen Phu Pa Phoom, Tambon Tha-Khanoon, Thong Phapoom. Tel: (034) 599035, 599048, 599063. 44 rooms.
Ban Suan Fon, 20/3 Mu 8, Tambon Gaeng Seant. Tel: (034) 513657/8. 18 rooms.
Jungle Raft Resort, Over Srinakharin Dam, Sisawat. Tel: (02) 2534504, 2535989, 22 rooms.
Kasem Island Resort, 27 Tambon Ban Tai. Tel: (034) 511359. 30 rooms.
Log Home Resort, 29/1 Mu 2, Tambon Pakprack. Tel: (034) 512282. 13 rooms.
Phukan Homtel, 209 Mu 2, Tambon Thamakham. Tel: (034) 512282. 16 rooms.
River Honey Well Resort, 208 Mu 8, Tambon Thamakham. Tel: (034) 514431, 514080 ext. 470. 20 rooms.
River Kwae Family Camp, 16/9 Mu 8, Tambon Gaeng Seant. Tel: (034) 512733. 5 rooms.
River Kwai Jungle House, 96/1 Mu 3, Sai Yok. Tel: (034) 561052. 80 rooms.
River Kwai Jungle Raft, Tambon Thasao, Sai Yok. Tel: (034) 2453069, 2475323, 76 rooms.
River Kwai Lodge, 164 Mu 2, Tambon Thamakham. Tel: (034) 513657/8. 54 rooms.
Sai Yok Valley Resort, Tambon Loom Soom, Sai Yok. Tel: (034) 591024. 30 rooms.
Suan Prasobsuk Resort, 6/1 Tambon Gaeng Seant. Tel: (034) 591024. 21 rooms.
Suan Sai Yok, Sai Yok. Tel: (02) 4124509, 4124869, 4129944. 25 rooms.
Three Pagodas Resort, 128 Mu 9, Tambon Nonghlu, Sangklaburi. Tel: (034) 595064. 53 rooms.

NAKHON NAYOK

(100 baht and over)
Cho Mamuang Cottage, 92 Mu 2, Tambon Sarika.
Tel: (01) 2120806. 11 rooms.
Chulachomklao Royal Military Academy Guest-house, Amphoe Muang. Tel: (037) 413010/4. 29 rooms.
Koblua Palace, 420 Thongchai Simuang Road.
Tel: (037) 311633, 311644. 96 rooms.
North Bungalow, 145 Mu 5, Sarika Road.
Tel: (037) 311814. 18 rooms.
Panchai Hotel, 342/1 Suwannason Road.
Tel: (037) 311399. 60 rooms.
Sida Resort, Amphoe Muang. Tel: (02) 2331552, 2239328. 160 rooms.
Suan Pho Daeng, 124 Mu 2, Tambon Sarika.
Tel: (037) 312086. 10 rooms.
Wang Takrai, 22/1 Mu 1, Nangrong Road.
Tel: (037) 311063. 14 rooms.

NAKHON PATHOM

(1,500 baht and over)
Rose Garden, 21 Mu 2, Sam Phran, Nakhon Pathom. Tel: (034) 322772/4. 116 rooms.

(500 baht and over)
Nakhon Inn, 55 Rajvithi Road. Tel: (034) 251152/4. 70 rooms.
Whale Hotel, 151/79 Rajvithi Road.
Tel: (034) 251020/4, 253855/63. 136 rooms.

(100 baht and over)
Mit Phaisan, 120/30 Phaya-Phan Road.
Tel: (034) 242422, 243122. 59 rooms.
Sutha Thip, 44/1 Thesaban Road.
Tel: (034) 242242. 54 rooms.

PHETCHABURI

(3,500 baht and over)
Dusit Resort & Polo Club, 1349 Phetkasem Road, Phetchaburi. Tel: (032) 520009. 308 rooms.

(3,000 baht and over)
Golden Sands, Phetkasem Road. Tel: (032) 471985/8. 226 rooms.

(2,000 baht and over)
The Regent Cha-Am Beach Resort, 849/21 Phetkasem Road. Tel: (032) 471480/90, 471493/95. 650 rooms.

(1,500 baht and over)
Beach Garden Hotel, 249/21 Phetkasem Road. Tel: (032) 471350/1, 471334/6, 471291/2. 230 rooms.
Cha-Am Methavalai, 220 Ruamchit Road.
Tel: (032) 471028/9, 471145/6. 118 rooms.
Cha-Am Royal Beach, 82/6 Phetkasem Road, Chao Samran Beach. Tel: (032) 427477, 427852. 75 rooms.

Chom Hat, 264/1 Ruamchit Road.
Tel: (032) 471325. 27 rooms.

(1,000 baht and over)
Cha-Am Lagoon Resort, Klong Khon-Cha-Am Road. Tel: (032) 471326/7.
Cha Am Marina Resort, 777 Phetkasem Road.
Tel: (032) 471851/7. 56 rooms.
Holiday Resort, Phetkasem Road. Tel: (032) 471473/4. 24 rooms.
Kaenchan, 241/3 Ruamchit Road.
Tel: (032) 471314, 471203. 48 rooms.

(500 baht and over)
Cha-Am Cabana Resort, 186 Khlong-Thian Road.
Tel: (032) 471861. 33 rooms.
Cha-Am Paradise, Ruamchit Road.
Tel: (032) 471072. 8 rooms.
Cha-Am Park Resort, 346 Chao Lai Road.
Tel: (032) 471181, 471736. 25 rooms.
Hat Petch Resort, North Cha-Am.
Tel: (032) 471630.
Narumon Lucky House, Ruamchit Road.
Tel: (032) 471220, 471440. 60 rooms.
Paisiri, 259/9 Ruamchit Road. Tel: (032) 471047, 471873. 59 rooms.
Rua Makham Villa, 236 Ruamchit Road.
Tel: (032) 471073/76. 48 rooms.
Rung Aran, 236/26 Ruamchit Road.
Tel: (032) 471226. 10 rooms.
Sam Resort, 246/9 Ruamchit Road.
Tel: (032) 471197. 22 rooms.
Santisuk, Ruamchit Road. Tel: (032) 471212/4. 62 rooms.
Taworn, Ruamchit Road. Tel: (032) 471359. 10 rooms.
Thiptharee Place, 274/34-35 Ruamchit Road.
Tel: (032) 471879. 21 rooms.

HUA HIN

(3,500 baht and over)
Royal Garden Village, 45 Phetkasem Road, Hua Hin. Tel: (032) 513412/5. 162 rooms.

(2,500 baht and over)
Royal Garden Resort, 107/1 Phetkasem Road, Hua Hin. Tel: (032) 511881/4. 220 rooms.
Sofitel Central, 1 Damnoenkasem Road.
Tel: (032) 512021/30. 218 rooms.

(1,500 baht and over)
The Chalet Hua Hin, 144/7 Nongkae-Takiap Road, Takiap Beach. Tel: (032) 511228. 14 rooms.
Club Aldiana, 9 Pak-Nam Pran Buri.
Tel: (032) 631235. 60 rooms.
Hua Hin Grand Hotel & Plaza, 222/2 Phetkasem Road, Hua Hin. Tel: (032) 511765, 511391. 168 rooms.
Hua Hin Sport Villa, 10/95 Phetkasem, Road, Hua Hin. Tel: (032) 511453, 511391, 512158. 9 rooms.

Melia Hua Hin, 33/3 Naretdmri Road, Hua Hin. Tel: (032) 511006, 51135/6. 297 rooms.
Sailom, 29 Phetkasem Rod, Hua Hin Beach. Tel: (032) 511890/1, 512017/8. 66 rooms.

(1,000 *baht* and over)
Ban Phutraksa, 16 Nabkehat. Tel: (032) 511062. 9 rooms.

(500 *baht* and over)
Anantasila Villa, 13/5 Huadon, Takiap Beach. 6 rooms.
Ban Boosarin, 8/8 Poonsuk Road Hua Hin. Tel: (032) 512076, 512089. 10 rooms.
Ban Khun Kung, 236/23 Mubn Jamjuree, Phetksem Road, Hua Hin. Tel: (032) 512079. 7 rooms.
Ban Somboon, 13/4 Damnoenkasem Road, Hua Hin. Tel: (032) 511538. 9 rooms.
Bangpu By Resort, 133 Mu 8, Tambon Samroiyot, Pran Buri. Tel: (032) 621664. 21 rooms.
Fongkluan Guesthouse, 29 Koh Takiap, Takiap Beach. Tel: (032) 512402. 5 rooms.
Had Kaew Beach Resort, 39 Mu 9, Phetkasem Road, Bangsaphan. Tel: (032) 601555. 34 rooms.
Had Thong, 7 Su-Suk Road. Tel: (032) 611960/7. 132 rooms.
Hua Hin Place, 55/6 Phetkasem Road, Hua-Hin. Tel: (032) 511151, 512436. 30 rooms.
Janchai Bunglow, 117/1-18 Phetkasem Road, Hua Hin. Tel: (032) 511461. 29 rooms.
Napapan Guesthouse, 144/4-6 Nongkae-Takiap Road, Takiap Beach. Tel: (032) 512331. 8 rooms.
Nongkae Cabin House, 79 Nongke-Takiap, Takiap Beach. Tel: (032) 511291. 40 rooms.
Sam Roi Yot National Park, Forestry Department. Tel: (02) 5790529, 5794842. 7 rooms.
Sirin, Damnoenkasem Road, Hua Hin. Tel: (032) 511150, 512045. 25 rooms.
Thip Urai Guesthouse, 113/27-28 Phetkasem Road, Hua Hin. Tel: (032) 512210. 8 rooms.
Yom Di Cottages Privacy, Pran Buri, Prachuap. Tel: (02) 2217753, 4270911. 11 rooms.

RATCHABURI

(100 *baht* and over)
Araya, 187/1-2 Kraiphet Road, Tambon Namuang. Tel: (032) 337782. 80 rooms.
Ban Pong Inn, 21 Saeng Chuto Road. Tel: (032) 211923. 70 rooms.
Friend Motel, 59 Mu 4, Tambon Khok-Mo. Tel: (032) 321221. 24 rooms.
House 78, 137 Mu 1, Phetkasem. Tel: (032) 321221. 30 rooms.
Nam Sin, 2/16 Kraiphet Road. Tel: (032) 337551. 75 rooms.
Noknoi, Tambon Damnoensaduak, Damnoensaduak. Tel: (032) 251382. 30 rooms.
Thai Nam Riverside, 19/50 Saeng Chuto Road, Ban Pong, Ratchaburi. Tel: (032) 211947/8. 60 rooms.

Villa Hotel, Tambon Tapa, Ban Pong. Tel: (032) 221312. 55 rooms.

RAYONG

(3,500 *baht* and over)
Swiss-Purimas Beach Hotel, 34 Payoon Namrin Road, Ban Chang. Tel: (038) 611593. 79 rooms.

(3,000 *baht* and over)
Payoon Resort, Ban Chang. Tel: (01) 2114726. 30 rooms.

(2,000 *baht* and over)
Hin Suai Nam Sai, 250 Mu 2, Charkpong, Klaeng. Tel: (038) 611952. 174 rooms.
Novotel Rim Phe Rayong Hotel, 4/5 Mu 3, Phe, Klaeng-Kram Road, Charkpong, Klaeng. Tel: (038) 614678, 614088. 120 rooms.
Palmeraie Beach, 177 Mu 1, Ban Phe, Laem Mae Phim Road, Klaeng. Tel: (01) 2116328, 2117763. 65 rooms.
Rayong Resort, Laemtarn, Ban Phe. Tel: (038) 651000/6. 170 rooms.

(1,500 *baht* and over)
Ban Pa Mai, 105/25 Mae Ramphung Beach Road, Amphoe Muang. Tel: (038) 615808. 10 rooms.
Ban Phe Cabana, 205/7 Mu 3, Amphoe Muang. Tel: (01) 2114888. 35 rooms.
Bungalow Kon Ao Sea Food, Ban Kon Ao, Me Ramphung Beach, Amphoe Muang, 9 rooms.
Chonnikarn, 77/2 Tapong, Amphoe Muang. Tel: (02) 3746220. 10 rooms.
Laem Ya Resort, 78/1 Mu 1, Phe, Amphoe Muang. Tel: (038) 651355. 18 rooms.
Milford Banchang Beach Hotel, 168/171 Payoon Beach, Pala, Ban Chang. Tel: (038) 603019/23. 156 rooms.
Rayong Chalet, 8/4 Mu 3, Charkpong, Klaeng-Kram Road, Klaeng. Tel: (02) 2603592/9. 92 rooms.

(1,000 *baht* and over)
Ban Hin Khao, 146/13 Mu 1, Mae Ramphung Beach, Amphoe Muang. Tel: (02) 2341573. 14 rooms.
Ban Sai Kaeo, 210 Mu 2, Charkpong, Klaeng. Tel: (02) 3902146, 3916937. 15 rooms.
Ban Sang Resort, 169 Mu 2, Phe-Klaeng-Karm Road, Charkpong, Klaeng. Tel: (038) 612447. 24 rooms.
Mae Phim Chalet, 116/2 Mu 4, Hat Mae Phim, Klaeng. Tel: (02) 3914348, 3920268. 12 rooms.
P.M.Y. Beach Hotel, Beach Road, Pak Nam Mai, Amphoe Muang. Tel: (038) 613002/3. 35 rooms.
Pines Beach Hotel, 38 Mu 1, Phe, Muang. Tel: (038) 651636/40. 134 rooms.
Sin Siam Resort, 235 Laem Mae Phim, Tambon Kram, Klaeng. Tel: (02) 4373648, 4391385/6. 70 rooms.

Song Ruen Villa, 78/17 Mu 1, Ban Kon Ao, Phe. Tel: (038) 651546/50. 21 rooms.

(500 *baht* and over)
Amornphan Villa, 147 Mu 3, Charkpong, Klaeng. Tel: (02) 5125591/4. 49 rooms.
Ban Prom Pong, 144/4 Mae Ramphung Beach Road, Tapong, Bkk. Tel: (02) 2341337. 24 rooms.
Ban Sinsamut, Mu 3, Tha Rua Klaeng, Muang, Rayong. Tel: (02) 2529467, 2587251. 12 rooms
Ban Thale Kram, Tha Rua Kleng Square, Kleng. Tel: (01) 2116092. 16 rooms.
Bang Bai Resort, 4/4 Mu 3, Charkpong, Klaeng. Tel: (02) 5131129, 5110840, 5121966. 30 rooms.
Chat Thong Beach, 78/37 Mu 1, Ban Kon Ao, Phe. Tel: (02) 3212242. 6 rooms.
Di Prathap Chit, 82 Beach Road, Tambon Paknam. Tel: (038) 613611, 614271. 14 rooms.
Hat Sai Thong, Mu 3, Tambon Maptaphut. Tel: (01) 9165446. 43 rooms.
Inthorn Cabana, 105/22 Mae Ramphung Beach. Tel: (038) 611578. 7 rooms.
Kao Laem Ya National Park, Ban Kon Ao, Amphoe Muang. Tel: (02) 5790529, 5794842. 9 rooms.
Kon Ao Bay Resort, 89/4 Mu 1, Mae Ramphung Beach, Phe. Tel: (038) 651758. 8 rooms.
Melody Hotel, 144/1 Ratbamrung Road. Tel: (038) 611259. 38 rooms.
Noree House, 82/12 Mu 1, Phe. Tel: (038) 651748.
Pakarang Resort, 115 Mu 3, Charkpong, Klaeng. Tel: (02) 2240062 ext. 84. 57 rooms.
Phimnipha Villa, 177 Tambon Kram, Klaeng. Tel: (02) 3902191/2, 3902132. 13 rooms.
Premvadee Sea View, 105/1 Mu 1, Phe. Tel: (038) 651740. 24 rooms.
Punksachart Resort, 144/3 Mu 1, Mae Ramphung Beach, Tapong. Tel: (02) 5850221. 50 rooms.
Raya Island Resort, Man Klang Island, Bkk. Tel: (02) 3166717. 17 rooms.
Rayong City Mansion, Ratbamrung Road, Soi 4, Muang. Tel: (038) 614872/3, 613887. 43 rooms.
Rayong Orchid, Sukhumvit Road. Tel: (038) 614340/9. 156 rooms.
Rungnapha Lodge, 154 Suan Son-Wang Kaeo Road, Klaeng. Tel: (038) 671729. 105 rooms.
Samet Resort, Samet Island, 9 rooms.
Samet Villa, Ao Thian. Tel: (038) 611035, 651681/2. 40 rooms.
Sap Singha, Ban Kon Ao, Phe. Tel: (038) 651559, 651560. 6 rooms.
Sea Wind Resort, Mae Ramphung Beach Road, Phe. Tel: (038) 651562. 50 rooms.
Star Hotel, 109 Rayong Trade Centre Lane No. 4. Tel: (038) 614901/7. 248 rooms.
Suan Thip Varee Hotel, 215 Mu 3, Tha-Rua Klaeng Road, Charkpong, Klaeng. Tel: (02) 2156600, 2167317. 29 rooms.
Thale Ngam Resort, 205/1 Mu 3, Klaeng. Tel: (038) 613833 ext. 300. 20 rooms.
Tup Samet Village, 164 Mu 1, Charkpong, Klaeng. Tel: (02) 2341314/5. 16 rooms.

Vanda Resort, 61/4 Mu 4, Klaeng-Kram Road, Tambon Klaeng. Tel: (01) 2131993. 18 rooms.
Wang Thong Resort, 77/12 Mu 1, Phe. Tel: (038) 651691. 19 rooms.
Wong Duan Resort, Ao Wong Duan. Tel: (038) 651777, 651819. 54 rooms.
Wong Duan Villa, Ao Wong Duan. Tel: (038) 652300. 51 rooms.

SAMUT SAKHON

(100 *baht* and over)
Kasem Hotel, 927/28 Sethakij Road, Mahachai. Tel: (034) 411078. 54 rooms.
New Friend, 69/2 Mu 1 Ekachai Road, Tambon Thachin. Tel: (034) 411477. 50 rooms.

SAMUT SONGKHRAM

(100 *baht* and over)
Alongkorn 2, 540 Pomkaew Road, Tambon Mae Klong. Tel: (034) 711709. 46 rooms.
Mae Klong Hotel, 546/10-13 Petchsamut Road, Tambon Maeklong. Tel: (034) 711150. 18 rooms.

SUPHAN BURI

(500 *baht* and over)
Kalapruk Hotel, 135/1 Pracha Tipatai Road. Tel: (035) 522555/7. 80 rooms.

TRAT

(3,000 *baht* and over)
Ko Kood Island Resort, 942/100 3rd Floor, Charn Issara Tower, Rama IV Road, Bangkok 10500. Tel: (02) 2337276, 2337287. 20 rooms.

(2,000 *baht* and over)
Lao Ya Island Resort, 44 Pokprai, Tambon Wangkrajae. Tel: (039) 512552, 511145 ext. 203. 24 rooms.

(1,000 *baht* and over)
Ko Chang Resort, 12-3 Mu 1, Laem Ngop. Tel: (039) 512818. 88 rooms.
Ko Kradat Resort, Ko Kradat. Tel: (039) 511145 ext. 32. 32 rooms.
Ko Mak Resort and Cabana, 1 Suanlamthong, Patanakarn Road, Suan Luang, Bangkok 10250. Tel: (02) 3196714. 20 rooms.
Ko Sai Khao Resort, 8-10 Vichit Chanya Road, Ko Phrao, Tambon Bang Pra. Tel: (039) 511429, 511824. 5 rooms.
Twin Island Beach Resort, Ko Ngam, Laem Ngop. Tel: (02) 3186073/4. 22 rooms.
Your Place Exclusive Island Resort, 44 Ponkapri Road, Ko Laoya. Tel: (039) 512552. 22 rooms.

(500 *baht* and over)
Suan Poo, 199 Tambon Nongkansong.
Tel: (039) 512400. 15 rooms.
TKK. Bungalow, 27/3 Tambon Bangplid, Amphoe
Laem Ngop, 8 rooms.

THE NORTH & NORTH-EAST

BURI RAM

(100 *baht* and over)
Chai Charoen, 114-116 Niwas Road.
Tel: (044) 611559. 35 rooms.
Grand, 137 Niwas Road. Tel: (044) 611089,
611179. 96 rooms.
Kasemsook, 41 Pracha Santisook Road, Nang-
Rong. Tel: (044) 631039. 8 rooms.
Tepnakorn, 139 Jira Road. Tel: (044) 613400,
613401/2. 30 rooms.
Thai Hotel, 38/1 Romburi Road.
Tel: (044) 612462, 611112. 96 rooms.

CHAIYAPHUM

(100 *baht* and over)
Charoen, 196/7 Soi 1 Yuttitham Road.
Tel: (044) 811194/5. 36 rooms.
Lertnimitra, 1/447 Niwetrat Road.
Tel: (044) 811522/3. 96 rooms.
Phaibun, 227/41-4 Yuttitham Road.
Tel: (044) 811021. 20 rooms.
Sirichai, 565 Nonmuang Road. Tel: (044) 811543,
812299. 102 rooms.

CHIANG MAI

(3,000 *baht* and over)
Chiang Mai Orchid, 100-102 Huay Kaew Road.
Tel: (053) 222091-9. 267 rooms.

(2,000 *baht* and over)
Chiang Mai Plaza, 22 Sridonchai Road.
Tel: (053) 270036/50. 444 rooms.
Holiday Inn Green Hill, 24 Super Highway Road.
Tel: (053) 214112, 211226. 168 rooms.
Novotel Suriwongse, 110 Changklan Road.
Tel: (053) 270051/63. 168 rooms.
Royal Princess (Dusit Inn), 122 Changklan Road.
Tel: (053) 281033/34. 198 rooms.

(1,500 *baht* and over)
Chiang Mai Hills, 18 Huay Kaew Road.
Tel: (053) 210030/5. 300 rooms.
Dusit Inn, 122 Chang Klan Road.
Tel: (053) 281033. 198 rooms.
Holiday Inn Green Hills Chiang Mai, 24 Chiang
Mai-Lampang Road, Tambon Changphuak. Tel:
(053) 224112, 221602, 217409, 211226. 200
rooms.
Lanna Palace, 184 Changklan Road.
Tel: (053) 270722/51. 205 rooms.

Lanna Ville, 555 Super Highway.
Tel: (053) 217784, 210740/4. 116 rooms.
Mae Ping, 153 Sridonchai Road. Tel: (053) 270160/
8. 374 rooms.
Mae Rim Lagoon, 65/1 Mu 6 Mae Rim-Samoeng
Road, Mae Rim District. Tel: (053) 297288/90. 30
rooms.
Rim Ping Garden, 411 Charoenprathet Road.
Tel: (053) 281050/60. 20 rooms.
The Empress, 199 Chang Klan Road.
Tel: (053) 270240, 272977, 272020. 373 rooms.

(1,000 *baht* and over)
Arcade Inn, 1 Kaewnawarat Road.
Tel: (053) 249721, 249723. 114 rooms.
Chiang Inn, 100 Chang Khlan Road.
Tel: (053) 270070/6. 170 rooms.
Chiang Mai Garden, 330 Super Highway Road, Soi
Lanna Hospital. Tel: (053) 210240/3. 106 rooms.
City Inn, 154 Rajmanka Road. Tel: (053) 279864,
275396. 136 rooms.
Northern Inn, 234/12 Maneenopparat Road.
Tel: (053) 270100/7. 100 rooms.
Pornping Tower, 46-48 Charoenprathet Road.
Tel: (053)270100/7. 325 rooms.
Poy Luang, 146 Super Highway Road.
Tel: (053) 242633. 227 rooms.
Rincome, 301 Huay Kaew Road. Tel: (053) 221044.
158 rooms.
River View Lodge, 25 Charoenprathet Road.
Tel: (053) 271110. 36 rooms.
Rung Arun, 1/5 Mu 7, Amphoe San Kamphaeng.
Tel: (053) 251191 ext. 2020. 36 rooms.
Wang Inn, 29/1 Mu 2, Charoenmuang.
Tel: (053) 249855. 135 rooms.

(500 *baht* and over)
Ban Chiang Roy, 23/1 Asrug Road.
Tel: (053) 213173, 222052. 80 rooms.
Chiang Mai, 502 Huay Kaew Road.
Tel: (053) 221418, 222052. 155 rooms.
Diamond (Petngam), 33/10 Charoenprathet Road.
Tel: (053) 270080/5. 135 rooms.
Erawan Resort, 30 Mu 2, Tambon Pongyang, Mae
Rim. Tel: (053) 251191/4, 59 rooms.
Garden Palm Resort, 133/1 Mu 7, Saraphi.
Tel: (053) 248441. 13 rooms.
Hod Resort, Chiang Mai-Maesarieng Road.
Tel: (053) 236548. 13 rooms.
Holiday Garden, 16/16 Huay Kaew Road.
Tel: (053) 210901/4. 170 rooms.
Iyara, 199 Chotana Road. Tel: (053) 222723. 100
rooms.
Kangsadarn Resort, Km 18.5, Mae Rim-Samerng
Road, Mae Rim. Tel: (053) 212209, 232551.
Krisadadoi Resort, Km 14, Hang Dong-Samerng
Road, Hang Dong. Tel: (053) 248419.
Lanna View, 558 Chiang Mai-Lamphun, Soi Lanna
Hospital. Tel: (053) 217785. 114 rooms.
Mae Hong Son Resort, 50-52 Tha Pae Road.
Tel: (053) 249066, 236269. 34 rooms.

Mae Sa Resort, Km 3, Mae Rim-Samerng Road, Muang Mai, 502 Huay Kaew Road.
Tel: (053) 222499. 155 rooms.
Park Inn Thana, Charoenprathet Soi 8.
Tel: (053) 242633. 120 rooms.
Prince, 3 Taiwang Road. Tel: (053) 236396, 236944. 108 rooms.
Providence Chiang Mai, 99/9 Huay Kaew Road.
Tel: (053) 221750, 222122. 125 rooms.
Sarapee Resort, 223 Super Highway, Chiang Mai-Lampang Road, Sarapee.
Sritokyo, 6 Boonruangrit Road. Tel: (053) 213899, 211100/3. 111 rooms.
Suan Doi, 38/3 Chantarasap Lane, Huay Kaew Road. 26 rooms.
Suan Rintr, Km 9, Mae Rim-Samerng Road. 21 rooms.
Top North Center, 42 Moonmuang Road.
Tel: (053) 210531. 43 rooms.
Utthayan Lanna Resort, 1 Mu 4, Hang Dong.
Tel: (053) 248434. 23 rooms.
Wangtarn Resort, 35/1 Tambon Ruang Nua, Doi Saket. Tel: (053) 211185-6 ext. 2534. 45 rooms.
Yod Doi Resort, Km 15 Hang Dong-Samerng Road, Hang Dong. Tel: (053) 236548, 232032. 9 rooms.

CHIANG RAI

(2,000 *baht* and over)
Delta Golden Triangle Resort, 222 Mu 1, Golden Triangle, Chiang Saen. Tel: (053) 777031, 777001-4. 73 rooms.
Dusit Island Resort, 1129 Kraisorasit Road.
Tel: (053) 715777-9. 270 rooms.
Le Meridien Baan Boran, Golden Triangle, Chiang Saen. Tel: (053) 716678, 716690. 110 rooms.

(1,500 *baht* and over)
Rimkok Resort, 6 Mu 4, Chiang Rai-Thaton Road.
Tel: (053) 716445-60. 256 rooms.

(1,000 *baht* and over)
Chiang Rai Inn, 661 Uttarakit Road,
Tel: (053) 712673, 711483, 717700-5. 77 rooms.
Little Duck Chiang Rai, 199 Phaholyothin Road.
Tel: (053) 715620-38. 330 rooms.
Rim Chan Resort, 17 Mae Chan. Tel: (053) 771882-3. 30 rooms.
Wang Come, 869/90 Pemawipat Road. Tel: (053) 711800, 713841-8. 220 rooms.
Wang Tong, 299 Phaholyothin Road, Mae Sai.
Tel: (053) 731248, 732231. 150 rooms.
Wiang Inn, 893 Phaholyothin Road.
Tel: (053) 711533. 258 rooms.

(500 *baht* and over)
Golden Triangle Inn, 590 Phaholyothin Road.
Tel: (053) 711339. 39 rooms.
Holiday Park, 216/2 Phaholyothin Road.
Tel: (053) 712243. 47 rooms.
Inn Come, 176/2 Rat Bamrung Road.
Tel: (053) 717850. 111 rooms.

Laan Tong Lodge, Mae Chan. Tel: (053) 772049, 772050. 24 bamboo cottages.
Linleepark Inn, 94/1 Super Highway Road.
Tel: (053) 711415. 16 rooms.
Maesalong Resort, Doi Maesalong, Mae Chan.
Tel: (053) 714047, 713400. 20 rooms.
Saenphu, 390 Banphraprakarn Road, Tambon Wiang.
Tel: (053) 717300-9. 121 rooms.
Thima Inn, 21/9 Ratchayotha Road.
Tel: (053) 717248. 80 rooms.
Wangcome Annex, Chiang Rai Trade Center.
Tel: (053) 711800, 711811m 712971-3, 43 rooms.
Yonok Lake View, 109 Mu 3, Bankotao, Tambon Yonok Chiang Saen. Tel: (01) 513129. 16 rooms.

KALASIN

(100 *baht* and over)
Sang Thong, 100-102 Kalasin Road,
Tel: (043) 811555. 31 rooms.
Suphak, 81/7 Saneha Road. Tel: (043) 811315, 811031. 52 rooms.
Phaibun, 125/1-2 Somphamit Road.
Tel: (043) 811661. 46 rooms.

KAMPHAENG PHET

(100 *baht* and over)
Chakangrao, 123/1 Thesa Road. Tel: (055) 711325. 116 rooms.
Navarat, 2 Soi Prapan, Thesa Road.
Tel: (055) 711106, 711211-9. 78 rooms.
Phet, 99 Soi 3, Wichit Road. Tel: (055) 712810-8. 259 rooms.

KHON KAEN

(500 *baht* and over)
Kaen Inn, 56 Klang Muang Road.
Tel: (043) 236276, 237744, 286888. 163 rooms.
Khon Kaen, 43/2 Phimphasut Road.
Tel: (043) 237711, 237766. 140 rooms.
Kosa, 250-252 Si Chan Road. Tel: (043) 225014-8. 92 rooms.
Rosesukon, 1/10 Klang Muang Road.
Tel: (043) 238576-9. 82 rooms.

(100 *baht* and over)
Grand, 39 Lang Muang Road. Tel: (043) 236690. 70 rooms.
Kaen Nakhon, 690 Si Chan Road.
Tel: (043) 224268, 224272. 100 rooms.
Muang Inn, 41/1-6 Na-Muang Road.
Tel: (043) 238667-8, 238477-8. 37 rooms.
Phu Inn, 26 Sathit Yuttitham Road.
Tel: (043) 243174-6. 98 rooms.
Roma, 50/2 Klang Muang Road.
Tel: (043) 236276, 237206. 109 rooms.
Sawaddi, 177/9 Lang Muang Road.
Tel: (043) 221600, 222433. 60 rooms.

LAMPANG

(500 baht and over)
Lampang River Lodge, 330 Mu 11, Tambon Chomphu. Tel: (054) 217054. 120 rooms.
Thipchang Lampang, 54/22 Takrao Noi. Tel: (054) 224273, 226501-6. 130 rooms.

(100 baht and over)
Arunsak, 90/9 Boonyawat Road. Tel: (054) 217344, 217532. 50 rooms.
Asia Lampang, 299 Boonyawat, Road. Tel: (054) 227844-7. 73 rooms.
Khelang Nakorn, 719-20 Suandok Road. Tel: (054) 226137, 222846-7. 102 rooms.
Kim, 168 Boonyawat Road. Tel: (054) 217588, 217721. 40 rooms.
Kiu Lom Resort, (38 km/24 miles from Town), Tambon Banlang. Tel: (054) 217186.
Mae Tha Resort, Km 45 Chiang Mai-Lamphun Road, Mae Tha. Tel: 01-2117712. 104 rooms.
Sakol, 139/9 Phaholyothin Road. Tel: (054) 217573. 40 rooms.
Siam, 260/26-29 Chatchai Road. Tel: (054) 217472, 217277, 217642. 82 rooms.
Sri Sanga, 213-215/1-2 Boonyawat Road. Tel: (054) 217070, 217811. 34 rooms.

LOEI

(100 baht and over)
Cotton Inn, 191/1-9 Charoenrat Road. Tel: (042) 811302, 812353. 63 rooms.
Kings, 11/9-12 Chumsai Road. Tel: (042) 811701, 811783. 50 rooms.
Phuluang, 55 Charoen Road. Tel: (042) 811532, 811570. 86 rooms.
Thai Udom, 122/1 Charoenrat Road. Tel: (042) 811763. 76 rooms.

MAE HONG SON

(1,500 baht and over)
Bai Yok Chalet, 90 Khumlumpraphat Road. Tel: (053) 611486. 40 rooms.
Holiday Inn, 114/5-7 Khumlumpraphat Road. Tel: (053) 611390, 612108, 612212, 612324-9. 114 rooms.
Mae Hong Son Mountain Inn, 112 Khunlumpraphat Road. Tel: (053) 611175, 611135. 80 rooms.
Tara Mae Hong Son, 149 Mu 8, Tambon Pang Moo. Tel: (053) 611473, 611272, 611483, 104 rooms.

(500 baht and over)
Mae Hong Son Resort, 24 Ban Huai Dua, Tel: (053) 611406. 40 rooms.
Sammok Villa, 28/1 Amphoe Muang. Tel: (053) 611478. 40 rooms.

(100 baht and over)
Ing-Doi Resort, Amphoe Muang. Tel: (053) 611074. 16 rooms.
Mae Sariang Resort, 41 Laeng Phanit Road, Amphoe Mae Sariang. Tel: (053) 681055, 681099. 10 rooms.
Mae Thee, 55 Khunlumpraphat Road. Tel: (053) 612141. 38 rooms.
Mit Aree Hotel & Guest House, 34 Mu 2, Viang Mai Road. Tel: (053) 681109, 681280. 70 rooms.
Mit Aree, 158 Mu 2, Mae Sariang Roa, Mae Sariang. Tel: (053) 681110, 681279. 50 rooms.
Rim Nam Klang Doi, 108 Ban Huai Dua, Mu 3. Tel: (053) 611142. 40 rooms.
Siam, 23 Khunlumpraphat Road. Tel: (053) 611148. 26 rooms.

MAHA SARAKHAM

(100 baht and over)
Wasu, 1096/3 Damnoen Nat Road. Tel: (043) 711046, 711202. 104 rooms.

NAKHON PHANOM

(500 baht and over)
The Mae Nam Kong Grand View, 527 Sunthon Wichit Road. Tel: (042) 513564-73. 114 rooms.

(100 baht and over)
Charoensuk, 250 Bumrung Muang Road. Tel: (042) 511130. 38 rooms.
First, 16 Si Thep Road. Tel: (042) 511253. 63 rooms.
Grand, 210 Si Thep Road, Tel: (042) 511526, 513788. 45 rooms.
Lim-Charoen, 167/67 Chayangkun Road, Amphoe That Phanom. Tel: (042) 541019. 23 rooms.
Nakhon Phanom, 403 Aphiban Bancha Road. Tel: (042) 511455, 511074. 79 rooms.
River Inn, 137 Sunthon Wichit Road. Tel: (042) 511305. 16 rooms.
Si-Thep, 197 Si-Thep Road, Tel: (042) 511343, 512395, 511679, 512284. 87 rooms.
Winsor, 272 Bamrung Muang Road. Tel: (042) 511946. 50 rooms.

NOKHON RATCHASIMA

(2,000 baht and over)
Golden Valley Resort, 188 Mu 5, Tharat Road, Pakchong. Tel: (01) 33508803. 86 rooms.

(1,500 baht and over)
Juldis Khao Yai Resort, 54 Mu 4, Thanarat Road, Pakchong. Tel: (02) 255 5070-4, 255 2480, 255 4960, 235 2414-21 ext. 71129. 56 rooms.
Sima Thani, Mittraphap Road, Tel: (044) 243812, 251102-4. 135 rooms.

(1,000 baht and over)
Rimtarn Inn, 430 Mittraphap Road, Pakchong. Tel: (044) 313364-8. 42 rooms.

(500 baht and over)
Chomsurang, 270/1-2 Mahadthai Road.
Tel: (044) 257081-9. 168 rooms.
Phuphaya, 400/4 Mittraphap Road, Pakchong.
Tel: (044) 313134-7. 56 rooms.
Sophanavej Resort, 112/4 Thanarat Road,
Pakchong. Tel: (02) 3772985, 3755013-4, 3755338.
30 rooms.
Wanree Resort, 7/5 Km 22.5 Thanarat Road,
Pakchong. Tel: (02) 3942112, 3847273. 29 rooms.

(100 baht and over)
Anachak, 62/1 Chomsurangyart Road.
Tel: (044) 243825, 245817. 99 rooms.
At-Sadang, 315 Atsadang Road. Tel: (044) 242514,
257330. 40 rooms.
Cathay, 3692/6 Ratchadamnoen Road.
Tel: (044) 242889, 252067. 48 rooms.
Chumphon, 124 Pho-Klang Road.
Tel: (044) 252453,257121. 71 rooms.
Eknakorn, 120 Jompol Road. Tel: (044) 242504,
255192. 53 rooms.
Empire, 62/1 Jomsurangyart Road.
Tel: (044) 243825, 245817. 99 rooms.
Far Sang, 112-114 Mukkhamontri Road.
Tel: (044) 242143, 243342. 77 rooms.
Farthai, 35-39 Poklang Road. Tel: (044) 242533-
4. 90 rooms.
First, 132-136 Burin Road. Tel: (044) 255203,
255201. 100 rooms.
Great Inn, 92 Mu 3 Mittraphap Road.
Tel: (044) 259544-6, 371332. 88 rooms.
K. Star, 191 Atsadang Road. Tel: (044) 242260,
253264. 52 rooms.
Kings, 1756 Mittraphap Road. Tel: (044) 253360,
241362. 64 rooms.
Korat, 191 Atsadang Road. Tel: (044) 242260,
242444, 253264. 115 rooms.
Muang Mai Korat, 191 Atsadang Road, 110 rooms.
Phimai, 305/1-2 Haruthairom Road.
Tel: (044) 471306, 471940. 40 rooms.
Phothong, 658 Ratchadamnoen Road.
Tel: (044) 256799, 251962. 42 rooms.
Phubade, 781/1 Sukhapibal 3 Road, Pakchong.
Tel: (044) 311979, 311301, 313025. 49 rooms.
Ratchasima, 294-296 Jompol Road.
Tel: (044) 242837, 258734. 72 rooms.
Sakol, 46-48 Atsadang Road. Tel: (044) 241260,
244502. 120 rooms.
Siri, 688-690 Poklang Road. Tel: (044) 241556,
242831. 60 rooms.
Sripattana, 346 Suranaree Road. Tel: (044) 242883,
242944. 185 rooms.
Srivichai, 13 Boarong Road, Tel: (044) 242194,
241382. 55 rooms.
Thai Pokaphan, 106-110 Atsadang Road.
Tel: (044) 242454, 242654. 27 rooms.
Thai, 646-650 Mittraphap Road. Tel: (044) 244613,
242253, 241613-4. 140 rooms.
Wanchai, 434 Mittraphap Road, Pakchong.
Tel: (044) 311862. 31 rooms.

NAKHON SAWAN

(500 baht and over)
Pimarn, 605/244 Asia Road. Tel: (056) 222097,
222099, 221443, 222473. 140 rooms.

NAN

(100 baht and over)
Amonsi, 97 Mahayot Road, Tambon Nai Wiang.
Tel: (054) 710510. 22 rooms.
Nan Fa, 438-440 Sumon Thewarat Road.
Tel: (054) 710284. 24 rooms.
Nan Resort Fishing Park, 78 Mu 13, Nan-Thung
Chang Road, Km 4, Thung Chang.
Tel: (054) 771034. 21 rooms.
Suk Kasaem, 29-31 Ananworaritdet Road.
Tel: (054) 711034. 42 rooms.
Thewarat, 466 Sumon Thewarat Road.
Tel: (054) 710078, 710094, 710212. 165 rooms.

NONG KHAI

(100 baht and over)
Phanthavy, 1049 Haisok Road. Tel: (042) 411568-
600. 74 rooms.
Pongwichit, 1244/1-2 Banthoengchit Road.
Tel: (042) 411583, 411958. 38 rooms.
Poonsub, 843 Nechai Road. Tel: (042) 411031.
Prachak Bungalow, 1178 Prachak Road.
Tel: (042) 411116, 412644. 27 rooms.
Sukaphan, 823 Banthoengchit Road.
Tel: (042) 411894. 27 rooms.

PHAYAO

(500 baht and over)
Phayao, 445 Phaholyothin Road. Tel: (054) 481970-
3. 75 rooms.

(100 baht and over)
Siripan, Phaholyothin Road. Tel: (054) 431319. 20
rooms.
Tanthong, 55 Donsanam Road. Tel: (054) 431302.
124 rooms.
Wattana, 69 Donsanam Road. Tel: (054) 431086.
32 rooms.

PHETCHABUN

(100 baht and over)
Burapa, 308 Saraburi-Lomsak Road.
Tel: (054) 711155-9, 721383-4. 106 rooms.
Khosit Hill, 39 Samakheechai Road.
Tel: (056) 711293. 66 rooms.

PHICHIT

(100 baht and over)
Okhanakhon, 2/91 Simala Road. Tel: (056) 611206,
611321. 85 rooms.

Rose Inn, 57-59 Chomthirawet Road.
Tel: (056) 621044, 621237, 622036. 100 rooms.

PHITSANULOK

(1,000 *baht* and over)
Wang Nam Yen Resort, Km 46, Phitsanulok-Lomsak Road. Tel: (055) 243124-5. 35 rooms.

(500 *baht* and over)
Amarintr Nakhon, 3/1 Chao Phraya Road.
Tel: (055) 258588, 258945. 130 rooms.
Nan Chao, 242 Baromtrilokanat Road.
Tel: (055) 252510-4. 150 rooms.
Pailyn Hotel, 38 Baromtrailokanat Road.
Tel: (055) 252411-5. 240 rooms.
Thep Nakhon, 43/1 Sri Thamtraipidok Road.
Tel: (055) 251817, 251837. 150 rooms.

(100 *baht* and over)
Chang Phuak, Pra-Ong Dam Road.
Tel: (055) 259188, 259638. 52 rooms.
Guest House, 99/9 Pra-Ong Dam Road.
Tel: (055) 259970. 78 rooms.
Indra, 103/8 Srithumtridok Road.
Tel: (055) 259188, 259638. 88 rooms.
Rajapruk, 99/9 Pra-Ong Dam Roa.
Tel: (055) 258788-9, 258477. 123 rooms.
Rajawong, 714 Mittraphap Road. Tel: (055) 259569. 80 rooms.

PHRAE

(1,000 *baht* and over)
Mae Yom Palace, 181/6 Yantarakitkoson Road.
Tel: (054) 522906-9. 104 rooms.

(100 *baht* and over)
Bua Khao, 32 Muang Hit Road Tel: (054) 511372.
30 rooms.
Busarakhum, 39/12 Ratdamnoen Road.
Tel: (054) 511437. 24 rooms.
Ho-Fa, 194-16 Charoen Muang Road.
Tel: (054) 511140. 26 rooms.
Kanchana, 102 Charoen Muang Road.
Tel: (054) 511504. 25 rooms.
Nakhon Phrae, 69 Ratdamnoen Road.
Tel: (054) 521901, 511024, 511122. 250 rooms.
Pharadon, 177 Yantarakitkoson Road.
Tel: (054) 511177, 511969, 511059. 50 rooms.
Sawaddikan, 76-78 Yantarakitkoson Road.
Tel: (054) 511032. 30 rooms.
Thep Wiman, 226-228 Charoen Muang Road.
Tel: (054) 511003. 52 rooms.
Tung Sri Phibun, 84 Yantarakitkoson Road.
Tel: (054) 511011. 60 rooms.

ROI ET

(100 *baht* and over)
Banchong, 99-101 Suriyadet-Bamrung Road.
Tel: (043) 511235. 30 rooms.
Mai Thai, 99 Haisok Road. Tel: (043) 511136, 511038. 112 rooms.
Petcharat, 66-104 Haisok Road. Tel: (043) 511741. 72 rooms.
Si Chumphoon, Haisok Road. Tel: (043) 511741. 106 rooms.

SAKON NAKHON

(100 *baht* and over)
Araya, 1432 Premprida Road. Tel: (042) 711097. 59 rooms.
Dusit, 1782-4 Yuwa-Phattana Road.
Tel: (042) 711198-9, 712200-1. 102 rooms.
Imperial, 1892 Sukkasem Road. Tel: (042) 711119, 711887. 180 rooms.

SI SA KET

(100 *baht* and over)
Phromphiman, 849/1 Lak Muang Road. Tel: (045) 611141, 611161, 612270. 123 rooms.

SUKHOTHAI

(500 *baht* and over)
Northern Palace, 43 Singhawat Road, Tambon Thanee. Tel: (055) 611193-4, 612252. 67 rooms.
Pailyn Hotel Sukhothai, Jarodvithithong Road,
Tel: (055) 613310-5. 238 rooms.

(100 *baht* and over)
Rajthanee, 229 Charodvithithong Road.
Tel: (055) 611031, 611308, 612877. 81 rooms.
Thai Village House, 214 Charodvithithong Road.
Tel: (055) 611049, 612275. 120 rooms.

SURIN

(500 *baht* and over)
Tarin, 60 Sirirat Road. Tel: (044) 514281-8. 240 rooms.

(100 *baht* and over)
Ammarin, Thesaban 1 Road. Tel: (044) 511407. 80 rooms.
Memorial, 646 Lakmuang Road. Tel: (044) 511288, 513288. 56 rooms.
New Hotel, 6-8 Thanasan Road. Tel: (044) 511341, 511322. 96 rooms.
Petchkasem, 104 Jitbamrung Road.
Tel: (044) 511274, 511470. 162 rooms.
Sang Thong, 279-281 Thanasan Road.
Tel: (044) 512099. 125 rooms.

TAK

(500 baht and over)
Mae Sod Hill, 100 Asia Road, Mae Sod.
Tel: (055) 532601-8. 120 rooms.

(100 baht and over)
Wiang Tak, 25/3 Mahadthai Damrung Road.
Tel: (055) 511910, 511950. 100 rooms.
Wiang Tak, Chumphon Road. Tel: (055) 512507,
512686-7. 50 rooms.

UBON RATCHATHANI

(500 baht and over)
Khongchiam Resort, 75 Mu 6, Ban Pakhuaykaen,
Pibun-Khongchiam Road, Khongchiam. Tel: (045)
351073. 7 rooms.
Pathumrat, 337 Chayangkool Road.
Tel: (045) 241501-8. 168 rooms.
Regent Palace, 256-271 Chayangkool Road.
Tel: (045) 255529, 242503. 116 rooms.
Srikamol, 26 Ubonsak Road. Tel: (045) 255804,
241136, 243793. 42 rooms.
Tohsang, 251 Palochai Road. Tel: (045) 241925,
244814. 76 rooms.

(100 baht and over)
Bordin, 14 Palochai Road. Tel: (045) 254290. 110
rooms.
Chitsakon Resort, 42 Mu 14, Tambon Bung,
Amnatcharoen. Tel: (01) 423 0199. 11 rooms.
Krungtong, 24 Srinarong Road. Tel: (045) 241609.
116 rooms.
New Nakornluang, 66-70 Yuttapan Road.
Tel: (045) 255768. 44 rooms.
Parisa Guest House, 4/1 Auparisan Road.
Tel: (045) 245075.
Racha, 19 Chayangkool Road. Tel: (045) 254155.
58 rooms.
Ratthani, 297 Khuanthani Road. Tel: (045) 244388-
90. 100 rooms.
Sanarmchai Guest House, Warin-Phibun Road,
Phibunmangsahan. Tel: (045) 441289. 22 rooms.
Sri I-San 2, 60 Ratchabut Road. Tel: (045) 241141.
36 rooms.
Suriyart, 302 Suriyart Road. Tel: (045) 241141. 50
rooms.
Tokyo, 360 U-Parat Road. Tel: (045) 241739. 62 rooms.
Ubon, 323 Ubonkit Road. Tel: (045) 241045-7. 120
rooms.

UDON THANI

(500 baht and over)
Charoen, 549 Phosri Road. Tel: (042) 248155,
246121-4. 221 rooms.

(100 baht and over)
Charoensri Palace, 60 Phosri Rod.
Tel: (042) 242611-3. 70 rooms.

Kings, 57 Phosri Road. Tel: (042) 221634, 222919,
241444. 132 rooms.
Paradise, 44/29 Phosri Road. Tel: (042) 221506,
221956. 90 rooms.
Siri Udon, 79-91 Amphoe Road, Tel: (042) 221658,
221816, 222330-2. 98 rooms.
Sri Chai, 480-484 Phosri Road. Tel: (042) 221903,
222621. 39 rooms.
Udon, 81-89 Nakkhang Road. Tel: (042) 246528-
30. 91 rooms.

UTHAI THANI

(100 baht and over)
Phiboonsuk, 336 Sri Uthai Road.
Tel: (056) 511048, 511647. 79 rooms.

UTTARADIT

(500 baht and over)
Seeharaj, 163 Borom Art Road. Tel: (055) 411106,
412223. 124 rooms.

(100 baht and over)
Chai Fa, 131-3 Borom Art Road.
Tel: (055) 411256. 20 rooms.
Numchai, 213/3-4 Borom Art Road.
Tel: (055) 411253-4, 411753. 50 rooms.
Pho Wanit 2, 1-3 Si Utra Road. Tel: (055) 411499.
66 rooms.
Pho Wanit 3, 47-51 Samran Ruen Road.
Tel: (055) 411559. 25 rooms.
Wiwat, 159 Borom Art Road. Tel: (055) 411778,
411791. 80 rooms.

YASOTHON

(100 baht and over)
Yot Nakhon, 141-143/1-3 Uthai-Ramrit Road.
Tel: (045) 711122. 75 rooms.

THE SOUTH

CHUMPHON

(500 baht and over)
Chumphon Sunny Beach Resort, Pak Nam Tako,
Aronothai Beach. Tel: (077) 536007. 18 rooms.
Jansom Chumphon, 188-65-66 Sala Daeng Road.
Tel: (077) 502502-11. 140 rooms.
Phornsawan House, 110 Mu 4, Pharadon Phap
Beach. Tel: (077) 521031, 521051. 75 rooms.
Sai Ree Lodge, 100 Mu 4, Sai Ri Beach.
Tel: (077) 502023. 20 rooms.

(100 baht and over)
Chumphon 99 Bay Resort, 9 Mu 4, Tambon Pak
Nam Lang Suan, Lang Suan. Tel: (077) 541481,
541681. 10 rooms.
Chumphon Cabana, Thung Wua Laen Beach, Tambon
Saphil. Tel: (077) 501990. 40 rooms.

Chumphon, 176/1-2 Sala Daeng Road.
Tel: (077) 511776. 30 rooms.
Jane, 127/5 Khao Ngoen Road. Tel: (077) 541330.
30 rooms.
Lang Suan, 28-30/1-2 Tambon Lang Suan, Lang
Suan, 22 rooms.
Paradon Inn, 180/12 Pharadon Road.
Tel: (077) 511500, 511598. 116 rooms.
Si Chumphon, 127/22-4 Sala Daeng.
Tel: (077) 511280, 511397. 95 rooms.
Suan Phadaeng, 102 Mu 1, Tambon Hat Sai Ri.
Tel: (077) 521143. 7 rooms.
Suriwong Chumphon, 125/27-9 Sala Daeng Road.
Tel: (077) 511203, 511397. 78 rooms.
Tha Taphao, 66/1 Tha Tahao Road.
Tel: (077) 511479, 511953. 85 rooms.
Thai Prasert, 202-4 Sala Daeng Road.
Tel: (077) 511250. 47 rooms.
Thawat, 67 Mu 12, Tambon Khan Ngoen, 70 rooms.
Thawat, Khan Ngoen Road, Lang Suan.
Tel: (077) 541341, 541569. 100 rooms.

KRABI

(2,000 *baht* and over)
Phra Nang Plantation Club (Phra Nng Group),
Khlong Muang Beach. Tel: (075) 612173-4. 60
rooms.

(1,500 *baht* and over)
Ao Nang Villa, 113 Phra Nang Beach.
Tel: (075) 612994. 76 rooms.
Krabi Resort, Mu 2, Tambon Ao Nang.
Tel: (075) 612161, 612420. 79 rooms.
Pee Pee International Resort, Laem Tong, Amphoe,
Ko Phi Phi. Tel: (075) 214297. 120 rooms.
Phi Phi Tonsai, 201/3-4 Uttrakit Road.
Tel: (075) 611496, 612514. 50 rooms.

(1,000 *baht* and over)
Beach Terrace, 154 Mu 2, Ao Nang.
Tel: (01) 7220060. 34 rooms.
Ko Hai Resort, Ko Hai. Tel: (075) 210317, 211045.
18 rooms.
Phi Phi Palm Beach Resort, Tambon Ao Nang, Ao
Luk. 78 rooms.
Phra Nang Inn (Phra Nang Group), Ao Phra Nang.
Tel: (075) 612173-4. 51 rooms.

(500 *baht* and over)
Ao Nang Palm Hill Valley, 88 Mu 2, Ao Nang, 10
rooms.
Ko Hai Village, 155-157 Uttrakit Road.
Tel: (075) 611188, 611288. 28 rooms.
Lame Hin, Ao Ko Don, Ao Luk, 15 rooms.
Pee Pee Island Cabana, 201/3-4 Uttrakit Road.
Tel: (075) 611496, 612514. 50 rooms.
Pee Pee View Point Resort, Tambon Ao Nang.
Tel: 01-7230483. 20 rooms.
Phi Phi Coral Resort, 55 Mu 8, Tambon Ao Nang,
51 rooms.

Phi Phi Pavillion Resort, 201/5 Uttrakit Road.
Tel: (075) 611496, 612514. 50 rooms.
Thai, 7 Issara. Tel: (075) 611122, 611474-6. 150
rooms.
Vieng Thong, 155 Uttrakit Road.
Tel: (075) 611188, 611592-3. 153 rooms.

(100 *baht* and over)
Chao Fa Valley Bungalow, 50 Chao Fa Road.
Tel: (075) 612499. 40 rooms.
Chao Ko Pee Pee Lodge, Ko Phi Phi.
Tel: (075) 215014. 30 rooms.
City, 15/2-3 Sukhon Road. Tel: (075) 611961. 53
rooms.
K.R. Mansion, 52/1 Chao Fa Road.
Tel: (075) 612761-2. 40 rooms.
Kitti Suk, 9/11 Phangnga Road. Tel: (075) 611087,
611466. 18 rooms.
Krabi Pee Pee Resort, Ao Ton Sai, Ko Phi Phi.
Tel: (075) 612188. 60 rooms.
Krabi Sea View Resort, 171-173 Uttrakit Road.
Tel: (075) 611648. 17 rooms.
Lanta Chalrie Beach, Ko Lanta Yai.
Tel: 01-7230876. 100 rooms.
Lanta Royal Resort, Ban Sala Dan, Ko Lanta Yai.
Tel: 01-7230876, 7210047. 53 rooms.
Naowarat, 403 Uttrakit Road, Tel: (075) 611581-
4. 58 rooms.
New, 9-11 Phatthana Road. Tel: (075) 611318,
611545. 12 rooms.
P.P. Family Co., Ltd., 37 Prachachon Road.
Tel: (075) 611717. 70 rooms.
P.P. Family Country Ao Nang Village, Ao Nang.
Tel: (075) 611717. 30 rooms.
Palm Beach Bungalow, Ko Lanta Yai, Krabi, 20
rooms.
Peace Laguna Resort, Mu 2, Ao Phra Nang, Krabi.
Tel: 01-7231005, (075) 611972, Fax: (66 075)
612196. 45 rooms.
Pee Pee Chalrie Bech Resort, 17 Prachachon Road,
Ko Phi Phi. Tel: 01-7230495. 40 rooms.
Pee Pee Paradise Pearl, Mu 7, Tambon Ao Nang.
Tel: 01-7230484. 120 rooms.
Phra Nang Bay Village, Ao Nang.
Tel: (075) 611944 ext. 14. 50 rooms.
Phra Nang Place, Ao Nang. Tel: (075) 611944,
612172 ext. 01. 36 rooms.
Railae Bay Bungalow, 64 Ao Nang.
Tel: (075) 611944 ext. 41. 55 rooms.
Rimna Villa, Mu 7, Tambon Ao Nang.
Tel: (075) 212901-4. 10 rooms.
River Side, 287/11 Uttrakit Road.
Tel: (075) 612128-9. 51 rooms.
Sun Sea Bungalow, Rai Lay Beach.
Tel: (075) 611944-55 ext. 40,41. 60 rooms.
Sun Set Beach, Rai Lay Bay. Tel: (075) 611944 ext.
30. 45 rooms.
Tap Kheak Resort, 11 Khong Kha Road, Phra
Nang Beach, 10 rooms.

NAKHON SI THAMMARAT

(500 *baht* and over)
Khanab Nam Diamond Cliff Resort, 99 Mu 8, Nai Phlao Beach, Khanom. Tel: (075) 529000, 529111, 529222. 25 rooms.

(100 *baht* and over)
Bua Luang, 1487/19 Soi Luang Muang, Chamroen Withi Road. Tel: (075) 341518, 341570. 84 rooms.
Choke Chai, Pho Sadet-Karom Road.
Tel: (075) 356508. 39 rooms.
Fern Bay, Nai Phlao Beach, Khanom.
Tel: (02) 246 5242. 18 rooms.
Khanom Beach Resort, Khanom Beach, Khanom,
Monthien, 1509/40 Yommarat Road.
Tel: (075) 341908-10. 110 rooms.
Muang Thong, 1459/7-9 Chamroen Withi Road.
Tel: (075) 356177. 52 rooms.
Nai Phlao Bay Resort, 51/3 Nai Phlao Beach, Khanom. Tel: (075) 529039, 529422-4. 20 rooms.
Nakhon Garden Inn, 1/4 Pak Nakhon Road.
Tel: (075) 344831-5. 50 rooms.
Nakhon, 1477/5 Yommarat Road.
Tel: (075) 356318. 42 rooms.
Neramit, 1629-31 Neramit Road. Tel: (075) 356514. 60 rooms.
Phetphailin, 1838/38-9 Yommarat Road.
Tel: (075) 341896-7. 80 rooms.
Prasansuk Villa, Hin Ngam Beach, Pak Nam, Sichon. Tel: (075) 342756. 30 rooms.
Siam, 1403/17 Charoen Withi Road.
Tel: (075) 356090. 69 rooms.
Supar Villa, Nai Phlao Beach, Khanom.
Tel: (075) 529237. 19 rooms.
Thai Hotel, 1357 Ratchadamnoen Road.
Tel: (075) 356505, 356416, 356451. 215 rooms.
Thai Lee, 1130 Ratchadamnoen Road.
Tel: (075) 356948. 20 rooms.
Thak Sin, 1584/23 Si Prad Road.
Tel: (075) 342790-4. 120 rooms.
Udom, 1461/8-9 Yommarat Road.
Tel: (075) 356310. 54 rooms.
Yaowarat, 1475 Yommarat Road. Tel: (075) 356089. 53 rooms.

NARATHIWAT

(500 *baht* and over)
Genting, 141 Asia 18 Road. Tel: (073) 613231-40. 190 rooms.
Grand Garden, 104 Arif Makkha Road. Tel: (073) 611219, 613501-4. 129 rooms.
Lilla, 28/32 Sarit Wong Road. Tel: (073) 611188, 613521-5. 72 rooms.
Tan Yong, 16/1 Sopha Phisai Road. Tel: (073) 511477, 511831-3. 84 rooms.

(100 *baht* and over)
Amarin, 295/6 Phracha Wiwat, Sungai Kolok.
Tel: (076) 611108. 34 rooms.

An An, 183/1 Phracha Wiwat Road, Sugai Kolok.
Tel: (073) 811058. 54 rooms.
Asia, 4 Charoen Khet Road, Sungai Kolok.
Tel: (073) 611101. 22 rooms.
Banggalow Kolok, 27 Wong Withi Road, Sungai Kolok. Tel: (073) 611218. 14 rooms.
Cathay, 43/1 Sai Thong 2 Road, Sungai Kolok.
Tel: (073) 611301. 33 rooms.
Chonan, 43/5-6 Soi Phuthon, Charoen Khet Road, Sungai Kolok. Tel: (073) 611421. 23 rooms.
Come In, 46-48 Sarit Wong Road, Sungai Kolok.
Tel: (073) 611187. 20 rooms.
Erawan, 21 Choen Makkha Road, Sungai Kolok.
Tel: (073) 612526. 11 rooms.
Family, 18/1 Choen Makkha Rod, Sungai Kolok.
Tel: (073) 611200, 611397. 132 rooms.
First, 1/3 Soi 1, Phracha Wiwat Road, Sungai Kolok. Tel: (073) 612026. 30 rooms.
Grand, 122 Phichit Bamrung Road.
Tel: (073) 511067. 14 rooms.
Inter Tower, 160-166 Phracha Wiwat Road, Sungai Kolok. Tel: (073) 611192, 611700-1. 80 rooms.
Krung Thong House, 2/2 Withi-Uthok Road, Sungai Kolok. Tel: (073) 611511. 23 rooms.
Lee, 102/1-3 Arif Makkha Road, Sungai Kolok.
Tel: (073) 611036. 13 rooms.
Marry, 143/1 Arif Makkha Road, Sungai Kolok.
Tel: (073) 581123-4. 25 rooms.
Masyar Resort, Muang Mai Taba, Tak Bai.
Tel: (073) 611391. 30 rooms.
Merlin, 40 Chroen Khet Road, Sungai Kolok.
Tel: (073) 611003, 611413. 96 rooms.
My House, 50/1-2 Sarit Wong Road, Sungai Kolok. Tel: (073) 611069, 613569. 24 rooms.
Nam Thai 2, 57/1 Soi Phuthon, Charoen Khet Road, Sungai Kolok. Tel: (073) 611163. 37 rooms.
Pacific, 41/1-2 Warakham Phiphit Road.
Tel: (073) 511076, 511259. 23 rooms.
Panan Resort, 71/2 Mu 5. Tel: (073) 611757.
Paris, 3/5 Sarit Wong Road, Sungai Kolok.
Tel: (073) 611757. 16 rooms.
Parkson, 501 Charoen Khet Road, Sungai Kolok.
Tel: (073) 612789, 612790. 44 rooms.
Pimarn, 76-4 Charoen Khet Road, Sungai Kolok.
Tel: (073) 611464. 17 rooms.
Plaza, 3 Thet Prathom Road, Sungai Kolok.
Tel: (073) 611875-6. 94 rooms.
Rama, 50/6-7 Sarit Wong Road, Sungai Kolok.
Tel: (073) 611487. 24 rooms.
Rex, 6/1-2 Chamrun Nara Road.
Tel: (073) 511134, 511190. 38 rooms.
Sai Thong, 122 Phichit Bamrung Road.
Tel: (073) 511067. 18 rooms.
Savoy, 8/2 Charoen Khet Road, Sungai Kolok.
Tel: (073) 611093. 27 rooms.
Stellar, 56-58 Waraman Amnuai Road, Sungai Kolok. Tel: (073) 611295. 28 rooms.
Thai, 102 Arif Makkha Road, Sungai Kolok.
Tel: (073) 611348, 611467. 38 rooms.
Thai Ek, 43 Wong Withi Road, Sungai Kolok.
Tel: (073) 611052, 613136. 37 rooms.

Thai Laem Thong, 193/8 Pracha Wiwat Road, Sungai Kolok. Tel: (073) 611094. 34 rooms.
Thai Liang, 12 Charoen Khet Road, Sungai Kolok. Tel: (073) 611132. 14 rooms.
Thak Sin 1, 30 Prcha Wiwat Road, Sungai Kolok. Tel: 611010, 611083. 39 rooms.
Thak Sin 2, 4 Pracha Wiwat Road, Sungai Kolok. Tel: (073) 611083, 611220. 49 rooms.
Thanee, 4/1 Choen Makkha Road, Sungai Kolok. Tel: (073) 611241. 52 rooms.
Thara Regent, 45 Soi Phuthon, Charoen Khet Road, Sungai Kolok. Tel: (073) 611401, 611801-2. 120 rooms.
Valentine, 2/1 Waraman Amnuai, Sungai Kolok. Tel: (073) 611229, 612299-300. 40 rooms.
Venice Palace, 18/1 Choen Makkha rpad, Sungai Kolok. Tel: (073) 611200, 611397. 130 rooms.

PATTANI

(100 *baht* and over)
Chong Ar, 190-4 Prida Road. Tel: (073) 349039. 32 rooms.
June, 308 Pattani Phirom Road. Tel: (073) 349021. 22 rooms.
My Gardens, 8/28 Charoen Pradit Road. Tel: (073) 348448, 348577, 348655, 348933. 135 rooms.
Palace, 38-40 Soi Prida, Prida Road. Tel: (073) 349171, 349711. 42 rooms.
Santisuk, 1/16 Phiphit Road. Tel: (073) 349122, 349209. 38 rooms.

PHANGNGA

(1,000 *baht* and over)
Sun Splendor Lodge, 40 Mu 7, Amphoe Takua Pa. Tel: (076) 421350. 22 rooms.

(500 *baht* and over)
Phang Nga Bay Resort, 20 Thadan, Ko Panyee. Tel: (076) 412067-70. 90 rooms.

(100 *baht* and over)
Amarin, 7/5-8 Montri 2 Road. Tel: (074) 421073, 421534. 52 rooms.
Extra, 46 Sena Rat Road, Takua Pa. Tel: (076) 421026, 421110. 75 rooms.
Kasem Suk, 82 Tambon Takua Pa, Takua Pa. 25 rooms.
Khao Luk Resort, 158 Si Takua Pa Road, Takua Pa. Tel: (076) 421064, 421105. 20 rooms.
Long Beach Village, 25/26 Mu 5, Ko Yao Noi, Ko Yao. Tel: (076) 212901-5 ext. 150. 49 rooms.
Luk Muang, 1/2 Phetkasem Road. Tel: (076) 411288, 412125. 23 rooms.
Nang Thong Bay Resort, Nang Thong Bay, Khao Luk, Takua Pa. Tel: 01-723 1181. 30 rooms.
New Luk Muang, 540 Phetkasem Road. Tel: (076) 411500, 412218. 24 rooms.
Phaduang, 36-38 Montri Road, Takua Pa. Tel: (076) 421132, 421985. 20 rooms.

Phadung, 22-4 Montri 2 Road, Takua Pa. Tel: (076) 421132. 35 rooms.
Phangnga Valley Resort, 5/5Phetkasem Road. Tel: (076) 412201. 31 rooms.
Rak Phangnga, 98 Phetkasem Road. Tel: (076) 411090. 36 rooms.
Rattanaphong, 111 Phetksem Road. Tel: (076) 411247. 26 rooms.
Yan Yao, 136/2 Si Muang Road, Takua Pa. Tel: (076) 421219. 25 rooms.

PHATTHALUNG

(100 *baht* and over)
Dina Inn, 1/20 Chai Buri Road. Tel: (074) 613029. 24 rooms.
Ho Fa, 28-30 Khuha Sawan Road. Tel: (074) 611645, 611920, 611922. 96 rooms.
Lampam Resort, 88 Mu 6, Tambon Lampam. Tel: (074) 611486. 17 rooms.
Phatthalung 2, 34/1 Ramet Road. Tel: (074) 611045. 15 rooms.
Thai Hotel, 14-14/1-5 Dissara Sakharin Road. Tel: (074) 611636, 611727, 611798. 56 rooms.

PHUKET

(3,000 *baht* and over)
Amanpuri Resort, 118/1 Pansea Beach, Tambon Choeng Thale. Tel: (076) 311394-9. 40 rooms.
Cape Panwa Sheraton, 27 Mu 8, Sakdidet Road. Tel: (076) 391123-5. 164 rooms.
Club Andaman Beach Resort,77/1 Patong Beach. Tel: (076) 340530. 75 rooms.
Dusit Laguna, 390 Si Sunthon Road, Tambon Choeng Thale, Amphoe Kathu. Tel: (076) 331320-9. 240 rooms.
Holiday Inn Phuket, 86/11 Thawiwong Road, Patong Beach. Tel: (076) 340608-9. 280 rooms.
Kamala Beach Estate, 33/6 Kamala Beach. Tel: (01) 7230379. 31 rooms.
Karon Beach Resort, 27 Rasada Road, Karon Beach. Tel: (076) 381527-8. 80 rooms.
Le Meridien, 8/5 Mu 1, Karon Noi Bech. Tel: (076) 321480-5. 470 rooms.
Pansea, Rasada Center. Tel: (076) 311249. 110 rooms.
Phuket Apartment, Mae Luang Road. Tel: (076) 220747. 30 rooms.
Phuket Arcadia, 78/2 Karon Beach. Tel: (076) 381038-9, 381040-4, 381433-41. 255 rooms.
Phuket Mansion, 3/37 Phuket Road. Tel: (076) 215161. 30 rooms.
The Boat House Inn and Restaurant, 2/2 Mu 2, Kata Beach. Tel: (076) 381557-60. 36 rooms.
The Maithon Resort, Ko Maithon. Tel: (076) 214954-8. 68 rooms.
The Phuket Yacht Club Hotel & Beach Resort, 23/3 Wiset Road, Nai Harn Beach. Tel: (076) 381156-63. 108 rooms.
Thevorn Palm Beach, 128/10 Karon Beach. Tel: (076) 381034-7. 210 rooms.

(2,500 baht and over)

Blue Canyon, Thepkasattri Road. Tel: (076) 311176. 40 rooms.

Club Mediterranée, 7/3 Mu 2, Tambon Karon. Tel: (076) 381455-59. 300 rooms.

Coral Beach, 104 Mu 4, Patong Beach. Tel: (076) 340106-15. 200 rooms.

Diamond Cliff Resort, 61/9 Kalim Beach, Kathu. Tel: (076) 340501-6. 220 rooms.

Karon View Point, 4/8 Karon Beach. Tel: (076) 381853, 381666. 81 rooms.

Kata Thani, 62/4 Rasada Road, Kata Noi Beach. Tel: (076) 381417-25. 183 rooms.

Pacific Island Club, 323 Si Sunthon Road, Bang Thao Beach. Tel: (076) 311620-7. 253 rooms.

Patong Merlin, 99/2 Thawiwong Road, Patong Beach. Tel: (076) 321070-4. 297 rooms.

Pearl Village, 93 Phuket Road, Nai Yang Beach. Tel: (076) 311338-9, 311376-83. 215 rooms.

Phuket Golf Resort, 131 Wichit Songkhram Road. Tel: (076) 321038.

Phuket Island Resort, 73/1 Rasada Road. Tel: (076) 215950-5, 381010-1. 300 rooms.

Royal Park Beach Resort, Si Sunthon Road, Bang Thao Beach, Tambon Choeng Thale. Tel: (076) 311243, 311453. 115 rooms.

The South Sea Resort, 36/2 Mu 1, Karon Beach. Tel: (076) 381611-7. 100 rooms.

(2,000 baht and over)

Andaman Orchid, Patong Beach. Tel: (076) 321036. 72 rooms.

Karon View Point, 4/8 Karon Beach. Tel: (076) 381666, 381853. 81 rooms.

Karon Villa-Karon Royal Wing, 36/4 Karon Beach. Tel: (076) 381139-48. 152 rooms.

Kata Beach Resort, 5/2 Patak Road. Tel: (076) 381530-3. 280 rooms.

Raya Pacific, Kata Beach. Tel: (076) 381710-2. 50 rooms.

Thavorn Bay Resort, 6/2 Mu 2, Nakale Beach. Tel: (076) 340486. 30 rooms.

Thavorn Grand Plaza, Dilok Uthit Road. Tel: (076) 222240-70. 149 rooms.

The Islandia Park Resort, Karon Beach. Tel: (076) 381604, 381492. 128 rooms.

The Royal Paradise, 70 Mu 3, Rat Uthit Road, Kathu. Tel: (076) 340566-70. 248 rooms.

(1,500 baht and over)

Coconut Village, Thawiwong Road, Patong Beach. Tel: (076) 340161. 64 rooms.

Duangjitt Resort, 99/4 Thawiwong Road, Patong Beach. Tel: (076) 340288. 173 rooms.

Kalim Guest House, Kalim Beach. Tel: (076) 340353. 11 rooms.

Patong Bay Garden Resort, 61/13 Thawiwong Road, Patong Beach. Tel: (076) 340297-8. 45 rooms.

Patong Beach, 94 Thawiwong Road, Patong Beach. Tel: (076) 340611-3. 245 rooms.

Patong Lodge, 61/7 Mu 5, Kalim road, Patong Beach. Tel: (076) 340286-7. 130 rooms.

Patong Resort, 94/2 Rat Uthit Road, Patong Beach. Tel: (076) 340333-5.

Pen Villa, Surin Beach. Tel: (076) 216811. 40 rooms.

Phuket Cabana, 94 Thawiwong Road, Patong Beach. Tel: (076) 340130-40. 75 rooms.

Phuket Fishing Lodge, Chalong Bay. Tel: (076) 381223. 42 rooms.

Phuket Island View, 175 Phuket Road, Karon Beach. Tel: (076) 381919-20. 81 rooms.

Phuket Kamala Resort, 74/8 Mu 3, Tambon Kamala. Tel: (076) 212901-4 ext. 078, 212775, 216167. 42 rooms.

Sand Resort, 53/7 Karon Beach. Tel: (076) 212901-4 ext. 036. 32 rooms.

The Metropole, 1 Montri Road. Tel: (076) 214020-9. 248 rooms.

Vises, 95/21 Wiset Road, Patong Beach. Tel: (076) 340174, 340473. 47 rooms.

(1,000 baht and over)

A.A. Villa, Patong Beach. Tel: (076) 321499, 01-723 0095. 21 rooms.

Ban Sukhothai Patong Beach, 95 Rat Uthit Road, Patong Beach. Tel: (076) 340195-6. 120 rooms.

Ban Thai Beach Resort, 89/71 Thawiwong Road, Patong Beach. Tel: (076) 340328-30, 340 388-9. 190 rooms.

Chaokuan Bungalow, 5/3 Patak Road, Kata Beach. Tel: (076) 381403. 18 rooms.

Daeng Plaza, 57 Phuket Road. Tel: (076) 213951, 216428, 216752. 75 rooms.

Green Valley Bungalow, 66/3 Patak Road, Karon Beach. Tel: (076) 381468. 40 rooms.

Jaroensuk, 136-138 Thalang Road. Tel: (076) 211203. 10 rooms.

Jungle Beach Resort, 11/3 Wiset Road, Ao Sane Beach. Tel: (076) 214291, 381108. 44 rooms.

Karon Bay Inn, Karon Beach. Tel: 01-723-0291. 30 rooms.

Karon Inn, 27 Rassada Road, Karon Beach. Tel: (076) 381519-20. 100 rooms.

Lame Sai Village, 119/5-21 Mu 2, Kata Beach. Tel: (076) 212901-4. 13 rooms.

Lone Pavillion, 47/5 Chalong Bay. Tel: (076) 381374, 381858. 28 rooms.

Marina Cottge, 143 Kata Beach. Tel: (076) 381516, 381625. 96 rooms.

Nai Harn Villa, Nai Harn Beach. Tel: (076) 381959-61. 40 rooms.

Neptuna, 82/49-50 Rat Uthit Road, Patong Beach. Tel: (076) 340188. 36 rooms.

Patong Beach Bungalow, 96/1 Thawiwong Road, Patong Beach. Tel: (076) 340117, 340213. 35 rooms.

Patong Inn, 98/3 Thawiwong Road, Patong Beach. Tel: (076) 340126. 40 rooms.

Patong Villa, 85/3 Thawiwong Road, Patong Beach. Tel: (076) 340132-3. 24 rooms.

Pearl, 42 Montri Road. Tel: (076) 211044, 211907-3. 200 rooms.
Phuket Merlin, 158/1 Yaowarat Road. Tel: (076) 212866-70. 180 rooms.
Phuket Ramada, Karon Beach. Tel: (076) 381391. 42 rooms.
Safari Beach, 83/12 Thawiwong Road, Patong Beach. Tel: (076) 340230-1. 37 rooms.
Sea Wind, 9/11 Kata Beach. Tel: (076) 381 564. 22 rooms.

(500 *baht* and over)
Beau Rivage, 77/15-17 Rat Uthit Road, Patong Beach. Tel: (076) 211239. 20 rooms.
Bougainvill Terrace House, Kata Beach. Tel: (076) 381060. 17 rooms.
City, 91/1 Thepkasattri Road. Tel: (076) 216910-7. 165 rooms.
Coconut Villa, 99/3 Thawiwong Road, Patong Beach. Tel: (076) 340161. 38 rooms.
Coral Island Resort, 53 Phuket Road. Tel: (076) 214779, 216381. 40 rooms.
Earl Inn, Luang Pho Road. Tel: (076) 220965-6. 66 rooms.
Holiday Resort, 61 Thawiwong Road, Patong Beach. Tel: (076) 340119, 340261. 105 rooms.
K Hotel, 82/47 Patong Beach. Tel: (076) 340124. 42 rooms.
K.S.R. Bungalow, 83 Mu 3, Thawiwong Road, Patong Beach. Tel: (076) 340322. 23 rooms.
Kampong Karon, Karon Beach. Tel: (076) 212901 ext. 103. 24 room.
Long Beach Bungalow, Ko Yao, Phuket, 40 rooms.
Manorah, 17/4 Kommalaphat Road. Tel: (076) 212003, 216079. 72 rooms.
Merlon Karon, Karon Beach. Tel: (076) 213310. 27 rooms.
Nai Harn Beach Resort, 14/29 Mu 1, Nai Harn Beach. Tel: (076) 381810. 20 rooms.
Naka Pearl Farm & Resort, 20/20 Mae Luang Road, Ko Nata Noi. Tel: (076) 212901-4, 213723.
Panorama Beach Club, 57 Patong Beach. Tel: (076) 340451. 43 rooms.
Patong Bay Inn, 85/5 Thawiwong Road, Patong Beach. Tel: (076) 340092-3. 27 rooms.
Patong Bay Shore, 32 Rat Uthit Road, Patong Beach. Tel: (076) 340602-7. 56 rooms.
Phuket Country Lodge, 56 Thepkasattri Road. Tel: (076) 212518, 212932. 60 rooms.
Phuket Garden, 40/2 Bangkok Road. Tel: (076) 216900-9. 132 rooms.
Phuket Golden Sand Inn, 8/6 Karon Beach. Tel: (076) 381493-5. 95 rooms.
Phuket Ocean Resort, 9/1 Karon Beach. Tel: (076) 381599, 381601. 85 rooms.
Pure Mansion, Chao Fa Road. Tel: (076) 211700. 48 rooms.
Rattana Mansion, Dilok Time Squre. Tel: (076) 222600, 222603. 34 rooms.
Rome Place, Phuket Road. Tel: (076) 213425, 213591. 96 rooms.

Seagull Cottage, Patong Beach. Tel: (076) 340238-40. 56 rooms.
Seaview, 102 Thawiwong Road, Patong Beach. Tel: (076) 340103. 74 rooms.
Sintawee, 81 Phangnga Road. Tel: (076) 211186. 260 rooms.
Summer Beach Mansion, Patong Beach. Tel: 01-723 0859. 28 rooms.
Tapao Yai Island Resort, Ko Taphao Yai. Tel: (076) 391217. 35 rooms.
Thamdee Inn, 69/4 Patong Beach. Tel: (076) 340452. 40 rooms.
Thara Patong Beach Resort, 81 Thawiwong Road, Patong Beach. Tel: (076) 340135, 340520. 118 rooms.
The Mansion, 4/7 Kata Noi Beach. Tel: (076) 381565-6. 33 rooms.
Tropica Bungalow, 94/4 Thawiwong Road, Patong Beach. Tel: (076) 340204-6. 63 rooms.

(100 *baht* and over)
Atlas Resort, 14 Wiset Road, Rawai Beach. Tel: (076) 381279, 381286, 381643. 41 rooms.
Black Margin Bungalow, Narisorn Road. Tel: (076) 213401. 90 rooms.
Crown Nai Yang Suite, 65/15 National Park Road, Nai Yang Beach. Tel: (076) 311516-8, 01-7230568. 58 rooms.
Crystal Beach, 36/10 Patak Road, Kata Beach. Tel: (076) 381580-5. 120 rooms.
Dam Rong, 52 Luang Pho Road. Tel: (076) 211704. 79 rooms.
Friendship Bungalow, 6/5 Mu 2, Kata Beach. Tel: (076) 381499. 23 rooms.
Imperial 2, 17/14 Luang Pho Road. Tel: (076) 213156. 50 rooms.
Imperial, 51 Phuket Road. Tel: (076) 212311. 39 rooms.
Karon Guest House, Karon Beach. Tel: (076) 381860. 35 rooms.
Karon Sea View, Karon Beach, Phuket, 60 rooms.
Kata Noi Rivera, 3/21 Kata Beach, Patak Road. Tel: (076) 381726. 30 rooms.
Kockchang Village, Kata Beach. Tel: (076) 381578. 30 rooms.
Montri, 12/6 Montri Road. Tel: (076) 212936. 72 rooms.
Nordic Bungalow, 82/25 Patong Beach. Tel: (076) 340284. 34 rooms.
P.S. 1, 50/2 Rat Uthit Road, Patong Beach. Tel: (076) 340184. 35 rooms.
P.S. 2, 76/59 Rat Uthit Road, Patong Beach. Tel: (076) 340184. 30 rooms.
P.S. Inn, 31-33 Ongsim Phai Road. Tel: (076) 212216. 117 rooms.
Patong Penthouse, Patong Beach. Tel: (076) 340350. 39 rooms.
Phuket Motel, 60 Phun Phon Road. Tel: (076) 211958. 39 rooms.
Pop Cottage, 2/12 Mu 2, Patak Road, Kata Beach. Tel: (076) 381794. 30 rooms.

Rawai Plaza & Bungalow, Rawai Beach.
Tel: (076) 381346-7. 50 rooms.
Raya Island Bungalows, Raya Island, 30 rooms.
Roongrawee Mansion, Yaowarat Road.
Tel: (076) 211446, 213275. 30 rooms.
Sirey Seaview Bungalow, 46 Mu 1, Tambon Rasada,
Ko Sirey. Tel: (076) 216973. 32 rooms.
Siri, 231 Yaowarat Road. Tel: (076) 211307. 107
rooms.
Subsiri, Pradiphat Road. Tel: (076) 211353. 63
rooms.
Suksabye, 82/9 Thepkasattri Road.
Tel: (076) 212287, 216089. 53 rooms.
T. Songsaeng, 72/5 Chao Fa Road.
Tel: (076) 212567. 32 rooms.
Thai Inter, 22 Phun Phon Road. Tel: (076) 214452.
63 rooms.
Thavorn, 74 Rasada Road. Tel: (076) 211333-5.
200 rooms.
The Residence, Patong Beach. Tel: (076) 340456.
51 rooms.

RANONG

(1,000 *baht* and over)
Jansom Thara Resort, Paknam Ranong.
Tel: (077) 821611. 41 rooms.

(500 *baht* and over)
Jansom Thara, 2/10 Phetkasem Road, Tambon
Bang Rin. Tel: (077) 811510, 821511. 230 rooms.
Spa Inn, Phetkasem Road. Tel: (077) 811715. 70
rooms.

(100 *baht* and over)
Asia, Ruang Rat Road. Tel: (077) 811113. 67
rooms.
Charoensuk, 225 Ruang Rat Road. 51 rooms.
Ranong Inn, Ruang Rat Road. Tel: (077) 821523,
822777. 75 rooms.
Rattanasin, 226 Ruang Rat Road.
Tel: (077) 811242. 44 rooms.
Sin Ranong, 26/23-24 Ruang Rat Road.
Tel: (077) 811454. 120 rooms.
Sinthawi, 81/1 Ruang Rat Road.
Tel: (077) 811213. 32 rooms.

SATUN

(500 *baht* and over)
Adang Marine National Park, Ko Adang, Tambon
Ko Sarhai, Tel: (02) 579 0529, 579 4842. 18 rooms.
Tarutao Marine National Park, Ko Tarutao,
Tambon Ko Sarhai. Tel: (02) 579 0529, 579 4842.
9 rooms.

(100 *baht* and over)
Lianthong, 124 Saman Pradit Road.
Tel: (074) 711036. 25 rooms.
Satun Thani, 90 Satun Thani Road.
Tel: (074) 711010. 50 rooms.

Slinda, 11 Wiset Mayur Road. Tel: (074) 711115,
711436. 60 rooms.
Udomsuk, 201 Hatthakham Suksa Road.
Tel: (074) 711006. 33 rooms.
Wang Mai, 43 Satun Thani Road.
Tel: (074) 711607-8, 711891. 108 rooms.

SONGKHLA & HAADYAI

(1,500 *baht* and over)
J.B., 99 Chuti-Anuson Road, Haadyai.
Tel: (074) 234300-28. 430 rooms.

(1,000 *baht* and over)
Haadyai Central, 180-181 Niphat Uthit 3 Road,
Haadyai. Tel: (074) 230000-11.
Manhattan Palace, 29 Chaikun Uthit Road, Haadyai.
Tel: (074) 230724, 230730. 180 rooms.

(500 *baht* and over)
Asian Haadyai, 55 Niphat Uthit 3 Road, Haadyai.
Tel: (074) 245271, 245455, 245938. 104 rooms.
Central Sukhontha, 26 Saneha-Anuson Road,
Haadyai. Tel: (074) 230094-99, 243999. 187 rooms.
Emperor, 1 Tanrattanakon Road. Tel: (074) 220215-
18. 108 rooms.
Grand Plaza, 24/1 Saneha Anuson Road, Haadyai.
Tel: (074) 234340-8. 145 rooms.
Hat Kaew Resort, 163 Kaew Beach, Haadyai.
Tel: (074) 331059-67. 143 rooms.
Holiday Plaza, 1-3 Chiwanuson Road, Haadyai.
Tel: (074) 243881, 243923. 106 rooms.
Indra, 94 Thammanun Withi Road, Haadyai.
Tel: (074) 243277, 245886. 90 rooms.
Kosit, 199 Niphat Uthit 2 Road, Haadyai.
Tel: (074) 234366. 182 rooms.
L.K., 150 Saeng Chan Road, Haadyai.
Tel: (074) 230120-9. 195 rooms.
Lee Garden, 1 Lee Phatthana Road, Haadyai.
Tel: (074) 231888, 245888. 122 rooms.
Merlin, 2 Chaiyakun Uthit 2 Road, Haadyai.
Tel: (074) 232030, 238586. 110 rooms.
Montien, 120-124 Niphat Uthit Road, Haadyai.
Tel: (074) 245399, 246968-9. 180 rooms.
Nora, 216 Thammanun Withi Road, Songkhla.
Tel: (074) 244944, 244982-3. 170 rooms.
President, 420 Phetkasem Road, Haadyai.
Tel: (074) 244069, 244477, Fax: (66 074) 244662.
110 rooms.
Ratchathani, 1 Thammanun Withit Road, Haadyai.
Tel: (074) 231020, 232288. 79 rooms.
Samila, 1/11 Ratchadamnoen Road, Songkhla.
Tel: (074) 311310-4. 75 rooms.
The Florida Haadyai, 8 Siriphuwanat Road.
Tel: (074) 233590, 234555, 243921. 119 rooms.
The Regency, 23 Prachathipat Road, Haadyai.
Tel: (074) 234400-9. 190 rooms.
The Royal, 106 Prachathipat Road, Haadyai.
Tel: (074) 232115, 232162, 243953-4. 136 rooms.

(100 *baht* and over)

Amarin, 285 Niphat Uthit Road, Haadyai.
Tel: (074) 244012, 244272. 140 rooms.
Chok Amnuai, 161/26-27 Sang Si Road, Haadyai.
Tel: (074) 246376. 44 rooms.
City, 533/1 Saiburi Road, Haadyai.
Tel: (074) 321020, 322364-5. 65 rooms.
Dusit, 25/3 Pracharom Road, Haadyai.
Tel: (074) 232141. 50 rooms.
First Orchid, 37 Pracharak Road, Haadyai.
Tel: (074) 231519, 245161. 125 rooms.
Hat Kaew Villa, Sai Kaew Beach, Ranong Road,
Songkhla. Tel: (074) 311614. 40 rooms.
Haadyai Ambassador, 23 Phadung Phakdi Road,
Haadyai. Tel: (074) 234411-7. 170 rooms.
Haadyai Garden Home, 51/2 Hoy Muk Road,
Haadyai. Tel: (074) 232283, 236047, 239736. 60
rooms.
Haadyai Green View, 85/4 Saeng Si Road, Haadyai.
Tel: (074) 244207, 244314. 165 rooms.
Haadyai Inter, 42-44 Niphat Uthit 3 Road, Haadyai.
Tel: (074) 231022, 244744, 246039. 210 rooms.
Hiage, 33/1 Phasawang 5 Road, Haadyai.
Tel: (074) 244227, 244376. 90 rooms.
Kenting, 263 Sam Chai Road, Haadyai.
Tel: (074) 239651-4. 72 rooms.
Kings, 126 Niphat Uthit Road, Haadyai.
Tel: (074) 233413, 243966. 88 rooms.
Laem Thong, 44 Thammanun Withi Road, Haadyai.
Tel: (074) 233413, 244433, 133 rooms.
Lido, 11 Montri 1 Road, Haadyai.
Tel: (074) 244974-5. 37 rooms.
Mandarin, 62-4 Niphat Uthit 1 Road, Haadyai.
Tel: (074) 243438. 32 rooms.
Metro, 86 Niphat Uthit 2 Road, Haadyai.
Tel: (074) 244266, 244422. 155 rooms.
My House, 600 Phetkasem Road, Haadyai.
Tel: (074) 243372, 244759. 137 rooms.
New World, 144-158 Niphat Uthit 2 Road, Haadyai.
Tel: (074) 230100, 246993. 148 rooms.
O.H., 136 Niphat Uthit 3 Road, Haadyai.
Tel: (074) 230142-44. 126 rooms.
Orchid Songkhla, 99/44 Kanchanawanit Road,
Songkhla. Tel: (074) 322811-2, 322821-2. 55
rooms.
Oriental, 137-9 Niphat Uthit 3 Road, Haadyai.
Tel: (074) 245674, 245977. 124 rooms.
Pacific, 149/1 Niphat Uthit 2 Road, Haadyai.
Tel: (074) 244062, 245202. 37 rooms.
Palm Inn, 880 Phetkasem Road, Haadyai.
Tel: (074) 233198. 50 rooms.
Phiman, 89 Rat Yindi Road, Haadyai.
Tel: (074) 246955. 60 rooms.
Rado, 59 Saneha-Anuson Road, Haadyai.
Tel: (074) 243858, 245266. 88 rooms.
River Inn, 65 Chon Thana Road, Haadyai.
Tel: (074) 231101-3, 244750. 90 rooms.
Royal Crown Songkhla, 38 Sai Ngam Road,
Songkhla. Tel: (074) 311918, 312174. 52 rooms.
Saeng Fa, 98-100 Niphat Uthit 3 Road, Haadyai.
Tel: (074) 243363, 243833. 78 rooms.

Sakol, 47-48 Saneha-Anuson Road, Haadyai.
Tel: (074) 245256, 245356. 104 rooms.
Sakura, 165/1 Niphat Uthit 3 Road, Haadyai.
Tel: (074) 233160, 246908. 60 rooms.
Scala, 43/42-43 Tanrattanakon Road, Haadyai.
Tel: (074) 234800-3. 80 rooms.
Seiko, 41 Saneha-Anuson Road, Haadyai.
Tel: (074) 243792. 45 rooms.
Tawan Ok, 131/1-3 Niphat Uthit 3 Road, Haadyai.
Tel: (074) 233265, 243071. 32 rooms.
Thai Pe, 43/5 Si Phuwanant Road, Haadyai.
Tel: (074) 244471. 48 rooms.
Thai, 31/4 Rat Uthit Road, Haadyai.
Tel: (074) 243771, 244371. 75 rooms.
Tong Nam, 118-120 Niphat Uthit 3 Road, Haadyai.
Tel: (074) 232078, 244023. 30 rooms.
Wang Noi, 114/1 Saeng Chan Road, Haadyai.
Tel: (074) 245633, 245729. 68 rooms.
Yong Di, 99 Niphat Uthit 3 Road, Haadyai.
Tel: (074) 234350-7. 107 rooms.

KO SAMUI, KO TAO, KO PHANGAN & SURAT THANI

(3,500 *baht* and over)

Santiburi Dusit Resort, Mae Nam Beach, Ko Samui.
Tel: (077) 286901. 79 rooms.
The Imperial Thong Sai Bay, Laem Ban Plai,
Tambon Bo Phut, Ko Samui. Tel: (077) 425015-24.
Thong Sai Hotel & Cottage, Thong Takian Bay, Ko
Samui. Tel: (077) 421451-60. 72 rooms.

(3,000 *baht* and over)

Chaweng Blue Lagoon, Chaweng Beach, Ko Samui.
Tel: (077) 422401. 61 rooms.
Samui Euphoria, Bo Phut Beach, Ko Samui.
Tel: (077) 286948. 124 rooms.
The Imperial Samui, Chaweng Noi Beach, Ko
Samui. Tel: (077) 422020-26. 155 rooms.

(2,500 *baht* and over)

Seafan Beach Resort, Mae Nam Beach, Ko Samui.
Tel: (077) 421350. 35 rooms.

(2,000 *baht* and over)

Beachcomber, Chaweng Beach, Ko Samui.
Tel: (077) 421388. 60 rooms.
Boat House Samui, Thong Takian Bay, Ko Samui.
Tel: (077) 425041-044. 216 rooms.
The Victorian Resort & Hotel, Chaweng Noi Beach,
Ko Samui. Tel: (077) 286943. 60 rooms.

(1,500 *baht* and over)

Central Samui Beach Resort, Chaweng Beach, Ko
Samui. Tel: (077) 421384. 50 rooms.
Chaba Samui Resort, 19 Chaweng Beach, Tambon
Bo Phut, Ko Samui. Tel: (077) 421380. 16 rooms.
Chaweng Cove, 17/4 Mu 2, Chaweng Beach, Ko
Samui. Tel: (077) 286957. 39 rooms.
Coral Bay Resort, 9 Mu 2, Chaweng Beach, Tambon
Bo Phut, Ko Samui. Tel: (077) 286902. 42 rooms.

Palm Reef, 14/3 Mu 2, Chaweng Beach, Tambon Bo Phut, Ko Samui. Tel: (077) 281000, 286947. 84 rooms.
Pansea Samui, Chaweng Beach, Ko Samui. Tel: (077) 422384. 50 rooms.
Samui Palm Beach Resort, Bo Phut Beach, Ko Samui. Tel: (077) 421358. 50 rooms.
Samui Park Resort, Lamai Beach, Ko Samui. Tel: (077) 421435. 61 rooms.
Samui Villa Flora, Chaweng Beach, Ko Samui. Tel: (076) 272222 ext. 225. 80 rooms.
The Pavillion Resort, 124/24 Lamai Beach, Mu 3, Ko Samui. Tel: (077) 421420. 47 rooms.
The Princess Village, Chaweng Beach. Tel: (077) 422382. 12 rooms.
Weekender Resort & Hotel, Chaweng Beach, Ko Samui. Tel: (077) 421428. 70 rooms.

(1,000 *baht* and over)
Aloha Resort, Lamai Beach, Ko Samui. Tel: (077) 421418-9. 26 rooms.
Chaweng Cabana, Chaweng Beach, Ko Samui. Tel: (077) 421377. 24 rooms.
Chaweng Resort, Chaweng Beach, Ko Samui. Tel: (077) 422378. 39 rooms.
Hilton Garden Resort, Lamai Beach, Ko Samui. Tel: (077) 421056. 40 rooms.
Nara Lodge, Phra Yai Beach, Ko Samui. Tel: (077) 421364. 44 rooms.
Samui Laguna Resort, Lamai Beach, Ko Samui. Tel: (077) 272222 ext. 233. 63 rooms.
Samui Yacht Club, Ao Thong Takian, Ko Samui. Tel: (077) 421400. 40 rooms.
The Village, Chaweng Beach, Ko Samui. Tel: (077) 422382. 19 rooms.
The White House, Chaweng Beach, Ko Samui. Tel: (077) 421382. 12 rooms.
Tropicana Beach Resort, Chaweng Beach, Ko Samui. Tel: (077) 421408. 50 rooms.

(500 *baht* and over)
Casanova's Resort, Lamai Beach, Ko Samui. Tel: (077) 421425. 20 rooms.
Central Bay Resort, Chaweng Beach, Ko Samui. Tel: (077) 272222 ext. 217. 40 rooms.
Chaweng Guest House Bungalow, Chaweng Beach, Ko Samui. Tel: (077) 421375. 33 rooms.
Chaya Rai Resort, Mae Nam Beach, Ko Samui. Tel: (077) 425290. 10 rooms.
Fare House Resort, Chaweng Beach, Ko Samui. Tel: (077) 421373. 39 rooms.
Farn Bay Resort, Phra Yai Beach, Ko Samui. Tel: (077) 425188. 425394. 88 rooms.
J.R. Bungalow, Chaweng Beach, Ko Samui. Tel: (077) 422402. 40 rooms.
J.R. Palace, Chaweng Beach, Ko Samui. Tel: (077) 421402. 70 rooms.
Ko Tao Cottage, Chalok Ban Kao, Ko Tao. Tel: (077) 286062. 24 rooms.
Laem Set Inn, Laem Set Bay, Ko Samui. Tel: 01-725 0267, 2122762. 15 rooms.

Mae Nam Inn, Mae Nam Beach, Ko Samui. Tel: 01-7250600. 30 rooms.
Phangan Central, Thong Sala, Ko Phangan. Tel: (077) 287052. 60 rooms.
Phloen Resort, Thong Yang Beach, Ko Samui. Tel: (077) 421083, 01-7250245. 15 rooms.
Samui Orchid Resort, Laem Set Bay, Ko Samui. Tel: (077) 421079. 64 rooms.
Samui Royal Beach, Chaweng Beach, Ko Samui. Tel: (077) 421402. 25 rooms.
Samui Silver Beach Resort, Chaweng Beach, Ko Samui. 20 rooms.
Sand Sea Resort, Lamai Beach, Ko Samui. Tel: (077) 421415. 28 rooms.
Sun Sand Resort, Choeng Mon Beach, Ko Samui. Tel: (077) 286946. 33 rooms.
The Royal Blue Lagoon Hilltop Beach Resort, Lamai Beach, Ko Samui. Tel: (077) 272222 ext. 991. 28 rooms.
Wang Tai, 1 Talad Mai Road, Surat Thani. Tel: (077) 283020-6. 230 rooms.
Win, Na Thon, Ko Samui. Tel: (077) 421500/1. 33 rooms.

TRANG

(500 *baht* and over)
Kradan Island Resort, 25/36 Sathani Road. Tel: (075) 211367, 219758. 44 rooms.
Thammarin, Thammarin Square. Tel: (075) 218157. 218296, 218944. 117 rooms.

(100 *baht* and over)
Cesar Bungalows, 65/1 Phloen Phithak Road. Tel: (075) 218026. 34 rooms.
Holiday, 2/2-3 Wiset Kun Road. Tel: (075) 218720. 28 rooms.
Huai Yot, Phetkasem Road, Tambon Huai Yot, Huai Yot. Tel: (075) 271008. 8 rooms.
Ko Teng, 77-9 Phraram Hok Road. Tel: (075) 218622. 56 rooms.
Maitri, 4-8 Sathani Road. Tel: (075) 218103. 23 rooms.
Plaza, Soi 1, Wiset Kun Road. Tel: (075) 218720. 28 rooms.
Queens, Wiset Kun Road. Tel: (075) 218229, 218422. 148 rooms.
Saha Thai, 111/1 Phatthalung Road. Tel: (075) 218072. 30 rooms.
Siri Chai, 132-4 Sathon Sathan Phithak Road. Tel: (075) 251172. 23 rooms.
Sitrang, 24 Lang Sathani Road. Tel: (075) 251172. 30 rooms.
Thap Thiang, 138 Kantang Road, Tel: (075) 218057. 23 rooms.
Trang, Wiset Kun Road. Tel: (075) 218703, 218451, 218944. 55 rooms.
Watthana, 127/3-4 Phraram Hok Road. Tel: (075) 218184, 218288. 39 rooms.

(100 *baht* and over)
Cathey, 17-21 Chantharo Thai Road.
Tel: (073) 230999. 99 rooms.
Cola, 15 Khotchaseni 1 Road. Tel: (073) 212208.
42 rooms.
Fortuna, 50-8 Phakdi Damrong Road, Betong.
Tel: (073) 230065, 230238. 72 rooms.
Hua An, 352/1 Siro Rot Road. Tel: (073) 212771,
212989. 64 rooms.
Kheng Thai, 33 Chaya Chaowalit Road, Betong.
Tel: (073) 230238, 230589. 32 rooms.
Khong Kha, 1 Thammawithi Road, Betong.
Tel: (073) 230441-3. 140 rooms.
Kings, 130/5 Rattanakit Road, Betong.
Tel: (073) 230299. 51 rooms.
My House, 27 Rattanakit Road, Betong.
Tel: (073) 230525-6. 64 rooms.
Rama, 39 Tanwira Road, Betong.
Tel: (073) 230011. 40 rooms.
Rung Arun, 45/8 Tanwira Road, Betong.
Tel: (073) 230116. 32 rooms.
Si Betong 2, 16/4 Chaya Chaowalit Road, Betong.
Tel: (073) 230355. 46 rooms.
Si Betong, Sukkhayang Road, Betong.
Tel: (073) 230192. 52 rooms.
Si Charoen, 17 Soi Praphan Phesat, Betong.
Tel: (073) 230537. 40 rooms.
Si Yala, 16-22 Chai Charat Road.
Tel: (073) 212045, 212170, 212299. 93 rooms.
Thai, 25 Rattanakit Road. Tel: (073) 230074,
230122. 81 rooms.
Thepwiman, 31-37 Si Bumrung Road.
Tel: (073) 212400, 212963. 84 rooms.
Venus, 303/28 Tanwira Road, Betong.
Tel: (073) 230156-7. 54 rooms.
Yala My House, 109 Ratkhamnung Road.
Tel: (073) 213147, 213875. 60 rooms.
Yala Rama, 21 Si Bumrung Road. Tel: (073)
212563, 212815, 212841, 213053. 126 rooms.

FOOD DIGEST

WHAT TO EAT

The dramatic rise in the number of Thai restaurants
opened around the world in the past decade says
something about the universality and uniqueness of
one of Asia's supreme cuisines. It is no surprise that
when gourmets arrive on these shores fresh from
Thai dining experiences at home, they fall into a
feeding frenzy that lasts their entire stay.

One would expect that a dish would taste better
on its own home ground, but what diners soon
discover is the diversity of tastes a single dish can
have. Varying chefs, varying types of ingredients and
a society that, if it knows nothing else, knows food,
ensure fresh taste experiences each meal, each as
individual as the chef.

The base for most Thai dishes is coconut milk.
Ginger, garlic, lemon grass and fiery chilies give
Thai dishes a piquancy that can set tender palates
aflame. While many of the chilies are mild, their
potency is in obverse proportion to their size; the
smallest, the *prik khii no* or "rat dropping chilies",
are guaranteed to dissolve your sinuses and cloud
your vision with tears. For those averse to spicy
food, chefs can bland the curries or serve one of the
dozens of non-spicy curries.

Dining Tips
Dining is a communal affair. Meals are best enjoyed
with friends in a convivial atmosphere, normally
lubricated with beer or whiskey. Thais dawdle over
their meals, talking and making an entire evening of
the affair. Since dishes are placed in the middle of
the table and shared by all, it makes sense to take
a half dozen friends so one can order more dishes and
sample more tastes.

Thai food is eaten with rice. Traditionally, the
curries were secondary to the meal, a means of
pepping up one's tastebuds so one would eat more
rice. Even today, rural Thais eat enormous quantities of rice with nothing more than bits of dried
salted fish to flavor them. Chilies are also a means
of spicing up Thai rice, even though it is, on its own,
one of the most flavorful rices in Asia. Try a few
spoonful of plain rice before you get into the meal
and discover just how delicious it is.

Affluent city Thais and foreigners have turned the
order of importance around so that rice is secondary
to an enjoyment of a curry. The rice serves to absorb

the curry or to clear the palate much in the way the French eat bread when drinking wine.

When dining, one heaps rice on one's plate and then ladles a spoonful or two of a curry onto it. It is considered polite to take one curry at a time, consuming it before ladling another curry onto the rice. Thais eat with the spoon in their right hand and fork in their left, the fork being used to shovel the food onto the spoon for transport to the mouth. Chopsticks are used only for Chinese noodle dishes.

There seems to be some confusion among those who have sampled their first Thai meals abroad, about the proper condiments to add to the food. Much to their surprise, they discover that "peanut sauce", an "indispensable" addictive to every dish in Western restaurants, is really of Malayan and Indonesian origin and is used in Thailand only for *satay*. Similarly, instead of salt, Thais rely on *nam plaa* or fish sauce for their salt intake, splashing a bit of it on the rice and mixing it in.

When ordering the dishes noted below, remember that the initial "K" letter is pronounced as a "G" and "Kh" as an aspirated "K".

Spicy Dishes

"*Gaeng*" means curry. The group includes the spiciest of Thai dishes and forms the core of Thai cooking. Among the green curries is *Gaeng Khiew Wan Gai*, a gravy filled with chunks of chicken and tiny pea-sized eggplants. A relative, *Gaeng Khiew Wan Nua*, has bits of beef in it. Gaeng *Luang*, a category of yellow curries, includes *Gaeng Karee* which is also made with chicken or beef.

Gaeng Phet is a red curry with beef. A close relative is *Penang Nua*, a so-called "dry" curry with beef in a tasty paste.

Among the fiery favorites is *Thom Yam Kung*, a lemony broth teeming with shrimp. It is served in a metal tureen that is wrapped around a mini-furnace heated by charcoal so that it remains piping hot throughout the meal. *Po Tak* ("The Fisherman's Net Bursts") is a cousin of *Thom Yam Kung* – the broth also has squid, mussels, crab and fish.

Gaeng Som is cooked in a sour soup but falls into the category of hot-sour soups. It is filled with bits of fish or shrimp.

Yam is generally translated as salad and is as much meat as vegetable. It is also one of the hottest dishes.

Mild Curries

Among the non-spicy dishes is a favorite among foreigners: *Thom Kha Kai*, a thick coconut milk curry of chicken chunks with lemon grass.

Plaamuk Thawd Krathiem Prik Thai is squid fried with garlic and black pepper. When ordering, ask that the garlic (*krathiem*) be fried crispy (*krawp krawp*). The dish is also prepared with fish.

Gaeng Joot is a non-spicy curry, a clear broth filled with glass noodles, minced pork and mushrooms.

Nua Phat Namman Hoi is beef in oyster sauce with a few chopped shallots to add variety.

Muu Phat Priew Wan, sweet and sour pork, is probably of Portuguese origin and arrived in Thailand via Chinese émigrés. It is also possible to order it with Red Snapper (*Plaa Krapong*), beef (*nua*) and shrimp (*kung*).

Homok Talay is a seafood casserole of fish and shellfish chunks in a coconut mousse steamed in a banana leaf cup.

Gaeng Musselman is an unspiced curry. It consists of pieces of beef or chicken, combined with potatoes and onions in a brown gravy and resembles a Western stew.

Of Chinese origin but having secured a place in Thai cuisine is *Plaa Jaramet Nung Kiem Bue*, steamed pomfret with Chinese plum and bits of ginger.

Pu Phat Pong Karee is pieces of unshelled, steamed crab slathered in a curry sauce laden with shallots.

Hoi Malang Pu Op Moh Din is a thick, savory coconut milk gravy filled with mouth-watering mussels.

Noodles & Others

Most noontime dishes are derived from Chinese cuisine. Noodle dishes, a Chinese invention, have been adopted by the Thais. Those served at streetside, open-front shops come in two varieties: wet and dry. When ordering either, specify the wetness by adding the word "*nam*" or "*haeng*" to the dish's name. Thus, a wet *Kuay Tiew* would be *Kuay Tiew Nam*.

Kuay Tiew is a lunchtime favorite, a soup of noodles with balls of fish or bits of beef. *Baa Mii* is egg noodles with bits of meat and vegetable.

The rice-based lunchtime dishes are also Chinese and include *Khao Mun Kai*, boiled rice topped with slices of chicken and bits of ginger; *Khao Moo Daeng*, the same dish with pork slices, and *Khao Kha Moo*, stewed pork with greens on rice.

Then, there are the variants using noodles. *Kuay Tiew Rawt Naa* is broad white noodles boiled and served in a dish with morning glory. *Phat Thai* is noodles fried in a wok with *tofu* and bits of vegetables. *Mii Krawp* is crisp-fried noodles coated in honey and served with bits of vegetables.

Served late at night and early in the morning are two soup-like dishes filled with boiled rice. The rice in *Khao Tom* is watery and is augmented by bits of minced pork and shallots. A close relative is *Jok* in which the rice has been cooked until the liquid becomes viscous like a porridge. Into this mix is tossed ginger, coriander and bits of meat.

Regional Dishes

Each of Thailand's other three regions has its own cuisine. Northern and northeastern cuisine are related to Lao dishes which are eaten with glutinous rice. Southern food is flavored with the tastes of Malaysia and Muslim cooking.

Northern Cuisine: Northern specialties are generally eaten with *Khao Niew* or "sticky rice" which is kneaded into a ball and dipped into various sauces and curries.

Sai Oua (also called *Naam*) is an oily, spicy pork sausage that epitomizes northern cooking. The sausage is roasted over a fire fueled by coconut husks which impart an aroma to the meat. Generally prepared hygienically, it is best to buy it only at better restaurants. Beware the *prik khii nuu* chilies that lurk inside waiting to explode on the tongues of the unwary.

Khao Soy originated in Burma. This egg noodle dish is filled with chunks of beef or chicken and is lightly curried in a gravy of coconut cream and sprinkled with crispy noodles.

Nam Prik Ong combines minced pork with chilies, tomatoes, garlic and shrimp paste. It is served with crisp cucumber slices, parboiled cabbage leaves, and pork rind (the latter another northern snack).

Larb is a minced pork, chicken, beef or fish dish normally associated with northeastern cuisine. While Northeasterners traditionally eat it raw, Northerners cook it thoroughly. It is served with long beans, mint leaves and other vegetables which contrast with its mellow flavor.

Gaeng Hang Lay, another dish of Burmese origin, is one of the spiciest of northern dishes and should be approached with caution. Pork and tamarind flesh give this curry a sweet and sour flavor. The curry is especially suited to dipping with a ball of sticky rice.

Mieng, or fermented tea leaves, is also Burmese and is eaten as an hors d'oeuvre.

Northeastern Cuisine: Northeastern food is simple and spicy. Like northern food, it is eaten with sticky rice which *I-sarn* (northeastern) diners claim weighs heavily on the brain and makes one sleepy.

Kai Yang or northeastern roasted chicken has a flavor found in no other chicken. Basted with herbs and honey, it is roasted over an open fire and chopped into small pieces. Two dips are served with it; one hot and the other sweet.

Larb (described above under "Northern Cuisine").

Nua Yang is beef dried like a jerky. One can chew for hours on a piece and still extract flavor from it.

Som Tam is the dish most associated with the northeast. It is a spicy salad made from raw shredded papaya, dried shrimp, lemon juice and chilies.

Southern Cuisine: *Khao Yam* is rice with *kapi* (a paste made of fermented shrimp).

Phat Phet Sataw. Sataw looks like a lima bean but has a slightly bitter but pleasant flavor. This dish is cooked with shrimp or pork with a sprinkling of chilies.

Khao Mok Gai, a Muslim dish, lays roasted chicken on a bed of saffron rice and mixes it with ginger which has been fried lightly to make it crisp.

Khanom Chin is found throughout Thailand but the South claims to have created it. Tiny bits of minced beef are stewed in a red sauce and then served atop rice noodles. It is generally sold in markets in the early morning.

Nam Prik Kung Siap or dried prawn on a stick, is grilled and served with chilies, *kapi* (fermented shrimp paste) and lime.

Gaeng Dtai Plaa was created by bachelor fishermen who wanted a dish that would last them for days. Fish kidneys, chilies and vegetables are blended in a curry sauce and stewed for up to seven days.

Homok Khai Plaa. Fish roe are stirred into a coconut mousse, wrapped in leaves and steamed.

Desserts

The traditional Thai dessert and the perfect counter to the heat of the meal and the heat of the night is a simple plate of fruit. A typical plate consists of papaya, pineapple and watermelon, peeled and cut into bite-sized chunks. It may also include banana, tangerine and seasonal fruits like jackfruit, rambutan and mangosteen. For a taste treat, try durian – the rich, spiky fruit whose smell and texture offends but whose taste transcends all its bad aspects.

Coconut milk, tapioca, vermicelli, lotus seeds, water chestnut and fruits are the prime ingredients of luscious sweets sold by sidewalk vendors. Try "ice cream kathit", made of coconut milk.

WHERE TO EAT

In Europe, the very best restaurants are not usually to be found in hotels. In Thailand, the reverse is true. There are, of course, exceptions to both these generalities. All the following restaurants contribute to making Thailand a gourmet's paradise.

BANGKOK

Thai Cuisine

All Gaengs, 173/8-9 Suriwongse Road. Tel: 2333301. Elegant, modern decor and delicious Thai cuisine.

Benjarong, Dusit Thani Hotel, 946 Rama IV Road. Tel: 2360450-9. Superlative Royal Thai cuisine served on exquisite *benjarong* ware.

Bon Vivant, Tawana Ramada Hotel, 80 Surawongse Road. Tel: 2360361. Splendid cuisine with a host of traditional Thai dishes, all beautifully prepared and presented.

Bussaracum, 35 Soi Pipat 2, Convent Road. Tel: 2358915. Extremely popular with local connoisseurs of classical Thai cuisine; pleasant, informal atmosphere.

Cabbages and Condoms, 8 Soi 12, Sukhumvit Road. Tel: 2527349. Value for money and first-class cuisine. If you are not familiar with Thai food, this should be among one of your first choices. The profits support various family planning and other charitable projects.

Celadon, Sukhothai Bangkok, 13/3 South Sathorn Road. Tel: 2870222. Exceptional cuisine in the setting of an exotic water garden.

Chilli House, Patpong 4, (near the Rome Club), Silom Road. Tel: 2372777. You can enter either via Silom Road or through the Patpong Car Park Building on Patpong 2. Everything expertly prepared and presented by a top Thai chef, especially the seafood dishes; reasonable prices.

D'Jit Pochana, 62 Soi 20 Sukhumvit. Tel: 2581597 with branches at 1082 Paholyothin Road. Tel: 2795000-2, and New Paholyothin Road. Tel: 5311644. A long established Thai restaurant with moderate prices.

Khunying, 55 Soi 63, Sukhumvit Road. Tel: 381 2830.

Laicram, 120/1-2 Soi 23, Sukhumvit Road. Tel: 2599604. Variety of Thai dishes at moderate prices.

Lemongrass, 5/1 Soi 24, Sukhumvit Road. Tel: 2588637. Well known for its excellent cuisine at medium prices.

Nathong Restaurant, 84 Rachadapisek Road. Tel: 2462160-1.

Nipa Thai, Landmark Hotel, 138 Sukhumvit Road. Tel: 2540404. As with all the many restaurants in this hotel, its Thai restaurant is of the highest standard.

Pan Kitchen, Tai-Pan Hotel, 25 Soi 23, Sukhumvit Road. Tel: 2609888. Tasty Thai cuisine at reasonable prices. Worth going out of your way to try the inexpensive buffet set lunch which also includes some European dishes.

Salathip, Shangri-la Hotel, 89 Soi Wat Suan Phlu. Tel: 2367777. Superb Thai dining on the river's edge.

Sara Jane's Larb Lang Suan, 36/2 Soi Lang Suan. Tel: 2526572. Traditional, spicy Northeastern dishes.

Sidewalk, 855/2 Silom Road. Tel: 2364496. The owner is French born Pierre Chaslin, the author of the best selling "Discover Thai Cooking". Superb cuisine, ordinary decor, reasonable prices.

Sorn Dang (at the Democracy Monument), 78/2 Rajadamnern Road. Tel: 2243088. One of the oldest restaurants in town, well-known for good Thai food.

Spice Market, The Regent Hotel, 155 Rachadamri Road. Tel: 2516127. Beautifully-decorated restaurant, with dishes that the chef can adapt to suit Western palates.

Thai Pavilion, 981 Holiday Inn Crowne Plaza. Tel: 2384300. Traditional Thai cuisine in a traditonal setting.

Thai Room, 37/20-5 Patpong 2 Road. Tel: 2337920. Serving Thai, Mexican, Chinese and European food. One of the oldest restaurant in the city.

Thanying, 10 Pramuan Road, Silom. Tel: 2364361. Serves excellent Thai food. Set in very pleasant surroundings.

The Glass, 22/3-5 Soi 11, Sukhumvit Road. Tel: 2543566. As well known for its food as its live music in the evenings.

Whole Earth Cafe, 93/3 Soi Lang Suan. Tel: 2525574. Branch at 71 Soi 26, Sukhumvit Road. Tel: 2584900. Bangkok's best known Thai vegetarian restaurant; comfortable and friendly. There is also a tasty menu of non-vegetarian fare with some excellent Indian dishes.

Seafood

Dusit Rimtarn Seafood Restaurant, Supakarn Shopping Center, Sathorn Bridge. Tel: 4379671. A view of the river. Seafood and other Thai and Chinese cuisine superbly prepared under the supervision of the Dusit Thani Hotel.

Kaloang Sea Food and Restaurant, 127/41 Leab-Menam Road (Riverside), Chongnonthri Yanna. Tel: 2941488, 2941799.

Lord Jim's, Oriental Hotel, 48 Oriental Avenue. Tel: 2360400. Top quality restaurant noted for its good atmosphere, excellent food and service; expensive prices.

Sammuk Seafood, 2140-4 Lardprao, Soi 90. Tel: 5392466-9. One of many inexpensive Thai seafood restaurants in Bangkok. This particular one has won many accolades for the quality of its food.

Sea Food Market, 388 Sukhumvit Road, (opp. Soi Asoke). Tel: 2580218. Pick out the seafood of your choice from a vast variety on ice and have it cooked to suit your taste; informal and can be expensive if you succumb to the temptation of ordering too much.

Sea Food Restaurant, 1980 New Petchburi Road. Tel: 3144312. Under the same management as Sea Food Market.

Talay Thong, Siam Inter-Continental Hotel, 967 Rama I Road. Tel: 2530355. High quality dining, decor and service.

Wit's Oyster Bar, 20/10-11 Soi Ruam Rudi, Ploenchit Road. Tel: 2521820. A plush English style oyster bar.

Thai Dinner & Cultural Shows

Baan Thai, 7 Sukhumvit Soi 32. Tel: 2585403. Pleasant atmosphere in a group of old Thai houses in a tropical garden. Open daily 7.30pm with Thai dancing starting at 9pm.

Maneeya Lotus Room, 518/4 Ploenchit Road. Tel: 2510382. Open daily. Lunch 10 am–2pm. Nightly 7pm with Thai classical dance performance at 8.15pm.

Sala Rim Nam, Oriental Hotel. Tel: 4376211. Located in a beautiful, temple-like building across the river from the Oriental – particularly good Thai dancing. Free boat service from Oriental Hotel landing.

Sala Thai, Indra Hotel, 120-126 Ratchaprarop Road. Tel: 2080022. Attractive reproduction of a classic building on an upper floor of the hotel.

Silom Village Trade Center, 286 Silom Road. Tel: 2339447. Open-air and indoor restaurants, traditional food stalls, Thai cultural show presented every Saturday & Sunday from 12.45am and Thai classical dance shows daily at 8pm. Informal atmosphere.

Food Centers

Most major department stores have created a variation of traditional Thai food market stalls in the air-conditioned comfort of their precincts. The inexpensive dishes range from 15–50 *baht* and payment is made with refundable coupons purchased as you enter.

Outdoor Thai Restaurants

When giving instructions to the taxi driver, tell him "Suan Aahaan" (garden restaurant) before giving him the name of one of the restaurants below.

Baanbung, 32/10 Soi Intramara 45, Rachadapisek. Tel: 2778609, 2777563.

Buatong, 30 Rajadapisek Road. Tel: 2455545.

Tum Nak Thai, 131 Ratchadapisek Road. Tel: 2761810-2. This restaurant has merited an entry in the *Guinness Book of Records* as the largest in the world. Waitresses on roller skates serve food from all regions of Thailand; very popular with tourists.

Riverside Restaurants

Baan Khun Luang, 131/4 Khaw Road. Tel: 2410521. Thai, Chinese and Japanese cuisine in a riverside setting.

Dusit Rimtam Seafood Restaurant, Supakarn Shopping Center (on Thonburi side of Sathorn Bridge). Tel: 4379671-2.

Sala Rim Nam, Oriental Hotel, 48 Oriental Avenue, New Road. Tel: 2360400.

Salathip, Shangri-la Hotel, 89 New Road. Tel: 2367777.

Savoey Seafood Restaurant, River City Complex, 23 Yotha Road. Tel: 2377557-8. Excellent Thai and Chinese seafood dishes.

Dinner & Day Cruises

Tassaneya Nava, Contact World Travel Service at: Oriental Hotel. Tel: 2361920. 700 *baht* per person for a Thai meal. Two trips per night: 6–8pm, 8–10pm. Passengers have to board at River City Shopping Center pier.

The **Mekhala** is a handsomely converted teak rice barge that cruises up-river to Ayutthaya and back leaving Bangkok at 8am. Candlelight Thai and European buffet dinners catering up to 30 persons can be organised, taking in the vistas of Wat Arun, the Royal Barges and the Grand Palace. Contact Asia Voyages (Tel: 2567168).

Hotel Buffets

Many hotels in Bangkok vie with each other to prove that their lunch and dinner buffets surpass that of their competitors both in quality and value-for-money. The result is an overwhelming choice at prices that range from 100–500 *baht*. You will not be disappointed wherever you choose to go and even the least expensive buffets still offer a bewildering variety of dishes. All are highly recommended.

Asian Restaurants

CHINESE

Canton Palace, Evergreen Laurel Hotel, 88 North Sathorn Road. Tel: 2349829. A new restaurant in an elegant new hotel that has already received many acolades for the high standard of its Cantonese cuisine.

Chinatown, Dusit Thani Hotel, 946 Rama IV Road. Tel: 2360450. Less expensive than the Mayflower also within the hotel, but just as delicious.

Chiu Chau, Ambassador Hotel, 171 Soi 11-13, Sukhumvit Road. Tel: 2540444. Delicacies from the Southern Chinese province of Chiu Chau (Guangchao).

Coca Noodles, 8 Soi Tantawan, Suriwong Road. Tel: 2369323, branches at Siam Square, 416/3-8 Henry Dunant Road. Tel: 2516337, The Mall 4, 1911 Ramkhamhaeng Road. Tel: 3180997, 1/1 Soi 39, Sukhumvit Road. Tel: 2598188. Cantonese hot pot, sukiyaki and noodle dishes.

Dynasty, Central Plaza Hotel, 1695 Phaholyothin Road. Tel: 5411234. Traditional cuisine with Peking duck, shark's fin and abalone all featured in the extensive menu.

Great Wall, Asia Hotel, 296 Phaya Thai Road. Tel: 2150808. The heart of any good hotel is in the kitchen and at the Asia Hotel, there are several different kinds of restaurants of which this is one of the best.

Hoi Tien Lao, 762 Laadya Road, (Thonburi bank of river, opp. Royal Orchid Sheraton Hotel). Tel: 4371121. Cantonese food; one of Bangkok's oldest and most popular Chinese restaurants.

Hong Teh, Ambassador Hotel, 171 Soi 11-13, Sukhumvit Road. Tel: 2540444. A favorite with local gourmets for banquet entertaining.

Jade Garden, Montien Hotel, 54 Suriwongse Road. Tel: 2348060. Southern Chinese dishes prepared bv Hong Kong chefs in an elegant setting.

Lin-Fa, Siam City Hotel, 477 Sri Ayutthaya Road. Tel: 2470130. An elegant Chinese restaurant in one of Bangkok's most stylish hotels.

Lok Wah Hin, Novotel, Siam Square. Tel: 2556888. Cantonese and Szechuan cuisine at its best.

Mayflower, Dusit Thani Hotel, 946 Rama IV Road. Tel: 2360450. Without doubt, one of Thailand's best hotel Chinese restaurants.

Ming Palace, Indra Regent Hotel, 120/126 Ratchaprarop Road. Tel: 2080022. Southern Chinese dishes.

Nguan Lee, 101/25-26 Soi Lang Suan, Ploenchit Road. Tel: 2518366, 2523614. Covered market; real atmosphere. One of the few restaurants where you can eat the famous Mekong giant catfish.

Rice Mill, Royal Garden Riverside Hotel, 257/1-3 Charoen Nakhon Road. Tel: 4760022. Built on the site of an old rice mill, this new, luxury riverside hotel has a splendid Chinese restaurant.

Royal Kitchen, 46/1 North Sathorn Road. Tel: 2343063-5. More elegant and expensive than others.

Scala Restaurant, 218-218/1 Soi 1, Siam Square, (near Scala Theater). Tel: 2542891. One of the house specialities is Peking Duck. The adjoining restaurant specialises in shark's fin.

Shang Palace, Shangri-La Hotel, 89 Soi Wat Suan Phlu. Tel: 2367777, ext. 1350 & 1358. Superb Cantonese and Szechuan specialities. The lunchtime *dim sum* is a real treat.

Shangarila, 58/4-9 Thaniya Road. Tel: 2340861, branches at 154/4-5 Silom Road. Tel: 2349147, 306 Yawarat. Tel: 2245933. Northern Chinese cuisine.

Silom Restaurant, 793 Silom Road. Tel: 2364442. One of the oldest Chinese restaurants in town; northern Chinese dishes.
Silver Palace Restaurant, 5 Soi Pipat, Silom Road. Tel: 2355118-9. Well known for the variety of its delicious *dim sum* menu. Cantonese cuisine in opulent surroundings.
Sui Sian, Landmark Hotel, 138 Sukhumvit Road. Tel: 2540404. Cantonese and other regional delicacies to the highest standards.
Tai-Pan, Imperial Hotel, 6 Wireless Road. Tel: 2540111, ext. 1473. Cantonese fare in elegant surroundings.
The Chinese Restaurant, Grand Hyatt Erewan, 494 Ratchadamri Road. Tel: 2541234. Sophisticated Cantonese specialities prepared by Hong Kong chefs.
The Empress, Royal Princess Hotel, 269 Lan Luang Ropad. Tel: 2813088. Delicious lunchtime *dim sum*.
Ti Jing, Monarch Lee Gardens Hotel, 188 Silom Roiad. Tel: 2381999. A dazzling array of *dim sum* and other Cantonese delicacies.
Tien Tien Restaurant, 105 Patpong I Road, Bangrak. Tel: 2348717, 2346006. Located in the middle of busy, bustling Patpong. Moderate prices. The decor takes second place to the food.

INDIAN/ARABIC/MUSLIM
Akbar Restaurant, 1/4 Soi 3, Sukhumvit Road. Tel: 2533479. Northern Indian food at very reasonable prices. Try the prawn *korma*.
Bangkok Brindawan, 44/1 Soi 19, Silom Road. Tel: 2334791. Simple decor and some excellent vegetarian dishes. Daily buffet lunch. Inexpensive.
Bukhara, Royal Orchid Sheraton Hotel, 2 Captain Bush Lane. Tel: 2345599. Superb Indian cuisine with impeccable service.
Cafe India, 460/8 Surawong Road. Tel: 2330419. Northern Indian cooking in handsomely-decorated surroundings.
Cedar, 4/1 Soi 49/1, Sukhumvit Road. Tel: 3914482. Lebanese and Greek cuisine.
Himali Cha Cha, 1229/11 New Road. Tel: 2351569. Northern cuisine by a master chef named Cha Cha; ask him what he recommends from the daily menu.
Maharajah's, 19/1 Soi 8, Sukhumvit Road. Tel: 2548876. Some tasty tandoor dishes. Inexpensive.
Moghul Room, 1/16 Sukhumvit Soi 11. Tel: 2534465. Popular, but more expensive than some.
Mrs. Balbir's, 155/18 Soi 11, Sukhumvit Road. Tel: 2532281. Excellent cuisine with medium prices.
Rang Mahal, Rembrandt Hotel, 19 Soi 18, Sukhumvit Road. Tel: 2617100. First-class cuisine and impeccable service.
Tandoor, Holiday Inn Crowne Plaza, 981 Silom Road. Tel: 2384300. North Indian cuisine of exceptional quality. Moderate prices.

INDONESIAN
Bali, 15/3 Soi Ruam Rudee, Ploenchit Road. Tel: 2543581. Customers can savor the best of Javanese cuisine at very reasonable prices.

JAPANESE
Benihana, Royal Garden Riverside Hotel, 257/1-3 Charoen Nakhon Road. Tel: 4760022. The preparation of the dishes is a combination of knife-wielding and juggling. The end result is always a superb meal.
Benkay, Royal Orchid Sheraton Hotel, 2 Captain Bush Lane. Tel: 2345599. The restaurant is noted for its exquisite Japanese cuisine served in an ambience of quiet elegance; a place for refined tastes.
Endogin, Shangri-La Hotel, 89 Soi Wat Suan Phlu. Tel: 2367777. All that you would expect from one of Bangkok's top hotels.
Genji, Hilton International Hotel, Wireless Road. Tel: 2530123, ext. 8141. Expensive.
Hagi, Central Plaza Hotel, 1695 Phaholyothin Road. Tel: 5411234. Popular and with reasonable prices.
Hanaya, 683 Siphya Road. Tel: 2348095. Clean and unpretentious.
Kagetsu, Asia Hotel, 296 Phaya Thai Road. Tel: 2150808. Traditional cuisine and setting. Popular and reasonable prices.
Kiku-No-Hana, The Landmark Hotel, 138 Sukhumvit Road. Tel: 2540404. First-class Japanese cuisine in a first-class hotel.
Miraku, Imperial Hotel, 6 Wireless Road. Tel: 2540023. Traditional Japanese dishes in a traditional Japanese setting.
Mizu's, 32 Patpong Road. Tel: 2336447. One of the oldest Japanese restaurants in the city. The house speciality is sizzling steak. Reasonable prices.
Nishimura, Siam City Hotel, 477 Sri Ayutthaya Road. Tel: 2470130. First-class dining in style.
Shogun, Dusit Thani Hotel, 946 Rama IV Road. Tel: 2360450. Sashimi and other Japanese delicacies; elegant decor.
Teikoku, Imperial Hotel, 6 Wireless Road. Tel: 2540111, ext. 1496. Superb Japanese dishes, traditional decor and surroundings.
Teio, Monarch Lee Gardens Hotel, 188 Silom Road. Tel: 2381999. Sophisticated Japanese dining. Special family buffet lunches on Saturday and Sunday.
Tokugawa, Ambassador Hotel, 171 Soi 11-13, Sukhumvit Road. Tel: 2540444, ext. 1569. The *teppanyaki* is delicious and fun to watch the chef displaying his skill.

KOREAN
Arirang House, 106-8 Silom Road (at the end of Patpong 3 across from Convent Road). Tel: 2341096. Wide selection of Korean food; inexpensive.
First Korean, 543 Silom Road. Tel: 2342636. One of the oldest and best if you want to sample fine Korean cuisine.
Korea House, 57/23 Wireless Road (behind Hoburger on corner with Ploenchit Road). Tel: 2522589. Good, simple Korean cooking served in an informal atmosphere.
Koreana Restaurant, 446-450 Soi 7, Siam Square. Tel: 2529398. An extensive menu of traditonal Korean fare. Popular with local Koreans.

POLYNESIAN
Trader Vic's, Royal Garden Riverside Hotel, 257/1-3 Charoen Nakhon Road. Tel: 4760022. The unique style of oven gives a different flavour to the dishes. A delightfully different dining experience.

VIETNAMESE
Cherie Kitchen, 593/13 Soi 33/1 Sukhumvit. Tel: 2585058. Medium prices.
Le Dalat, 47/1 Soi 23, Sukhumvit Road. Tel: 2584192 and on 2nd floor, Patpong Building, Surawong Road. Tel: 2340290. Two of the best in town in the medium price range.
Le Danang, Central Plaza Hotel, 1695 Phaholyothin Road. Tel: 5411234. A long established Vietnamese restaurant renowned for its authentic cuisine.
Saigon, Asia Hotel, 296 Phaya Thai Road. Tel: 2150808. Luxury dining in an elegant setting under the supervision of a Vietnamese chef.
Saigon Bakery, 313 Silom Road. Tel: 2310434. A Vietnamese restaurant and bakery; inexpensive.
Saigon-Rimsai, 413/9 Soi 55, Sukhumvit Road. Tel: 3811797. Small, beautifully decorated and the Vietnamese chef produces a variety of inexpensive dishes.
Vietnam, 82-4 Silom Road, (opp. Convent Road). Tel: 2346174. Southern style Vietnamese cuisine.

Continental Cuisine
ENGLISH/AMERICAN & GRILL
Angus Steak House, 9/4 5 Thaniya Road. Tel: 2343590 and at 595 Soi 31/1, Sukhumvit Road. Tel: 2594444. A mixed menu but juicy prime cuts of imported beef are the house speciality. The lunchtime set menu is particularly good value.
Bécassine, 43 Soi 31, Sukhumvit Road. Tel: 2584592. Some expertly prepared English dishes that taste better than you will find in their country of origin. Elegantly furnished and decorated. Reasonable prices.
Bobby's Hot Dog Stand, Patpong 2. Tel: 2341549. The name belies the fact that it is a splendid New York style deli and diner serving American sandwiches with a choice of over 50 different filling, their own 100% pure beef burgers and much more.
Captain Bush Grill, Royal Orchid Sheraton Hotel, 2 Captain Bush Lane. Tel: 2345599. Superb cuisine with an extensive continental menu and charcoal grilled steaks. The decor is reminiscent of an old sailing ship.
Fireplace Grill, Le Meridien President Hotel, 136/26 Gaysorn Road. Tel: 2530444. Renowned for its excellent food and service.
Gourmet Gallery, 6/1 Soi Promsri (which joins Sois 39 and 41), Sukhumvit Road. Tel: 3914811. It lives up to its name.
Hamilton's, Dusit Thani Hotel, 946 Rama IV Road. Tel: 2360450. High quality dining, decor and service.
Hard Rock Café, Soi 11, Siam Square. Tel: 2510792-4. A branch of the well-known international chain.

La Rotonde Grill, Narai Hotel, 222 Silom Road. Tel: 2370100-39. Thailand's only revolving restaurant. The view from atop the hotel is unique. The menu of international fare is expertly prepared and presented.
Le Gourmet Grill, Montien Hotel, 54 Suriwongse Road. Tel: 2348060. An intimate, quiet restaurant with excellent food and good service.
Neil's Tavern, 58/4 Soi Ruam Rudee. Tel: 2566875. Recommended for good steaks and seafood.
Regent Grill, Regent Bangkok, 155 Ratchdamri Road. Tel: 2516127. Light, innovative cuisine in a tropical garden ambience. Extensive wine cellar.
Savoury, 60 Soi Wat Khaek, Pan Road. Tel: 2364825-30. Extensive continental food menu.
The Cup, 2nd floor, Peninsula Plaza. Tel: 2524568. Gourmet lunches only, closes 6.30pm.
Tiara, Dusit Thani Hotel, 965 Rama IV Road. Tel: 2360450. On the top floor of the hotel, offering a superb view of the city. The menu features a delightful combination of Asian and Western dishes that are the unique creation of the inventive chef.

FRENCH
Avenue One, Siam Inter-Continental Hotel, 967 Rama I Road. Tel: 2530355. Authentic traditional and nouvelle cuisine.
Bécassine, 43 Soi 31, Sukhumvit Road. Tel: 2584592. The menu features international cuisine with some excellent French dishes. Stylish surroundings and reasonable prices.
Café de Paris, Patpong 2 Road, (next to Trattoria da Roberto). Tel: 2372776. A cosy Parisian style café with authentic French cuisine and decor. Sit outside on the small patio in front and watch the world go by in busy Patpong. Reasonable prices.
Chez Daniel Le Normand, 1/9 Soi 24, Sukhumvit Road. Tel: 2588636. The French master chef despises nouvelle cuisine, so be prepared for traditional French sauces and filling portions in the setting of a Normandy Inn. The casual atmosphere, fine food and reasonable prices have earned this restaurant an envied reputation.
Chez Serge, 4 Soi Thonglor 25, Soi 55, Sukhumvit Road. Tel: 3812187. One of the best French restaurants in Bangkok. Very stylish, friendly atmosphere, good choice of wines and very reasonable prices.
Kempinski Terrace, Mansion Kempinski, 75/23 Soi 11, Sukhumvit Road. Tel: 2532655. It rivals the best known and longer established French restaurants in Thailand both in the quality of the food and the service. The innovative menu is a credit to the talented chef.
La Brasserie, Regent Bangkok, 155 Ratchdamri Road. Tel: 2516127. Overlooking a fish pond and waterfall; excellent food and service.
La Noppamas, Sukothai Bangkok, 13/3 South Sathorn Road. Tel: 2870222. Innovative gourmet dishes; overlooking a water garden.
La Paloma, 26/2 Mahaesak Road. Tel: 2333853. Good food and a quiet atmosphere; moderate prices.

La Tache, Shangri-La Hotel, 89 Soi Wat Suan Phlu. Tel: 2367777. All that you would expect from one of Bangkok's top hotels.

Le Bistrot, **20/**17-19 Soi Ruam Rudee. Tel: 2512523. A classical and elegant French restaurant and very popular.

Le Bordeaux, 1/38 Soi 39, Sukhumvit Road. Tel: 2509766. An interesting menu of traditional fare with some of the chef's own creations. Moderate prices and some good wines.

Le Cristal, Regent Bangkok, 155 Ratchadamri Road. Tel: 2516127. A place for one to see and be seen; unique Franco-Siamese interior.

Le Normandie Grill, Oriental Hotel, 49 Oriental Avenue. Tel: 2360400, ext. 3380. One of the finest restaurants in the world, with a spectacular view of the river. High class; jacket and tie required.

Ma Maison, Hilton International Hotel, Wireless Road. Tel: 2530123, ext. 8026. Elegant and expensive.

Mon Séri, Soi Ruam Rudee, Ploenchit Road. Tel: 2517879. A new French restaurant with an inventive menu.

Palais de Monarch, Monarch Lee Gardens Hotel, 188 Silom Road. Tel: 2381999. First-class European cuisine with a French flavour and live music.

Stanley's French, Soi Ruam Rudee, Ploenchit Road. This soi has several excellent restaurants and this is one of them. Apart from the French dishes, there are some Cajun/Creole house specialities. Superlative cuisine and service.

GERMAN

Bier-Kutsche, 7 Soi 3 Sukhumvit. Tel: 2532063. Basic and inexpensive.

By Otto, 1 Soi 20, Sukhumvit Road. Tel: 2526208. One of the best German restaurants in Thailand with everything from the sausages to the bread freshly made on the premises.

Singha Bier Haus, 179 Soi 21, Sukhumvit Road. Tel: 2583951. A faithful re-creation of a Bavarian beer house, with a German chef.

HUNGARIAN

Nick's No. 1, 17 Soi 16, Sukhumvit Road. Tel: 2594717. Bangkok's only Hungarian restaurant but with only a few traditional Hungarian dishes. Kobe steak is an added attraction; eccentric atmosphere.

ITALIAN

Don Giovanni, Central Plaza Hotel, 1695 Phaholyothin Road. Tel: 5411234. The best Italian restaurant in this part of Bangkok.

Giorgio's, Royal Orchid Sheraton Hotel, 2 Captain Bush Lane. Tel: 2345599. Fine dining enhanced by spectacular views of the Chao Phya River.

L'Opera, Soi 39 Sukhumvit. Tel: 2585605. Highly regarded by all and very popular. Warm, friendly atmosphere.

Paesano, 96/7 Soi Ton Son, Ploenchit. Tel: 2522834. Casual atmosphere and medium prices.

Pan Pan, 591 Sukhumvit (corner Soi 33). Tel: 2589304 and at 45 Soi Lang Suan. Traditional Italian fare and reasonable prices.

Peppino, Shangri-La Hotel, 89 Soi Wat Suan Phlu. Tel: 2367777. First-class cuisine and impeccable service. You will pay a little more but well worth it. Try the Parma ham – it is made in the hotel with local pork and tastes as good as the imported variety.

Pizzeria, **Nara**i Hotel, 222 Silom Road. Tel: 2370100. Unpretentious, but serving some of the best Italian food in Bangkok.

Roberto's 18, 36 Soi 18 Sukhumvit. Tel: 2581327. Good pasta. Friendly atmosphere.

Sorrento, 66 North Sathorn Road. Tel: 2349841. Located in an old Neapolitan style villa. Superb Italian cuisine in the heart of Bangkok.

Spasso, Grand Hyatt Erewan Hotel, 494 Ratchadamri Road. Tel: 2541234. Expert Italian chef, authentic Italian cuisine including clay oven-baked pizzas. Live music from a top band and one of the "in" places.

Trattoria da Roberto, 37/9 Plaza Arcade, Patpong 2 Road. Tel: 2345987. Very good Italian food in the middle of Bangkok's bar belt.

Vito's, 20/2-3 Soi Ruam Rudee, Ploenchit Road. Tel: 2521820. Pizza, pasta and traditional Italian fare in the most elegant surroundings.

MEXICAN

El Gordo's, 130/8 Silom Road (in lane opposite Bangkok Bank's head office building). Tel: 2345470. Mexican specialities in an old Mexican atmosphere. Live music.

Senor Pico, Rembrandt Hotel, 19 Soi 18, Sukhumvit Road. Tel: 2617100. Authentic Mexican fare with everything from snacks to a full meal; live band.

SCANDINAVIAN

The Two Vikings, 2 Soi 35, Sukhumvit Road. Tel: 2588843. Established over 20 years ago and still pleasing its customers.

The Wall, 120/20-22 Soi Pramote 3, Mahesak Road. Tel: 2358041. Very reasonable prices and one of the friendliest restaurants in Bangkok. Inexpensive.

Tea Rooms

Afternoon tea is an English custom that is followed in several of the major hotels. The most famous is in the Author's Lounge at the prestigious Oriental Hotel. The buffet style afternoon teas in some of the hotels are so lavish and the choice so varied that they may easily be mistaken for a full gourmet dinner.

Fast Food

There are several internationally known fast food chains such as **McDonalds, Burger King, Dunkin Donuts, Mr. Donut, Pizza Hut, Swensons, Shakey's, Kentucky Fried Chicken**, and **A & W Family Restaurant** in all the major urban areas of Bangkok.

Thai
Bain's Garden, 2/2 Wat Gate Road, Soi 1, offers a range of Thai dishes in a garden setting.
The Gallery, on Charoenrat Road combines an art gallery with a Chinese garden and riverside terrace.
Krua Khun Phan, 80/1 Indrarot Road (near Suan Dok Gate), displays a variety of ready-made Thai dishes.
Ma-Prang (Star Fruit), at 25 Charoenprathet Road, across from Pornping Hotel, serves Thai food in a garden setting.
Nang Nual is also a riverside restaurant but is downriver off the Chiang Mai-Lamphun Road, near Wat Chedi Si Liem.
Riverside Restaurant on Charoenrat Road serves excellent meals on the banks of the Ping River. Good live music.
Six Poles on Charoenrat Road, across from The Gallery, is an old northern-style restaurant serving Thai and Continental meals.

There are also Lanna Khantoke dinners where you can dine on northern Thai Khantoke cuisine and then sit back to enjoy a program of northern dances and music. **The Diamond Hotel** on Charoenprathet Road serves a nightly Lanna Khantoke dinner with classical Lanna and hilltribe dancing. Tel: 234155 for reservations. **Old Chiang Mai Cultural Center** also presents a Khantoke dinner with a program of Northern and hilltribe dances. Offered nightly from 7pm–10pm in a beautiful Northern Thai style house at 185/3 Wua Lai Road. Tel: 235097 for reservations. The fee is 200 *baht* and it begins at 7pm. Reserve beforehand.

Whole Earth, 88 Sridonchai Road. Tel: 232463, serves vegetarian and non-vegetarian Thai dishes in a garden setting.

Rabbit, cobra, deer, eels, frogs, tortoises, lambs and other exotic meats are offered at **Kaithong Restaurant**, 67 Kotchasarn Road. Tel: 236584.

Asian
Musashi (Japanese), 53/6 Inthawarot Road. Tel: 210944.
Naina (Indian), 138 Charoenrat Road. Tel: 248663.

European
Beer Stube (German), 33/6A Moonmuang Road (near Tapae Gate). Tel: 210869.
Cafe de Paris (French), 14-16 Kotchasan Road. Tel: 234804.
German Beer Garden (German), 48 Charoenprathet Road. Tel: 236179.
Papillion (French), 12/1 Rotfai Road, next to the railway station. Tel: 243187.
Pensione La Villa (Italian), 145 Ratdamnern Road. Tel: 215403.
The Pub (English), Huay Kaew Road, near the Rincome Hotel (Tel: 211550), has English meals and a fireplace.

Thai
Deeprom, 503 Pattaya Klang Road. Tel: 418937.
Krua Suthep, Pattaya 2 Road. Tel: 419888.
Nang Nual, South Pattaya. Tel: 418478, 418708.
Sugar Hut, Chomtien Beach. Tel: 422600.

Asian & Continental
Akamon (Japanese cuisine), Pattaya 2 Road, North Pattaya. Tel: 419598, 423727.
Dolf Riks (Indonesian and Continental), Regent Marine complex, Pattaya 2 Road. Tel: 418269.
Orient Express (Continental), Nipa Lodge, Beach Road. Tel: 418195, 418321. Continental favorites in a refurbished railway car.

Thai
• PHUKET TOWN
Tunk-ka Cafe atop Rang Hill on the north end of town. Southern specialities.
Kaw Yam Restaurant at 1/1 Thoon Ka Road. Southern Thai dishes.
• PATONG
Two superb restaurants are next-door to each other on Soi Bangla: **No. 4** and **Tum**.
Malee's Seafood Village on Thaviwong Road. Try shark steak.
• KARON
Sunset Restaurant, opposite Karon Supermarket on Soi Bangla. Good food and economical prices.
• KATA
Boathouse Restaurant, Boathouse Inn. Superb dining by the sea.
Kampong Kata, on a hill above the Kata Center. Traditional Thai dishes.
• NAI HARN
On the Rocks, beyond the Phuket Yacht Club Hotel.
• CHALONG
Gan Eng 1, end of the Chalong Road, by the sea.

Asian
• PATONG
Fuji (Japanese), halfway down Soi Patong Post Office on the right. Patronized by Japanese.
Shalimar (Indian) at 89/59 Soi Patong Post Office. Serves northern Indian specialties.
• KATA ROAD
Hayashi Thai House (Japanese), atop the hill on H 4028 (Patak Road). Superb views.
No vegetarian restaurants but **Shalimar** has Indian vegetarian dishes.

European
• PATONG
K. Hotel (German) on Rat-uthit Road. German chef.
Paciugo (Ice Cream), 30m in Soi Patong Resort (off Soi Bangla) on the left. Italian creations.

Pizzeria Napoli (Italian), Soi Patong Post office. Pizza, pasta and a host of other Italian dishes.
• KARON
Ristorante Italiano (Italian), next to Coco Cabana. Northern Italian cuisine.

DRINKING NOTES

Many restaurants catering to western tastes whip up a delicious shake made of pureed fruit, crushed ice and a light syrup. Chilled young coconuts are delicious; drink the juice, then scrape out and eat the tender young flesh. Soft drinks like Coca-Cola are found everywhere. Try Vitamilk, a health drink made from soya bean milk. For a refreshing cooler, order a bottle of soda, a glass of ice and a sliced lime. Squeeze the lime into the glass, add the soda and instantly, your thirst is slaked.

Sip the very strong Thai coffee flavored with chicory. The odd orange Thai tea is sticky sweet but delicious. On a hot day, Chinese prefer to drink a hot, very thin tea believing that ice is bad for the stomach. Try all three over ice anyway.

Beers include Kloster, Carlsberg, Amarit, Singha and Singha Gold. Of the many Thai cane whiskeys, Mekhong is the most popular. It is drunk on the rocks, with soda and lime or with a bit of honey added to it. Most foreign liquors are available. Large restaurants have wine lists.

THINGS TO DO

SIGHT-SEEING TOURS

CITY

Bangkok
After touring the famous attractions like the Grand Palace, Wat Phra Kaew, Wat Po, Wat Arun, Chatuchak Weekend Market, and the Floating Market, visit these lesser-known sites:

See Buddhist monks on their morning alms round by visiting **Wat Benjamabophit** at about 6.30am. Here, in contrast to the normal practice, Buddhists take food to monks who wait silently outside the gates of the temple. Some excellent photo opportunities arise here.

Tour **Vimarn Mek**, the world's largest Golden Teak Palace, and its superb collection of crystal, gold and silver art objects. Open Wednesday–Sunday, 9.45am–3pm. Admission is 50 *baht* or free

with an entrance ticket to the Grand Palace.

Early in the morning, wander through Bangkok's largest wet market, **Phak Klong Talad**, near the foot of the Memorial Bridge. Then visit the flower market on nearby Chakkapet Road.

Enjoy a traditional Thai massage in the *sala* (pavilion) near the eastern wall of the **Wat Po** compound.

Board an express boat from the Oriental Hotel or Tha Chang near the Grand Palace and ride 45 minutes upriver to Nonthaburi with its bustling market. Have a drink or a meal at the floating restaurant next to the beautiful old provincial office. Alternatively, take the boat downstream to the last stop near the Krung Thep Bridge.

Take a free guided tour of the **National Museum**, Tuesday–Thursday at 9.30am.

Enjoy the educational snake show (where cobras are milked) at the **Snake Farm** (Saowapha Institute) on Rama 4 Road at 11am and 2pm.

On Saturdays and Sundays, explore the **Weekend Market** at Chatuchak Park. Start early to avoid the midday heat.

Walk down **Sampeng Lane** in the heart of Chinatown. Explore all the side alleys.

Stroll through a former century of gracious living at the **Jim Thompson House**. Or visit the complex of old houses at **Suan Pakkad Palace**.

Visit the **Ancient City** with its miniature replicas of the kingdom's chief architectural masterpieces.

Rent a private boat at The Oriental Hotel and cruise through Klong Bangkok Noi, stopping at the **Royal Barge Museum**. Take the long route home, through the smaller canals to Klong Bangkok Yai and back to The Oriental.

Attend a **Thai boxing match** at Rajdamnern or Lumpini Stadium.

Have your fortune told by an astrologer at the Montien Hotel.

Watch a free **likay performance** at Lak Muang.

Make a wish and an offering at the **Erawan Shrine** at Rajprasong.

COUNTRY

Central Plains
Take the train to the **Bridge on the River Kwai**. The State Railways of Thailand offers a day trip each Saturday. If you have several days, stay on one of the rafthouses farther up the river.

Ride the **Oriental Queen** up the Chao Phya River to Ayutthaya, visiting Bang Pa-in along the way.

Enjoy the water sports in **Chomtien** or the nightlife in **Pattaya**.

Take a bus to Petchburi to explore **King Mongkut's palace and observatory** on top of the hill.

Drive to **Rajburi** to look at the beautiful ceramics crafted and sold there.

Visit **King Narai's old palace** at Lopburi.

The Northeast
Drive to the Northeast to see **Khmer temples** at Phimai, Phanom Wan, Phanom Rung and Muang Tham.

Take a day trip to **Khao Yai National Park**. The State Railways of Thailand conducts a one-day trip on Saturdays.

Travel the road from Nong Khai along the Meklong River to Ubon.

The North
Take the train to Phitsanuloke to see the Phra Buddha Jinnarat image in **Wat Mahathat**. Continue to Sukhothai to see Thailand's first capital city. Then to Si Satchanalai for some quiet beauty. Complete the journey by dropping south to the walled city of Kampaengphet before returning to Phitsanuloke.

Visit the hilltop temple of **Doi Suthep** at sunset for a panoramic view of Chiang Mai Valley.

Explore the **crafts studios** along the road to Borsang.

Drive the tree-lined road to Lamphun to visit **Wat Phra That Haripunchai** and **Wat Chamathewi**.

Visit the orchid farms and butterfly farms of **Mae Sa Valley**. Then ride for two hours on an elephant through the hills.

Take a trek to visit **hilltribes** outside of Chiang Mai or Chiang Rai.

Attend the demonstration of elephant's skills in moving teak logs at the **Young Elephant's Training School** at Lampang or the **Chiang Dao Elephant Camp**.

Ride a longboat 3½ hours down the **Kok River** from Tha Ton to Chiang Rai.

Visit Mae Sai on the Burmese border and then drive to the **Golden Triangle** where the borders of Laos, Thailand and Myanmar meet in the middle of the Meklong River.

The South
Visit the islands of **Pang-nga Bay**.

Ride the train from Bangkok to **Penang** in Malaysia.

Roam the farm areas and coastal roads of **Phuket** in a rented jeep.

Rent a motorcycle and visit all the beaches of **Ko Samui**.

Cruise around Phuket on a **Chinese junk**.

BEACH

Beach facilities range from the rustic to the well-developed, each attracting a different clientele. On a rating of 1–3 (1 = basic facilities only; 2 = adequate but not luxurious facilities; 3 = first-class hotels with restaurants, sports, shopping and sightseeing facilities).

Pattaya & Chomtien
The Queen of Thailand's beaches offers a full range of activities. Hotels run from the very luxurious to fan-cooled rooms in shophouses off the main street. There are Continental, Asian and Thai restaurants, extensive land and water sports facilities, a golf course, cultural shows, a somewhat tatty nightlife, and all the accoutrements of a full-blown resort. (3)

South Coast
Resorts running east from Ban Phe comprises of groups of bungalows set in beautiful tropical gardens. Dining and entertainment are found within the confines of each complex with few attractions outside the resort. Limited water sports facilities. This is ideal for families and those who want a quiet, relaxing vacation. (2)

Koh Samet
While it is changing, this beautiful island is still a backpacker's retreat with rustic bungalows along lovely beaches. There are a few up-market hotels but the lack of connection with the mainland other than scheduled ferry boats means that the island attracts a hardier crowd. Water sports facilities are limited and there is little nighttime entertainment other than beachside restaurants. This is a place to spend several quiet days. (1)

Hua-Hin & Cha-am
In former times, royalty gathered here and there is still an air of grandeur to its wide beaches. The area generally attracts families and older vacationers but there are young couples as well. Excellent for quiet relaxation, strolling the fishing docks, a leisurely round of golf, riding ponies on the beach, or just sitting in a beach chair. (2.5)

Phuket
One of the fastest-growing success stories in Asia has combined natural beauty with a complete range of resort facilities to turn this into a magnet for Asians and Europeans alike. Gone are most of the budget accommodations but there are still low-priced as well as luxury hotels. It has land and water sports, a golf course, cultural shows, nightlife, drives around the island, in short, a full-fledged beach resort. (3)

Phi Phi
For years, its natural attractions were muted by its remoteness so that only budget travelers stayed in its thatched bungalows. It is still bungalow accommodation for the most part but it has begun to move up-market. Superb snorkeling, limited water sports, virtually no land sports, little nightlife, trips to nearby islands, restaurants and surpassing beauty is what it offers. (1.5)

Krabi
Wide beaches and a laid-back lifestyle formerly drew only budget travelers. A new airstrip has made the island accessible and first-class hotels made it comfortable for better-heeled tourists. Some water sports and cultural activities. (2)

TRAVEL PACKAGES

Thai Airways International (THAI) offers Royal Orchid Holiday tours that provide individual traveler benefits at package tour prices. Arrange with Thai International before arrival, they last 2 days but can be extended. Choose from tours of Bangkok, Chiang Mai and Phuket.

Tour Operators

Bangkok and Chiang Mai abound in tour agencies which offer a dozen trips to see temples, craft workshops, canals and other attractions.

CULTURE

Modern pop culture seems to have gained ascendancy over traditional Thai arts and while government support for Thai arts and performers is growing, the old culture is far from being a vital force in the society. Foreign culture is promoted by the respective country cultural organizations but little is done to attract foreign performers in the manner of, say, Hong Kong's Art Center and the annual Hong Kong Arts Festival.

There many museums in Bangkok and in major towns around the country are devoted to preserving the past and contain some superb specimens. Exhibitions of modern art are arranged by private gallery owners, foreign government cultural centers, or by corporate patrons, usually banks, who sponsor annual shows.

Museums

The **National Museum** at 4 Phra Athit Road, Tel: 2212522, next to Sanam Luang in the heart of the old royal city, is a repository of archaeological finds, Buddha images, old royal regalia, ceramics and art objects (usually Buddhist) from neighboring countries. The walls of the Buddhaisawan Chapel in the museum grounds are covered in some of the finest Buddhist murals in Thailand.

The National Museum offers free guided tours of Buddhist and other art and conducts them in a number of languages. The schedule is:

English: Thai Art and Culture (Tuesday, Thursday); Buddhism (Wednesday).

French: Pre-Thai and Thai Art (Wednesday).

German: Thai Art and Culture (Tuesday, Thursday).

Japanese: Thai Culture and Pottery (first two Tuesdays of the month); Buddhaisawan Chapel (third Tuesday of the month); Pre-Thai and Thai Art (fourth and fifth Tuesday of the month).

Mandarin and Spanish: On request (groups only). Tel: 2241402.

Tours last about 2 hours. Whatever tour you take, be sure to visit the Buddhaisawan Chapel and the Cremation Chariot Hall (Hall 17) afterwards.

Art Galleries

The **National Gallery** to the north of the National Museum across the approach to the Phra Pinklao Bridge at 4 Chao Fa Road, Tel: 2812224, displays works by Thai artists and offers frequent film shows. Open daily from 9am–noon, 1–4pm except on Monday and Friday.

Silpakorn University, opposite the Grand Palace on Na Phralan Road is the country's premier fine arts college. It frequently stages exhibitions of students' work. Other promoters of Thai art and photography are the British Council, Goethe Institute and Alliance Francaise, all of which sponsor exhibitions.

Art galleries seem more interested in selling mass market and "tourist" works than in promoting experimental art; but one, **Visual Dhamma**, takes an active role in ensuring that talented artists exhibit their works. As its name implies, it is interested primarily in a new school of Thai art which attempts to re-interpret Buddhist themes. It is located on Soi Asoke in a lane opposite the Singha Beer House.

Concerts

The Fine Arts Department periodically offers concerts of Thai music and dance/drama at the **National Theatre**. On Saturday afternoons at 2pm, programs of Thai classical dance are presented at the auditorium of the **Public Relations Building** on Rajdamnern Klang Avenue opposite the Royal Hotel. Each Friday, Bangkok Bank offers traditional Thai music on the top floor of its **Pan Fah** branch (Rajdamnern Avenue at the intersection with Prasumane Road) at 5pm.

Concerts of European music and dance are few and far between and are generally sponsored by foreign cultural organizations. Other concerts feature Thai musicians playing European music. In deference to local tastes, the fare is generally standard compositions rather than wildly avant garde, but the musicianship is of a high level. English-language newspapers announce upcoming programs.

Theaters

The **National Theater** presents Thai works and, occasionally, big name foreign ensembles like the New York Philharmonic. For more experimental works, Thai or foreign, look to the **Thailand Cultural Center**. The Center, which is a gift of the government of Japan, is located on Ratchadapisek Road north of Bangkok. Its three stages present everything from pianists to puppets. See the newspapers for announcements of forthcoming performances.

It is also possible to find Chinese opera (*ngiew*) performed as part of funeral entertainment or during the Vegetarian Festival each September in Chinatown. These performances are normally not announced but are an unexpected surprise one stumbles across when wandering back alleys. It is hard to miss; the clash of cymbals and drums and the screech of violins identify it.

So, too, has *Likay* bitten the dust. *Likay*, the village version of the great *lakhon* and *khon* dance/dramas of the palace, was once staple fare at temple fairs. Alas, most of the fairs have faded away in the city and are found only in rural areas. Even there, *likay* performances are often given second billing to popular movies shown in the open air on big screens. About the only place one can see truncated *likay* performances is at Lak Muang where successful supplicants pay a troupe to perform for the gods of the heavens and the angels of the city.

Movies

Bangkok movie theaters present Thai, Chinese and Western films. The Western films are either megahits or are filled with violence – gore being substituted for dialogue; pretty grim fare, generally. Thai films, city Thais will tell you, are either based on a set theme (good versus evil with pathos, rowdy humor, ugly villains and plenty of fisticuffs) that appeal only to up-country audiences (and indeed are made primarily with them in mind) or are silly comedies on the theme of young love. Only rarely does a film of social significance appear.

Unfortunately, no film is translated or subtitled in English so one must either go with a Thai friend or guess the dialogue and plot (often easier than you think). The third option is to attend a Chinese movie, usually made in Hong Kong or Japan and on the theme of kung fu vengeance, mob violence, cutesy mom-pop-and-baby comedies or young love. These are subtitled and make for good, light entertainment.

Diary of Events

For a listing of daily events, see the *Bangkok Post, Thailand Times* and *The Nation* features sections and week-long diaries of coming events in the Sunday editions.

Libraries

For reading or reference, stop in at one of these Bangkok libraries. All carry books in English on Thailand.

A.U.A., 179 Rajdamri Road, Tel: 2528953. Open from 8.30am–6pm on Monday–Friday; and from 8am–1pm on Saturday. The library is sponsored by the US Information Service.

British Council, 428 Siam Square, Soi 2, Tel: 2526136. Open from 10am–7pm on Tuesday–Friday; and from 10am–5pm on Saturday.

Neilson Hayes, 195 Suriwong Road, Tel: 2331731. Open from 9.30am–4pm on Monday–Saturday; and from 9.30am–12.30pm on Sunday.

Siam Society, 131 Soi 21, Sukhumvit Road, Tel: 2583491. Open from 9am–5pm on Tuesday–Saturday.

Bookstores

Bangkok has many good bookstores with a wide selection of books for information and for entertainment. If you want to read about something you have encountered in Bangkok or just want a good, light read for the beach, try one of these bookshops. Alternatively, your hotel bookstore may have something you want.

Asia Books, 221 Sukhumvit Road (between Sois 17 and 19) and 2nd fl., Peninsula Plaza, Landmark Hotel. Art books, coffee table books, travel books, bestsellers in English.

D.K. Books, jocularly known as the "Patpong University", is in the basement of the CCT Building, 999 Suriwongse Road (around the corner from Patpong and open until 1.30am). The most complete bookstore in Bangkok with books in English on nearly every subject under the sun.

Central Department stores, all branches, have good book departments.

NIGHTLIFE

For years, Thailand enjoyed a lusty reputation as a center for sin and sex. While the reputation was not altogether undeserved, times and clienteles have changed a bit. The GIs of the 1960s and the German, Japanese and Arab sex tourists of the 70s, have been replaced by more up-market tourists, usually traveling as couples and interested in sex shows more as dabblers than as gourmands.

The nighttime scene in Bangkok and, to some extent, in big up-country towns has thus changed considerably to accommodate them. While there has been no diminution in the number of massage parlors and bars, there has been an increase in other activities to meet the needs of the new breed of travelers, most of them in the 20–50 age range. Jazz clubs, videotheques, discos and open air restaurants have found a clientele in the towns.

In cities like Phuket and Chiang Mai, "barbeers" or open-squares enclosing bargirls and ringed outside by patrons on barstools, have become popular with both sexes. Only Pattaya does not seem to have gotten the message and continues to pander to sex voyeurs, despite pleas it is catering to a family trade.

A sign of the drastic changes is that the queen of nighttime activities is shopping. Night markets have sprung up along Sukhumvit and Silom roads. Even that wrinkled old harlot of a street, Patpong, has not been immune to the breezes of change. Vendors' tables choke the street, drawing more patrons than the bars. A wealth of cheap goods, some of them counterfeit – fake Rolex watches, fake Benetton shirts, fake cassette tapes – vie with faked orgasms at seedier upstairs sex shows.

The change has rubbed off on the bars as well. Many of Patpong's bars have metamorphosed into discos which begin to throb with life after 11pm. To find nightlife as it used to be, one has to go to Soi Cowboy or Nana Entertainment complex.

Up-country, the scene is essentially the same. Chiang Mai's Chang Klang night market attracts more tourists than the bars along Chaiyaphum Road. In Phuket, "barbeers" line the streets of

Patong beaches' Soi Bangla and similar areas of Karon and Kata; but the hard sex of Bangkok's yesteryear has never established a foothold there.

Outside of these major urban areas, there is little to appeal to the foreign visitor because their numbers are generally too small to warrant developing special facilities for them. Here, one must be content with more shopping, wandering through the Thai markets, or going to a Thai nightclub which features murky lighting, singers crooning Thai pop hits and, in the more sophisticated clubs, chorus lines dressed in outrageous costumes. Most visitors use the evening to rest up for another exhausting trek to ruins, hilltribes or the beach the following day.

BANGKOK

Bars

There are three key areas in Bangkok where the types of entertainment for which the city has become famous can be found. Their former rowdiness has been somewhat tamed as more and more Western women have begun invading what were formerly male-only bastions. Not that you won't find plenty to keep you amused; but most of it will not be found on the ground floor.

Patpong Road describes three streets: Patpong itself and Patpong 2 which is a welter of bars and bright lights, and Patpong 3 which is almost exclusively gay. Patpong offers a go-go bars in which bikini-clad bargirls balanced precariously on high heels on tiny platforms just above the bar, dance to rock music for the amusement of the patrons who ring the bar. There is no cover charge and the main drink is beer although cocktails can be ordered.

Bargirls will cadge drinks in exchange for conversation, but one is under no obligation and can simply sit and watch the strange activities of one's fellow humans. The bargirls can be taken out for the night (see below) at a price she arranges with the client. **King's Castle**, **Safari**, **Thighbar**, **Queen's Castle**, **Pussy Galore** and others offer essentially the same fare.

Tips

For Men: Bargirls can be taken out for extracurricular activities, but if it is before the bar closes (2am), he must pay the bar a fee. Other negotiations are entirely between the girl and him and the girl very much has the upper hand (it is a seller's market). If she decides she does not like the man, she simply will not go with him.

Most first-class hotels are nervous about letting bargirls onto the premises, primarily for security reasons. The hotel will normally demand that the girl deposits her Identification Card at the desk until she leaves. Girls do occasionally walk away with watches and cash, so it is not a good idea to leave valuables lying on the night table. Similarly, with AIDS on the rise, do not be foolish; there is a drug store just down the street.

For the Single Women: Bangkok nightlife is not really for single women. Most, however, feel comfortable in small groups in places like **Limelight**. There is nothing to fear; foreign women are accepted by the bargirls.

Sex Shows

Patpong touts offer menus of the shows in second story establishments. Read the menu if you want but don't accept their help; the street is not so long that you cannot find your way to one of these bars. The **Kangaroo**, **Firecat** and others offer shows which are more freakish than erotic. Not to everyone's taste, they seem to be patronized by as many Western women as men.

Beware of the live sex shows off Patpong or along Patpong 2. Most, but not all are rip-off bars where one is handed an enormous bill and immediately surrounded by large bouncers if he protests.

If such should happen to you, hand over the money. Get a copy of the bill if you can, and head straight for the police box on the Suriwongse Road, end of Patpong 2, or to the Tourist Police at the intersection of Silom and Rama 4 Road. The police do not tolerate this activity and if you act quickly, you can often get your money back.

Other Nightlife Areas

Soi Cowboy is a somewhat downmarket version of Patpong. Here, the entertainment is more basic and more in keeping with what Patpong and the old New Petchburi Road area once offered. The emphasis here is on pick-ups with wall to wall bargirls.

Without the bother of Patpong style touts, Nana Entertainment Plaza off Soi 4, Sukhumvit Road, though smaller than Patpong now has the busiest and most popular go-go bars in Bangkok. A fourth area, the **Grace Hotel** area on Soi 3, Sukhumvit, appeals primarily to a Mideastern clientele.

Escort Agencies

The ads look inviting but these are generally fronts for brothels. The women are usually dressed to be escorted to the better nightclubs. If you are worried about your reputation, try them. Otherwise, wander down to Patpong.

Massages

Massages fall into two categories: regular and irregular. Establishments billing themselves as "Traditional Thai Massage" and "Ancient Thai Massage" offer therapeutic services according to age-old traditions. The best place for this, however, is at Wat Po.

The second type of massage is given in massage parlors where the emphasis is upon total relaxation. You pick a girl from behind a one-way mirror and then spend the next hour getting a bath and whatever you arrange with the girl. In B-course massages, the girl uses her naked body to massage yours. Again, take prophylactic precautions should things get out of hand.

Discos

Patpong also offers discos like the **Peppermint Bistro**, many of which continue to throb long after the bars have closed down. Here, everyone is on his own and there is no solicitation nor expectations.

Rachadapisek Road has developed into a new magnet for Bangkok's young sybarites. The discos appeal more to Thais than to foreigners, but there is room for both. The biggest and most frequented is Capital City.

Full-fledged discos like NASA **Spacedome** are spread around the city. NASA, which claims to hold 3,000 people, sits in a former rice paddy at the far end of New Petchburi Road. Like its sisters elsewhere in the world, it is filled with flashing lights, loud music and video screens.

Also, try **Bubbles** in the Dusit Thani Hotel and **Diana's** in the Oriental Plaza. The very chic **Rome Club** on Patpong 3 functions as a gay bar most of the evening but becomes a videotheque about 10pm. All have cover charges of between 120 and 180 *baht* and remain open until 3am.

Music Clubs

This is not the kind of jazz you will find in New York, London or Tokyo but it is very listenable and some of it is very innovative. Jazz clubs proliferate along Sois Sarasin, Lang Suan, and elsewhere. They differ from their murky, hostess-filled counterparts in being open – usually glass-fronted and with sidewalk tables – with the emphasis on good live music and good conversation.

These clubs appeal as much to young professional Thais as they do to young Westerners. Among the most popular with mixed nationality crowds is **Brown Sugar** (Soi Sarasin) and **Round Midnight** (Soi Lang Suan). Musicians at **Saxophone** at the Victory Monument (3/8 Phya Thai Road) play jazz standards. Open until 3am

If you like Dixieland jazz and a lively atmosphere, **Bobby's Arms** at 8.30 Sunday evenings is where you should head. The band comprises local residents who play for the fun of it. Bobby's offers good British cuisine and lots of beer in a convivial setting. Located on the first floor of the carpark behind Foodland on Patpong 2 Road.

Most of the more sophisticated nightclubs are found in first class hotels. Classy and classic, the Oriental Hotel's famed **Bamboo Bar** nightclub is for dressier occasions. The scene is chic, normally with jazz singers from the United States playing long-term engagements. You can also find imported acts at the Dusit Thani Hotel's **Tiara Lounge**. Most hotels have lounge bars with good musical acts.

For other nighttime activities, check the daily newspapers for announcements of concerts, art shows, lectures and other offerings around the city. The Sunday morning *Bangkok Post, Thailand Times* and *The Nation* carry listings for the following week.

CHIANG MAI

Chiang Mai nightlife is subdued by comparison to that of Bangkok. Perhaps it is the fatigue induced by trekking, the calmer nature of the town, or simply the calmer nature of the traveler; but in the evenings, Chiang Mai is very quiet.

Music Clubs & Bars

The normal evening entertainment is to sit in a restaurant or pub and listen to local musicians sing soft tunes. **Riverside Restaurant** on Charoenrat Road and **Chiang Mai Tea House** on the Chiang Mai-Lamphun Road are two examples of this kind of entertainment. Bars along Chaiyaphum Road in the vicinity of Tapae Gate offer live and recorded music. The latter also have bargirls but not in the numbers of Bangkok or Pattaya.

During the dry season, most of Chiang Mai's evenings are spent in outdoor restaurants like **Old House** and **Maprang** on Charoenprathet Road, in the sidewalk cafe in front of the **Novotel Hotel**, the **Beer Garden** on Soi 4, Charoenprathet Road, and **Daret's House** on Chaiyaphum Road.

Massages

Traditional massages are available at **Diamond Hotel**, Charoenprathet Road, for 80 *baht* per hour; or at **Rin Kaew Phovej**, 183/4 Wua Lai Road. (beside the Old Chiang Mai Cultural Center), Tel: 234565, 235969. Open from 8am–midnight. Not-so-traditional massages are at **Saiyuri** on Soi 3, off Bamrungrat Road.

PATTAYA

Pattaya's nightlife is still in the old mold with bars proliferating in the South Pattaya area. Here, the emphasis is on picking up bargirls and drinking. There are one or two music clubs, where one can sip a beer and listen to 60s rock and roll. Simon and Marine bars have discos upstairs.

Hotels have lobby bands and bars with lounge singers. The Beach Road and Pattaya 2 Road are lined with barbeers which differ little from their cousins in South Pattaya.

PHUKET

The pace of Phuket's balmy nights matches that of its lazy days. On most beaches, nighttime means bedtime. There are barbeers but none of the rowdy, raunchy nightlife of Bangkok and Pattaya nor of the anything-goes massage parlors. In Phuket town, the entertainment is primarily for Thais with nightclubs, movies, massage parlors and little else.

Hotels provide cocktail bars and lounge musicians but visitors generally prefer to wander in the balmy air in search of fun. As in large hotels in other metropolitan centers, Phuket hotels have in-house videos but except for big hotels, expect to see third-run features.

Patong is the most developed and nighttime means a trek down to Soi Bangla barbeers with names like **Eat Joe's Bar**, **Dog and Duck**, and **Bamboo Benz**. For dancers, there is **Le Crocodile Music Hall** on Soi Bangla and **Banana Disco** at 94 Thaviwong Road (next to the Patong Beach Hotel).

There are also quiet hang-outs with darts, video and good music. **Paradise Bar** on Thaviwong Road (the Beach Road) next to Holiday Inn, is one of the best.

Nightlife in **Karon** and **Kata** is still in its infancy but is growing rapidly. **Karon's** barbeers are located down a narrow lane off the Beach Road next to a huge Fuji sign. **Kata's** are clustered around the main intersection. It also has a live music club called **Easyrider** where the 1960s are alive and well.

In Phuket town, go bowling at **Pearl Bowl** on Montri Road or to a Thai movie at the corner of Montri and Ranong roads or at the **Paradise Theater** off Phuket Road.

Massages

The **Pearl Massage** in the Pearl Hotel on Montri Road is the only parlor on the island in which naughty activities are allowed. For a traditional massage, go to the **Daeng Plaza Hotel** on Phuket Road.

SHOPPING

Whatever part of your budget you have allocated for shopping, double it or regret it. Thailand could easily be pronounced "Toyland" for all the wonderful things there are to buy in it. Keep a tight grip on your wallet or you will find yourself being seduced by the low prices and walking off with more than you can possibly carry home. If you cannot resist, see the "Export" section for an inexpensive way to get souvenirs home.

Over the years, there have been two major changes in the shopping picture. For one, there have been subtle design alterations to make the items more appealing to foreign buyers. The purists may carp but the changes and the wider range of products have found welcome reception by shoppers. At the same time, new products have been introduced which have found popular reception among visitors.

The other change is that while regional products were once found only in the towns that produced them, there has been a homogenization of distribution so that it is now possible, for example, to buy Chiang Mai umbrellas in Phuket. The widest range of items are found in Chiang Mai and Bangkok but if you never have a chance to leave Bangkok, do not despair; nearly everything you might want to buy in up-country towns can be found in the capital city.

Shopping Hours

Large department stores in Bangkok are open from 10am–9pm. Most ordinary shops are open from 9am–6pm.

Complaints

The customer is (nearly) always wrong might be the most candid way of putting it. Except for very large shops, expect that once you have paid for an item and left the store, or that unless the defect is very glaring and there is no possible way you could have caused it, the moment you walk out the door, you no longer exist. You can report the shop to the Tourist Police but they are not usually interested. Shop carefully. *Caveat emptor.*

WHAT TO BUY

Antiques & Neo-Antiques

Wood, bronze, terracotta and stone statues from all regions of Thailand and Myanmar can be found in Bangkok's and Chiang Mai's antique shops. There are religious figures and characters from classical literature, carved wooden angels, mythical animals, temple bargeboards and eave brackets.

Although the Thai government has banned the export of Buddha images, there are numerous deities and disciples which can be sent abroad. Bronze deer, angels and characters from the Ramakien cast in bronze do not fall under the export ban. It is also possible to buy and export Burmese Buddha images.

Chiang Mai produces beautiful wooden replicas modeled on antique sculptures. Sold as reproductions with no attempt to pass them off as genuine antiques, they make lovely home decor items. Animals, Buddha's disciples and dozens of items range in size from 10cm to life-sized.

Chiang Mai also produces a wide range of beautifully-crafted wooden furniture. Cabinets, tables, dining room sets, elephant *howdahs*, bedroom sets or simple items like wooden trays are crafted from teak or other woods and carved with intricate designs.

Basket

Thailand's abundant bamboo, wicker and grasses are transformed into lamps, storage boxes, tables, colorful mats, handbags, letter holders, tissue boxes and slippers. Wicker and bamboo are turned into storage lockers with brass fittings and furniture to fill the entire house. Shops can provide the cushions as well.

Yan lipao, a thin, sturdy grass, is woven into delicate patterns to create purses and bags for formal occasions. Although expensive, the bags are durable, retaining their beauty for years.

Ceramics

Best known among the distinctive Thai ceramics is the jade green celadon which is distinguished by its finely crazed surface. Statues, lamps, ashtrays and other items are also produced in dark green, brown and cobalt blue hues.

Modeled on its Chinese cousin, blue-and-white porcelain includes pots, lamp bases, household items and figurines. Quality varies according to the skill of the artist and of the firing and glazing.

Bencharong (five colors) describes a style of porcelain derived from 16th-century Chinese art. Normally reserved for bowls, containers and fine chinaware, its classic pattern features a small religious figure surrounded by intricate floral designs. The whole is rendered in five colors – usually green, blue, yellow, rose and black.

Earthenware includes a wide assortment of pots, planters and dinner sets in a rainbow of colors and designs. Also popular are the big, brown glazed Shanghai jars bearing yellow dragons which the Thais use to hold bath water and which visitors use as planters. Antique stoneware includes the double-fish design plates and bowls originally produced at Sawankhaloke, the kilns established near Sukhothai in the 13th century.

Some of the best ceramics come from Ratchaburi, southwest of Bangkok. The wide variety makes a special trip there worthwhile.

Decorative Arts

Lacquerware comes in two styles: the gleaming gold and black variety normally seen on temple shutters, and the matt red type with black and/or green details which originated in northern Thailand and Myanmar. The lacquerware repertoire includes ornate containers and trays, wooden figurines, woven bamboo baskets and Burmese-inspired Buddhist manuscripts. The pieces may also be bejeweled with tiny glass mosaics and gilded ornaments.

Black lacquer is also the base into which shaped bits of mother-of-pearl are pressed. Scenes from religious or classical literature are rendered on presentation trays, containers and plaques. Beware of craftsmen who take shortcuts by using black paint rather than the traditional seven layers of lacquer. On these items, the surface cracks, often while the item is still on the shelf.

Fabrics & Clothes

Thai silk is perhaps Thailand's best known craft. Brought to world attention by American entrepreneur, Jim Thompson, Thai silk has enjoyed enduring popularity. Sold in a wide variety of colors, its hallmark is the tiny nubs which, like embossings, rise from its surface. Unlike sheer Indian silks and shiny Chinese patterned silks, Thai silk is a thick cloth that lends itself to clothes, curtains and upholstery.

It is more popular as blouses, ties and scarves. It is also used to cover purses, tissue boxes and picture frames. Lengths printed with elephant, bamboo, floral and dozens of other motifs are turned into decorative pillowcases to accent rooms.

Mudmee is a northeastern silk whose colors are somber and muted. A form of tie-dyed cloth, it is sold in lengths or as finished clothes.

Cotton is popular for shirts and dresses since it "breathes" in Thailand's hot, humid air. Although available in lengths, it is generally sold already cut into frocks and shirts. The South is a batik center and offers ready-made clothes and batik paintings.

Burmese in origin and style, *kalaga* wall hangings depicting gods, kings and mythical animals have gained increasing popularity in the past few years. The figures are stuffed with *kapok* to make them stand out from the surface in bas relief.

Gems & Jewelry

Thailand is one of the world's exporters of cut rubies and sapphires. The rough stones are mostly imported from Cambodia and Myanmar, as local mines are not able to meet the demand.

Thailand is now regarded as the world's leading cutter of colored gemstones and is a leader in diamond cutting, the "Bangkok cut" rapidly becoming one of the most popular. Thai artisans set the stones in gold and silver to create jewelry and bejeweled containers. Artisans also craft jewelry that satisfy an international clientele. Light green Burmese jade (jadeite) is carved into jewelry and art objects. The island of Phuket produces international-standard natural, cultured, Mob (teardrop), and artificial pearls (made from pearl dust glued to form a globule). They are sold as individual items or are set into gold jewelry.

Costume jewelry is a major Thai business with numerous items available. A related craft which has grown rapidly in the past decade is that of gilding Thai orchids for use as brooches.

Hilltribe Crafts

Meo or Hmong, Mien or Yao, Lisu, Lahu or Musur, Akha, Karen and other northern hilltribes produce brightly-colored needlepoint work in a wide variety of geometric and floral patterns. These are sold either by themselves or are incorporated into shirts, coats, bags, pillowcases and other items.

Hilltribe silver work is valued less for its silver content (which is low) than for the intricate work and imagination that goes into making it. The genre includes necklaces, headdresses, bracelets and rings the women wear on ceremonial occasions. Enhancing their value are the old British Indian rupee coins which decorate the women's elaborate headdresses.

Other hilltribe items include knives, baskets, pipes and gourd flutes that look and sound like bagpipes.

Home Decor Items

Thailand's handcrafted artificial flowers and fruits made of organdy, poplin rayons, cotton, velvet, satin acetate, plastic, polyester and paper are virtually indistinguishable from garden blooms and produce.

Animals, containers, vases, screens and tables are crafted in papier mâché as gifts and home decor items. Seashells are used to decorate lampshades, boxes and picture frames.

Leatherware

The items are prosaic enough – shoes, bags, wallets, attaché cases, belts – but the animals who have contributed their hides are the oddest assortment: snake, armadillo, crocodile, cow hide stamped to look like crocodile, lizard, frog, chicken and even elephant.

Metal Art Objects

Although Thai craftsmen have produced some of Asia's most beautiful Buddha images, modern bronze sculpture tends to be of less exalted subjects and execution. Minor deities, characters from classical literature, deer and abstract figures are cast up to 2 m (7 ft) tall and are normally clad with a brass skin to make them gleam. Bronze is also cast into handsome cutlery and coated in shiny brass.

Silver and gold are pounded into jewelry items, boxes and other decorative pieces; many are set with gems. To create nielloware boxes and receptacles, a design is incised in silver or gold. The background is cut away and filled with an amalgam of dark metals leaving the figures to stand in high relief against the black background.

Tin, mined near Phuket, is the prime ingredient in pewterware of which Thailand is a major producer. Items range from clocks and steins to egg cups and figurines.

Paintings

Modern Thai artists paint everything from realistic to abstract art, the latter often a weak imitation of Western art. Two areas at which they excel are depictions of everyday village life and of new interpretations of classical Buddhist themes. Artists can also work from live sittings or photographs to create superb charcoal or oil portraits. A family photograph from home can be transformed into a painting. The price depends on size: a 40cm x 60cm (16" x 24") charcoal portrait costs around 1,000 *baht*. There are several street-side studios in Bangkok, Phuket and Pattaya that specialize in this art.

Theater Art Objects

Papier-mâché *khon* masks like those used in palace dance/drama are painted, accented with lacquer decorations and gilded to create superb works of art.

Shadow puppets cut from the hides of water buffaloes and displayed against backlit screens in open air theaters also tell the Ramakien story. Check to be sure the figure is actually cut from hide and not from a sheet of black plastic.

Nang Thalung: These bright-colored shadow puppets cut from buffalo hide make excellent wall decorations.

Inspired by the Ramakien, craftsmen have fashioned miniature models of chariots and warriors in gilded wood or glass sculpture. These two materials are also employed to create reproductions of the famous Royal Barges.

Umbrellas

Chiang Mai produces lovely umbrellas and fans made from silk or "*Sa*" paper, a fine parchment often confused for rice paper but made from pounded tree bark.

SHOPPING AREAS

If you cannot find it in Bangkok, you will not be able to find it anywhere else in the country. Aside from the traffic problems, Bangkok is the most comfortable place to shop. Shopping venues range from huge air-conditioned malls to tiny, hole-in-the-wall shops to crafts sections of large department stores.

Huge air-conditioned malls like **Amarin Plaza**, **Siam Center**, **Mahboonkrong**, **Oriental Plaza** and **Central Plaza** are filled with shops selling a variety of items. Some malls specialize in particular types of items; **River City**, for example, has dozens of shops selling superb antiques.

Queen Sirikit's Chitralada stores sell the rare crafts she and her organization, SUPPORT, have worked so diligently to preserve by teaching the arts to village women. There are branches in the airport, Grand Palace, Oriental Plaza, Hilton Hotel and Pattaya. The Thai government's handicraft center, **Narayana Phand**, at 127 Rajdamri Road, displays the full array of Thai handicrafts.

Most major department stores have special handicrafts departments carrying a wide selection of items. **New Road** between Silom and Suriwong, **Silom Road** in the vicinity of the Narai Hotel, the upper section of **Suriwongse Road**, and **Sukhumvit Road** are lined with crafts shops. Traditional shopping areas like **Sampeng Lane**, the **Thieves Market**, the Buddha amulet markets at **Tha Prajan** and **Wat Rajanadda** have lost some of their allure over the years as new businesses have moved in, but one can still find the occasional bargain. By far the most challenging (and often most rewarding) is the huge weekend market at Chatuchak which has special sections for porcelain, brassware and a number of old oddities that don't fit into any particular category.

Chiang Mai also has its air-conditioned department stores that sell household and personal products. Handicrafts can be found at studios along the 9-km road to Borsang and along Wua Lai Road. For pseudo antiques, you must travel farther, to **Baan Tawai** on the highway to Chom Thong. The famous **Chang Klang** night market is also a place to pick up bargains.

Phuket offers fewer shopping areas and most are concentrated on Highway 402 between the airport and Phuket town. **Thai Village** (Km 2.5), **Native Handicraft Center** (Km 8.5), **Shinawatr** (Km 9) and **Cheewa** (Km 10.6) offer both local handicrafts and those imported from other regions of Thailand. Thai Village has workshops where you can watch the artisans at work. For casual wear, check the shops and vendors along Patong's Beach Road and Soi Bangla and in Kata and Karon.

Pattaya has malls like **Thai Pan** and others on the Beach Road but most of the casual items are found on the Beach Road. Shops sell a good selection of casual wear.

Street Shopping

Visitors are beginning to find out what Thailand shoppers discovered long ago: that some of the best shopping is found on the street. More and more merchandise is being marketed on the streets of Bangkok, Chiang Mai, Pattaya, Phuket and all the small towns.

You will not find high ticket items nor will the quality equal that found in finer stores; but for gift items, there are few better places to look. In Bangkok look in **Pratunam market** – one of the city's oldest and largest – and along both sides of **Rajaprarop Road**. Try both sides of **Sukhumvit Road** between Soi 3 and 11 where you will find Burmese puppets, handicrafts and perhaps most important, suitcases and bags to put it all in.

The upper end of **Silom Road**, the small market in **Gaysorn Road** near Rajprasong, the Pratunam end of **Rajdamri Road** and its inner sois, the area called **Bangkok Bazaar** are where you will find finely-tailored shirts and T-shirts for around 150 *baht*.

In Chiang Mai, try the **Chang Klang Night Market** and the vendors along **Tapae Road**. In Phuket town, browse vendors and shops along **Ranong Road**. In Pattaya, there are street vendors along the **Beach Road** and in **South Pattaya**.

EXPORT

Shipping

Most shops will handle documentation and shipping for your purchases. Alternatively, the General Post Office on New Road offers boxes and a packing service for goods sent by sea mail. Packages can be shipped from most post offices. Post offices in most towns sell cardboard boxes specially created for shipping packages.

Thai International in Bangkok also offers a special service called THAIPAC that will air freight your purchases (regardless of the mode of transportation or the airline you are using) to the THAI destination closest to your home for 25 percent of the normal rate. Just take your goods to the THAI office at 485 Silom Road. They must fit into THAI's special box and weigh no more than 33 kg per box. THAI will also handle the documentation and customs clearance for a small charge.

Export Permits

The Fine Arts Department prohibits the export of all Thai Buddha images, images of other deities and fragments (hands or heads) of images dating from before the 18th century.

All antiques and art objects, regardless of type or age, must be registered with the Fine Arts Department. The shop will usually do this for you. If you decide to handle it yourself, take the piece to the Fine Arts Department on Na Prathat Road across from Sanam Luang, together with two postcard-sized photos of it. The export fee ranges between 50 and 200 *baht* depending on the antiquity of the piece.

Fake antiques do not require export permits, but Airport Customs officials are not art experts and may mistake it for a genuine piece. If it looks authentic, clear it at the Fine Arts Department to avoid problems later.

SPORTS & LEISURE

Thailand has developed its outdoor sports facilities to a considerable degree and air-conditioned the ones played indoors. Nearly every major hotel has a swimming pool and a fitness center; some have squash courts and jogging paths.

PARTICIPANT SPORTS

Bowling

In Bangkok, bowl at **Star Bowl** on New Petchburi Road near Soi 3 or at **Ploenchit Bowl** above Foodland Supermarket on Ploenchit Road near the intersection with Wittayu Road. 20 *baht* per game.

In Chiang Mai, **Chiang Mai Bowl** is at 102 Chang Klang Road, in front of Chiang Inn Hotel, Tel: 236005. Open 11am–midnight. 18 *baht* per game (up to 6pm), 20 *baht* per game from 6pm–midnight.

Pearl Bowl next to the Pearl Hotel on Montri Road in Phuket town has twelve lanes and an assortment of ball sizes. 20 *baht* per game including ball rental; shoes are 5 *baht*. Open 11am–midnight. In Pattaya, bowl at **Pattaya Bowl**.

Driving Ranges

In Bangkok, a driving range is found at the **Siam Inter-Continental Hotel**, Tel: 2530355 ext. 7636. The fee from 7am–5pm is 90 *baht* per hour; 5pm–10pm, 140 *baht* per hour. **The Army Golf Course** driving range on Ram Intra Road, Tel: 5211530, is open 6am–9pm. The cost is 10 *baht* per tray of balls. **Golden Golf & Tennis**, 7 Soi Soonvijai 1, New Petchburi Road, Tel: 3181651. Open from 6am–10pm. The fee is 20 *baht* per tray of balls. The **Railway Training Center Golf Course**, on Phaholyothin Road, Tel: 2710130, west of the Hyatt Central Plaza Hotel, is open 6am–8pm. The fee is 20 *baht* per tray of balls.

The Chiang Mai Driving Range is at 239/3 Wua Lai Road, Tel: 5100492. Open 6am–midnight. 20 *baht* per bucket of balls.

In Phuket, the **Phuket Golf and Country Club** driving range is across the road from the Phuket Country Club Golf course. Open 8am–6.30pm. One bucket of balls: 30 *baht*. One driver: 30 *baht*.

In Pattaya, there is a driving range at **The Siam Country Club**. Fees are 20 *baht* for a bucket of 40 balls.

Deep Sea Fishing

For deepsea fishing, go to Phuket or to Bang Saray south of Pattaya. At Bang Saray, marlin, king mackerel, cobia, yellow jack, barracuda, bonito, giant groupers, red snapper, rays and black tip sharks lurk among submerged rocks. Boats, tackle and guides are available for very reasonable fees. There are small hotels in Bang Saray but most fishermen spend the night in Pattaya and head out early in the morning. Fishing trips can be arranged by telephoning Bang Saray Fishing Lodge at its Bangkok office, Tel: 2337719, 2343094.

The waters off Phuket offer numerous challenges to deepsea fishermen. Sailfish, barracuda, albacore, marlin, wahoo, tuna and king mackerel are just a few of the many varieties awaiting a baited hook near Chicken or Raja Islands east of Phuket. **The Travel Company** on Patong Beach near Soi Patong Post Office, Tel: (032) 321292, offers daily cruises aboard converted 16–22 m (52–72 ft) long Thai fishing trawlers equipped with fixed sockets to hold the rods. The 1,500 *baht* price per person includes boat, rods and reels, bait, lunch, dinner, soft drinks and fruits. No minimum number of persons is required and the cruise is offered year-round.

Travel Company also offers night fishing tours that leave Patong at 4pm and return at 9am the following day. The 1,500 *baht* price covers the same services and amenities as above.

Pond Fishing
Koongten Ram Indra, 56/19 Ram Indra Road, Tel: 5102636, (open daily from 10am–11pm) lets you catch the main course. Pay by the weight of the fish plus a fee to have the restaurant cook it for you. Take your own rod and tackle. Catfish and Snake's-Head fish are the prey.

Koongten Fishing Hut at 113/1 Thessasamphan Road, Tel: 5816689, 5815379, offers fishing for 25 *baht* an hour. It will then clean and cook the fish and serve any other course you desire. Hours are 7am–10pm, Monday–Friday; 7am–midnight, Saturday–Sunday.

Fitness Centers
In Bangkok, the Asia-wide **Clark Hatch** has a branch in the Hilton Hotel. **Fitness International** is located in the Dusit Thani Hotel. Part-time membership is available. All the top hotels in Bangkok have well-equipped fitness centers.

In Phuket, there is a **Clark Hatch Fitness Center** in Le Meridien Hotel, Tel: 321480/1 ext. 1428, that is open from 7am–8.30pm. The **Holiday Inn** in Patong also has a fitness center.

Fitness Parks
One corner of Bangkok's **Lumpini Park** boasts a fitness park. In Chiang Mai, there is a free fitness park on **Nimmanhaemind Road** that is open from 5am–10pm. In Phuket, the fitness park sits atop **Rang Hill** in the middle of Phuket town while in Pattaya, it is located on the slopes of Pattaya Hill.

Golf
Thais are great golfing buffs, going so far as to employ some of world golfing's stellar architects to design international-class courses. The best courses are in Bangkok, Phuket and Pattaya with other courses in Chiang Mai, Khao Yai and Hua Hin. Greens fees range from 250 to 750 *baht* per round on weekends and it is generally not difficult to reserve a time. Caddy fees run from 90 to 150 *baht* per round.

Among Bangkok's courses is the **Navathanee Golf Course** (22 M.1, Sukhapibal 2 Road, Tel: 3747077) designed by Robert Trent Jones Jr. It is open from 6am–6pm. The **Army Golf Course** at 459 Ram Intra Road, Tel: 5211530, is open from 5am–9.30pm. The **Railway Training Center Golf Course**, on Paholyothin Road, Tel: 2710130, west of the Hyatt Central Plaza Hotel opens at 6am, closes at 8pm. The **Krungthep Sports Golf Course**, 516 Krungthep Sports Road, Tel: 3746063, opens at 5am, closes at 5pm.

In Chiang Mai, the **Lanna Golf Course** on Chotana Road, Tel: 221911, is open 6am–6pm. Greens fees on weekdays: 150 *baht*; weekends: 150 *baht*. Caddy: 100 *baht*. Club rentals: 200 *baht*.

Phuket has a brand-new course, the beautiful 18-hole **Phuket Country Club Golf Course** located between Phuket town and Patong beach (Tel: 321038 or 321039). It opens at 6.30am, closes at 6pm. Greens fees: 600 *baht* (low season: 400 *baht*). Caddy: 100 *baht*. Clubs and bag: 300 *baht* (250 *baht* in low season).

In Pattaya, **Siam Country Club Golf Course** 10km (6 miles) east of town in rolling hills charges 700 *baht* for greens and caddy fees.

Mini-Golf
Bangkok does not have mini-golf courses but there is a putting green at the **Siam Inter-Continental Hotel** that is open 7am–10pm. The fee from 7am–5pm is 30 *baht* per 30 min.; from 5pm–closing: 50 *baht* per 30 min. Shoes and clubs can be rented.

In Phuket, a modern mini-golf course, **Chalong Bay Mini Golf**, operates on the Chalong Road, 100m (110yds) from the Chalong junction. 18 challenging holes cost 25 *baht* per game; 30 *baht* if you want a caddy. Open 9am–sunset.

Hash House Harriers
Several towns in Thailand have chapters of the famous Hash House Harriers, the cross-country running organization that originated among British soldiers in Malaysia. Participants (called "Hounds") follow a paper trail laid down through rice paddies and coconut plantations by the "hare". There are plenty of false clues and opportunities to run through muddy fields and across canals to relocate the trail.

The pack is kept from getting hopelessly lost by a bugle-blowing leader who shouts "On, on" when the trail has been found. The real objective of the exercise is to reach a large supply of cold beer at the trail's end, thereby negating all efforts to lose weight along the route. Everybody is welcome. Good, not-so-clean fun.

In Bangkok, members gather each Saturday at 4.30pm, Monday evenings at 5.15pm and Wednesday at 5pm at a site announced in the sports sections of the *Saturday Bangkok Post*.

In Chiang Mai, the Chiang Mai branch departs from the Black Cat Bar on Moon Muang Road every second Monday at 4pm. Telephone Tony at 216793 for more information.

In Phuket, a van leaves from the Expat Bar on Soi Bangla in Patong each Saturday at 3.30pm. Or contact the **Expat Hotel** at 89/14 Moo 3, Ratuthit Road, Tel: 321300, for more information.

In Pattaya, check at BJ's Bar in South Pattaya.

Horse Riding

There are no public horse riding facilities in Bangkok but in Chiang Mai there is a stable on Chotana Road near the new provincial hall. It is open on Saturday and Sunday from 6am–noon and the cost is 200 *baht* per hour. Telephone 247478 for more information.

In Phuket, ride at **Crazy Horse Club** at 17 Moo 2, 1km (0.6 miles) down the back road connecting Kakata Inn with H 4028. Instructors accompany riders through rice fields and down the beach. Morning rides into the jungle are also offered. During the dry season, owners take riders on 2-hour trips into the hills. 300 *baht* per hour.

Jogging

Two jogging sites for those wise enough not to challenge Bangkok's traffic for right-of-way are in **Lumpini Park** and **Chatuchak Park**. The Siam-Intercontinental Hotel, Rama Gardens and the Hilton hotels have jogging paths.

In Chiang Mai, joggers run up the hill to **Doi Suthep** and catch a mini-bus back. In Phuket, jog up **Rang Hill**, a 1.3km (0.8-mile) jaunt. There is a fitness park at the top. In Pattaya, jog up **Pattaya Hill**.

Petanque

This ancient sport (also called *peton*) has found a following among Thais over the past year or so. Two hotels, the **Siam Inter-Continental** and the **Rama Gardens**, have installed outdoor lanes.

Shooting

There are no ranges in Bangkok but in Chiang Mai go to the **Chiang Mai Physical Education College**, 68/1 Sanamkila Road, Tel: 214237. Open Tuesday–Sunday from 9am–5pm. 20 *baht* fee; 20 *baht* for gun rental.

In Phuket, **Phuket Shooting Range** (Tel: 273755) offers recreational rifle and pistol shooting. Weapons include AK-47s, M-16s, Colt .45s, Smith and Wesson .38s, 9 mms, and .22 magnums. Bullseye, human and outdoor falling plate targets are available. Fees are pegged according to the type and number of bullets used and cover a target, the gun, use of the range, bullets, ear protectors and an instructor. It is located at 82/2 Patak Road (H 4028 to Kata) 800 m (870 yds) from Chalong junction. Open from 9am–6pm.

In Pattaya, **Tiffany's** on Pattaya 2 Road, Tel: 419642, has 19 galleries and a variety of pistols and rifles. Open 11am–9pm.

Ice Skating

Strange as it seems, Bangkok has two ice skating rinks. **Ice Skate** occupies the 2nd floor of The Mall Shopping Center, 1911 Ramkamhaeng Road, Tel: 3181001, in the eastern suburbs. Rental fees for the 2,300 sq m (24,750 sq ft) rink are 55 *baht* for 2 hours, including skate rental. Hours are: noon–10pm, Monday–Thursday; noon–midnight, Friday; 10am–midnight, Saturday; 10am–10pm, Sunday. A new ice skating rink has now opened at the World Trade Center on Rajadamri Road.

Roller Skating

The Skate is located on the ground floor of Central Department Store, Lard Prao branch (adjoining Hyatt Central Plaza Hotel) on Phaholyothin Road, Tel: 5411020 ext. The Skate. Open daily from noon–5pm. Ticket prices, including skate rental are: Monday–Friday: 20 *baht*; Saturday–Sunday, 30 *baht* (including one free soft drink).

Snooker

In recent years, Thailand has produced some excellent snooker players who are currently nipping at the heels of world champions in international competitions. As a result, parlors have sprung up everywhere in Thailand as budding aspirants focus their eyes on complex shots and potential riches. In Bangkok, there are numerous snooker parlors around the city. The "Rooks" chain is the most popular and dozens of its snooker parlors can be found.

In Chiang Mai, there is the **Plaza Snooker Club** on the First Floor of the Chiang Mai Plaza Hotel. Open 11am–1.30am 90 *baht* per hour.

In Phuket, reserve a table at **Vee Vee Snooker Parlor** 50 km (550yds) south of Patong on the road to Karon (across from Andaman Hospital) by telephoning 211066, 211077. **New Wave Snooker Club** in the Kata Center on Kata beach also has tables.

In Pattaya, there are billiards tables at **Pattaya Bowl** in Pattaya 2 Road.

Squash

Squash courts are found exclusively at hotels. The courts at **Rama Gardens**, **Dusit Thani** (or members of Fitness International gyms), **Hilton** (or members of Clark Hatch gyms) are open only to guests. The Oriental courts are also open to Royal Orchid Sheraton Hotel guests.

Courts open to non-guests are at the **Shangri-la** and **Imperial** hotels. The Shangri-la courts (Tel: 2367777) are open from 7am–9am. Open air courts are 50 *baht* per hour for guests (100 *baht* per hour for non-guests). Air-conditioned courts are 75 *baht* per hour for guests, 150 *baht* per hour for non-guests). The Imperial Hotel courts (Tel: 2540111) are open 8am–8pm at 100 *baht* per 45 minutes. There is a changing room by the swimming pool.

In Chiang Mai, squash is played at the **Gymkhana Club**, Chiang Mai-Lamphun Road, Tel: 2410035. Open 6am–8pm daily. 40 *baht* per hour. No rental equipment available.

In Phuket, **Clark Hatch** in Le Meridien Hotel (Tel: 321480, 321481 ext. 1428) rents squash courts and equipment. Pattaya does not have squash facilities.

Tennis

Tennis has become so popular among Thais that it is wise to reserve a court beforehand. Court rental for daytime games ranges from 30 to 60 *baht* per hour; for night games it rises to 70 to 90 *baht* per hour. Unless otherwise noted, you must supply your own racket and balls. Instructors are available at most courts.

In Bangkok, **Central Tennis Court** at 13/1 Soi Attakarnprasit, S. Sathorn Road, Tel: 2867202, is open from 7am–midnight. **Sawasdee Courts**, (between Sois 27 and 29, deep in Soi 31 from Sukhumvit Road, Tel: 2584502) are open daily 6am–11pm.

Golden Golf & Tennis at 7 Soi Soonvijai 1, New Petchburi Road, Tel: 3181651, opens 6am, closes 10pm. Racket rental: 20 *baht* per hour. **A.U.A.** at 179 Rajdamri Road, Tel: 2528953, is open daily 6am–9pm.

Several hotels open their courts to outsiders. **The Ambassador Hotel** (Tel: 2510404) is open from 9am–9pm. The **Siam Inter-Continental Hotel** (Tel: 2530355) is open 7am–10pm. Rackets rent for 30 *baht* per hour, balls for 150 *baht* for three, tennis shoes for 20 *baht* per hour.

Hilton Hotel (Tel: 2530123) is open for non-guests from 10am–4pm at 100 *baht* per hour. Racket rental: 20 *baht* per hour. **Shangri-la Hotel** and **Oriental Hotel** courts are open only to guests.

In Chiang Mai, the **Rincome Hotel** has courts for its guests' use. If they are not being used, they can be rented to outsiders. Otherwise, go to **Anantasiri Court**, 90/1 Superhighway (opp. Chiang Mai Museum), Tel: 222210. Open 7am–8pm on Monday, Wednesday, Friday and Saturday; 7am–7pm on Tuesday, Thursday and Sunday. 50 *baht* per hour; 70 *baht* with lights. Racket rental: 20 *baht* per hour; balls: 10 *baht* per hour; instructor: 70 *baht* per hour.

In Phuket, large hotels like **Holiday Inn**, **Phuket Yacht Club**, **Coral Beach** and **Phuket Meridien** maintain courts for their guests' use. If they are not in use, they can be rented by outsiders. **Holiday Inn** on Thaviwong Road (the Beach Road) in Patong charges outsiders 200 *baht* per hour (after 6pm, there is an extra 75 *baht* per hour charge for lights). Racket rental is 30 *baht* per hour; new balls are 200 *baht* per can. Open 7am–9pm.

In Pattaya, tennis can be played at any one of several hotels. Fees are comparable to those elsewhere with a nighttime charge for lights.

Boogie Boards

Large hotels like **Holiday Inn** in Phuket's Patong rent them for 50 *baht* per hour.

Jet Skis

Only marginally safer than water scooters. If you fall off, the machine will slow down and return to you so you can remount. 800 *baht* per hour.

Para Sailing

Strapped into a parachute, one is towed aloft by a powerboat for a 5-minute ride high over the bay. Be warned that this is not the safest sport in the world and injuries are common. Check that the wind is not too strong and that the boat driver is not too young. 500 *baht* per trip. Pattaya and Phuket.

Sailing

Catamarans (Prindles and Hobie Cats) rent for 300–500 *baht* per hour in Pattaya and Phuket. Or hire a boy for 50–100 *baht* per hour to take you out. Single-handed Lasers are 200 *baht* per hour.

Scuba Diving

Shops in Pattaya and Phuket's Patong beach provide comprehensive courses leading to internationally-recognized PADI or NAUI certification from Open Water up to Divemaster. The latter course costs up to 16,500 *baht*. In Pattaya, try **Seafari** and **Dave's Divers Den**, both on the Beach Road (see telephone numbers below). In Phuket, **Fantasea** is located on Patong's Beach Road next to the Holiday Inn.

Diving trips: In Pattaya, **Seafari Sports Center** on the Beach Road. (Tel: 419060), and **Dave's Divers Den** at Soi 6 on the Beach Road offer PADI and NAUI courses and diving trips to the outer islands. The water in the bay is murky and visibility is limited.

In Phuket, regular diving cruises are conducted to the Similian Islands; private trips can be arranged to other prime diving areas as well. **Fantasea** has some of the best but other dive shops in Patong offer similar itineraries and prices. Guaranteed departures and no minimum number of persons required.

Off the West Coast of Phuket. A day-trip to explore soft and hard coral reefs that contain a wide variety of colorful tropical fish. Good close-up photography opportunities. One dive costs 500 *baht*; two dives cost 750 *baht*. The price includes boat, tanks, air, back pack, weights, belt and fruit. Non-divers in the party receive a 50 percent discount. There are other trips to Shark Point, Koh Dok Mai, Raja Islands and Phi Phi islands. Nightdiving expeditions can also be arranged.

Asia Voyages offers a 3-day, 2-night scuba diving charter on the June Bahtra junk for 42,000 *baht* for four persons which includes all accommodations, transfers, scuba equipment, meals and the services of a divemaster. Contact Asia Voyages at 216137, 216528 in the Rasda Center on Rasda Road in Phuket town.

Similan Islands: **Fantasea** offers 6-night, 5-day dive cruises aboard the 16-m (17-yd) ketch, the *Andaman Explorer*. Weekly departures from December to April from Patong beach at 8pm, returning to Patong at 6am of the seventh day. The 12,500 *baht* fee includes unlimited diving, accommodation on board and all meals. Equipment costs are extra.

Snorkeling

Near Bangkok, only the waters around Sattahip are clear enough to snorkel. The good places on Phuket are off Kata and Kata Noi beaches; otherwise, head for Phi Phi or the Similans. Mask, fins and snorkel cost about 100 *baht* per day.

Surfing

None in Pattaya. Phuket's surf is low except during the rainy season (June–November); even then it is less than 1 m (3 ft). The best surfing beaches are Karon and Kelim on the northern end of Patong. On Karon's Soi Bangla, "Of Foreigner" shop rents surfboards for 100 *baht* for 2 hours.

Water Scooters

The inherent instability of water scooters means they tend to flip on waves or their riders clothesline themselves on anchor ropes and the number of fatalities rises each year. Because of their safety record, hotel owners have tried unsuccessfully to have them banned. If you insist on renting one, be sure it is in good condition, that you keep the speed down, and that you can swim (if you fall off, the machine keeps on going). Be aware that there is a scam on Pattaya beaches to send the rider out on a faulty scooter and then to claim he has damaged it and must pay a heavy repair bill. 300 *baht* per hour

Water Skiing

1,500 *baht* per hour for boat and skis is the normal price in Pattaya and Phuket.

Wind Surfing

Boards in Pattaya and Jomtien rent for 180 *baht* per hour and 400–500 *baht* for half a day. The owner will generally give free lessons. Prices are the same in Phuket's Patong and Karon beaches.

SPECTATOR SPORTS

Despite the hot climate, Thai men and women are avid sports enthusiasts, actively playing both their own sports and those adopted from the West according to international rules.

The king of foreign sports is soccer and is played both by men and women. Following a close second is badminton with basketball, rugby, track and field, swimming, marksmanship, boxing, tennis and golf trailing only a short way behind.

The principal sports venues in Bangkok where one can watch the Thais in action are the National Stadium on Rama I Road just west of Mahboonkrong

Shopping Center; the Hua Mark Stadium east of the city next to Ramkamhaeng University; and the Thai-Japanese Sports Center at Din Daeng near the northern entrance to the expressway.

In Phuket, games are played at the Phuket Stadium on Vichaisongkhram Road and in Chiang Mai at the Chiang Mai Stadium and at Chiang Mai University. Check the English-language newspapers for schedules.

Thailand has also created a number of unique sports and these are well worth watching as much for the grace and agility displayed as for the element of fun that pervades every competition.

Kite Fighting

The heat of March and April is relieved somewhat by breezes which the Thais use to send kites aloft. **Sanam Luang** in Bangkok and open spaces everywhere across the country are filled with young and old boys clinging to kite strings. The Thais have also turned it into a competitive sport, forming teams sponsored by major companies.

Two teams vie for trophies. One flies a giant star-shaped male Chula kite nearly 2 m (6½ ft) high. The opposing teams (there may be more than one) fly the diminutive diamond-shaped female Pakpao kites.

One team tries to snare the other's kite and drag it across a dividing line. Surprisingly, the odds are even and a tiny female Pakpao stands a good chance of pulling down a big lumbering Chula male (just like life). The teamwork and fast action make for exciting viewing. Competitions at Bangkok's Sanam Luang start at 2pm.

Horse Racing

Horse racing is not unique to Thailand but it is no less exciting. Betting is according to the Western system with Win, Place and Show but without the various permutations of Quinella or Trifecta. Bets begin at 50 *baht* and run as high as 200,000 *baht*. Bangkok has two racecourses that alternate in offering meets every Sunday except during the monsoon season.

The **Royal Turf Club** is at 183 Phitsanuloke Road across from Chitrlada Palace, Tel: 2823770; and the **Royal Bangkok Sports Club** is at No. 1 Henri Dunant Road, Tel: 2823770, 2822008. Post time is 12.15pm; the last race is at 6pm. Check the newspapers for dates and tipsheets.

Takraw

With close relatives in Malaysia and Indonesia, *takraw*, somewhat like Thai boxing, employs all the limbs except the hands to propel a woven rattan ball (or a more modern plastic ball) over a net or into a hoop. In the net version, two three-player teams face each other across a head-high net like that used in badminton. As the match heats up, it is not unusual for a player to turn a complete somersault to spike a ball across the net.

In the second type, six players form a wide circle

around a basket-like net suspended high in the air. Using heads, feet, knees and elbows to keep the ball airborne, they score points by putting it into the net. A team has a set time period in which to score as many points as it can after which it is the opposing team's turn.

Tournaments are held at the **Thai-Japanese Sports Center** (Tel: 4655325 for dates and times) four times a year; admission is free. Competitions are also held in the northwest corner of Bangkok's **Sanam Luang** during the March–April kite contests. Free admission. During the non-monsoon months, wander into a park or a temple courtyard anywhere in the country late in the afternoon.

Thai Boxing

One of the most exciting and popular Thai sports is "Thai Boxing." In Bangkok, **Rajdamnern Stadium** on Rajdamnern Nok Avenue next to the TAT, offers bouts on Monday, Wednesday, and Thursday at 6pm and on Sunday at 4.30 and 8.30pm. The Sunday matinee at 4.30pm is recommended as it has the cheapest seats. Ticket prices run between 500 and 1,000 *baht* for ringside seats (depending on the quality of the card), running downwards to 100 *baht*.

Lumpini Boxing Stadium on Rama 4 Road, 300 m (330 yds) east of the Wireless intersection stages bouts on Tuesday and Friday at 6.30pm and on Saturday at 1 and 6.30pm. Ticket prices are the same as at Rajdamnern. As above, weekend afternoon matinees are the cheapest.

There are also televised bouts on Saturday and Sunday and at 10.30pm on some weeknights. For many visitors this will be sufficient introduction to the sport. The **Rose Garden** and Phuket's **Thai Village** offer short demonstrations of Thai boxing but these are played more for laughs than for authenticity.

Thai boxing bouts ceased in Chiang Mai several years ago but bouts are staged each Friday at 8pm at the **Phuket Boxing Stadium** at Saphan Hin (to the right of the tin dredge memorial where Phuket Road meets the sea). Tickets are 30, 50 and 70 *baht*. Most large rural towns have their own boxing gyms and stage weekly bouts by young hopefuls.

LANGUAGE

Like the Thais, the Thai language was formed in the crucible of southern China with its host of tonal phenomena. It was only after the Thais crossed the mountains and came into contact with Indian influences, that it gained polysyllabic terms, a more formal structure and a written form. The result is a language which is grammatically simple but vocally complex (thanks to five tones) and frustratingly difficult to read, especially as the words are all run together so that a single sentence looks like a single word.

The key is in the tones. Misinformed Westerners will claim that tones are not important. They soon discover that when they mispronounce, they aren't simply saying a word incorrectly, they are saying another word entirely, substituting confusion for communication.

From the languages of India have come the lexicon of literature and the terms used in the royal court. Thai names are among the longest in the world. Every Thai first name and surname has a meaning. By learning the meaning of the name of everyone you meet, you will acquire a formal, but quite extensive vocabulary.

There is no universal transliteration system from Thai into English which is why names and street names can be spelled three different ways. For example, the surname "Chumsai" is spelled "Chumsai," "Jumsai" and "Xoomsai" depending on the family. This confuses even the Thais.

The way Thai consonants are written in English often confuses foreigners. An "h" following a letter like "p" and "t" gives the letter a soft sound; without the "h", the sound is more explosive. Thus, "ph" is not pronounced "f" but as a soft "p". Without the "h", the "p" has the sound of a very hard "b". The word Thanon (street) is pronounced "tanon" in the same way as "Thailand" is not meant to sound like "Thighland". Similarly, final letters are often not pronounced as they look. A "j" on the end of a word is pronounced "t"; "l" is pronounced as an "n".

Vowels are pronounced like this: "i" as in sip, "ii" as in seep, "e" as in bet, "a" as in pun, "aa" as in pal, "u" as in pool, "o" as in so, "ai" as in pie, "ow" as in cow, "aw" as in paw, "iw" as in you, "oy" as in toy.

In Thai, the pronoun "I" and "me" use the same word but is different for males and females. Men use the word *Phom* when referring to themselves; women say *chan* or *diichan*. Men use the word *Khrap* at the end of a sentence when addressing either a male or a female i.e. *Pai (f) nai, khrap (h)?* (Where are you going, sir?). Women append the word *Kha* to their statements i.e. *Pai (f) nai, kha (h)?*.

To ask a question, add a high tone *mai* to the end of the phrase i.e. *Rao pai (We go)* or *Rao pai mai (h)?* (Shall we go?). To negate a statement, insert a falling tone *mai* between the subject and the verb i.e. *Rao pai* (We go), *Rao mai pai* (We don't go). "Very" or "much" are indicated by adding *maak* to the end of a phrase i.e. *ron* (hot), *ron maak* (very hot).

Here is a small vocabulary intended to get you on your way. The five tones have been indicated by appending letters after them viz high (h), low (l), middle (m), rising as when asking a question (r), and falling as when suddenly understanding something such as "ohh, I see" (f).

GREETINGS & OTHERS

Hello/goodbye	*Sawasdee* (a man then says *Khrap*; a woman says *Kha*; thus *Sawasdee, Khrap*)
How are you?	*Khun sabai dii, ruu (r)*
Excuse me	*Khaw (r) thoat (f)*
Well, thank you	*Sabai dii, Khap khun*
Thank you very much	*Khapkhun maak*
Please come in	*Chern khao (f)*
Please sit down	*Chern nang*
May I come in?	*khao dai (f) mai (h)*
May I take a photo?	*Kaw thai roop (f) noi, dai (f) mai (h)*
Never mind	*Mai (f) pen rai*
I cannot speak Thai	*Phom (r) (Chan) phuut Thai mai (f) dai (f)*
I can speak little Thai	*Phom (r) (Chan) phuut a Thai dai (f), nit (h) noi*
Where do you live?	*Khun asai yoo thii (f) nai (r)*
What is this called in Thai?	*Nii (h), koo kaw riak away phasa Thai*
How much?	*Thao (f) rai*
When	*Mua (f) rai*

DIRECTIONS & TRAVEL

Go	*Pai*
Come	*Maa*
Where	*Thii (f) nai (r)*
Right	*Khwaa (r)*
Left	*ai (h)*
Turn	*Leo*
Straight ahead	*rong pai*
Please slow down	*Cha cha noi*
What street is this?	*Nii thanon arai*
What town is this?	*Nii muang arai*
How many kilometers to...?	*Kii kiilo by...*
Stop here	*Yood thii (f) nii (f)*

Fast	*Raew*
Hotel	*Rong raam*
Street	*Thanon*
Lane	*Soi*
Bridge	*Saphan*
Police Station	*Sathanii Dtam Ruat*
Market	*Talad*

USEFUL PHRASES

Yes	*Chai (f)*
No	*Mai (f) chai (f)*
Good	*Dii (m)*
Bad	*Mai (f) dii*
Do you have?	*Mii Mai (h)*
Expensive	*Phaeng*
Do you have something cheaper?	*Mii arai thii thook (l) kwa nii (h)*
Can you lower the price a bit?	*Kaw long noi dai (f) mai (h)*
Do you have another color?	*Mii sii uhn mai (h)*
Too big	*Yai kern pai*
Too small	*Lek kern pai*
Do you have bigger?	*Mii arai thii yai kwai nii (h) mai (h)*
Do you have smaller?	*Mii arai thii lek kwa nii (h) mai (h)*
Where is the toilet?	*Hong nam (h) yuu hii (f) nai (r)*

OTHER HANDY WORDS

Hot (heat)	*Ron (h)*
Hot (spicy)	*Phet*
Cold	*Yen*
Sweet	*Waan (r)*
Sour	*Prio (f)*
Delicious	*Aroy*
Coconut	*Ma-prao*

NUMBERS

One	*Nung (m)*
Two	*Song (r)*
Three	*Sam (r)*
Four	*Sii (m)*
Five	*Haa (f)*
Six	*Hok (m)*
Seven	*Jet (m)*
Eight	*Pat (m)*
Nine	*Kow (f)*
Ten	*Sip (m)*
Eleven	*Sip Et (m, m)*
Twelve	*Sip Song (m, r)*
Thirteen	*Sip Sam (m, r)*
Twenty	*Yii Sip (m, m)*
Thirty	*Sam Sip (r, m)*
100	*Nung Roi (m, m)*
1,000	*Nung Phan (m, m)*
10,000	*Muan*

Monday	*Wan Jan*
Tuesday	*Wan Angkhan*
Wednesday	*Wan Phoot*
Thursday	*Wan Pharuhat*
Friday	*Wan Sook*
Saturday	*Wan Sao*
Sunday	*Wan Athit*
Today	*Wan nii (h)*
Yesterday	*Mua wan nii (h)*
Tomorrow	*Prung nii (h)*
Every day	*Thuk (h) wan*

GLOSSARY OF THE TERMS

Bot: The ordination hall, usually open only to the monks. A *bot* is marked by six "*bai sema*" or boundary stones around the outside of the building which define the limits of sanctuary. Many *wats* do not have *bots*, only *viharns*.

Chedi: Often interchangeable with *stupa*. A mound surmounted by a spire in which relics of the Buddha or revered religious teachers are kept.

Chofah: The bird-like decoration on the ends of a *bot* or viharn roofs.

Naga: A mythical serpent, usually running down the edge of the roof. In sculpture, it sheltered Buddha as he meditated.

Prang: An Ayutthayan-style *chedi* that looks somewhat like a vertical ear of corn.

Sala: An open-sided pavilion.

Viharn: The sermon hall; the busiest building in a *wat*. A *wat* may have more than one.

Wat: Translated as "temple" but describing a collection of buildings and monuments within a compound wall.

FURTHER READING

History

Chakrabongse, Prince Chula. *Lords of Life*. London: Alvin Redman, 1960. A history of the Chakri kings.

Kasetsiri, Charnvit. *The Rise of Ayudhya*. London: East Asian Historical Monographs, 1976. A narration of the history of early Ayutthaya.

Coedes, George. *The Indianized States of Southeast Asia*. Trans. Susan Brown Cousing. Ed. Walter F. Vella. Honolulu: East-West Center Press, 1968. Well written scholarly work.

Hall, D.G.E. *A History of South-east Asia*. 3rd ed. London: Macmillan, 1968. The classic text.

Hutchinson, E.W. *1688: Revolution in Siam*. Hong Kong University Press. The events leading to the expulsion of the foreigners from Ayutthaya.

Moffat, Abbot Low. *Mongkut, the King of Siam*. Ithaca, New York: Cornell University Press, 1961. Superb history of one of Asia's most interesting 19th-century men.

Van Beek, Steve. *Bangkok Only Yesterday*. Hong Kong: Hong Kong Publishing, 1982. Anecdotal history of Bangkok illustrated with old photos.

Vella, Walter F. *Chaiyo!* Honolulu: University of Hawaii Press, 1979. The life and times of King Vajiravudh (1910–1925).

Wyatt, David K. *Thailand: A Short History*. Bangkok/London: Thai Wattana Panich/Yale University Press, 1984. Concise and well-written.

People

Aylwen, Axel. *The Falcon of Siam*. London: Methuen, 1988. A fictionalized story of Constant Phaulkon, Greek adventurer in Siam in the late 1600s.

Campbell, Reginald. *Teak-Wallah*. Singapore: Oxford, 1986. Adventurers of a teak logger in northern Thailand in the 1920s.

Collis, Maurice. *Siamese White*. London: Faber, 1965. Fictionalized account of a contemporary of Constant Phaulkon in 1600s Siam.

Lewis, Paul and Elaine. *Peoples of the Golden Triangle*. London: Thames and Hudson, 1984. Excellent text and photos on the hilltribes.

Seidenfaden, Erik. *The Thai Peoples*. Bangkok: Siam Society, 1967. Solid work by long-time resident.

Skinner, G. William. *Chinese Society in Thailand*. Ithaca, New York: Cornell University Press, 1957. Gives an insight into an important segment of Bangkok's history.

Religion

Bunnag, Jane. *Buddhist Monk, Buddhist Layman.* Cambridge: Cambridge University Press, 1973. Gives an insight into the monastic experience.

Nivat, Prince Dhani. *A History of Buddhism in Siam.* Bangkok: Siam Society, 1965. One of Thailand's most respected scholars.

Art & Culture

Diskul, M.C. Subhadradis. Art in Thailand: A Brief History. Bangkok: Silpakorn University, 1970. Dean of the Fine Arts University.

Klausner, William J. *Reflections on Thai Culture.* The Siam Society: Bangkok, 1987. Observations of a longtime resident anthropologist.

Rajadhon, Phya Anuman. *Essays on Thai Folklore.* Bangkok: D.K. Books. A description of Thai ceremonies, festivals and rites of passage.

Van Beek, Steve. *The Arts of Thailand.* Hong Kong: Travel Publishing Asia, 1985. Lavishly illustrated, includes the minor arts.

Warren, William. *The House on the Klong.* Tokyo: Weatherhill. The story of the Jim Thompson House.

Wray, Joe, Elizabeth Wray, Clare Rosenfeld and Dorothy Bailey. *Ten Lives of the Buddha; Siamese Temple Paintings and Jataka Tales.* Tokyo: Weatherhill, 1974. Well illustrated, valuable for understanding Thai painting and the Tosachat (Jataka Tales).

General

Amranand, Pimsai. *Gardening in Bangkok.* Bangkok: Siam Society. Good work on plants though could do with more photos.

Cooper, Robert and Nanthapa. *Culture Shock: Thailand.* Singapore: Times Books, 1982. Very useful look at Thai customs and how to avoid *faux pas.* Written and illustrated in highly amusing manner.

Hollinger, Carol. *Mai Pen Rai.* Boston: Houghton Mifflin. Expatriate life in the 1950s.

Ingram, J.C. *Economic Change in Thailand 1830–1970.* Palo Alto, California: Stanford University Press, 1971.

Segaller, Denis. *Thai Ways.* Bangkok: Thai Wattana Panich, 1979. Collection of columns on Thai customs by a longtime resident .

———. *More Thai Ways.* Bangkok: Allied Newspapers, 1982. More reprinted columns on Thai customs.

Siam Society, Culture and Environment in Thailand. Siam Society: Bangkok, 1989.

Sternstein, Larry. *Thailand: The Environment of Modernisation.* Sydney: McGraw-Hill, 1976. Excellent geography text.

Stockmann, Hardy. *Thai Boxing.* Bangkok: D.K. Books, 1979. Excellent, well illustrated book on the basics of Thai boxing.

Warren, William. *The Legendary American.* Boston: Houghton Mifflin. The intriguing story of American Thai silk king Jim Thompson.

OTHER INSIGHT GUIDES

From the *Insight Guide* collection comes a range of travel guides, specially designed to help make your visit an unforgettable one.

Insight Guide: Southeast Asia is the definitive guidebook that unravels the complexities of regional travel in Southeast Asia.

Personalized recommendations for the active and inquisitive visitor.

Itineraries designed for an idyllic stay in this island paradise.

Antiquities and forest splendor await you in this ancient capital.

ART/PHOTO CREDITS

INDEX

A

B

Borsang-Sankamphaeng Road 209
bot (main chapel) 101, 107
Bowling alleys 266
brahmins 28
Brazen Palace (Sri Lanka) 109
Bridge on the River Kwai 163, 164
Broken-Hearted Mountain 314
Bronze-making Civilization 250
Bualuang hotel 312
Bubbles (in Dusit Thani Hotel) 133
Buddha 104, 107, 112, 179, 184, 243, 261, 262,
Buddhaisawan Chapel 104
buffaloes, water 171
bullfights 315
Bung Boraphet 175

C

Cabbages and Condoms (restaurant) 90
Cape Phanwa Sheraton Hotel 301
Captain Light 297
Cathedral of St. Joseph 155
Cave of Tham Kung 165
Central Plains 22, 171, 191, 277
Central 129
Cha-am (beach resort) 283
Chachoengsao (town) 258
Chachoengsao 142
Chai Pattana (hotel) 249
Chaing Dao 219
Chaiya (town) 288
Chakrapetch Road 312
Chakrawat Road 115
Chakri Dynasty 49, 97, 284
Chakri kings 284
Chakri Maha Prasad 96
Chakri Throne room 97
chalk quarry 288
Chama Dewi (Lopburi Princess) 198
Chamlong Srimuang 66, 112
Chan and Muk (warrior women) 297
Chandrakasem Palace 154, 155
Chang Klan Road 209
Chanthaburi (town) 258, 262, 271, 273
Chanthaburi (hotel) 271
Chanthburi, river 271
Chantra Paisan Pavilion 158
Chao Lay (Sea Gypsy Village) 301
Chao Phya Chakri 39
Chao Phya Museum 155
Chao Phya River 22, 38, 142, 197, 258, 263, 272
Chao Phya Sarasih 39
Chao Phya 171
Chao Sam Phya Museum 155
Chao U-Thong ("Prince of the Golden Crib") 32
Chartered Bank (building) 298
Chatichai Choonhavan (former Prime Minister) 54
Chatuchak Flower Market 119
Chatuchak Park 67, 103
Chatuchak Weekend Market 112
Chawaeng Bay 304
Chedi Phu Khao Thong (Golden Mount Chedi) 157
Chedi 34, 100, 108
Chiang Dao Cave 220
Chiang Dao Elephant Camp 219
Chiang Dao Mountain 219
Chiang Kaishek's Kuomintang Army 220

Chiang Khon (town) 252
Chiang Khong 195, 229
Chiang Mai ("New Town") 30
Chiang Mai (Khon Kaen) 88
Chiang Mai (town) 271
Chiang Mai Flower Festival 207
Chiang Mai Museum 215
Chiang Mai University 205
Chiang Mai Zoo 205
Chiang Mai 200, 219, 223, 230
Chiang Rai 39, 223, 225
Chiang Rui 211
Chiang Saen 225, 229
Chicken island 311
Chinatown 87, 115
Chinese Buddhist Society 261
Chinese Shrines 298
Chinese 70
Chitralada Palace 61, 112
Chok Chai 245
Chom Thong 214
Chomtien (resort) 265, 257
Chon Buri (town) 257, 258, 261, 262
Chulachomklao Royal Military Academy 67
Chulalongkom University 48, 127
Chulalongkorn, King 46, 48, 87, 162, 176
Chum Phae (town) 252
Chumbhot, Princess of Nagara Svarga 119
Chumbhot, Princess 151
Chumphon (town) 287
Chumphon River 287
Church of Immaculate Conception (Catholic church)
    271
Constantine Phaulkon 36
Continental/Asian Cuisines 266
Crocodile Farm 149, 163
crocodiles, Siamese 149
Cruises (evening) 143
Cuisine
    northeast 78, 79
    southern 79

D

Damnern Saduak Floating Market 142
Damnern Saduak 142
Damrong, Prince 47
dance form 76
    Lakhon 76
    Likay 76
Dao Khanong 141
Darling (a barbershop) 90
de Albuquerque, Alfonso 34
Death Railway 27
Democracy Monument 95, 108
democracy 49
Den Chai 232
Department of Fine Arts 240
devaraja 33
devas (gods) 261
Devawongse, Prince 47
dharma 53
Dharmaraja (Lo Thai) 30
Dharmayuthi sect 246
dhotis 48
Diana's (Oriental Plaza) 133
discos 133

L

M

Q & R

S

T

He'll take you to paradise and back for just 50 pesc

When you need cash, use the GlobalAccess Card. Local currency from more than 170,0

Y–Z

A
B
C
D
F
G
H
I
J
a
b
c
d
e
f
g
h
i
j
k

ash only, of course.